Australian Reflections

Bruce D. Prewer

Ian Morris

Aub Podlich

Ideas into Books: Westview®
P.O. Box 605
Kingston Springs, TN 37082 USA

Cover Photograph by Ian Morris:
Djarrdjarr Billabong, Magela Creek

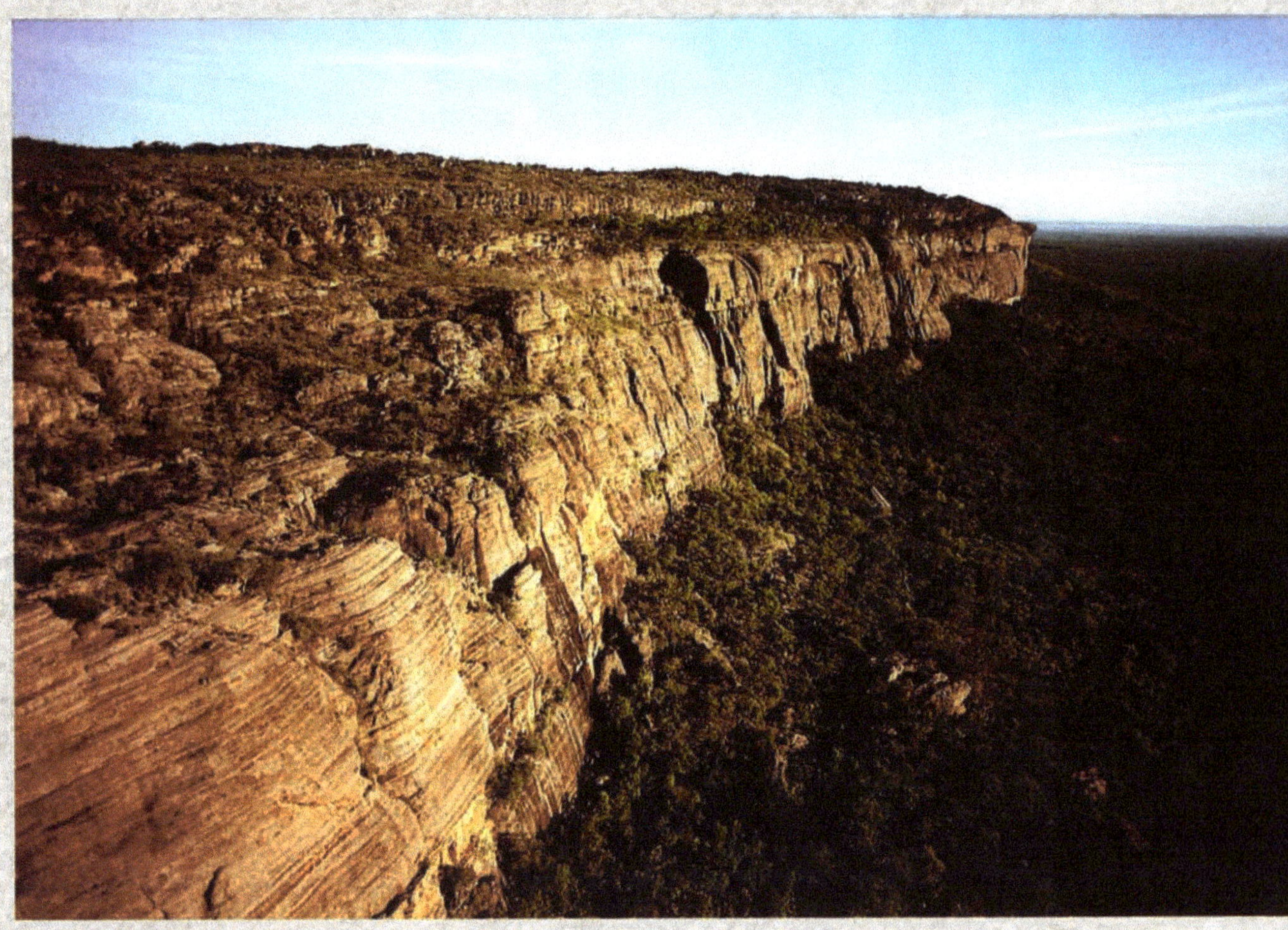

Text by Bruce Prewer and Aub Podlich; Photographs by Ian Morris, Jocelyn Burt, and Bruce Prewer; Graphic Design by Graeme Cogdell.

Australian Reflections First Edition, Easter 2018, ISBN 978-1-62880-144-6

Ideas into Books: Westview®, P.O. Box 605, Kingston Springs, TN 37082 USA

Digitally printed on acid free paper.

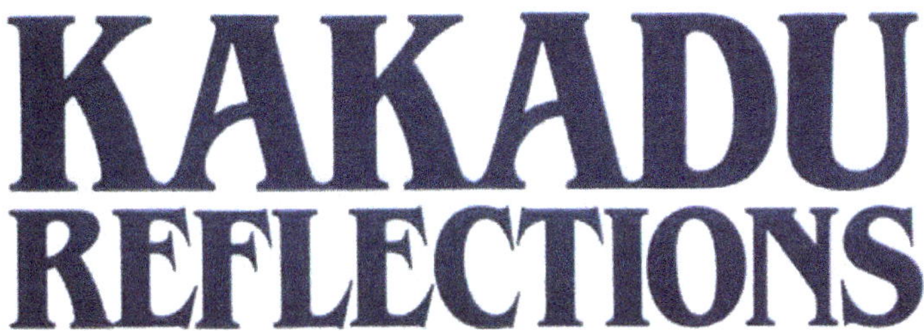

BRUCE PREWER

with photography by
IAN MORRIS

LEFT: *Kakadu escarpment near East Alligator River*

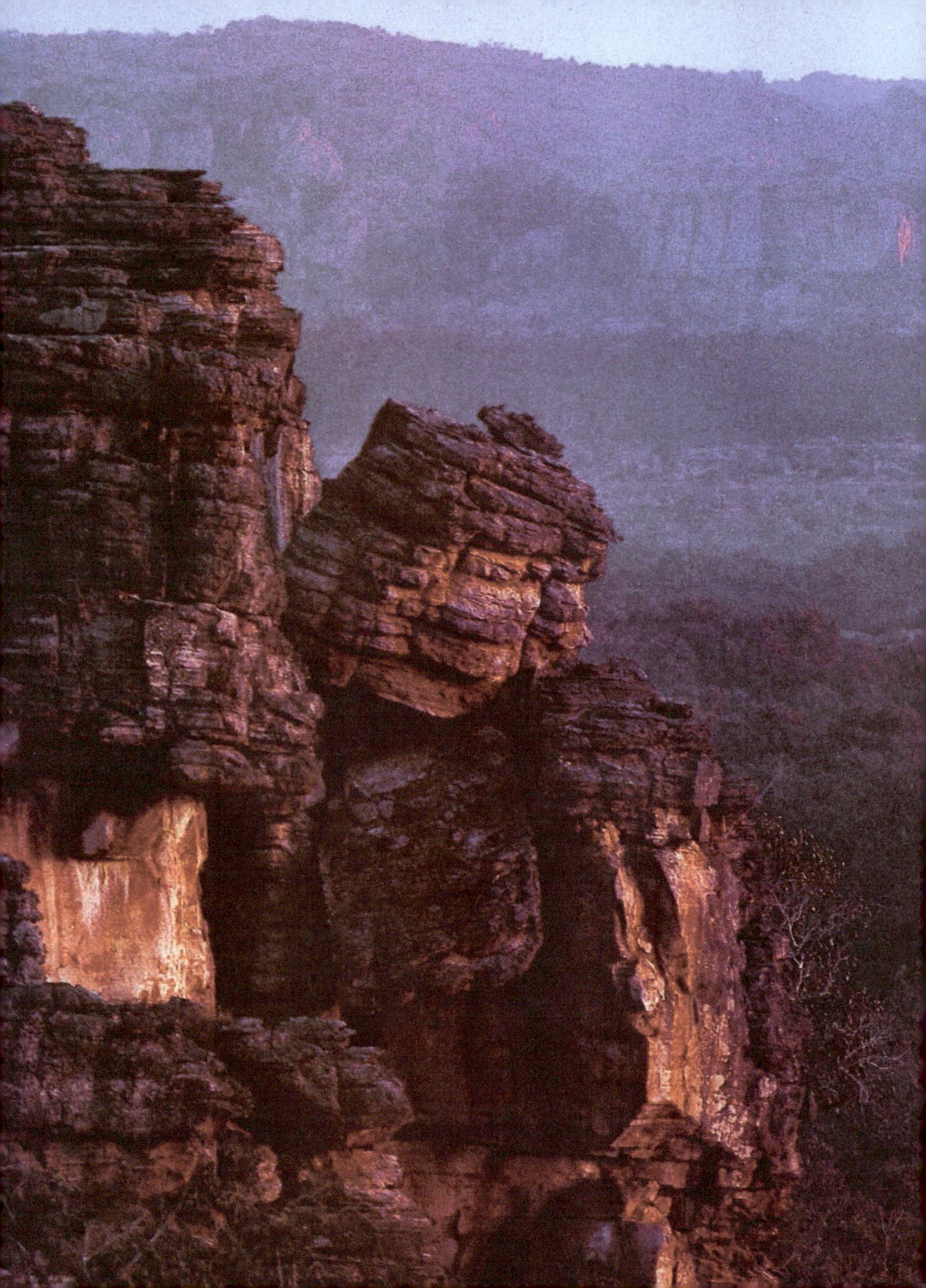

INTRODUCTION

By an act of grace — a rare thing in this greedy world — Kakadu is there for us all to enjoy, thanks to the Aboriginal owners. Having first fought to establish their rights as owners, with typical generosity they leased the area back to the National Parks and Wildlife Service in November 1978 so that we could all come and appreciate their home country.

The Park is about 220 kilometres east of Darwin, and consists of 19,000 square kilometres of tidal flats, floodplain, lowlands, and plateau country. Features that stand out are rivers, billabongs, and waterfalls (in the wet season), and especially the rugged, sandstone uplands of the Arnhem Land escarpment. Kakadu has many faces, many moods, and is home to a multitude of life-forms.

To the casual eye, much of the Park appears to be uninteresting bushland and savannah grassland, with gum trees and occasional stands of palms. What seems to make it even more uninteresting for some folk is that during the dry season many areas are deliberately burned, leaving them charred and smoking, with kites circling overhead looking for prey. But to the trained eye, all is not as it seems. The unspectacular bushland is home to a complex plant and animal kingdom which merges with and relates to the sedgland, the paper bark forests, the mangroves, monsoon forests, and the woodlands of the plateau. All are parts of one tapestry. Even the burning-off follows an ancient Aboriginal rotational system which does not destroy life, but stimulates and protects it.

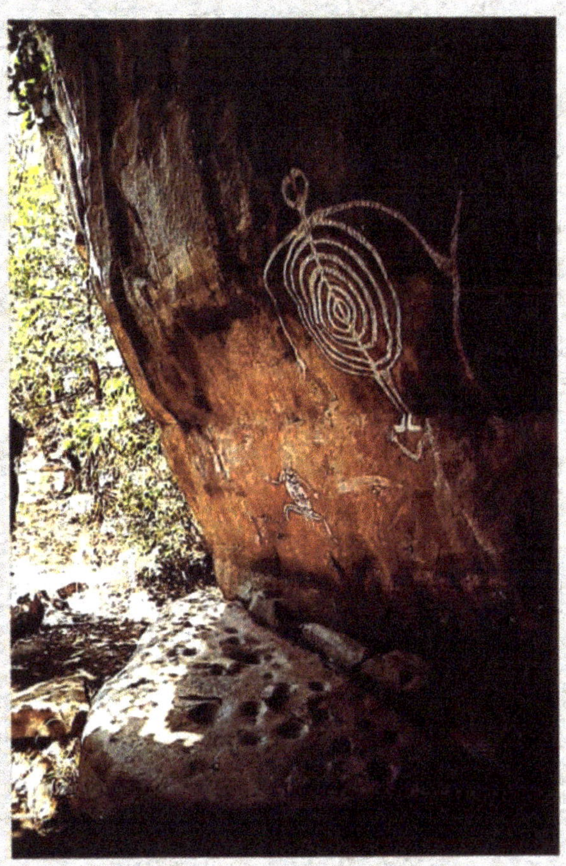

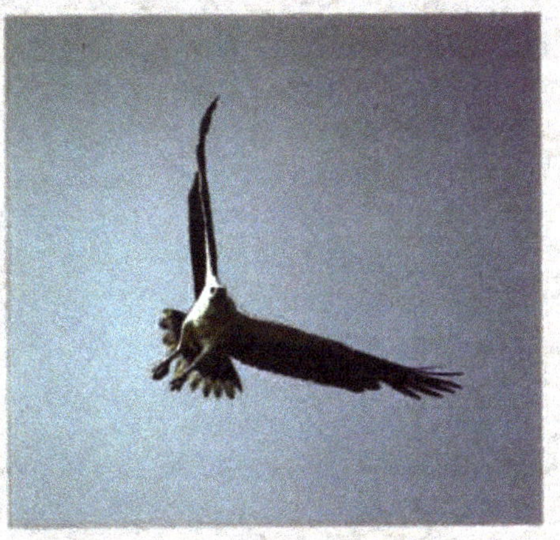

LEFT *Lightning Dreaming (Namarrkurn)*
UPPER RIGHT *Indjuwanydjuwa painting*
LOWER RIGHT *White-breasted Sea Eagle*

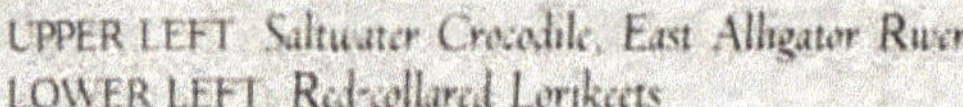

UPPER LEFT *Saltwater Crocodile, East Alligator River*
LOWER LEFT *Red-collared Lorikeets*

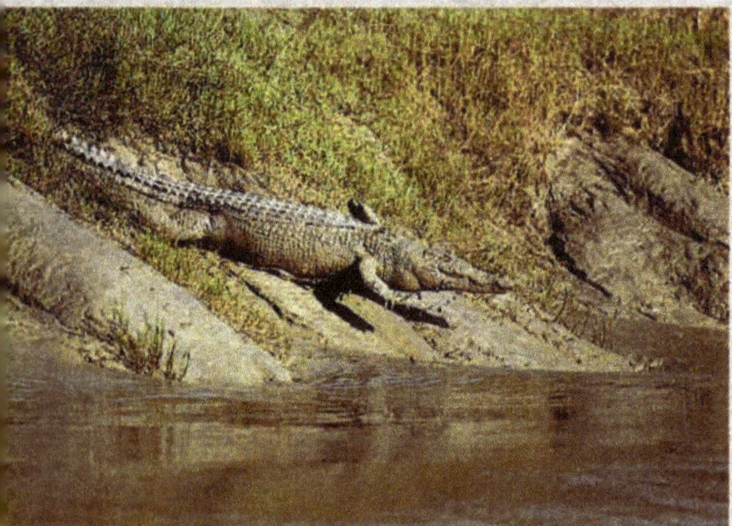

Kakadu is a rare survivor. It is one part of the 'top end' of Australia which as yet has not suffered irreparable damage from European settlement. Plant and animal life are generally intact. Those who visit this National Park are seeing a part of Australia almost as it has been for thousands of years — and that is precious! It imparts a sense of timelessness which is absent in our cities and in much of our devegetated countryside.

Wildlife is prolific in Kakadu. Tourists get excited by large flocks of magpie geese, whistling ducks, or pygmy geese. They stand amazed at trees so covered with cockatoos or parrots that they seem like trees in full blossom. The elegant stork, the jabiru, catches the attention as it wades in shallow waters gathering food. But what is noticed is only a small part of the population of 275 bird species which frequent this region.

Reptiles also come into the abundant category. There are 75 species, of which the usual visitor sees but a few. It is the crocodiles which provide most interest. Freshwater streams and billabongs are the habitat of the small Johnston crocodiles, shy and elusive.

However, it is the big saltwater crocs that most people come to see. They are tender parents, formidable hunters, and possess a speed and agility which is amazing in such bulky creatures. Although their habitat is usually the saltwater areas, they are also found in some streams and billabongs elsewhere, even as far as Jim Jim Falls. The wisest way to get a close look at these leviathans in the wild is in the company of guided tours for this purpose. The Rangers rightly warn that, because the crocodiles have not been hunted for many years, they are losing the fear of human

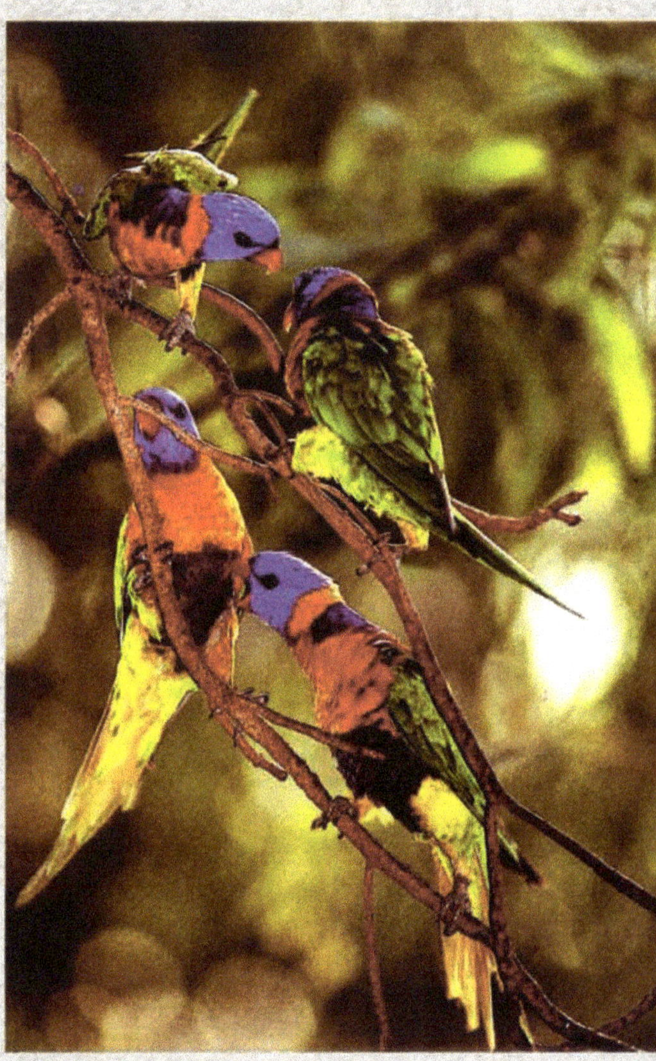

UPPER RIGHT: *Green Ants at Ubirr*
LOWER RIGHT: *Monsoon Forest, Gulungul Creek*

beings. Visitors are well advised to take no risks by staying clear of them.

Although crocodiles and birds are the most easily seen in Kakadu's wildlife, there are 50 species of mammal, 25 of frogs, and 55 of fish — to say nothing of the many colourful and spectacular insects which fly, crawl, and swim during various seasons. In fact, it is the prodigal dimension to the variety and abundance of life in Kakadu which leaves one quite overwhelmed.

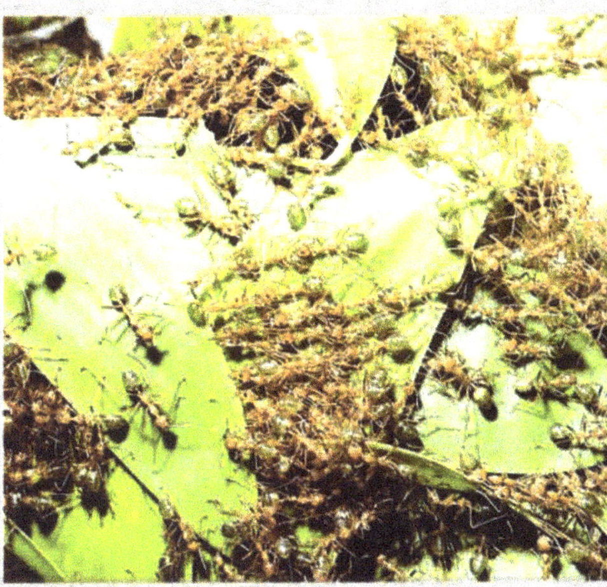

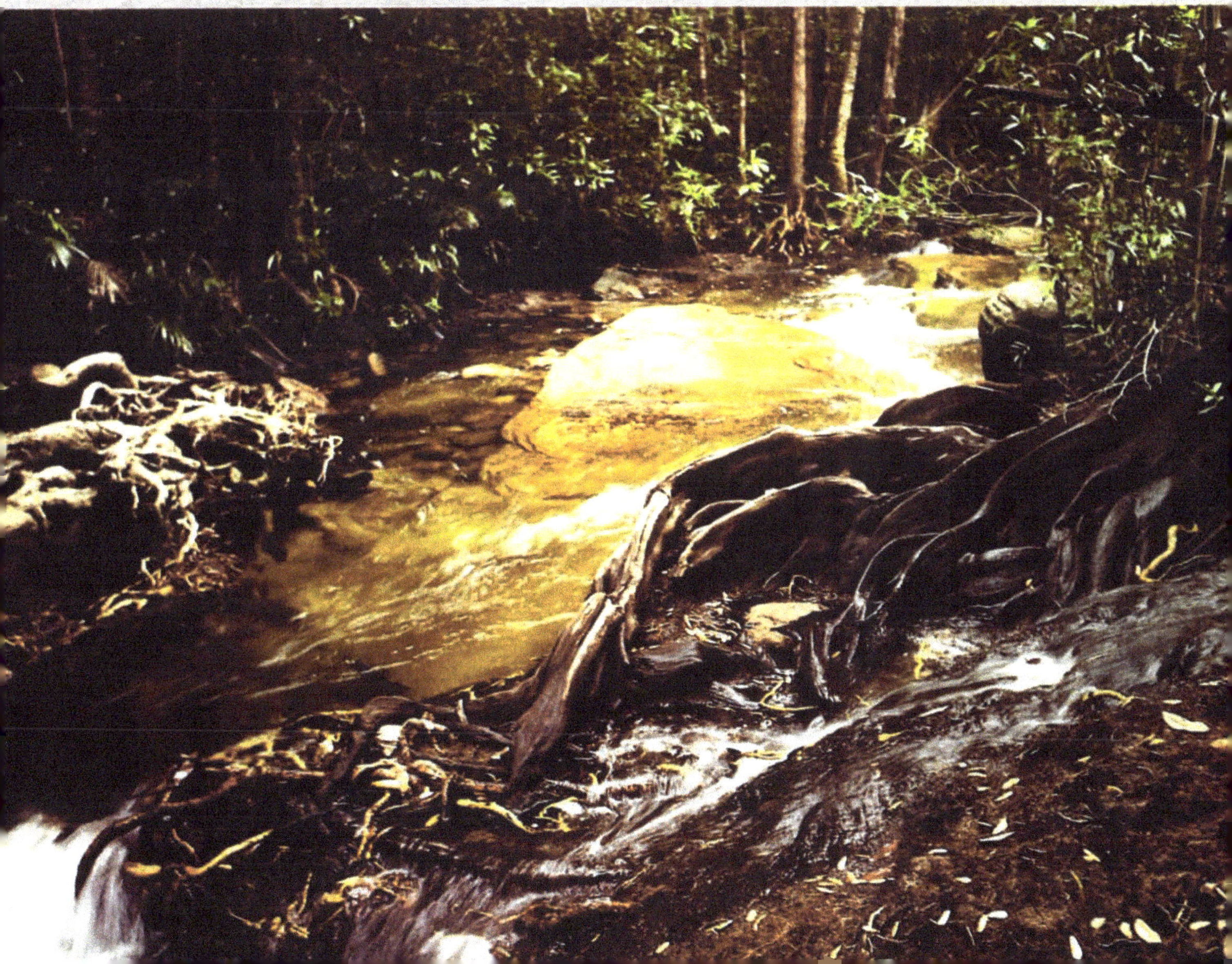

LEFT: *Jabiru fishing*
RIGHT: *Nourlangie Rock (Burrunggu) from Anbangbang Billabong*

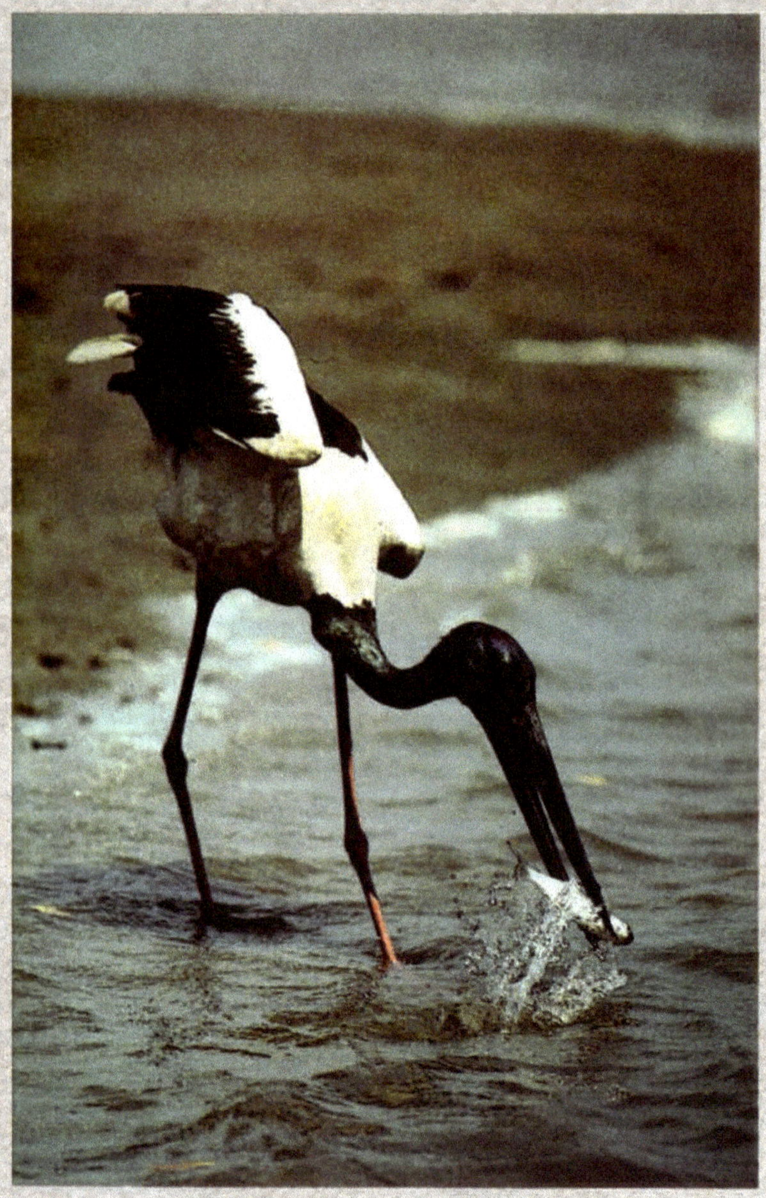

For many residents and visitors, the most notable and profound aspect of Kakadu is the Aboriginal heritage, including over 6,000 rock art sites. Kakadu is a people place. Archeologists who have examined some of the old camp-sites claim that the human story goes back at least 23,000 years, perhaps even 50,000. To be able to visit and stand within an ancient camp-site, such as the Anbangbang Shelter, can be an exciting and awesome experience.

Two of the best-known, and most-accessible, rock art sites are at Ubirr in the north, and at Nourlangie in the south, where the Parks and Wildlife Service have provided walking tracks and information about art styles and mythology. Beside the fascination of the changing art styles, there are surprises. At Ubirr one can see the painting of a Tasmanian Tiger, or of European visitors who came into the region in the last century — complete with rifles in their hands, and pipes in their mouths! Experts say that the art styles found in the area span a period of about 20,000 years — something one cannot find anywhere else in the world. Such art sites are a national treasure. They link us with the long, long story of humanity. Australians are, indeed, an ancient and spiritual people.

Over 250 of the descendants of those ancient artists still live within the boundaries of the Park. Most are out of sight, glad to see others enjoying their country, but reluctant to be on the tourist agenda themselves! Some have become well-trained and much-valued Rangers, keen to help visitors explore, understand, and appreciate the place which they love and treasure like a mother.

The most stunning land-form is the great, 500-kilometre-long Arnhem Land escarpment, with its buttresses, pillars, cliffs, and outliers (the remains of the plateau which centuries of erosion have left standing out on the lowlands). The weather has sculptured much of the sandstone into intriguing shapes. To be in the stone country near dawn or dusk, when the rock is radiant with colour, is among the special experiences which Kakadu can offer.

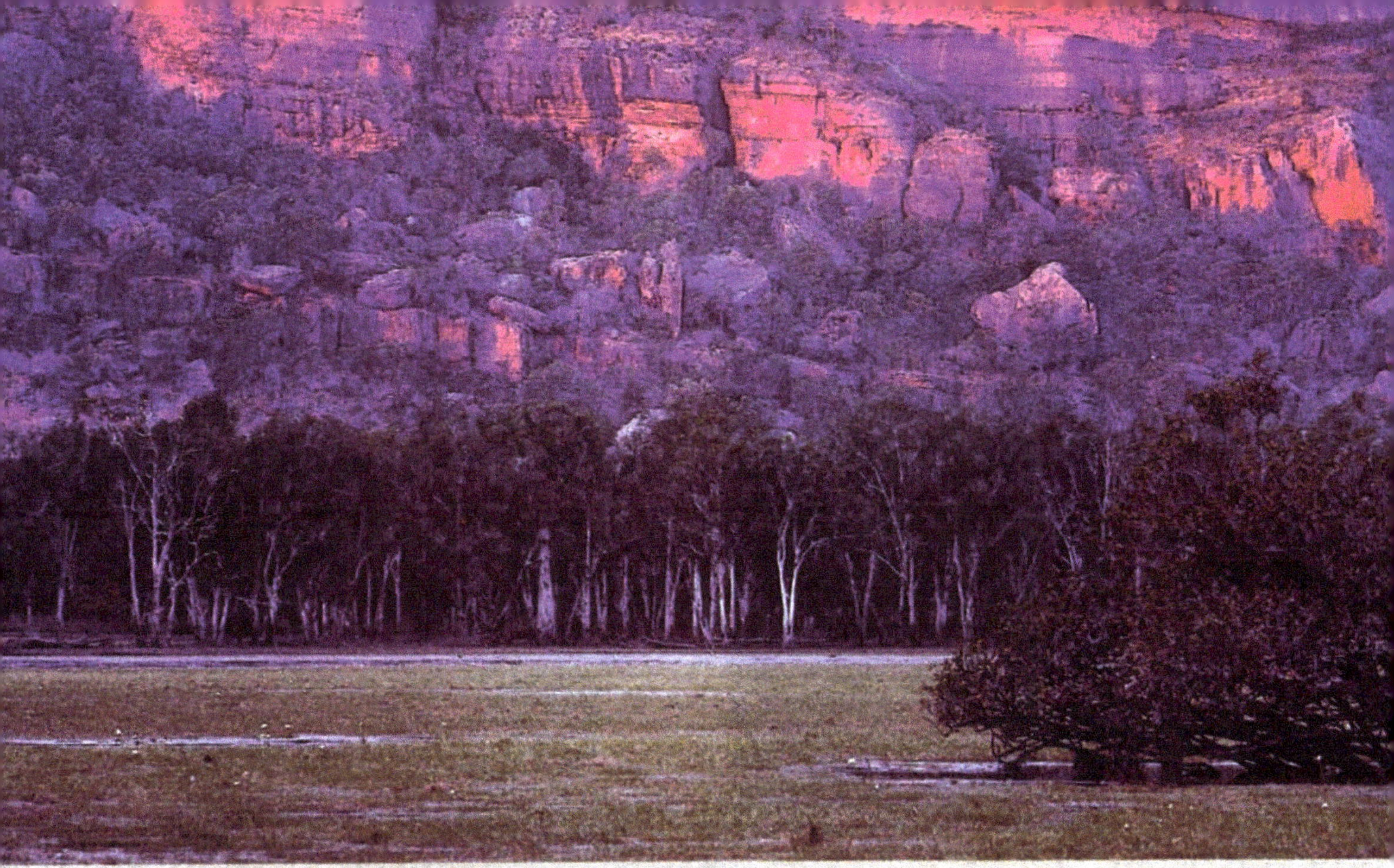

Of course, a visitor can see only a little, and understand even less. For fuller familiarity one would need to stay there often, to experience the changing moods and seasons. The thunder and lightning displays of November are a vivid contrast to the clear days of June. The dry, dusty lowlands and dried-up wetlands of August-September are almost another world compared with the torrential rain and waterways of December-March. Only those who actually reside at Kakadu can really begin to understand its many treasures. That is not possible for most of us —nor is it desirable for the Park!

Kakadu is not for everyone. Some tourists come and go, wondering what all the excitement is about. Bored to tears, they can hardly wait to get back to the bustle of Sydney, New York, or Tokyo. That is not surprising, for Kakadu is a place with a special, subtle quality which is hard to define. Some call it a spiritual quality. It is there for those who approach it gently, respectfully, and with time to absorb its mystique.

Whatever glimmers of appreciation I have for Kakadu National Park are largely due to Ian Morris, a Park Officer whose photography is featured in this volume. Ian has a profound affection and respect for the land and its people. He also has a deep and abiding love for the Creator. One can sense these qualities in the pages of this volume.

Together we present *Kakadu Reflections* with gratitude to the One who has provided places like Kakadu.

Easter 1988

Bruce Prewer,
Pilgrim Church, Adelaide

HOW MUCH MORE

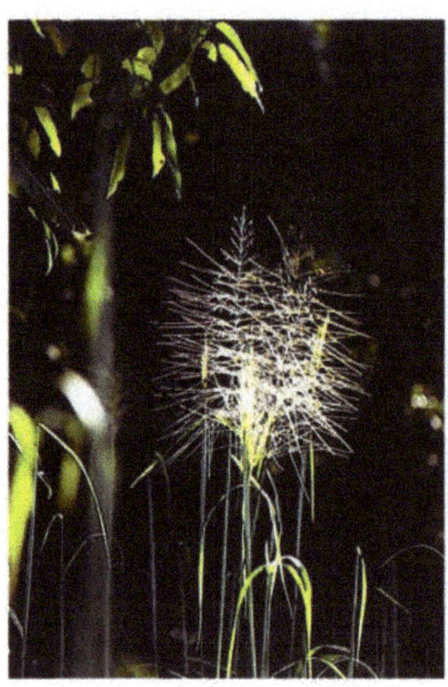

If my eye is excited
by teeming life
in due season,
  how much more
  by the abundant Life
  of all seasons.

If my ear delights
in the song
of a butcher bird
at dawn,
  how much more
  in the love-song
  of the Spirit.

If the handiwork
is awesomely beautiful
beyond words,
  how much more
  the beauty
  of the Hands.

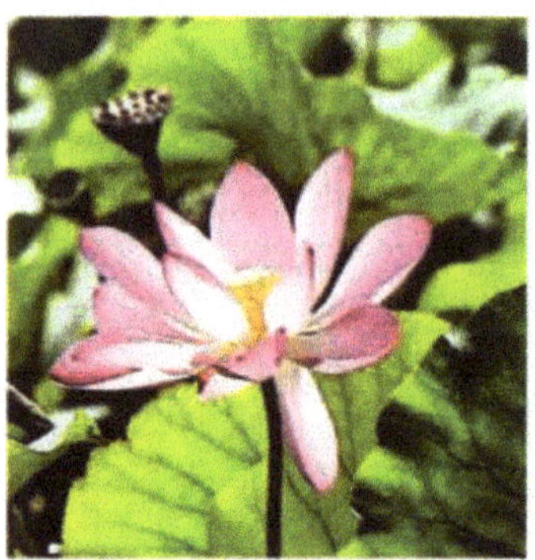

UPPER LEFT *Sorghum seed-head*
LOWER LEFT *Lotus at Cannon Hill Billabong*
RIGHT *Grey-backed Butcher Bird singing at dawn*

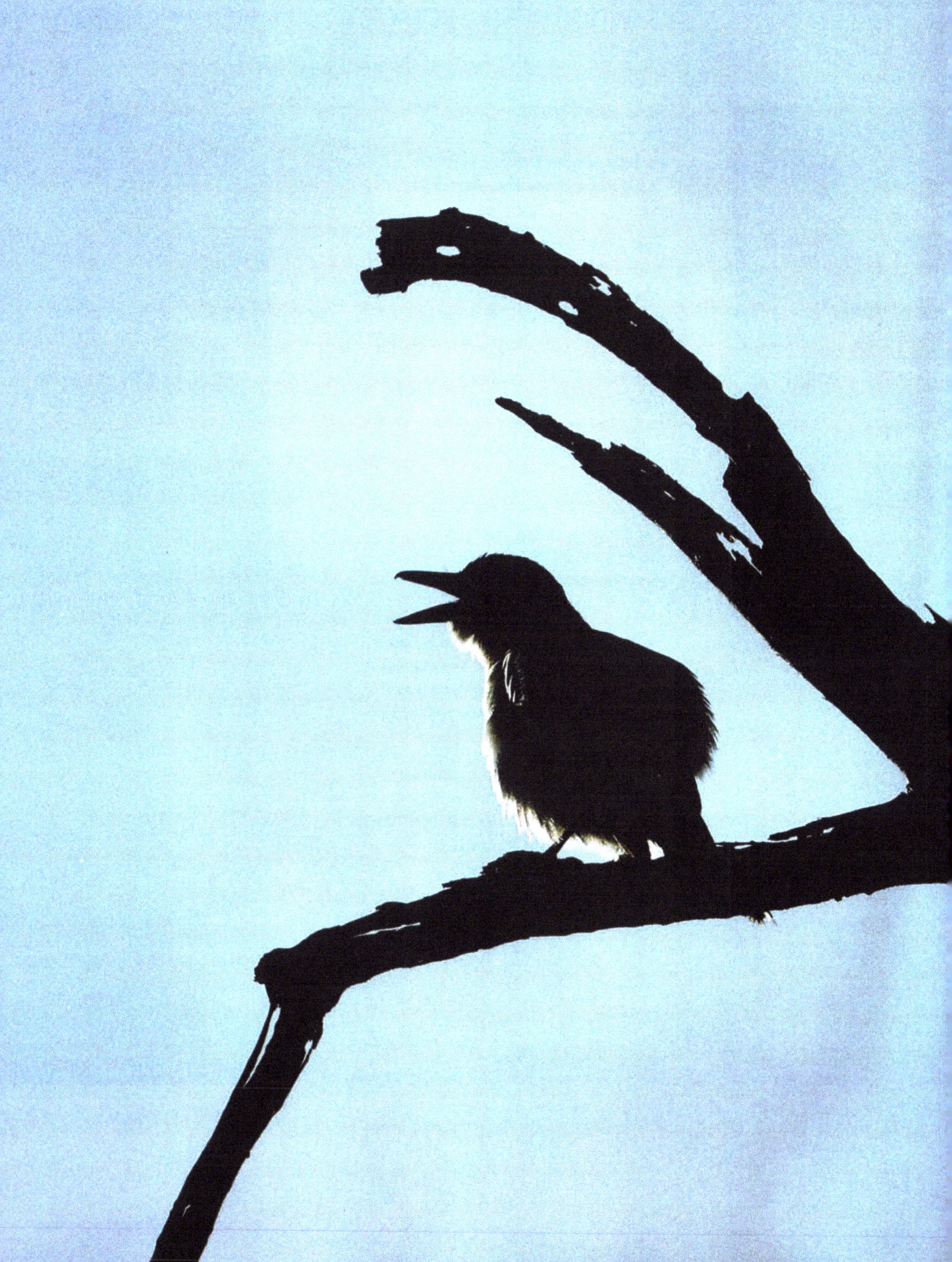

SUNRISE IN STONE COUNTRY

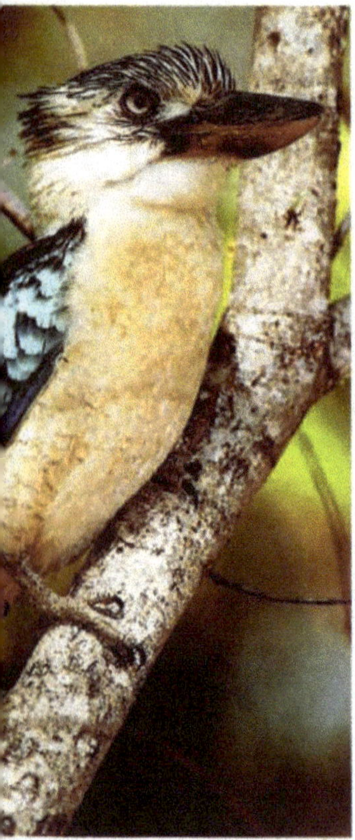

Sandstone outliers
lift their rugged turrets
through the enchanting dawn
like castles of another kingdom.

The dependable old sun
pushes his way up
over the great escarpment
and touches peaks with red gold.

Bats take shelter in caves,
agile wallabies seek rest
on the rocky slopes,
termites begin relentless labour.

It's time for the singing of the birds:
the bar-shouldered dove,
the call of the honeyeater,
the strident joy of the kookaburra.

Now the light reaches the lowlands,
the distant swamps and billabongs,
glazing across bird-lined waters
and suffusing lush grasses and reeds.

This one small parcel of creation
is awake with the glory of a new day —
awake to serve the Wisdom that made it
and the Love that sustains it!

LEFT: *Blue-winged Kookaburra*
RIGHT: *Kakadu Dawn from Jabiru Dreaming (Djagarna)*

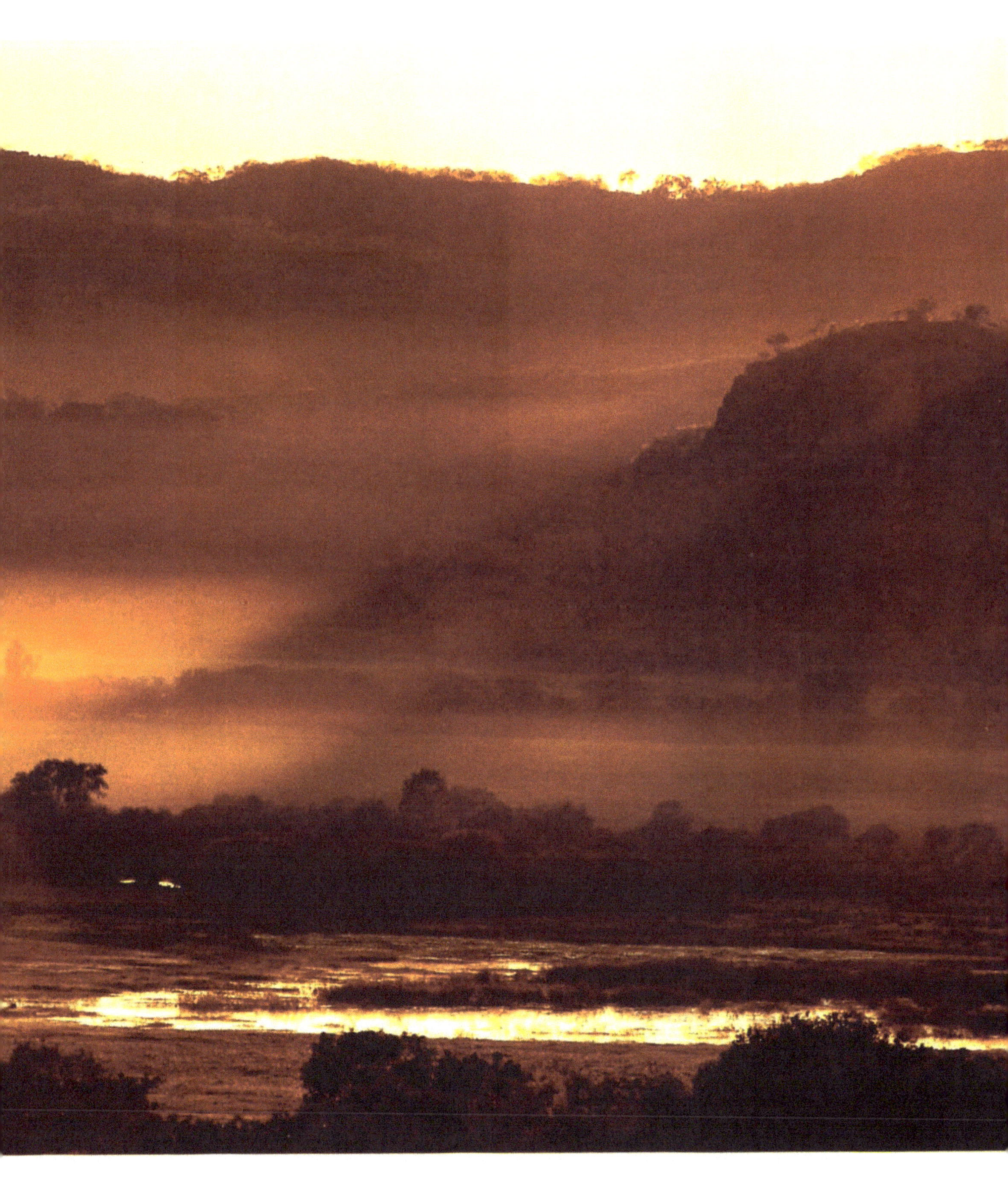

THE DOVE

Dove in the stone country
calling at daybreak.
Sign of the Mystery,
Spirit of love.

Dove among mangroves,
enjoying the morning.
Sign of belonging,
Spirit of love.

Dove over waters,
descending like light.
Sign of the Holy One,
Spirit of love.

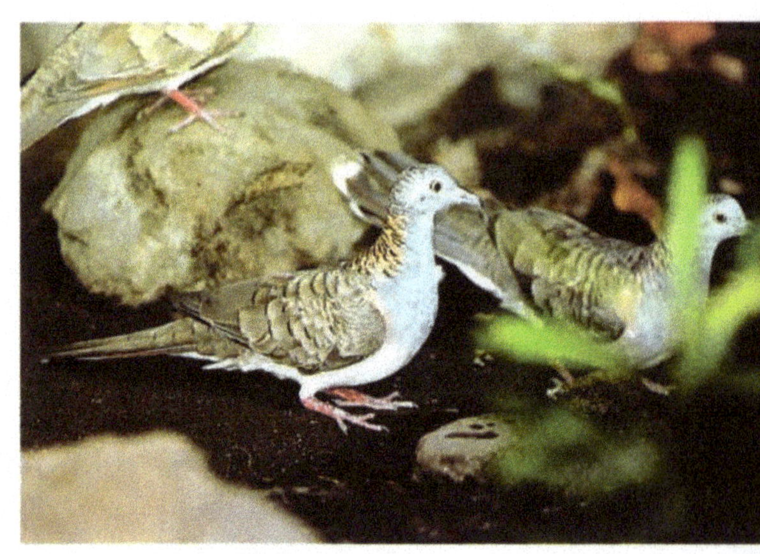

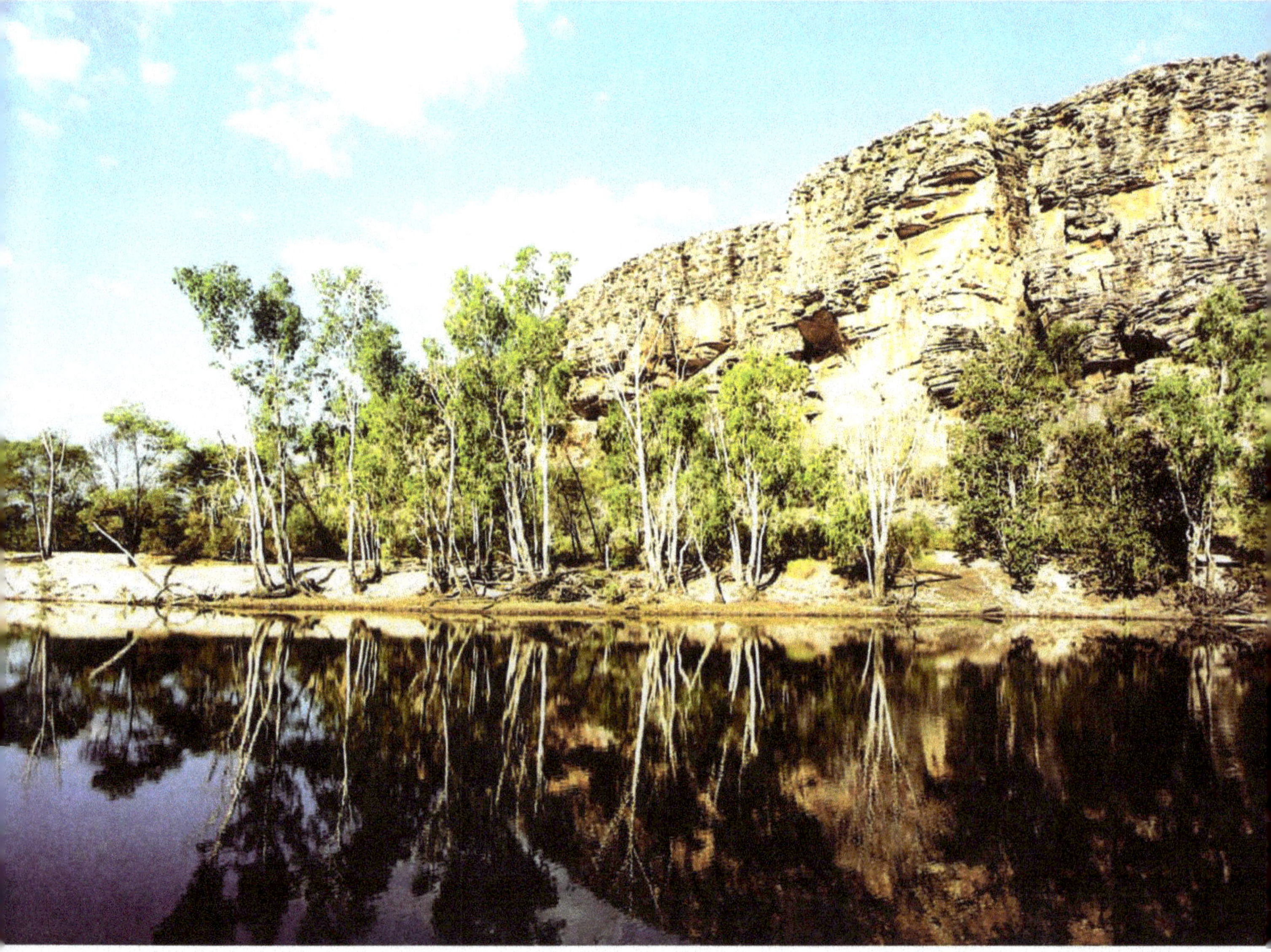

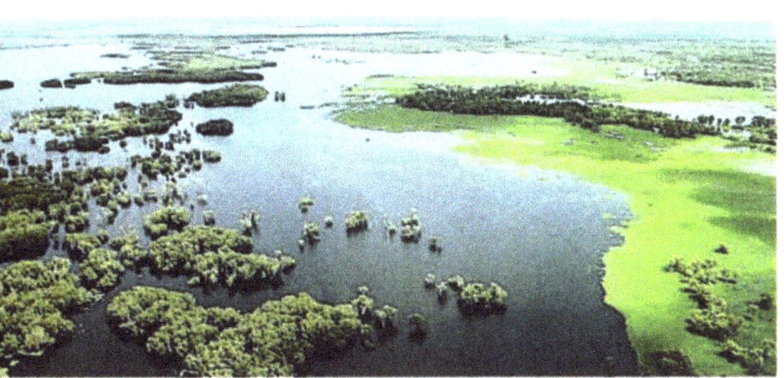

LOVE-LIGHT

God, the most holy,
God, the most beautiful,
said:
Let there be light.
And it was so.

Star-light glistening
  on smooth rock pools.
Moon-light caressing
  lilies in billabongs.
Green-light filtering
  to forest floors.
White-light viewed
  from the mouth of a cave.
Fierce-light bouncing
  off rockcliffs at noon.
Multi-light flashing
  on a swooping rainbow bird.
Dusk-light gentling
  over wide floodplains.
Dawn-light cresting
  over many-tiered stone country.

Love-light embracing
  all things,
  all people,
from you, most glorious God!
Aflame is the world
  with your glory!
Alight are your people
  with holy joy!

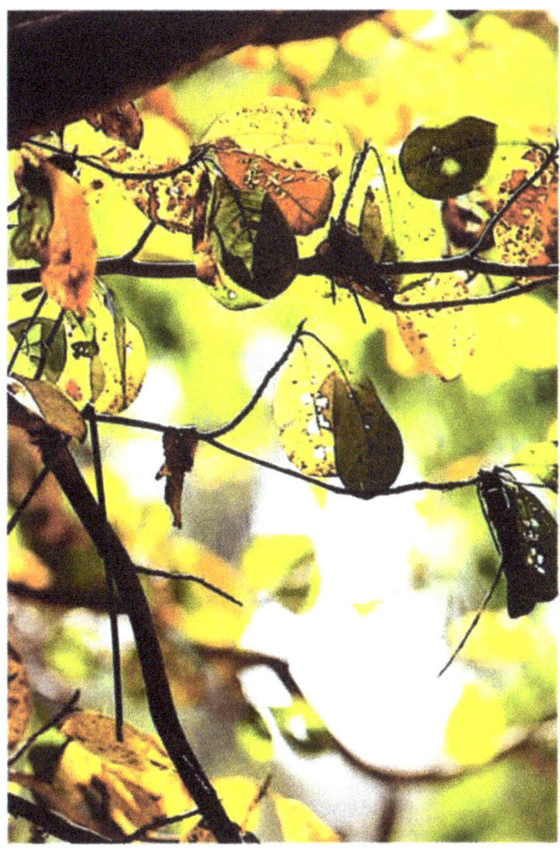

UPPER LEFT: *Bar-shouldered Doves*
LOWER LEFT: *Djuwarr Billabong, Deaf Adder Gorge*
UPPER RIGHT: *Kakadu wetlands in flood, South Alligator River*
LOWER RIGHT: *Light through leaves*

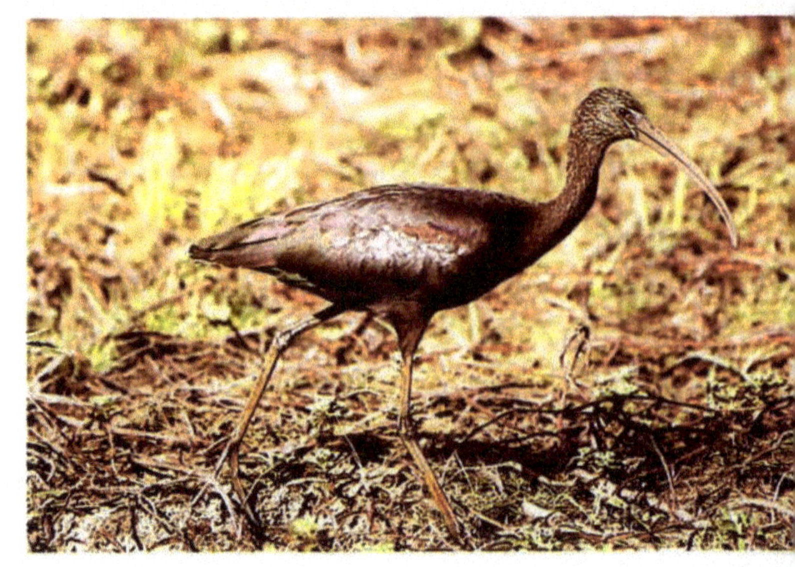

UPPER: Glossy Ibis, Yellow Waters
LOWER: South Alligator floodplain (Gumunkuwuy)

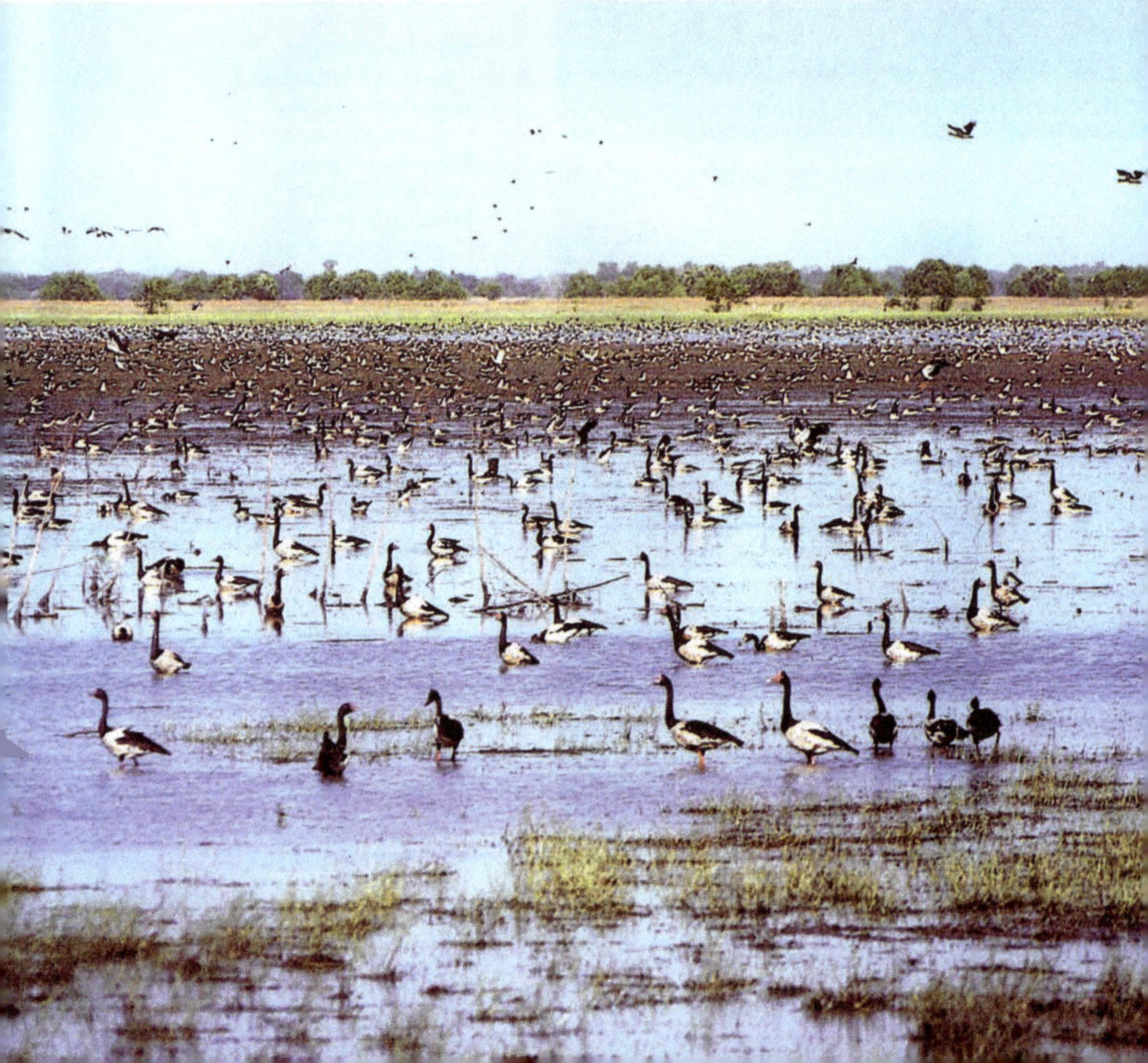

NEAR EDEN?

A small cloud of pigmy geese take wing,
wheeling over the wetlands,
green-sheening in the afternoon sun.

Watching us, yet not alarmed,
bulky magpie geese, legs red-knobbly,
stand massed in the shallows.

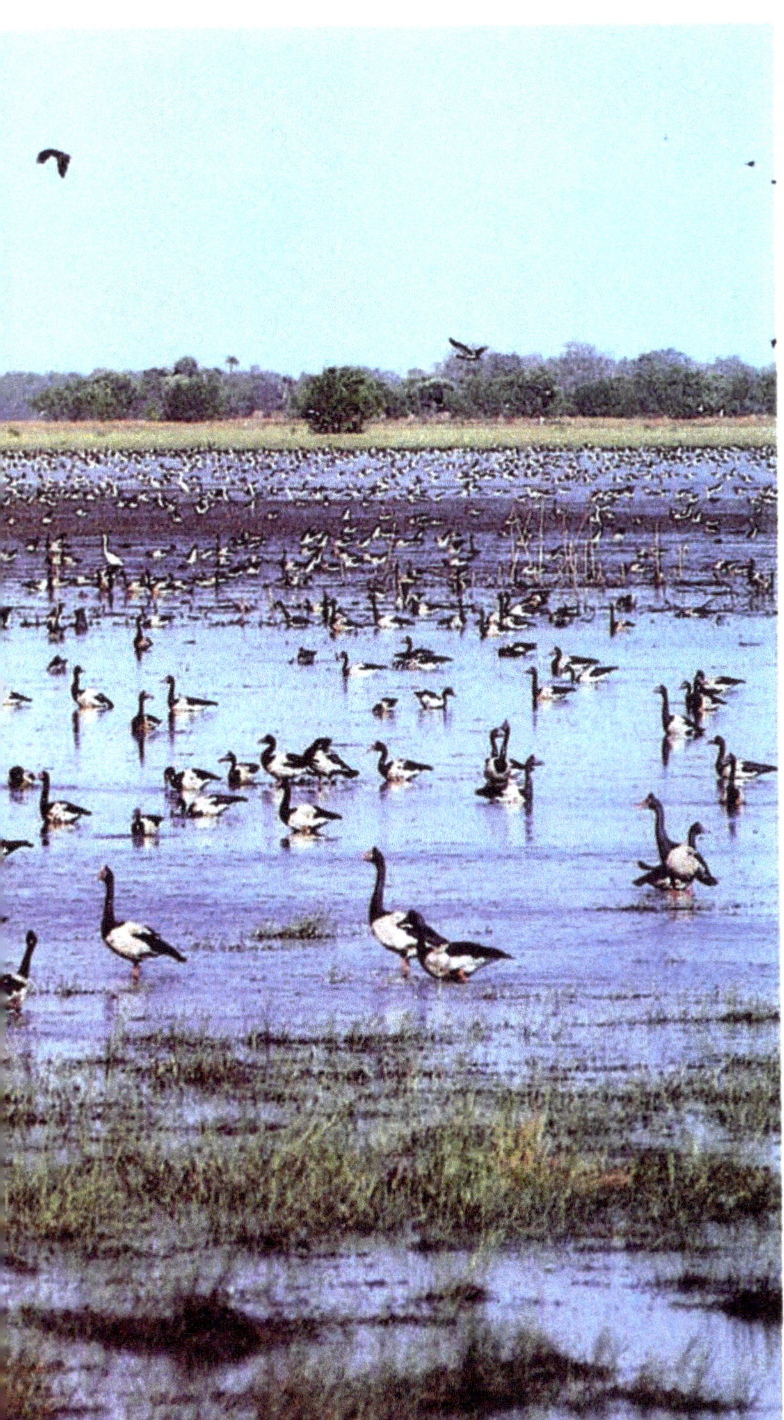

A light wind dusts the water's face
and ruffles the heads of tall grasses
which stretch to where paper barks stand tall.

Now a tribe of Burdekin ducks,
brown backs sloping, glistening,
twist necks, warily watching.

Glossy ibis pretend we are not here
as they stalk around the margins
with sickle-beaks ready for prey.

Their neighbours, more distant, the egrets,
outstretch elegant white necks
and stand like Michelangelo marble.

A gross of whistling ducks catch panic,
rise like a swarm of offended bees
and flurry away to the east.

Some tall jabiru, reserved and remote,
keep stalking up and down a mudbank
out in the swamp near a mangrove.

All the while, lotus birds
in pairs mime messiah convincingly
across weed and lily leaves.

My senses are in a tumult of joy
at the liberality of it all!
Am I somewhere near Eden?

O Wonderful is your name, loving Creator!
Blessed are the works of your hands!

FIRST THINGS FIRST

Asleep in the folds of night,
long have I joyfully dreamed
the wonder of flight.

Yet next day I am found
plodding, and sometimes crawling,
across the lowly ground.

Lord, take not away
the glory of that dream
as I begin each day.

But tell me surely
that walking truly
across uneven soil
without despairing
is faith's
first goal.

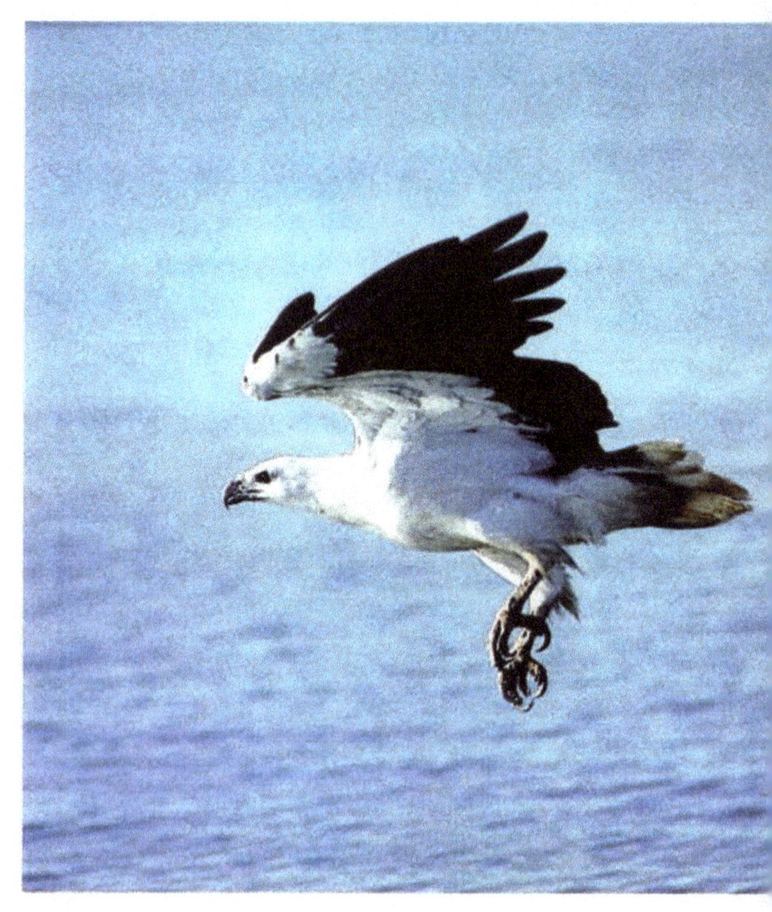

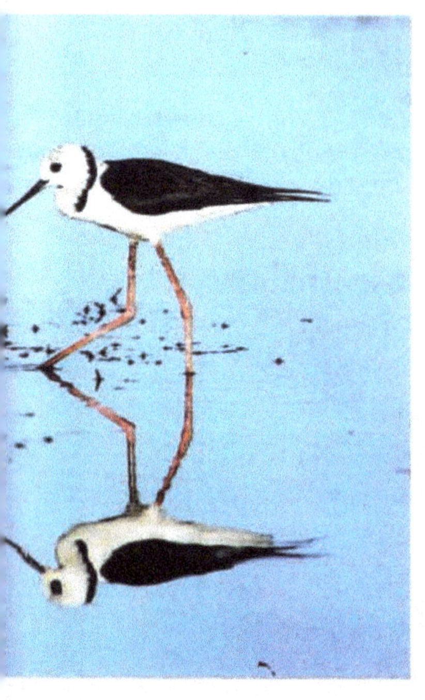

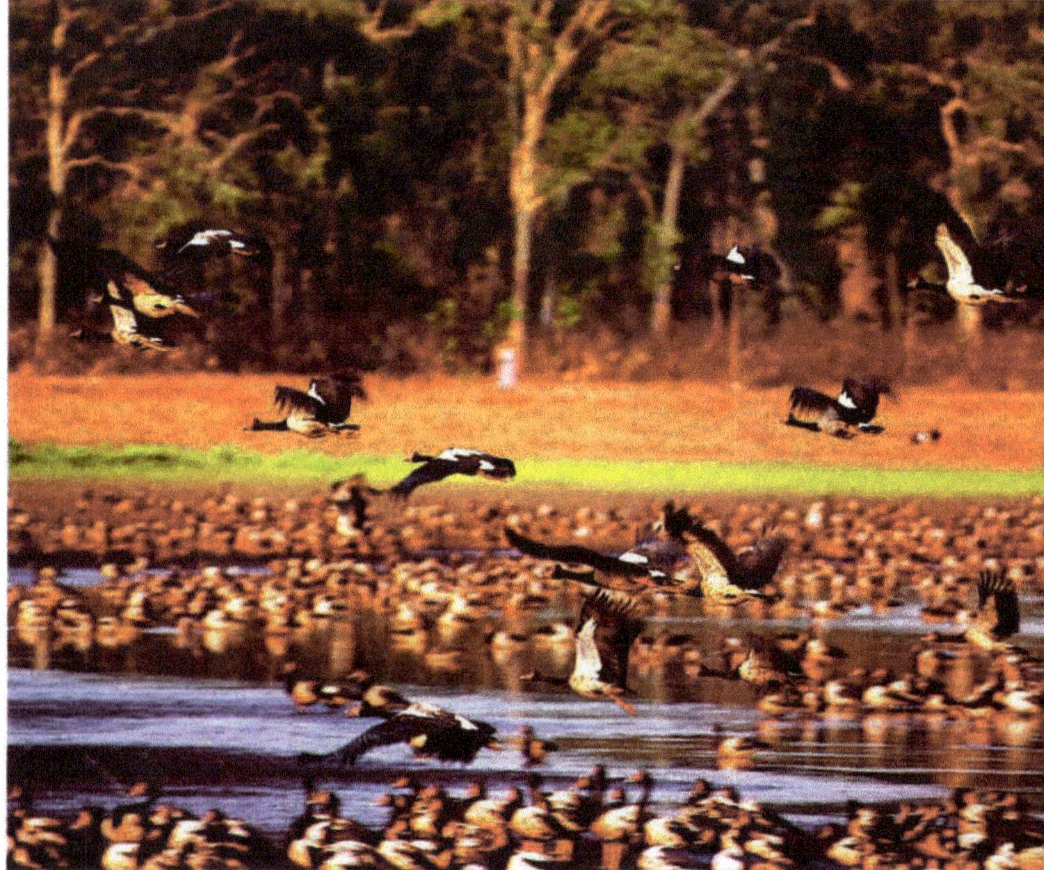

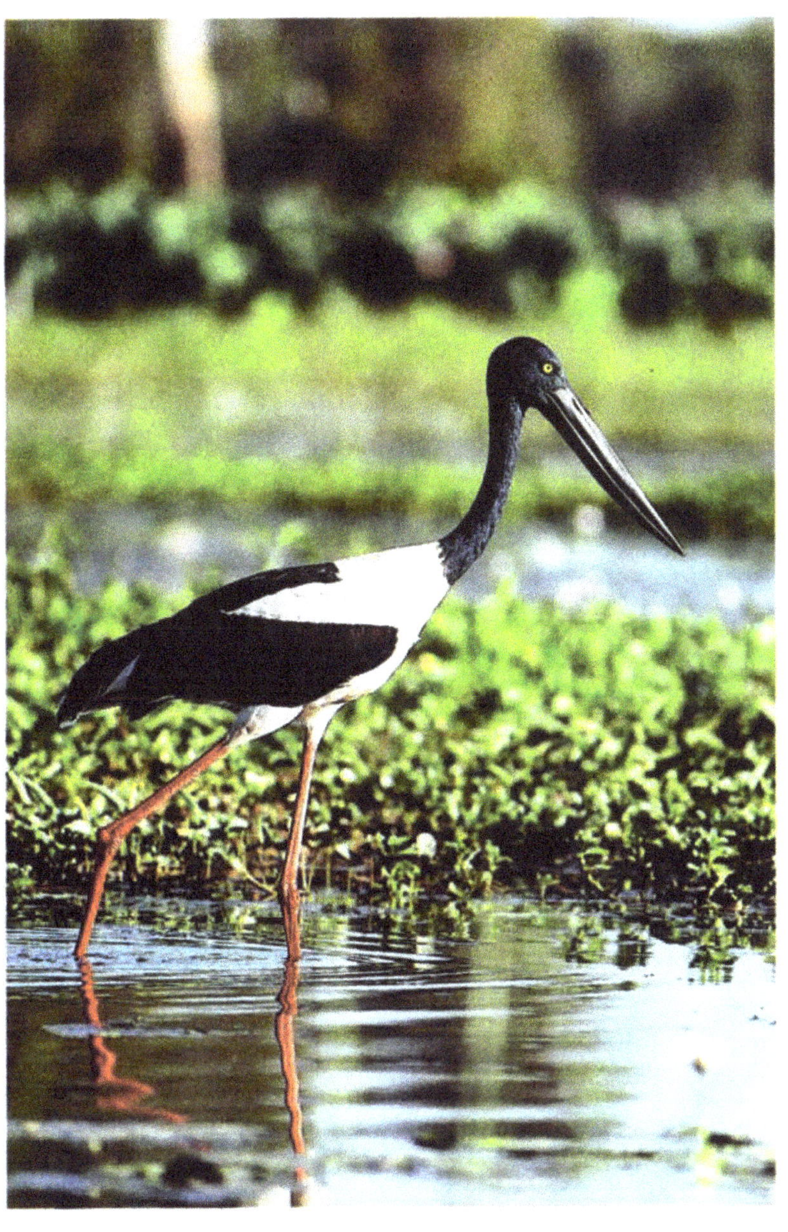

KNOWING

The jabiru knows her world
   and is nourished in abundance.
The turtle and swallow read seasons.
   And the brolga knows when to rejoice.

But do we yet read the times
   and know the possibilities in change?
Do we discern the winds
   and love the mystery of light?

Come, day of fulfilment —
   when knowledge is inward written,
and from the greatest to the least
   all shall know their inheritance!

(Inspired by Jeremiah 8:7 & 31:34)

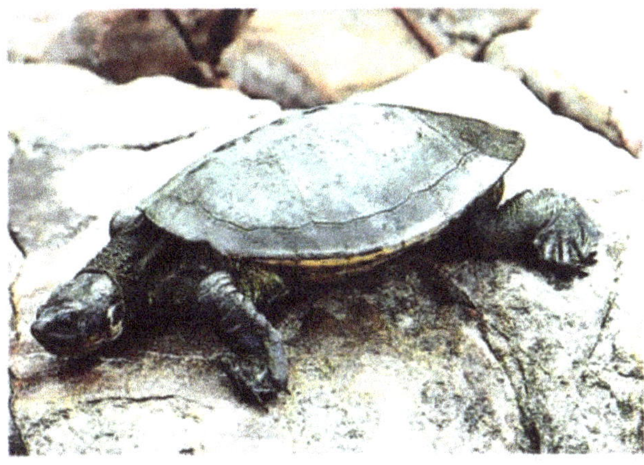

UPPER LEFT *White-breasted Sea Eagle*
FAR LEFT *Pied Stilt, Bamboo Creek*
NEARER LEFT *Magpie Geese on Angurrapal Billabong*
UPPER RIGHT *Female Jabiru, Yellow Waters*
LOWER RIGHT *Short-necked Turtle*
OVERLEAF *Malangangerr*

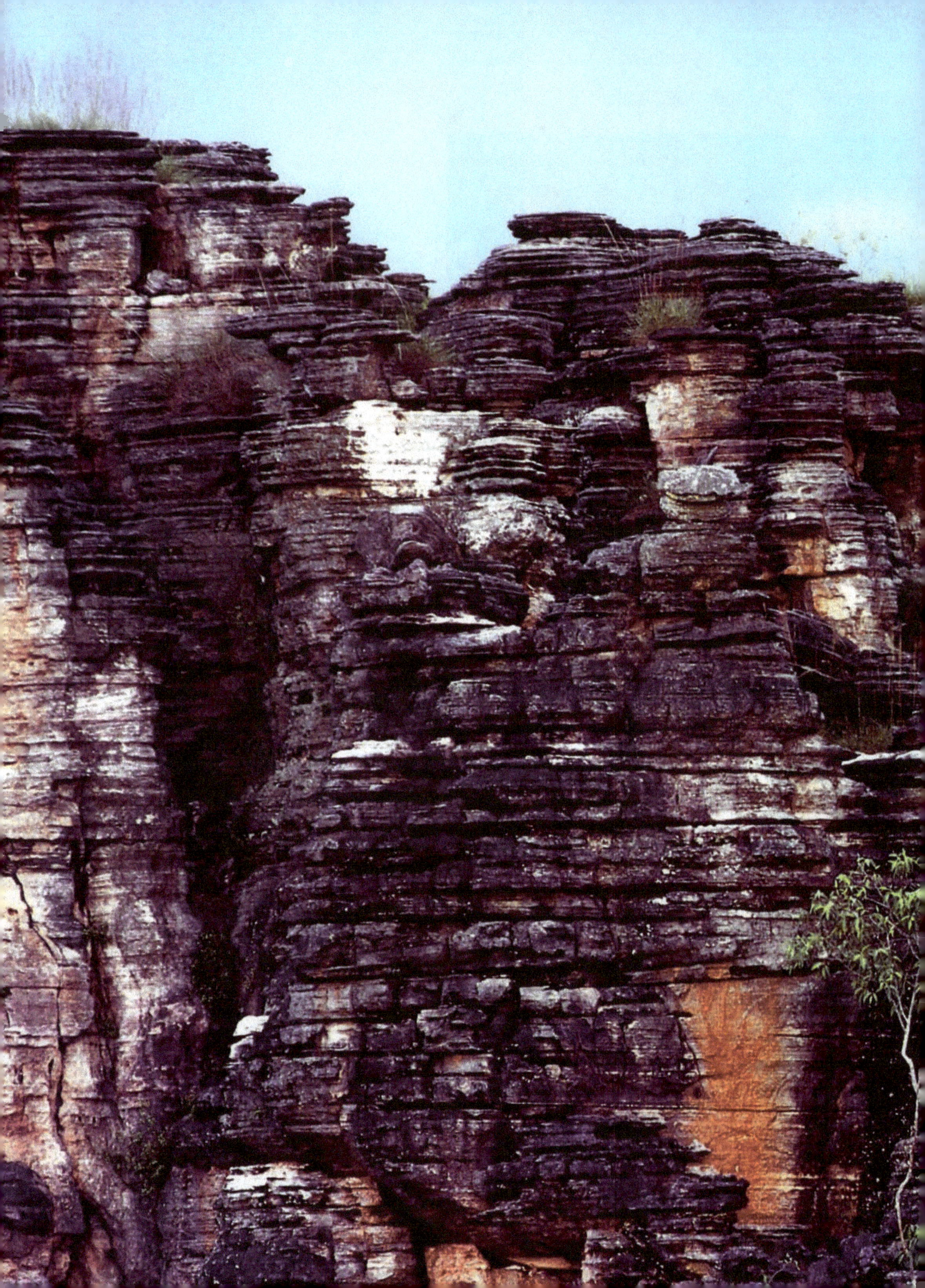

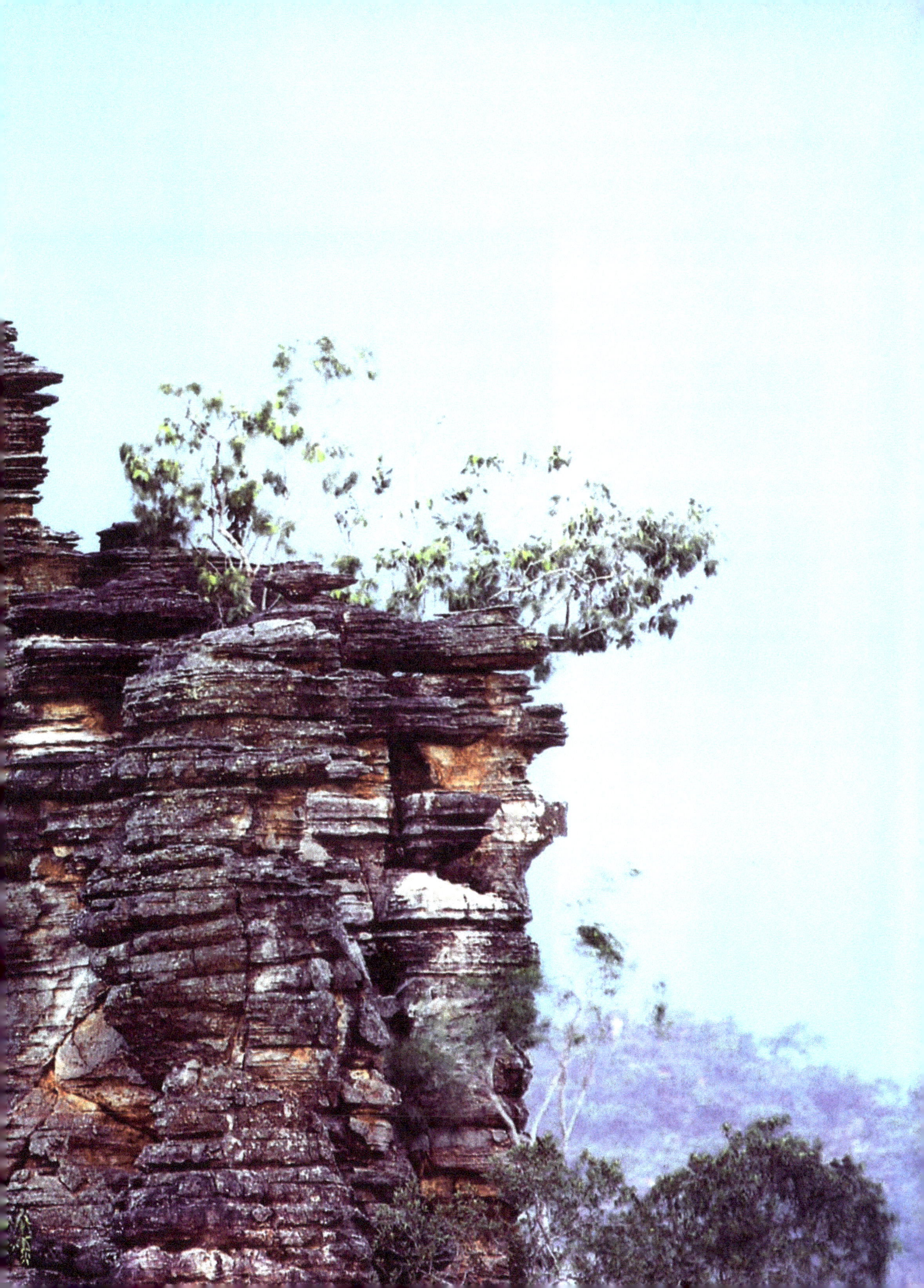

SEEING GOD

God is on the waters,
  God is in the land,
God is on the mountain,
  God is in your hand.

God is in the forest,
  God is on the plain,
God is in the desert,
  God is in your brain.

God is in the sunlight,
  God is in the air,
God is on a falcon's wing,
  God is in your prayer.

God is in our laughter,
  God is in sad loss.
God is in forgiveness,
  God is on the Cross.

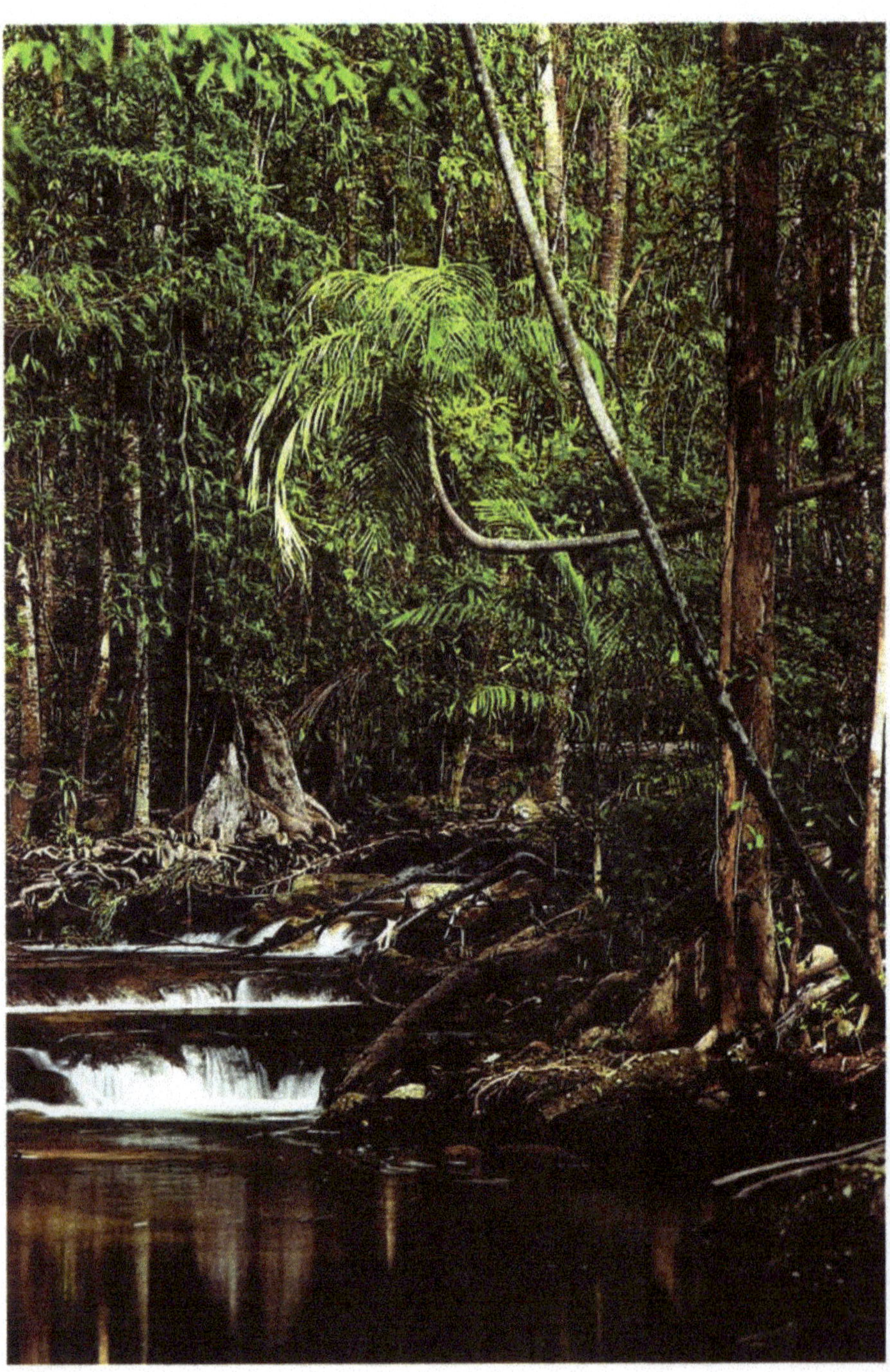

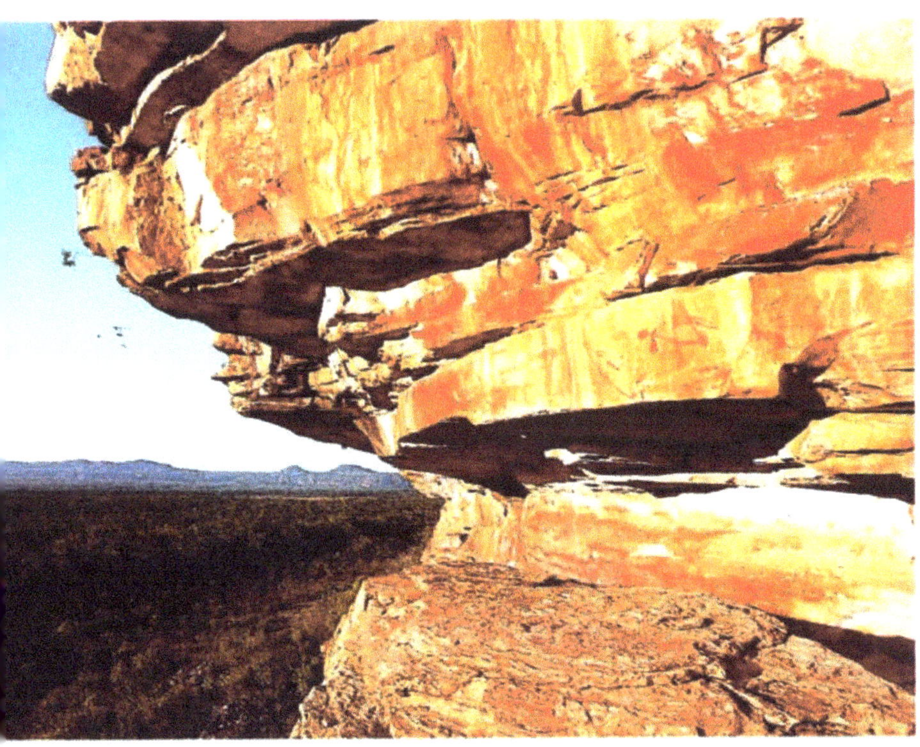

LEFT *Gulungul Creek, Mt Brockman*
UPPER RIGHT *Deaf Adder Gorge from Djuwarr*
LOWER RIGHT *Jim Jim Falls*

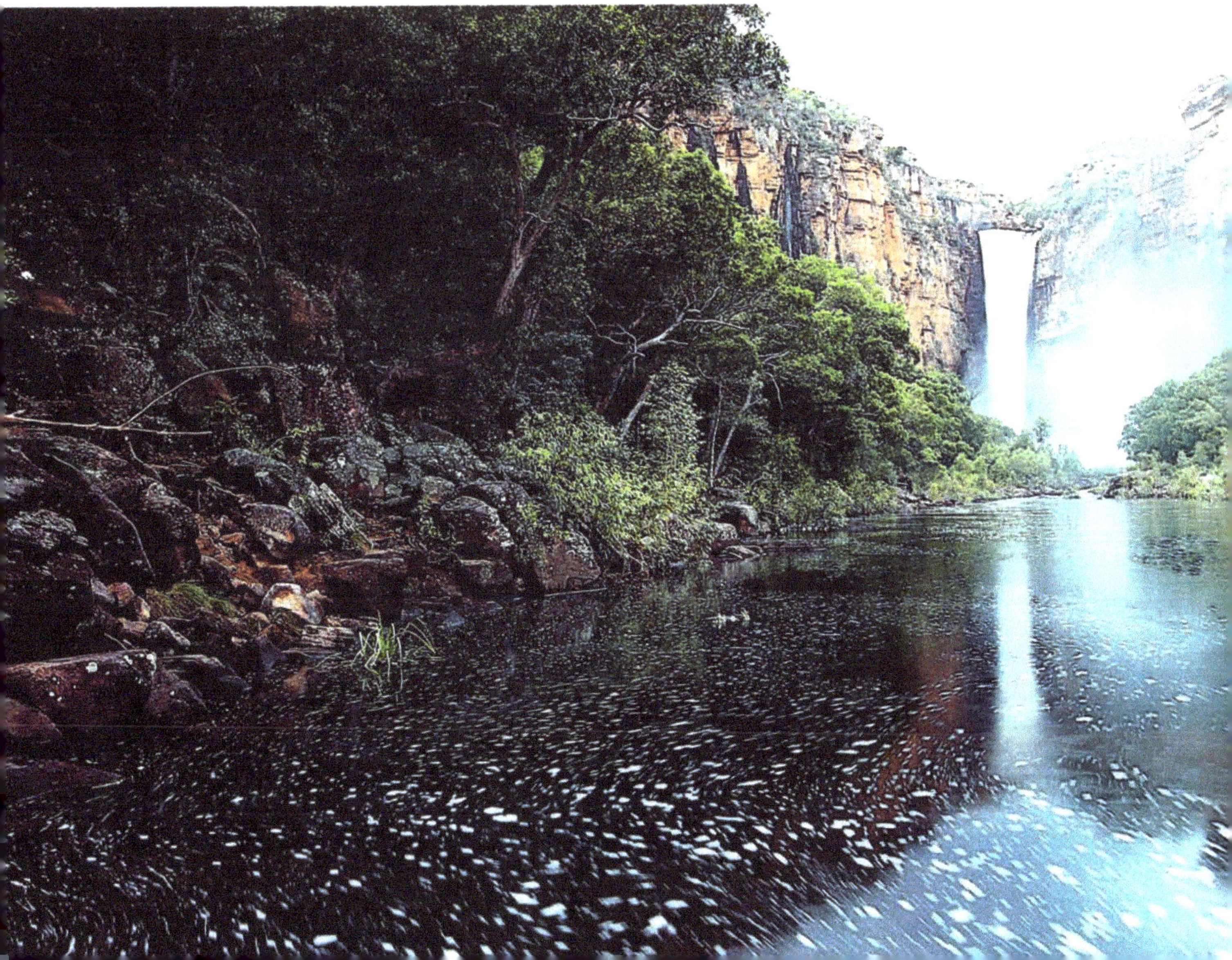

LOVE'S ENERGY

Your energy, O Lord, is infinite,
your authority everlasting.
You divide many rivers,
you thunder in the waterfall,
you surge in the flood,
and even tame the crocodile.

Yet you have many enemies —
numerous in our land —
fools who mock your existence,
or mix your name with obscenities.

Save us, O Lord, from their power,
deliver us from their wounding.
We are in their midst like peaceful doves
surrounded by fierce hawks.

O Lord, rescue all who are endangered;
remember the homeless poor.
You alone are True God,
Love from the very beginning,
Friend of living creatures,
Saviour of all people!

UPPER LEFT: *Escarpment pool*
LOWER LEFT: *Saltwater Crocodile, East Alligator River*
RIGHT: *Twin Falls*

(Inspired by Psalm 74:12–20)

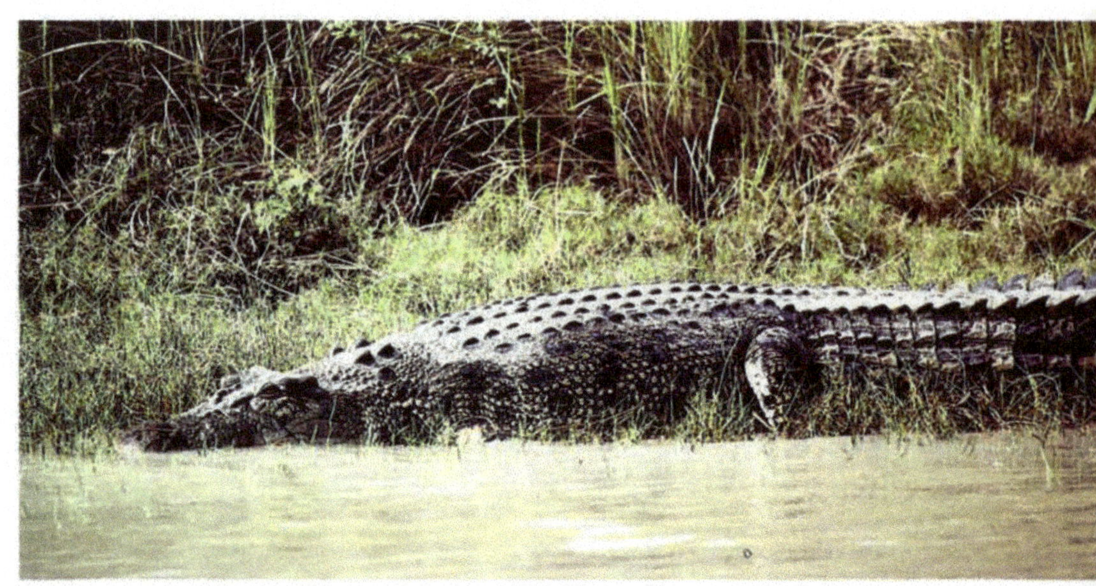

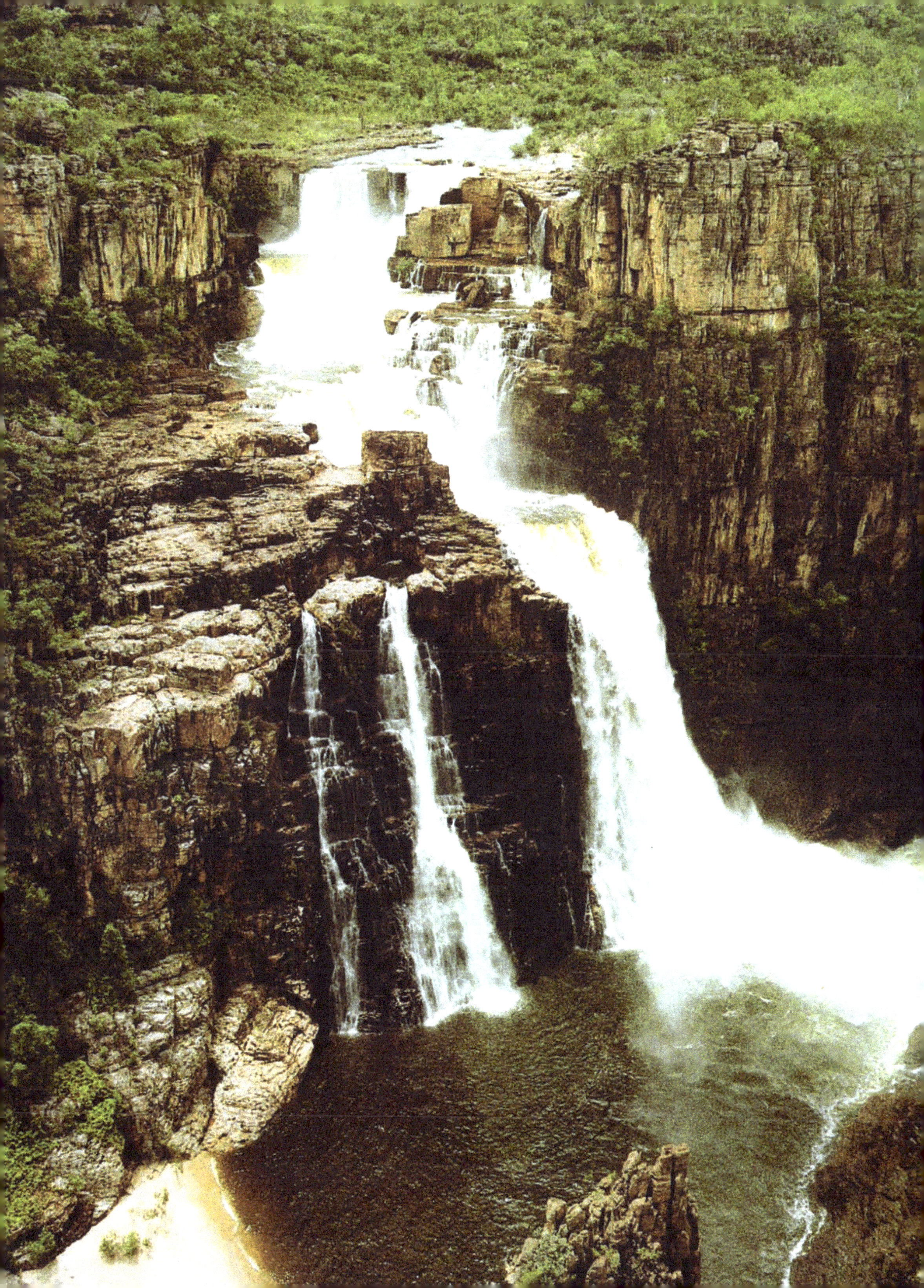

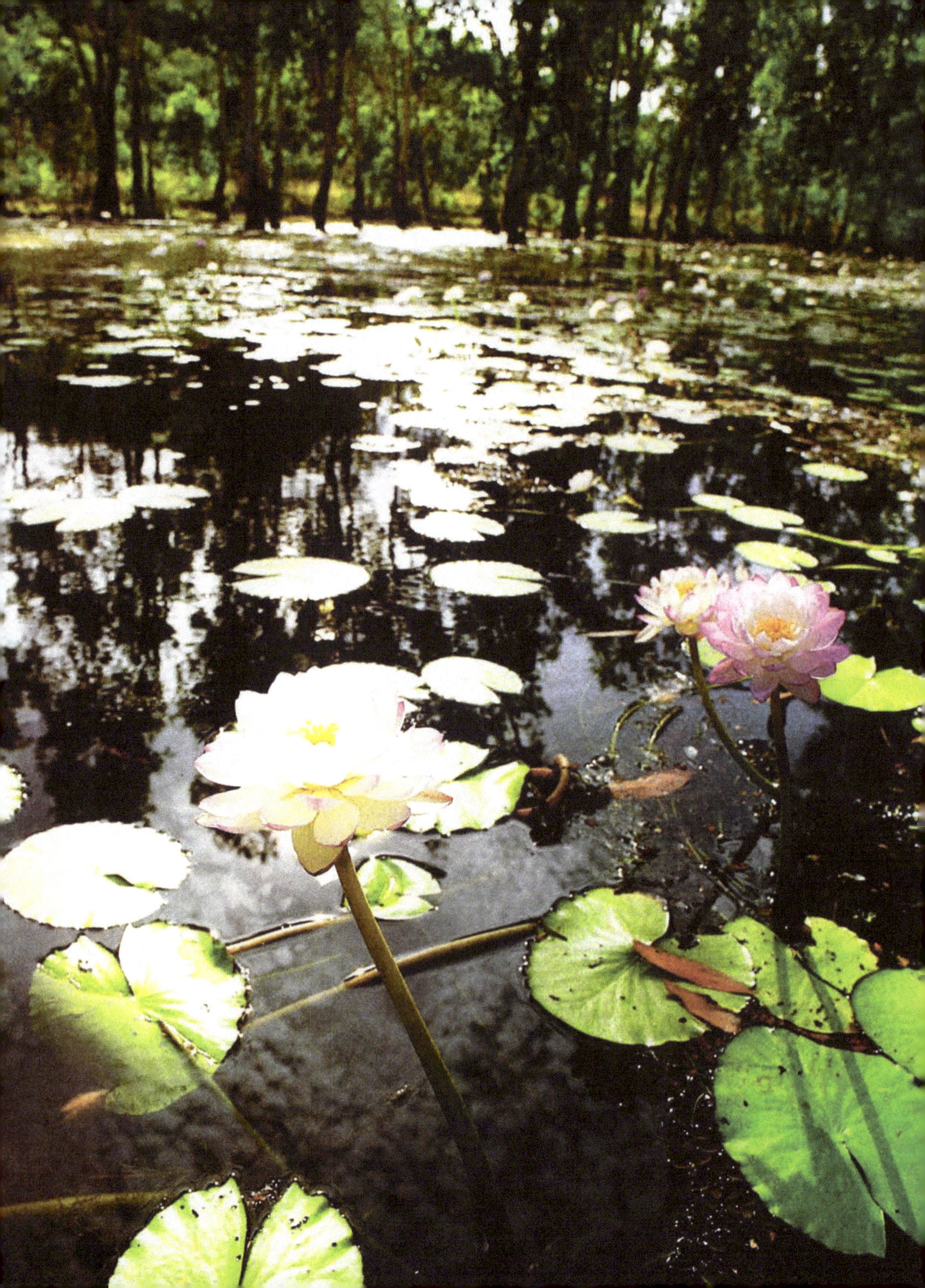

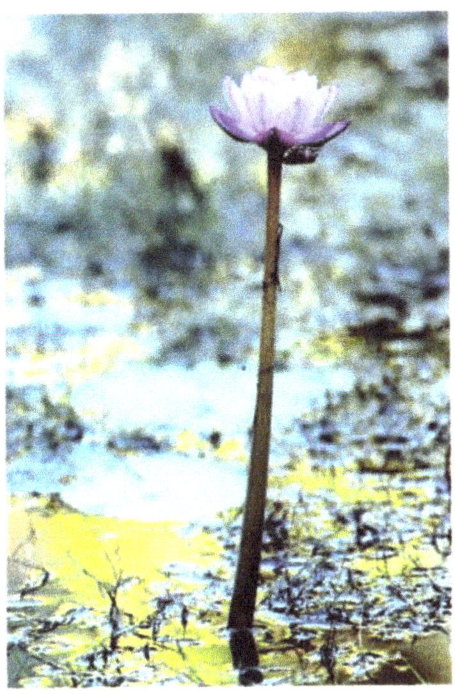

LEFT *Buyuwk Goluy Billabong*
UPPER RIGHT *Water Lily* (Nymphaea violacea)
LOWER RIGHT *Young Lotus Bird, Yellow Waters*

WATER LILY

The good Lord said
to his most skilful
angel:

Take a billabong,
grow some slender paper barks
on one side,
and place
a red-rock face
on the other.
Then add tall reeds
where fowl may nest.

Now within the water
fashion a special plant
with long limbs,
and leaves
wider than hands,
on which birds may walk.

Then carefully
raise from the roots
of this plant
a long, firm stem
on which to set
a matchless flower
in due season.

Let the sun
at dawn or dusk
outline the flower's
pure shape,
and tint it with colour
from the lips
of cherubim.

For eyes not yet created
shall one day come,
discover,
and marvel
at this fair
but faint reflection
of amazing grace.

MORNING

Whatever the Lord does,
he does well
through mountain and valley
on floodplain and billabong.

He makes the morning mist
rise around sandstone outliers.
He sends the wallaby to rest,
and wakes the dove and kingfisher.
He tints the peaks with crimson,
and calls the world to worship.

UPPER LEFT *Forest Kingfisher*
LOWER LEFT *View from Jabiru Dreaming (Djagarna)*
UPPER RIGHT *'From plateau to plain' (Djuwarr)*
LOWER RIGHT *Great Egret*

Let all who have eyes to see,
let all who have ears to hear,
greet the Lord
who does all things well!

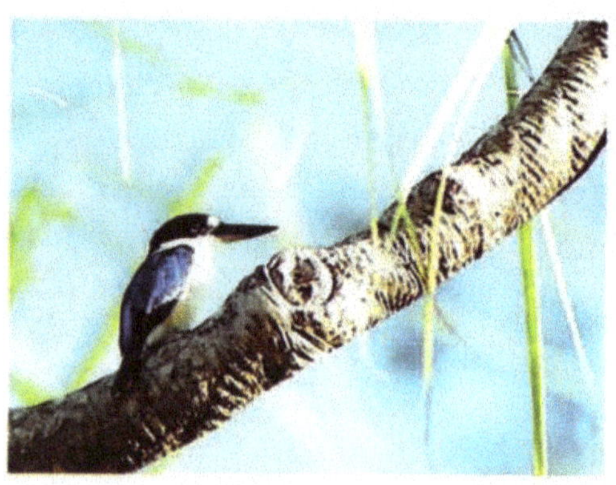

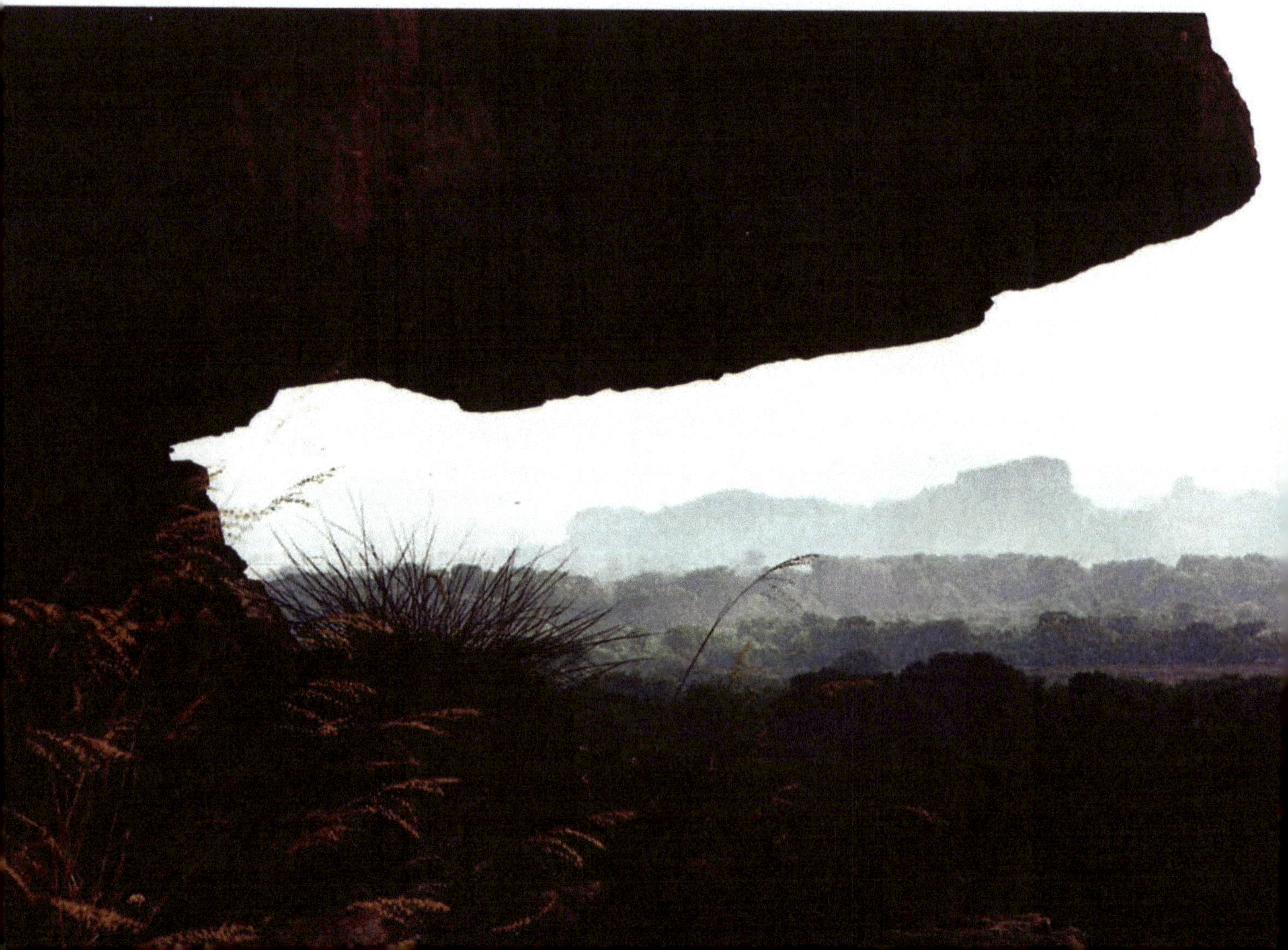

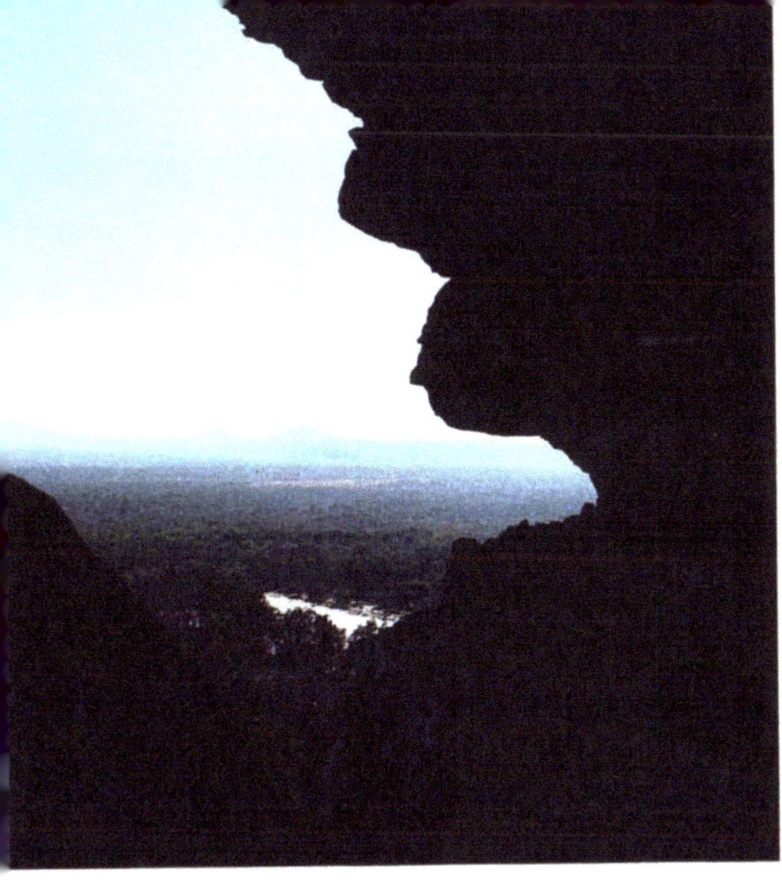

PRAYER OF THE DUST

Come, dayspring from on high,
come to your own
and fashion a generation
of seers.

Spread the dawn
over grey horizons,
and prepare eyes
for the first light.

Come as you came
on a cloud of yesterdays,
and touch the dust
with a radiant image.

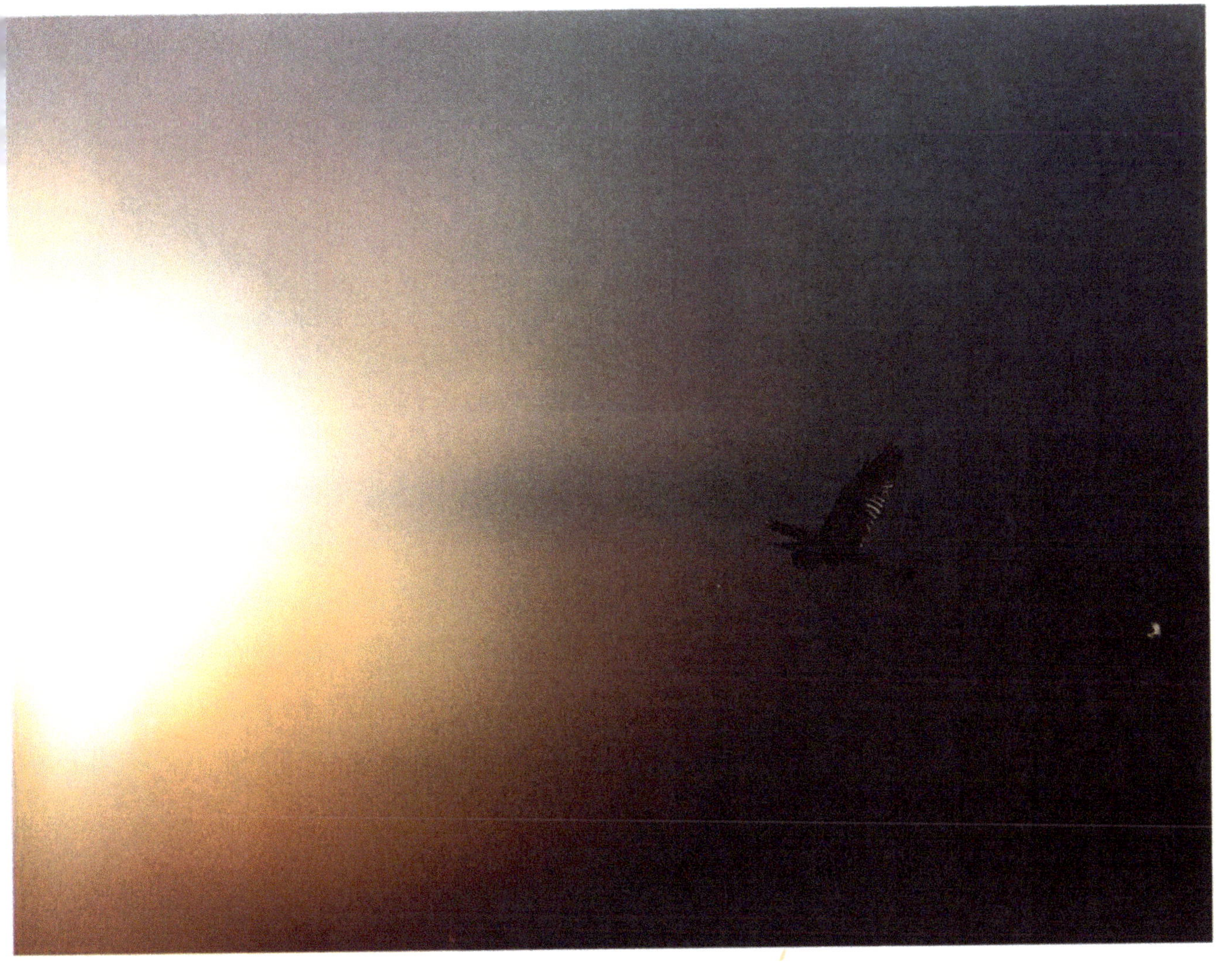

SIMPLE HAPPINESS

Is not this happiness:
To rise in the company
of a good friend;
to eat a simple breakfast
with gratitude;
to say one's prayers
outdoors in the sun
with a rowdy choir
of red-collared lorikeets;
to pick up a book without haste
and savour rich meditations
from wise ones
who lived long ago;
to remember loved ones
far away or near;
to know it is the very truth
when the Nazarene says:
'Be of good cheer'.

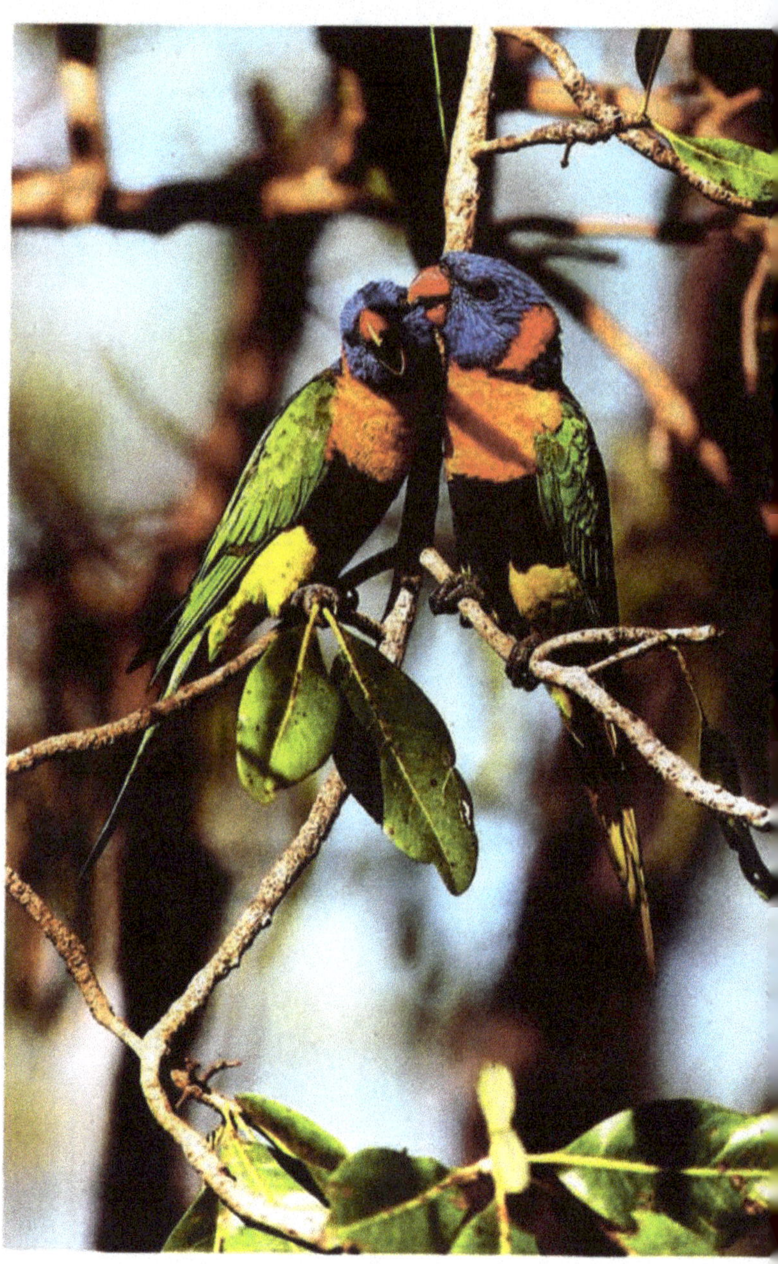

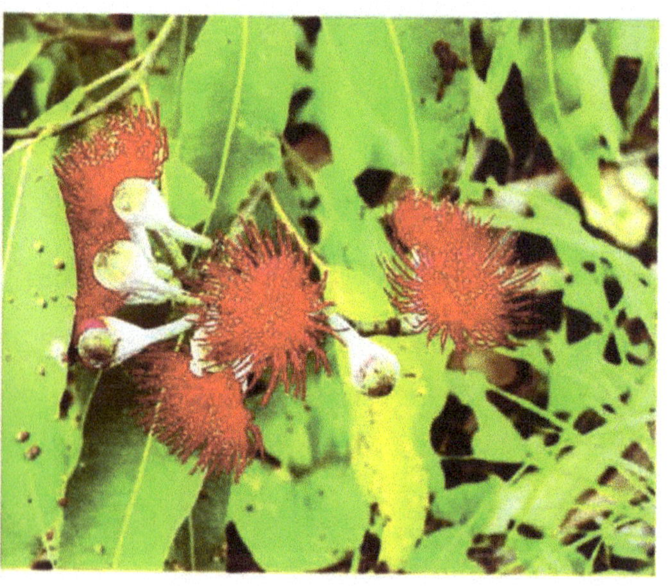

UPPER: *Red-collared Lorikeets*
LOWER: *Eucalyptus ptychocarpa* (Malangangerr)

MONSOON

Sound in our ears
   like a mighty rushing wind;
Light in our eyes
   like tongues of lightning;
New breath in our lungs
   like the gift of a Risen One;

Then weariness is washed away
and everything sings with joy
at the renewing of life.

LOWER: *Kapok Tree at Umudal, East Alligator River*
OVERLEAF: *Magpie Geese, Yellow Waters*

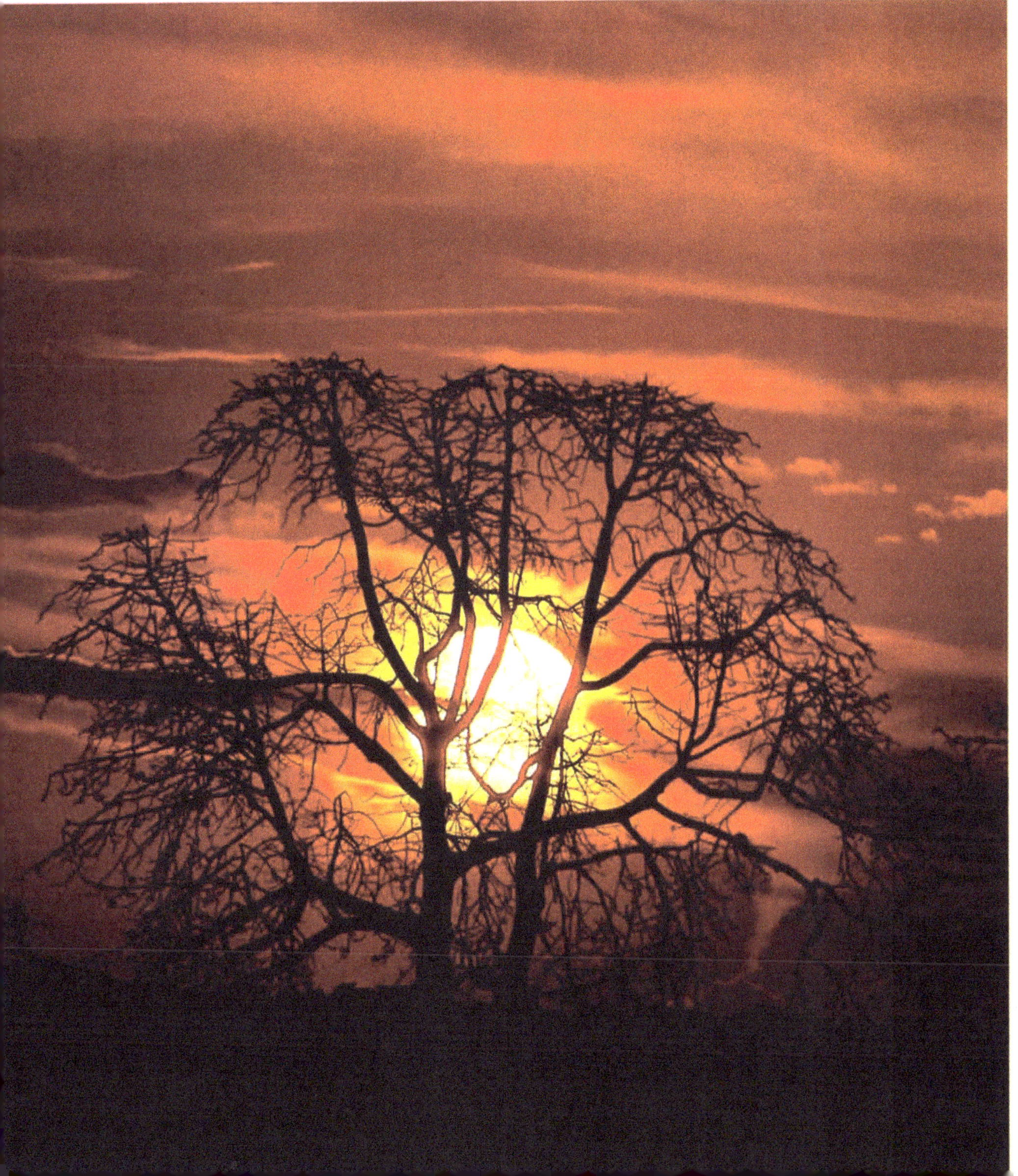

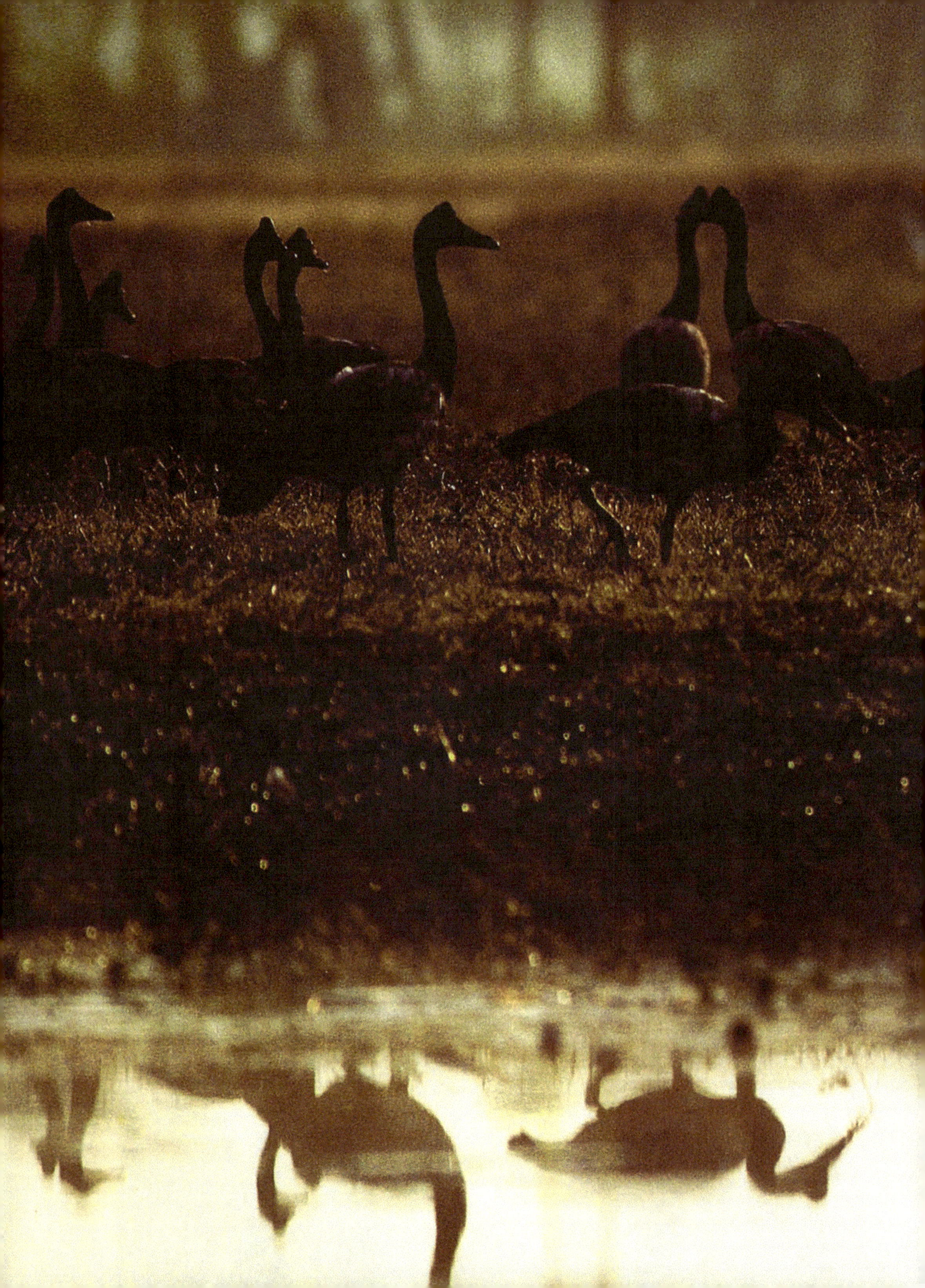

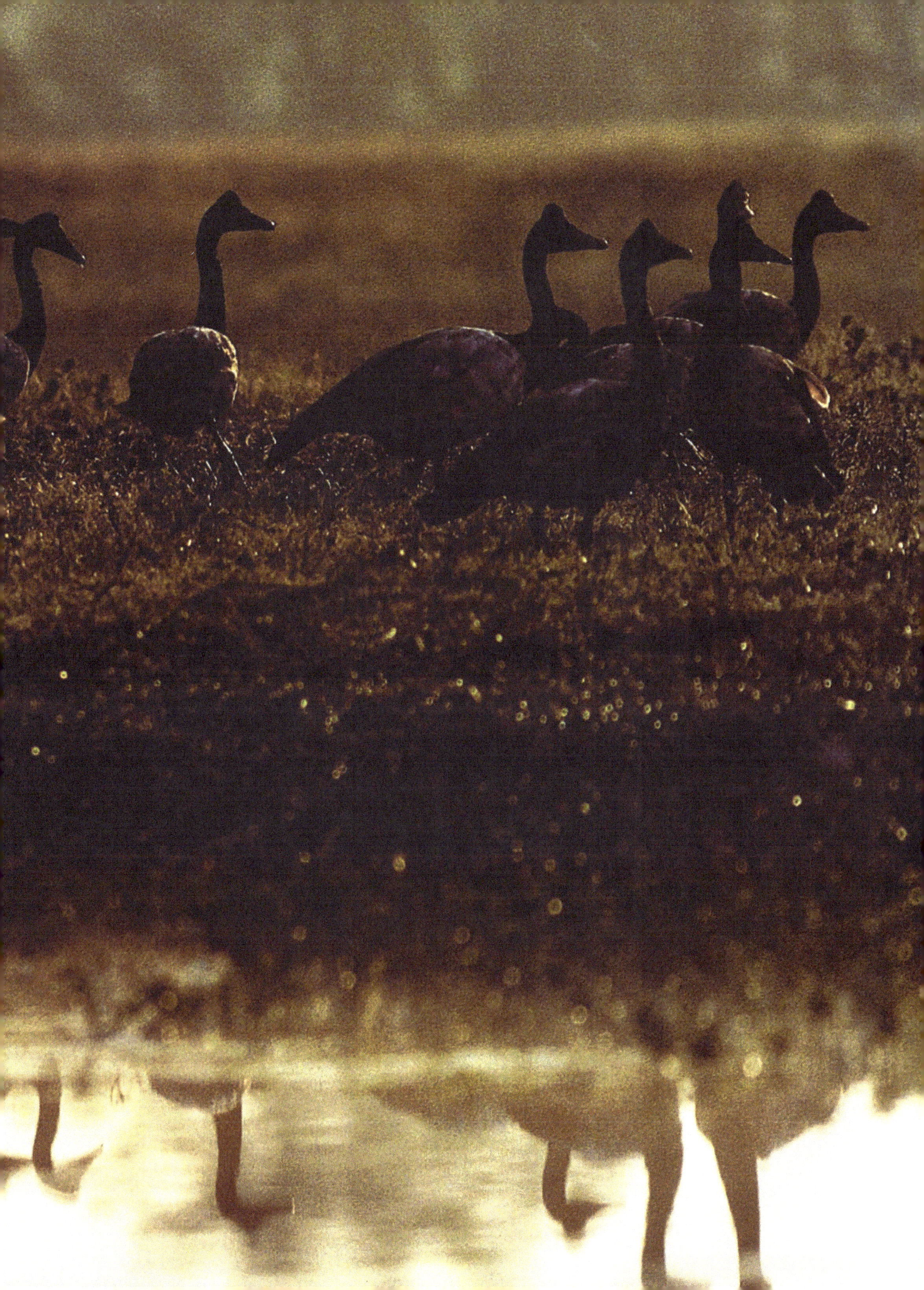

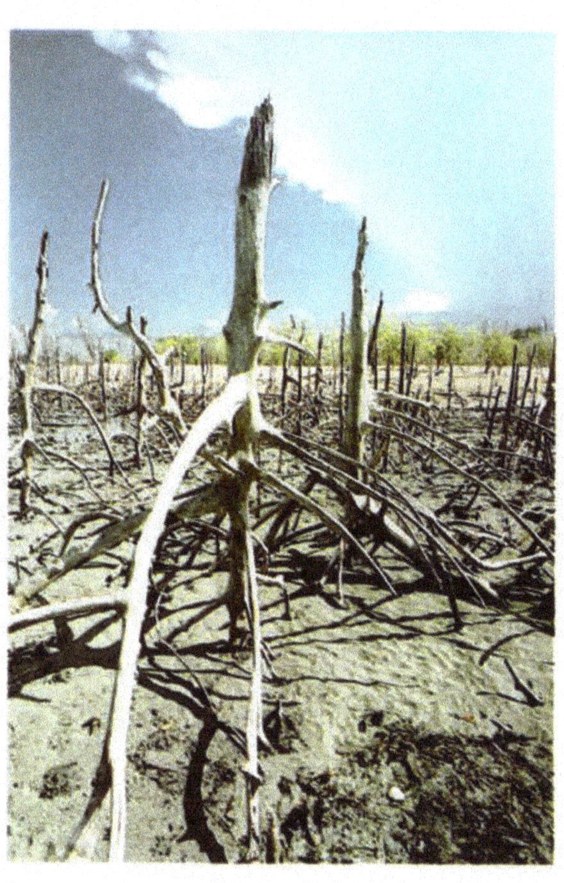

MUDDY FEET

When events
flow sluggishly,
forcing me
to spend time
in muddy places,

Lord,
give me the grace
to make use
of mud
as successfully
as does
the mangrove.

LEFT *Dead Mangrove Forest*
RIGHT *Mangrove Tree, East Alligator Mouth*

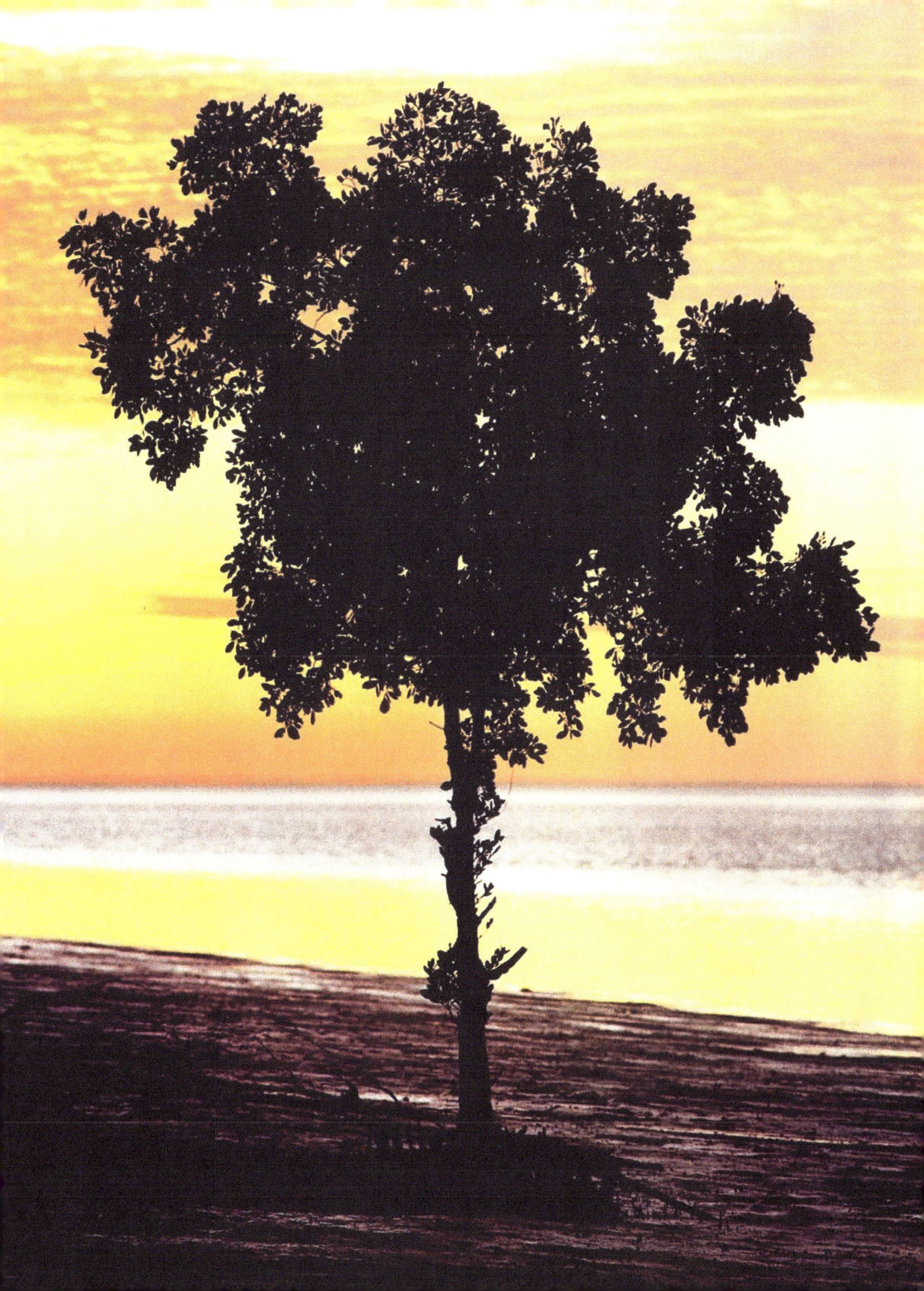

NONE SO BLIND?

O eye of Australian,
beguiled by the movements
on the stock exchange,
can't you see
the 'many-splendoured thing'?

O eye of Australian,
lured with the fiction
and fashion of self-fulfilment,
can't you see
the surge of the Spirit?

O eye of Australian,
programmed for lust
and lost in its wasteland,
can't you see
the light of Life?

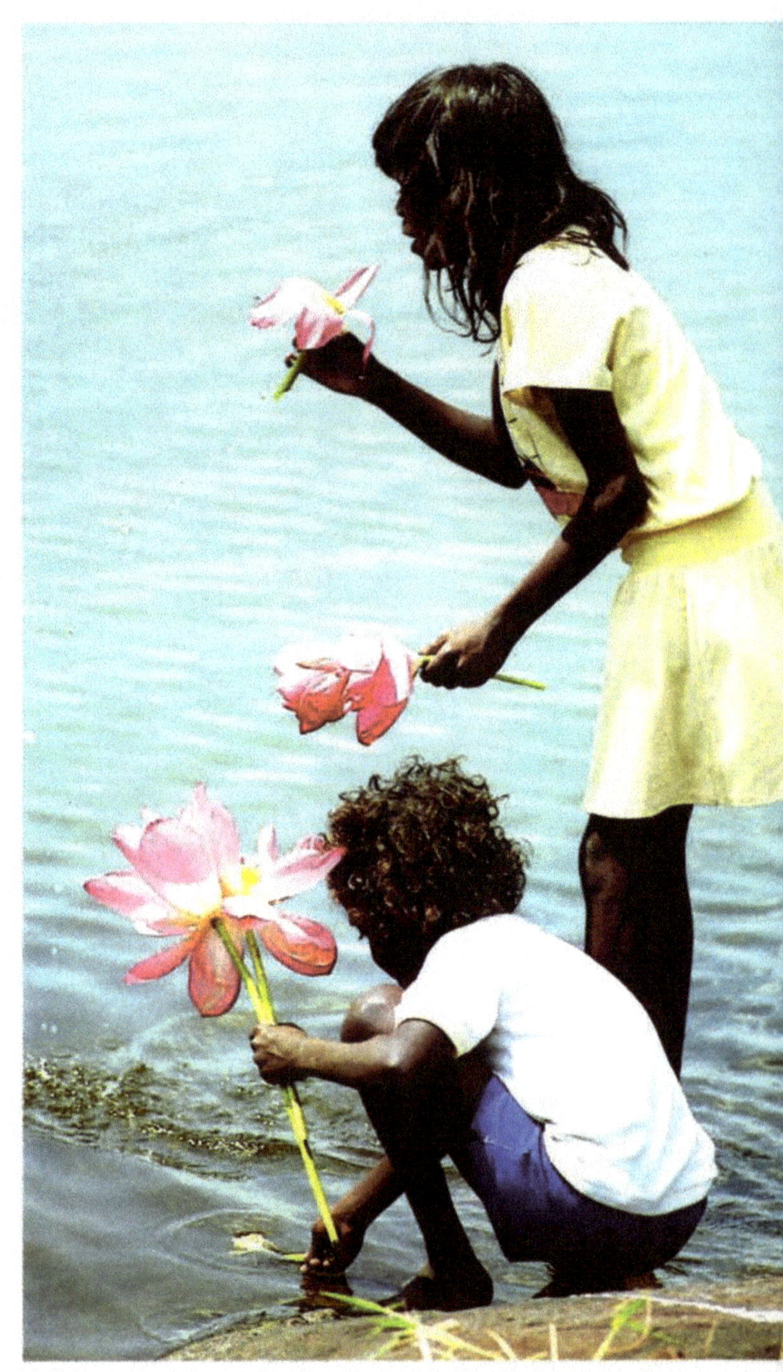

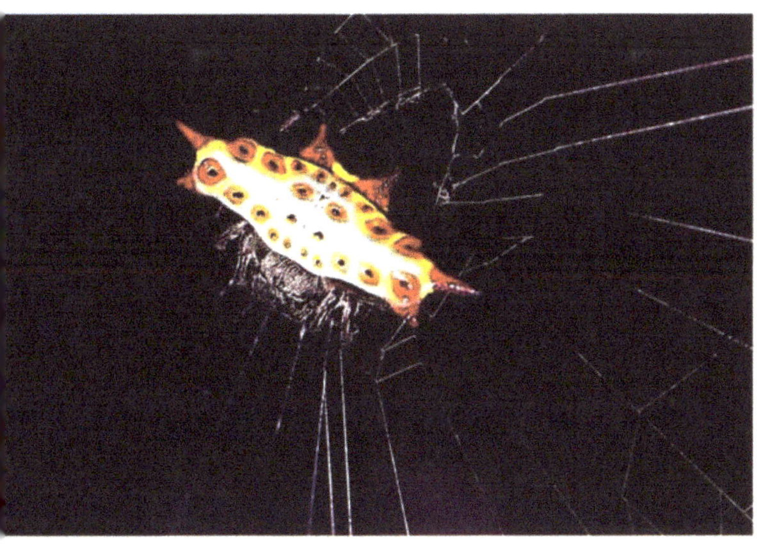

LEFT *Oenpelli Primary School children at Cannon Hill Billabong*
UPPER RIGHT *Monsoon Forest Spiny Spider*
LOWER RIGHT *Children playing in the Arafura Sea*

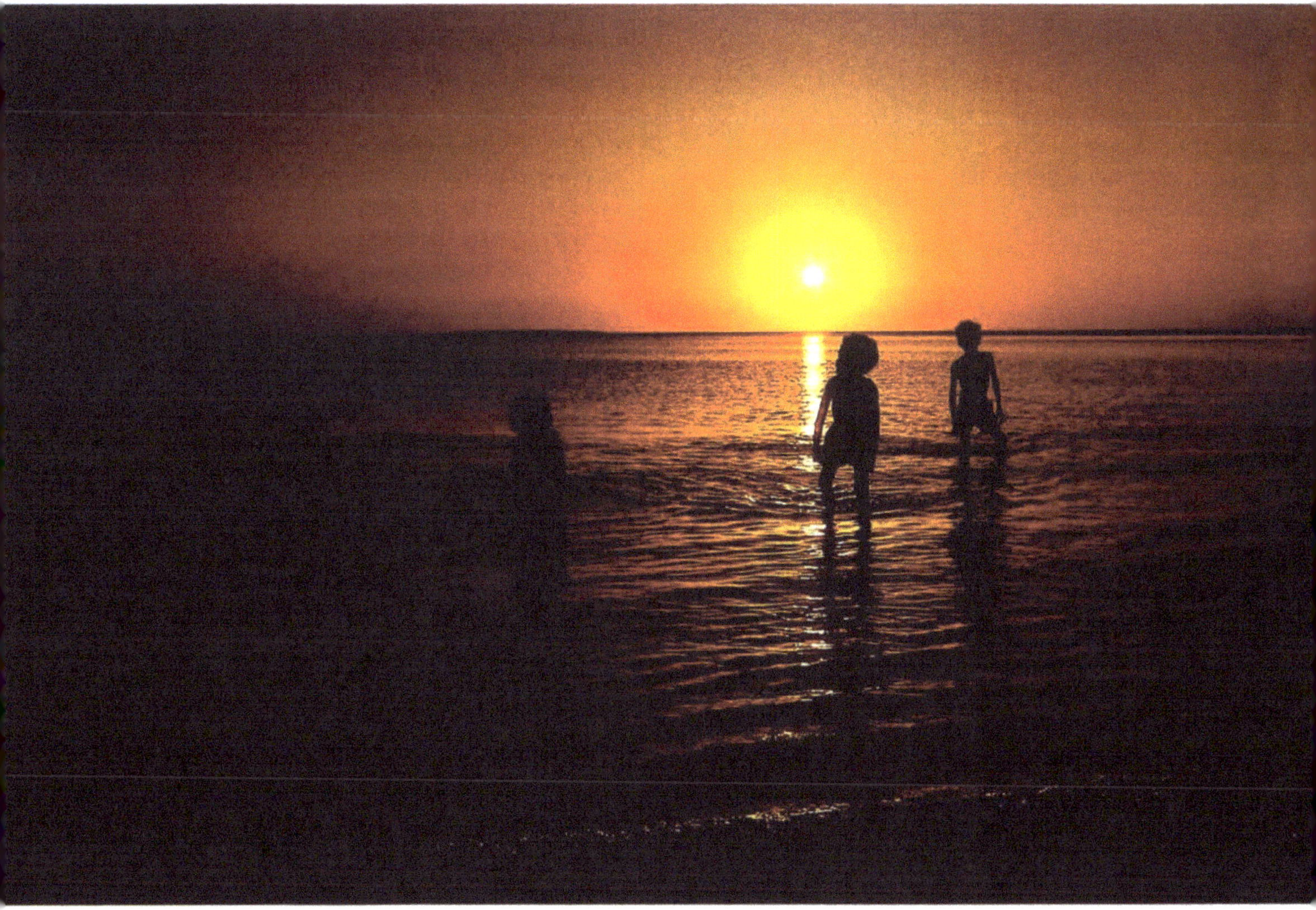

THE WORD

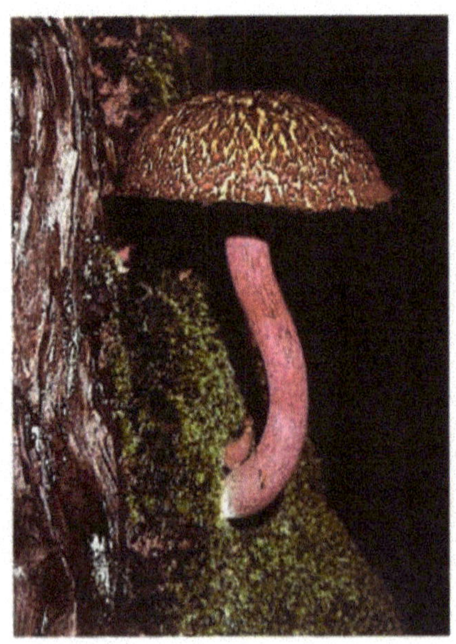

This whole world
is a remarkable word
spoken by a Lover
into the darkness.

Within that word
many small words:
some passive
like stones,
some beautiful
like orchids,
some surprising
like python patterns,
some perplexing
like hunted perchlets.

Mightier, and loveliest,
one incomparable Word
was enfleshed
among us;
a word far greater
than the world
of which it is a part,
yet leaving nothing —
not one fragment —
untouched
by its glory.

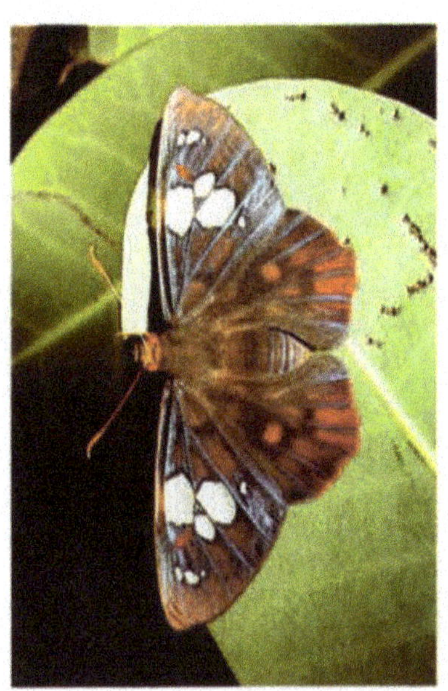

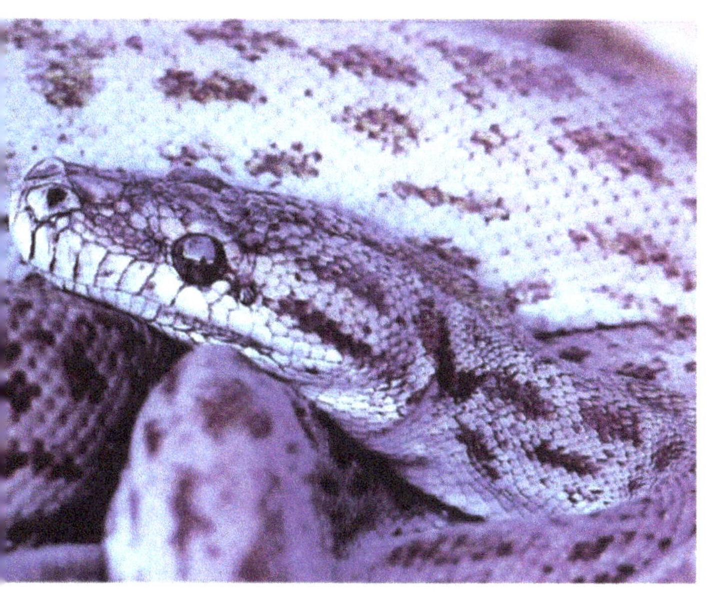

UPPER LEFT *Fungus growing out of mossy tree trunk, monsoon forest*
LOWER LEFT *The Rare Red-eye Butterfly, Arnhem Land*
UPPER RIGHT *Nawaran, the Oenpelli Python*
LOWER RIGHT *Cannon Hill view*

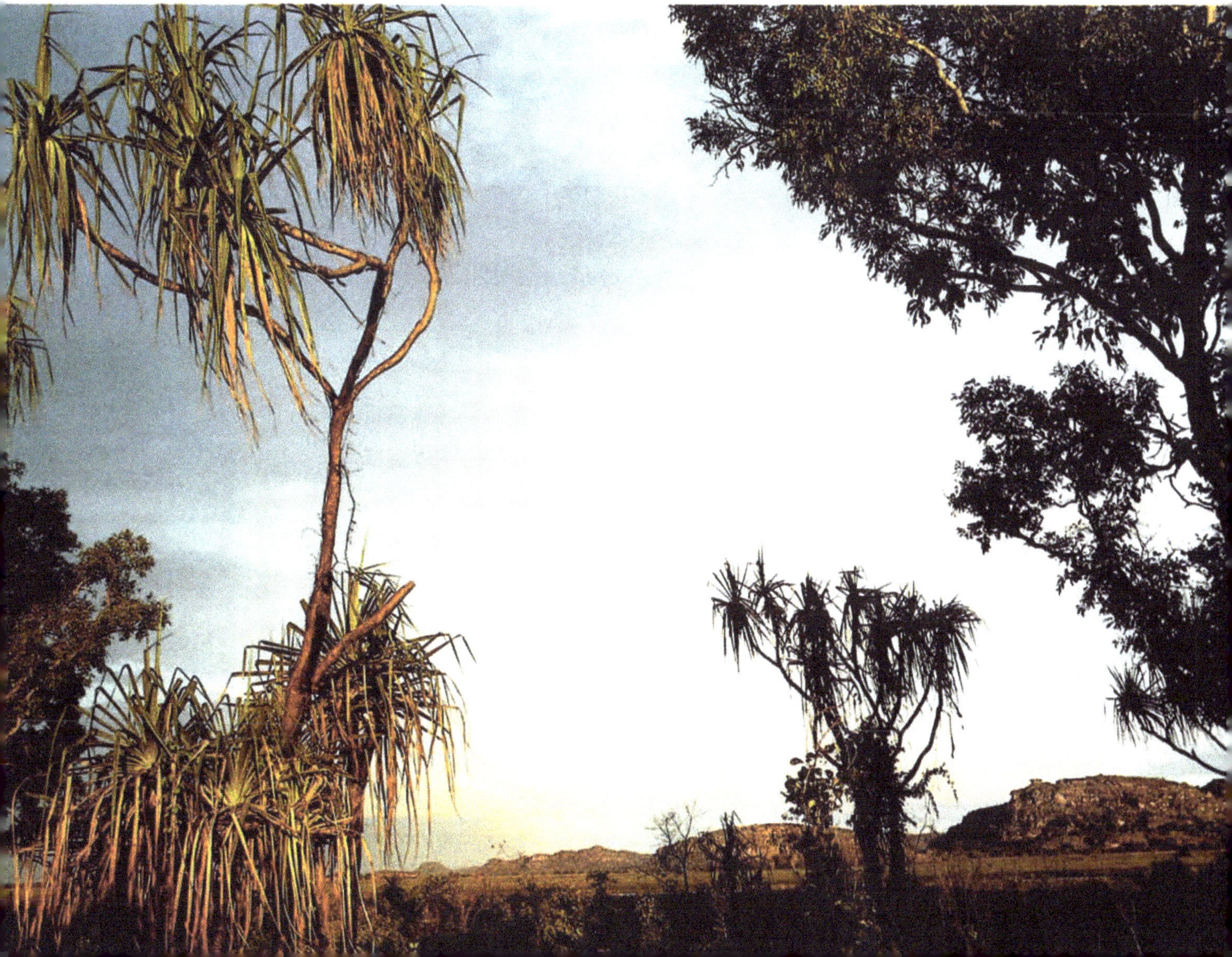

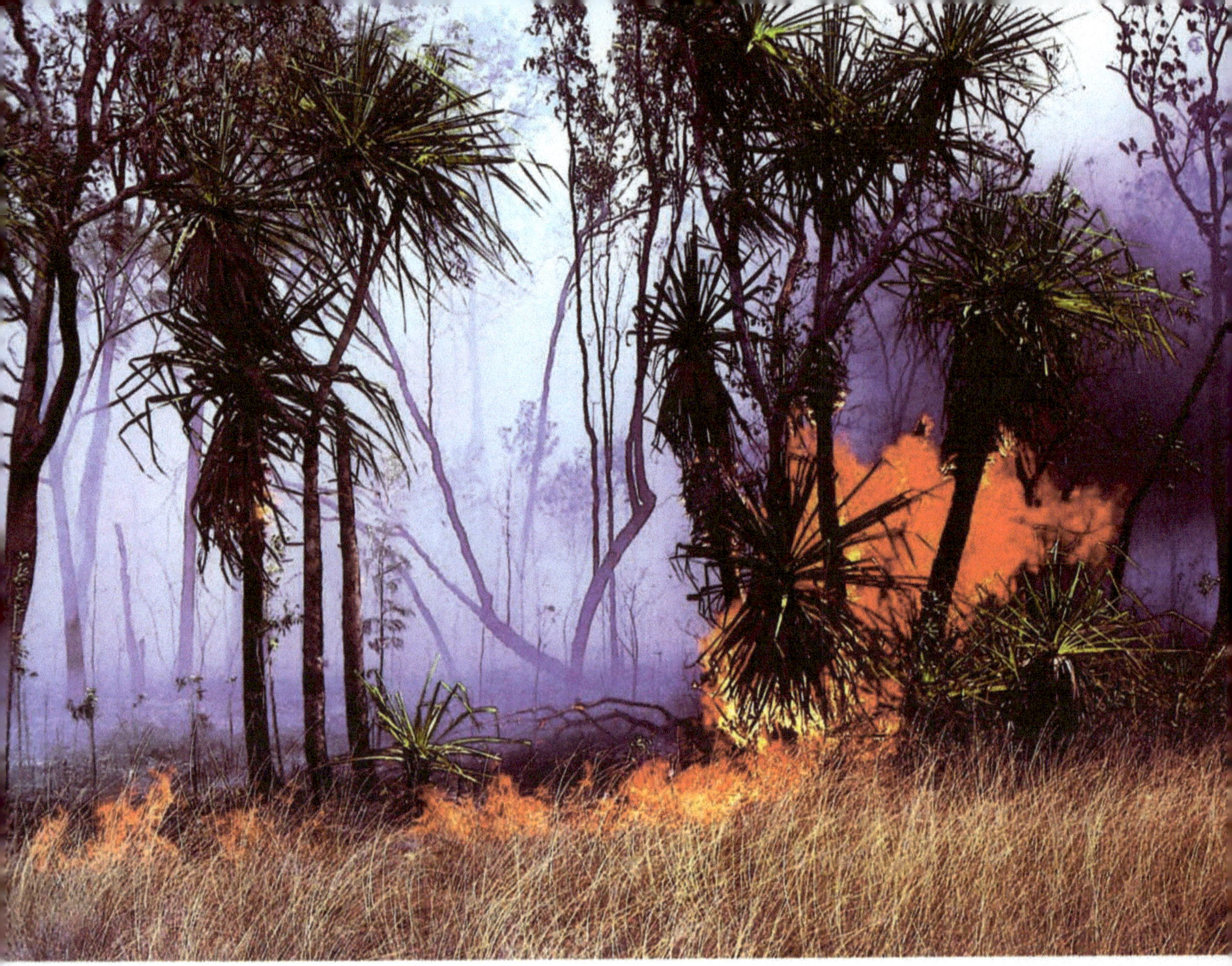

UPPER LEFT *Open woodland fire (Mambirri)*
LOWER LEFT *Freshwater Mangrove flowers*
UPPER RIGHT *View from Bluetongue Dreaming*
LOWER RIGHT *Sandstone Melaleuca flower*

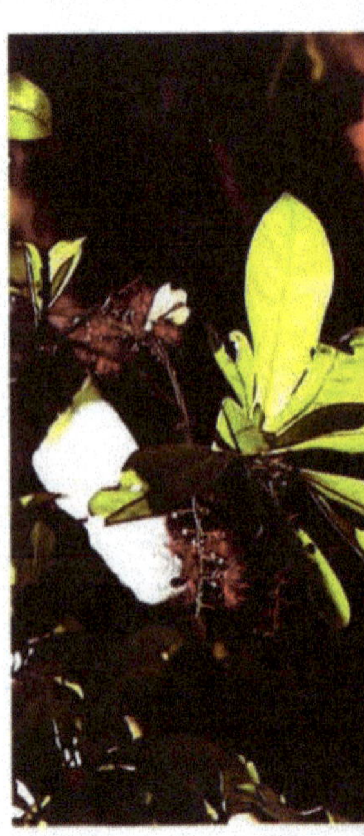

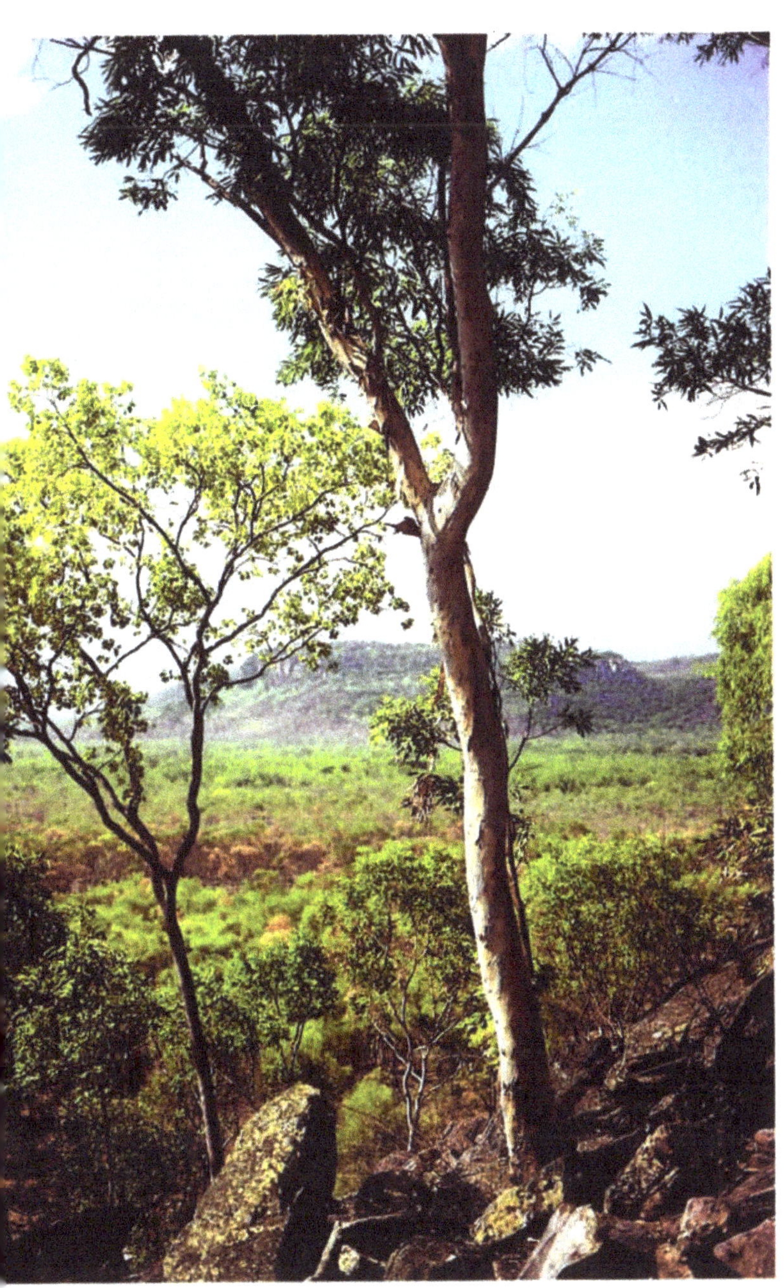

THE TIME OF FIRES

Lord, my stiff mind
finds it hard to accept
that fire is your servant.

Our black folk say
it is the necessary agent
for life, old and new.

But for white folk,
zealous in dodging discomfort,
fire seems offensive.

Yet my own eyes witness
to the vigorous greening
that follows the flames.

That flames can be
an expression of love,
Lord, help me to believe.

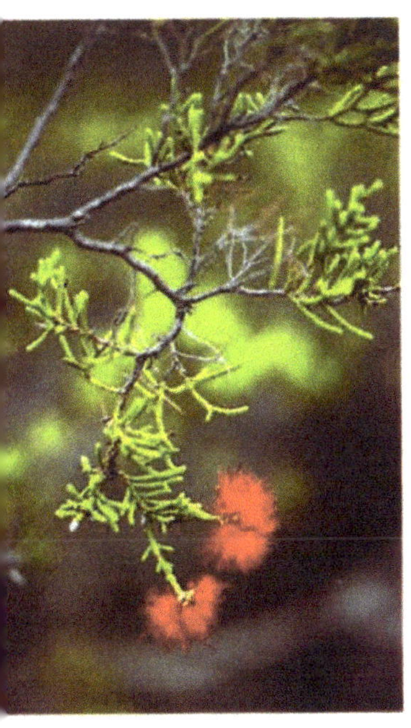

NEARNESS

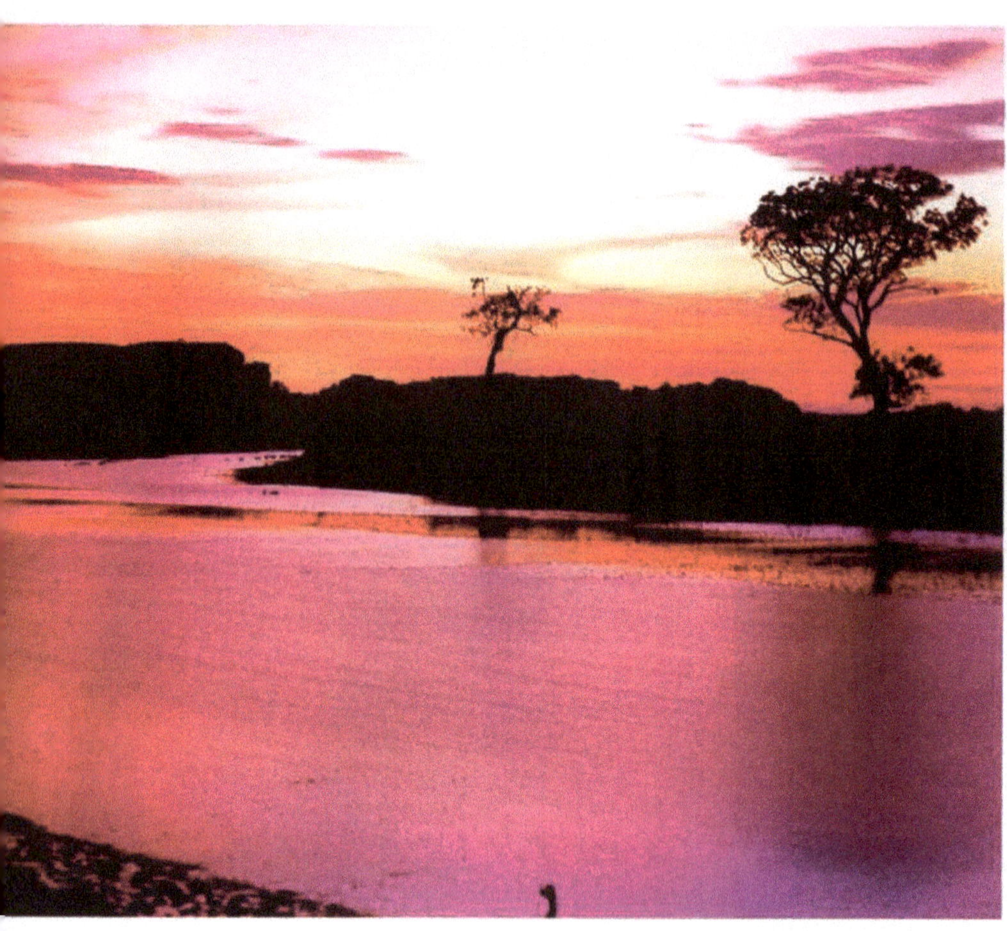

Near is the Mind
which frames all,
   limitless
   for ever the same
   for ever changing.

Near is the Power
which leavens all,
   limitless
   for ever covenanting
   for ever free.

Near is the Love
which embraces all,
   limitless
   for ever perfect suffering
   for ever perfect joy.

Near is the Nearness
which is our dreaming,
   limitless
   for ever our quest
   for ever our rest.

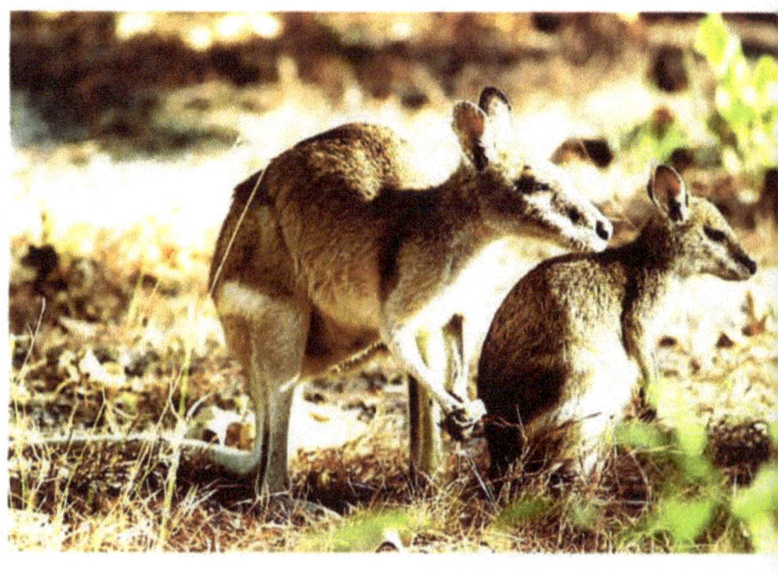

LORD OF THE STORM

At tranquil dawn
I dare not profess you,
unless within the storm
I also confess you.

In friend
I cannot claim you,
unless in enemy
I also name you.

Healthy, I dare not
say I know you,
unless diseased
I still adore you.

Nowhere shall I
truly greet you,
unless upon the Cross
I meet you.

UPPER LEFT: *Cannon Hill Billabong*
LOWER LEFT: *Agile Wallaby (Gonobolo) and young at foot, open woodland*
RIGHT: *Storm north of Cannon Hill*
OVERLEAF: *Saltwater Crocodile, Yellow Waters*

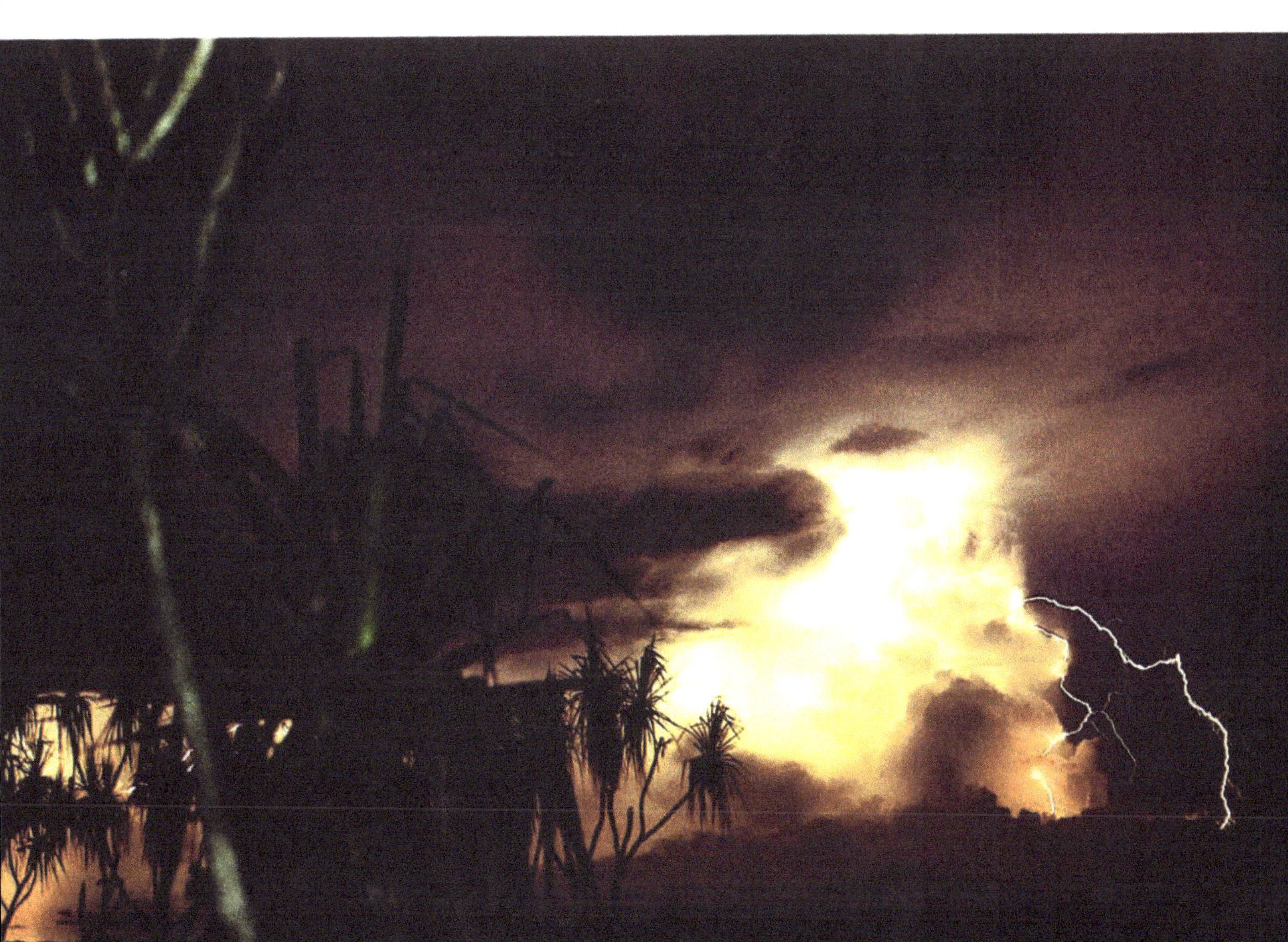

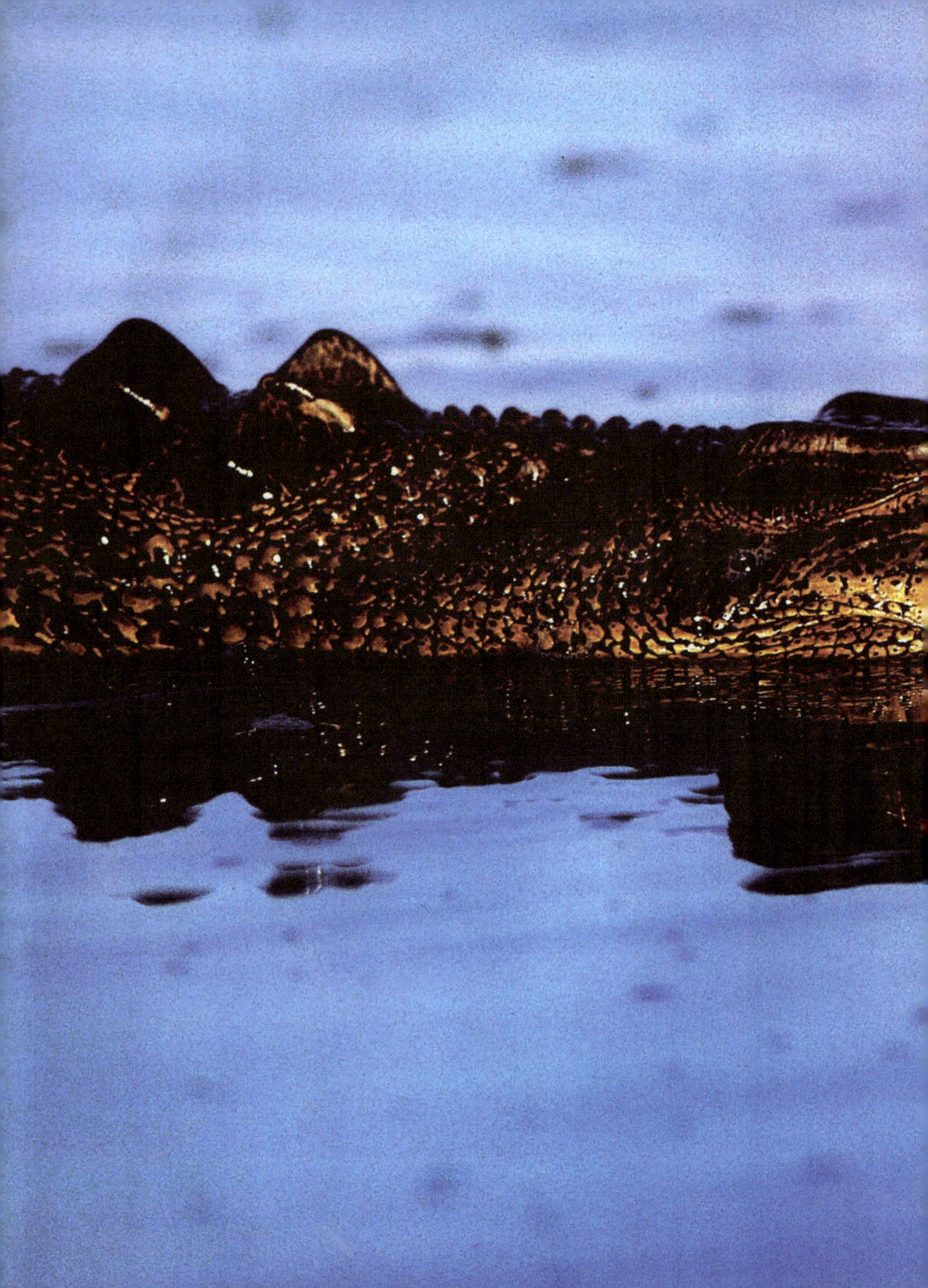

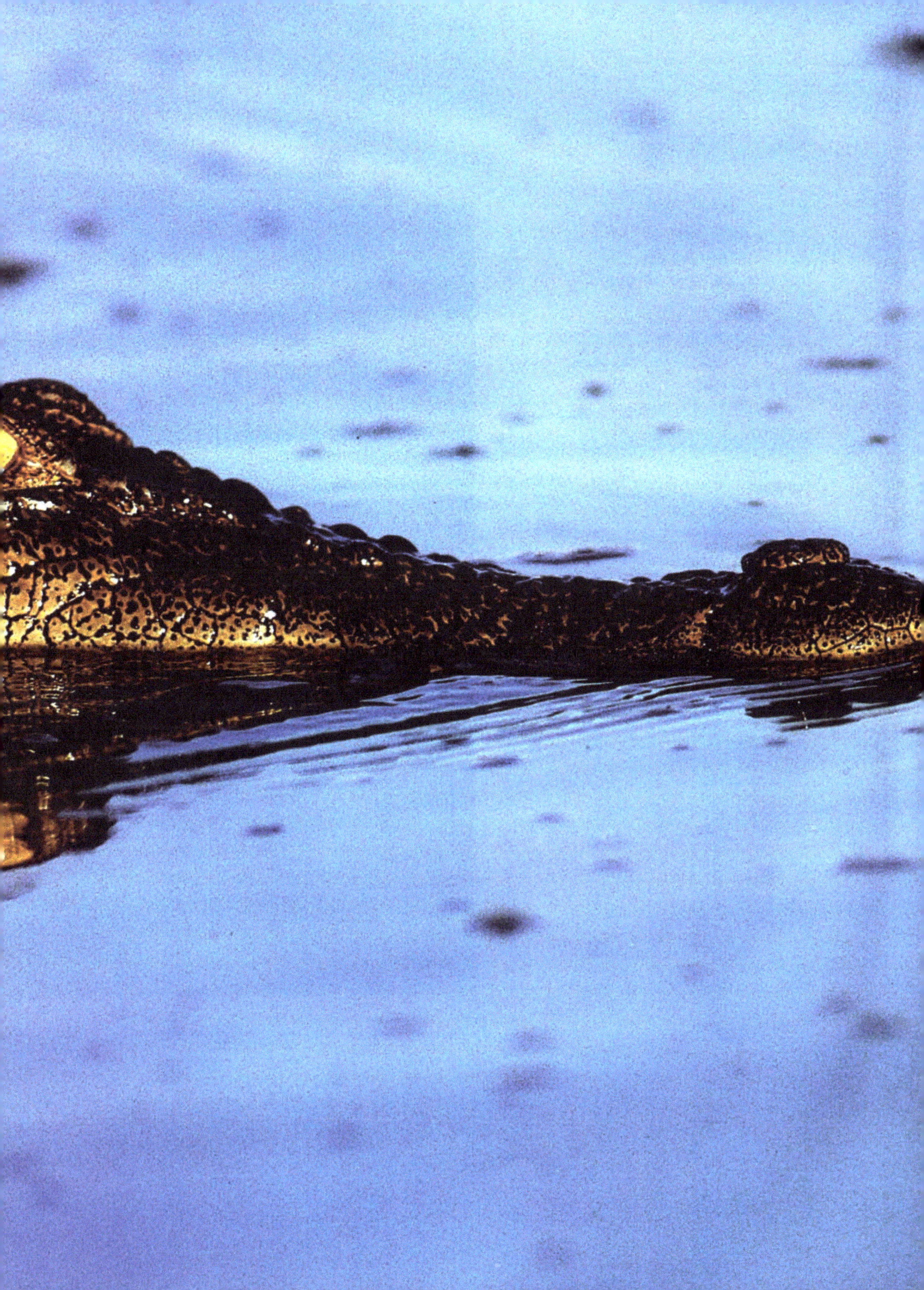

CREATURES OF LIGHT

And the Word was:
'Let there be light —
the sun to rule by day,
the moon and stars by night.'

God made things to enjoy it:
butterflies, buffaloes, and bees,
eagles riding on the wind,
and turtles in the seas.

Then God took some clay,
and said: 'Now, this is fun!'
He gave it the kiss of life
and placed it in the sun.

Up into life it leapt —
child, woman, man.
God said: 'Now, this is good,
the best since things began.'

'Now, this is good
by day or night,
now, this is good,
creatures of light!'

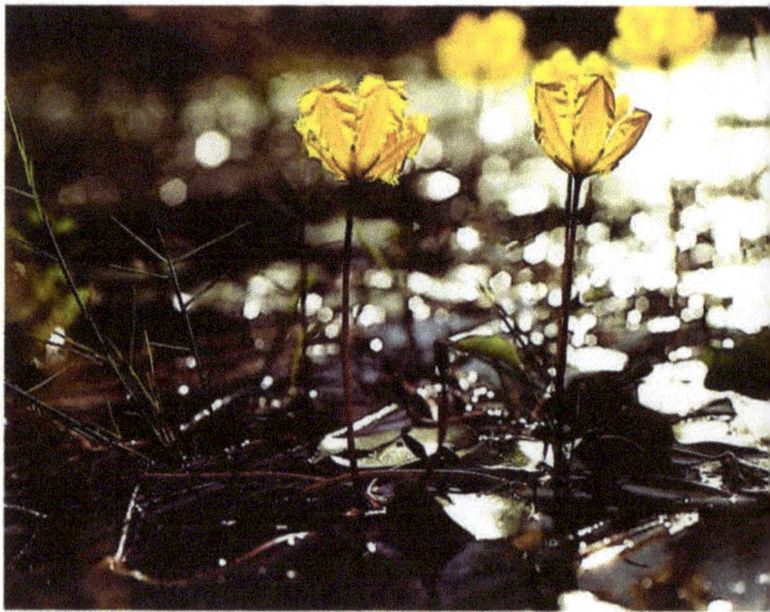

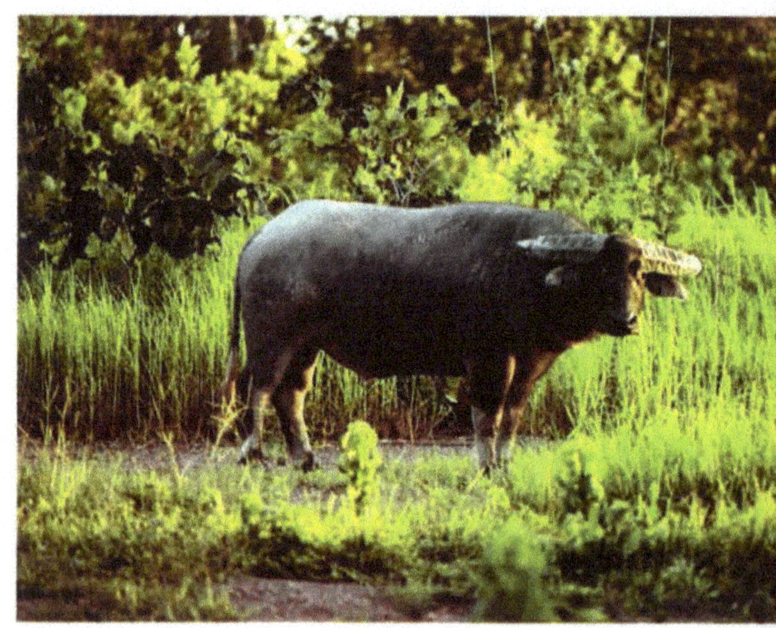

UPPER LEFT: *Yellow Lilies, Magela Creek*
LOWER LEFT: *Bull, Asian Water Buffalo*
RIGHT: *Kevin Buliwana, Deaf Adder Gorge*

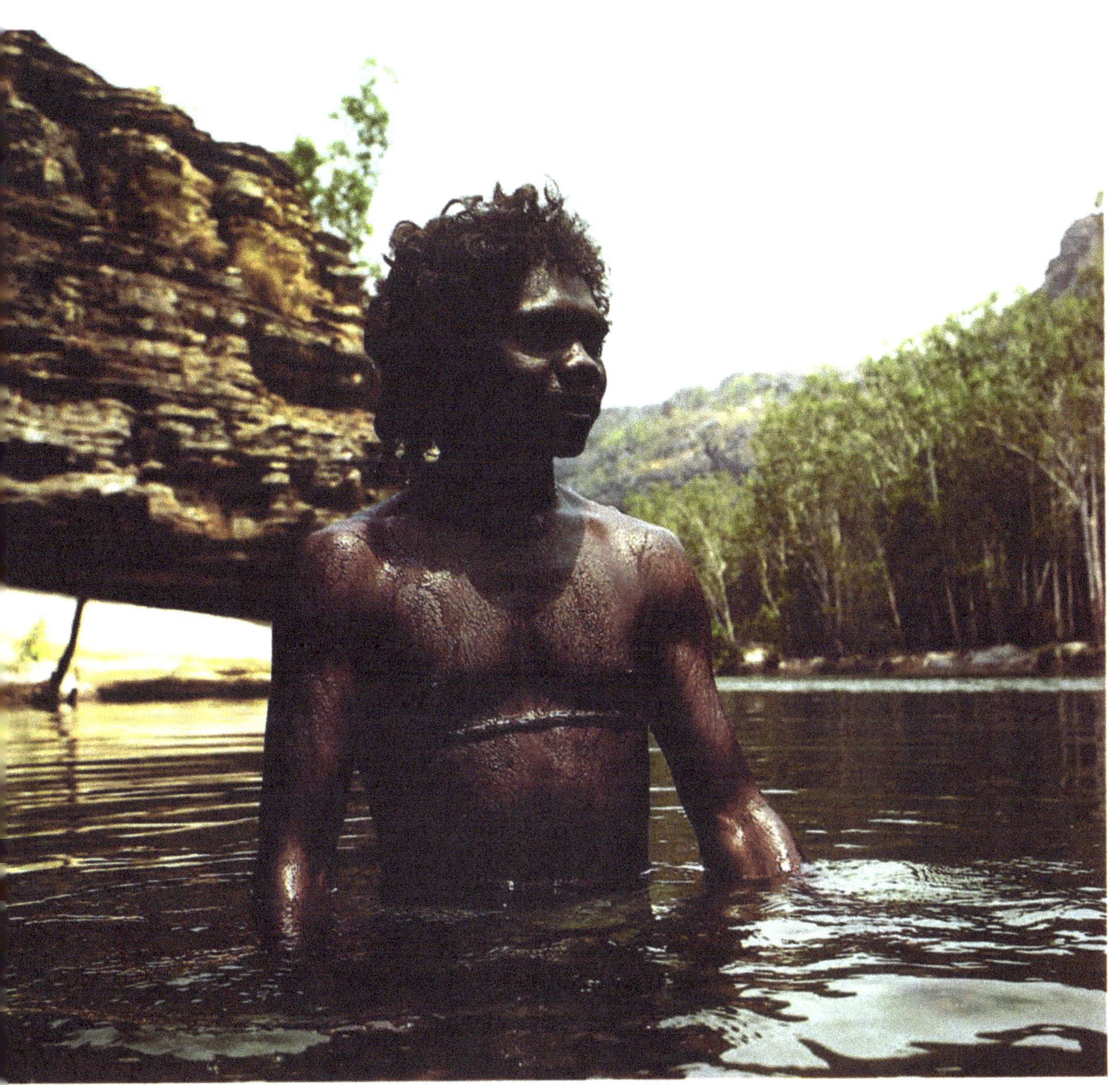

EMMAUS

If this collection
of shapes and colours
were life's only light,
sole ground of faith,
   how wretched
   we would be.

If we must deduce
from this alone
the first cause
and the final goal,
   how confused
   we would be.

If you, Lord,
had not met us
on the way
and opened the Scriptures,
   how lost
   we would be.

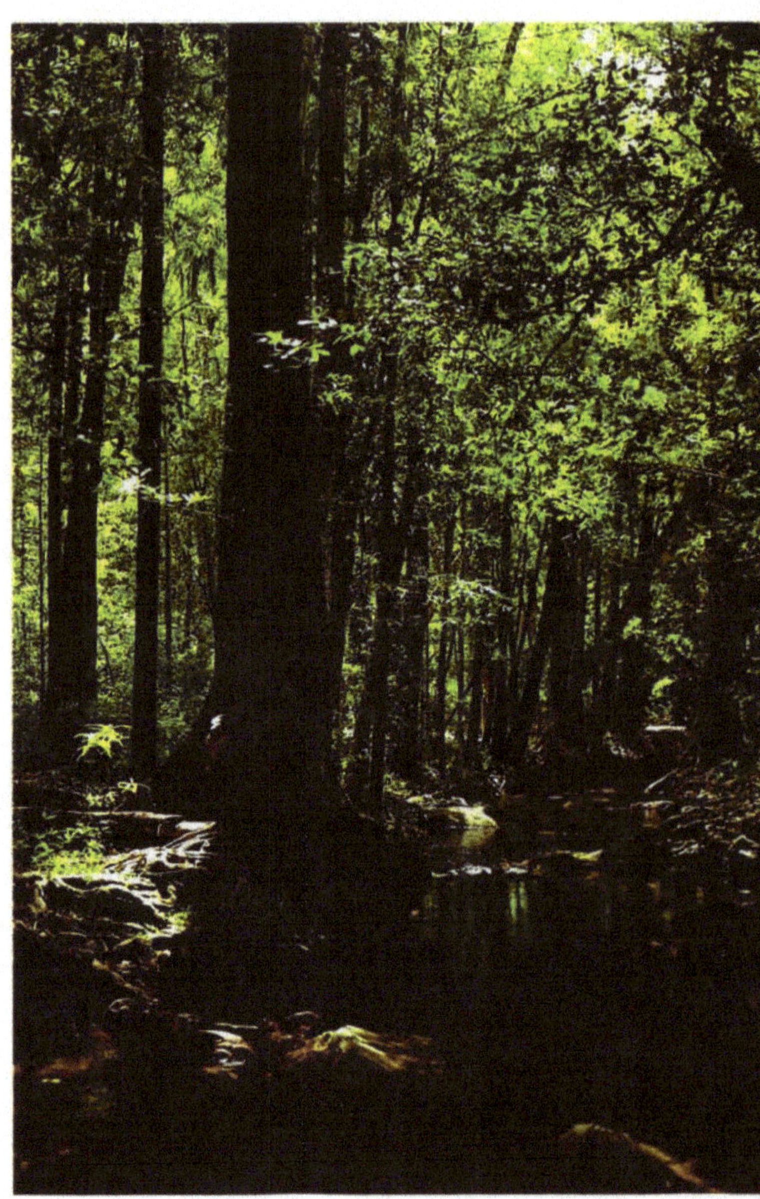

LEFT: *Gulungul Creek forest*
UPPER RIGHT: *Gould's Goanna*
LOWER RIGHT: *Aldjurr, the Leichhardt's Grasshopper*

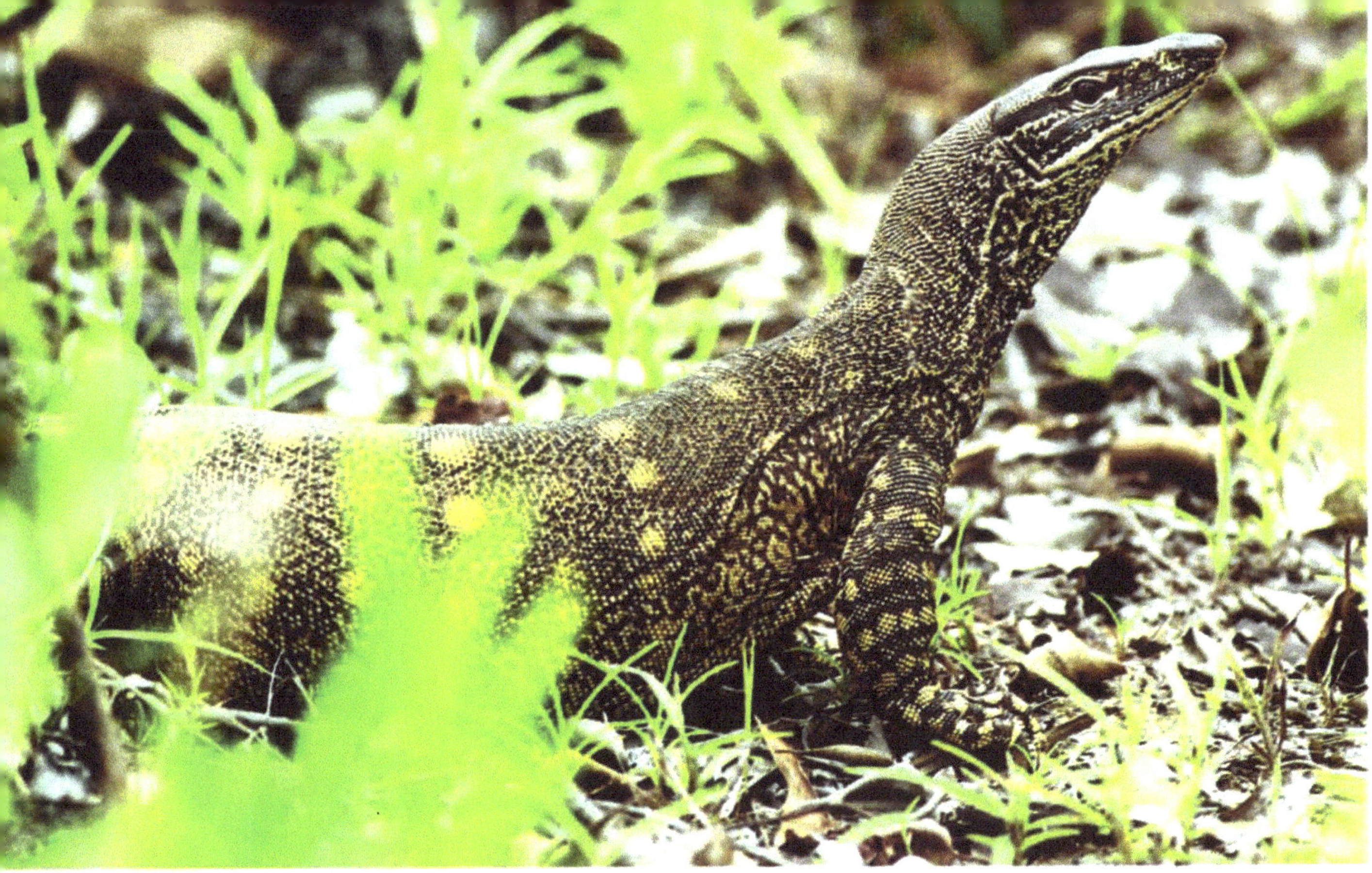

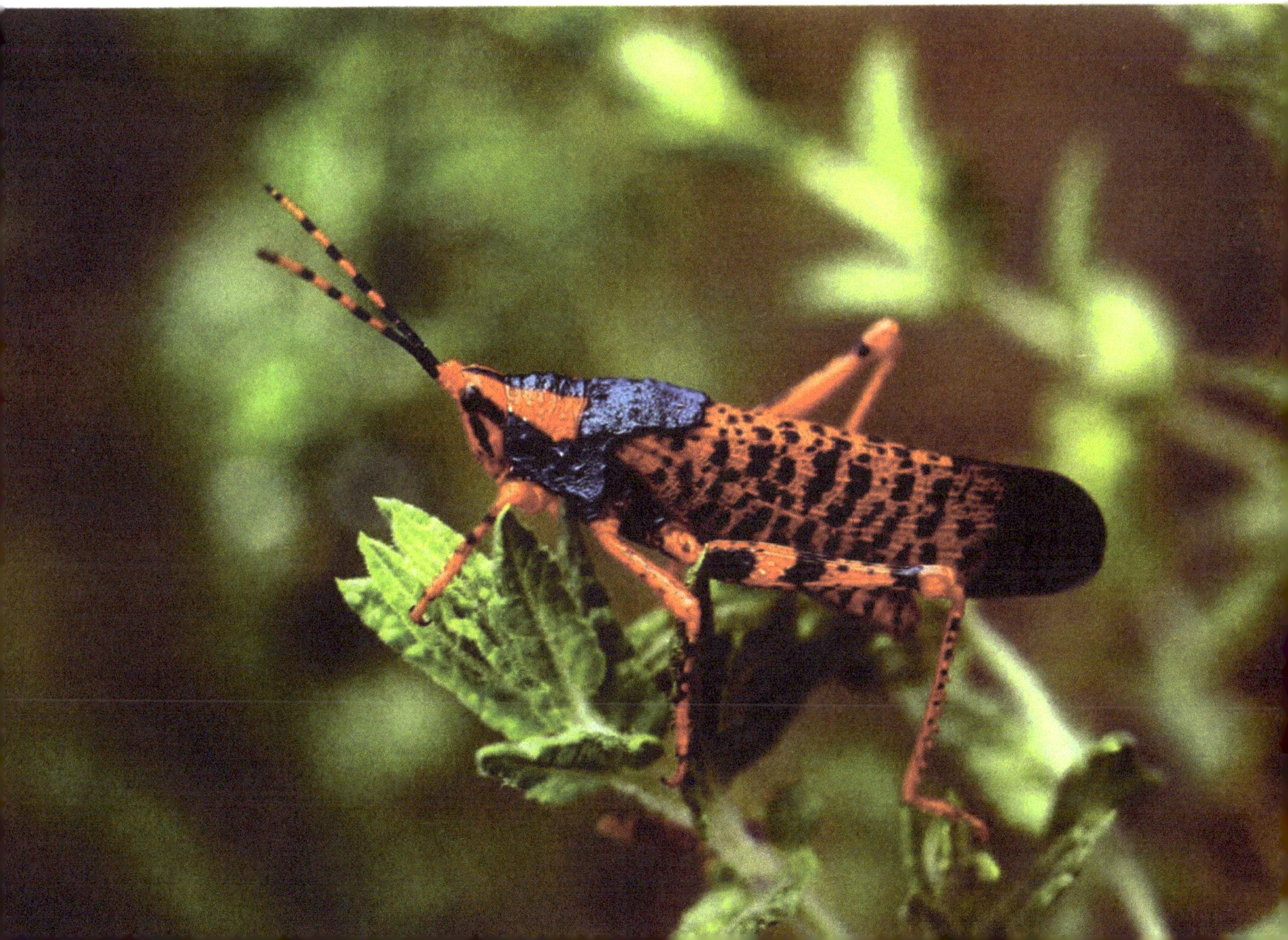

THANKS FOR THE COMICAL

For all things bright and beautiful,
we thank you, loving Creator,
but also for the surprise and delight
of creatures odd and comical:

Embarrassed-looking goanna
tree-wrapped above the floods.

Cumbersome crocodile diving
without splash or ripple.

Willy wagtail in angry display
ejecting a trespassing kite.

Curled-up death adder
imitating a crocheted scarf.

Great bower-bird rushing around
like a bossy school prefect.

Spiny anteater sunbaking
on its back and snoring.

Lotus birds on the waters
busily playing messiah.

White spoonbills earnestly shovelling
like labourers on a muddy building site.

Bulky buffalo bull threatening
but making a noise like a piglet.

Thank you, Lord, for giving us
eyes to see them,
lips to tell,
and the capacity to laugh!

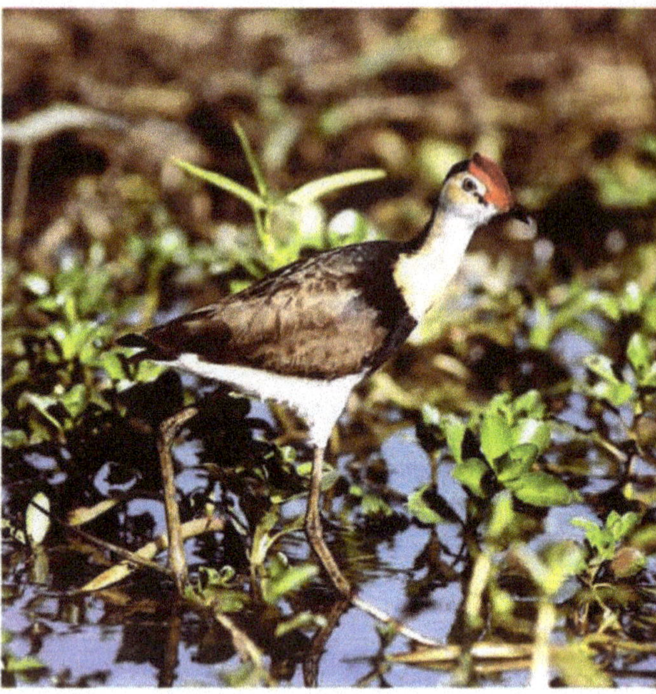

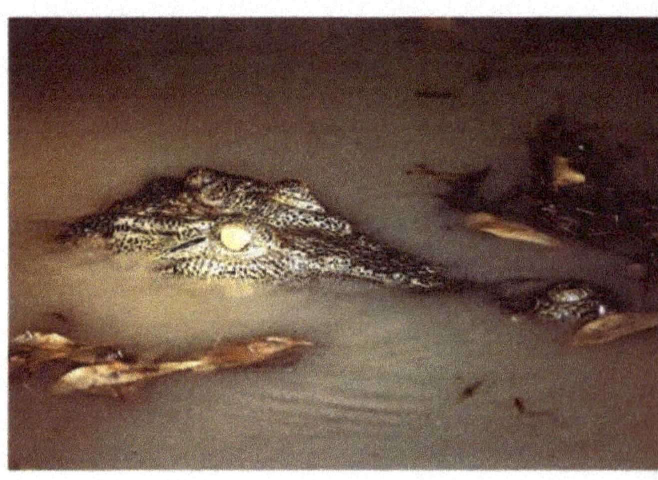

UPPER LEFT: *Lotus Bird*
LOWER LEFT: *Crocodile*
RIGHT: *Goanna stranded in flood*

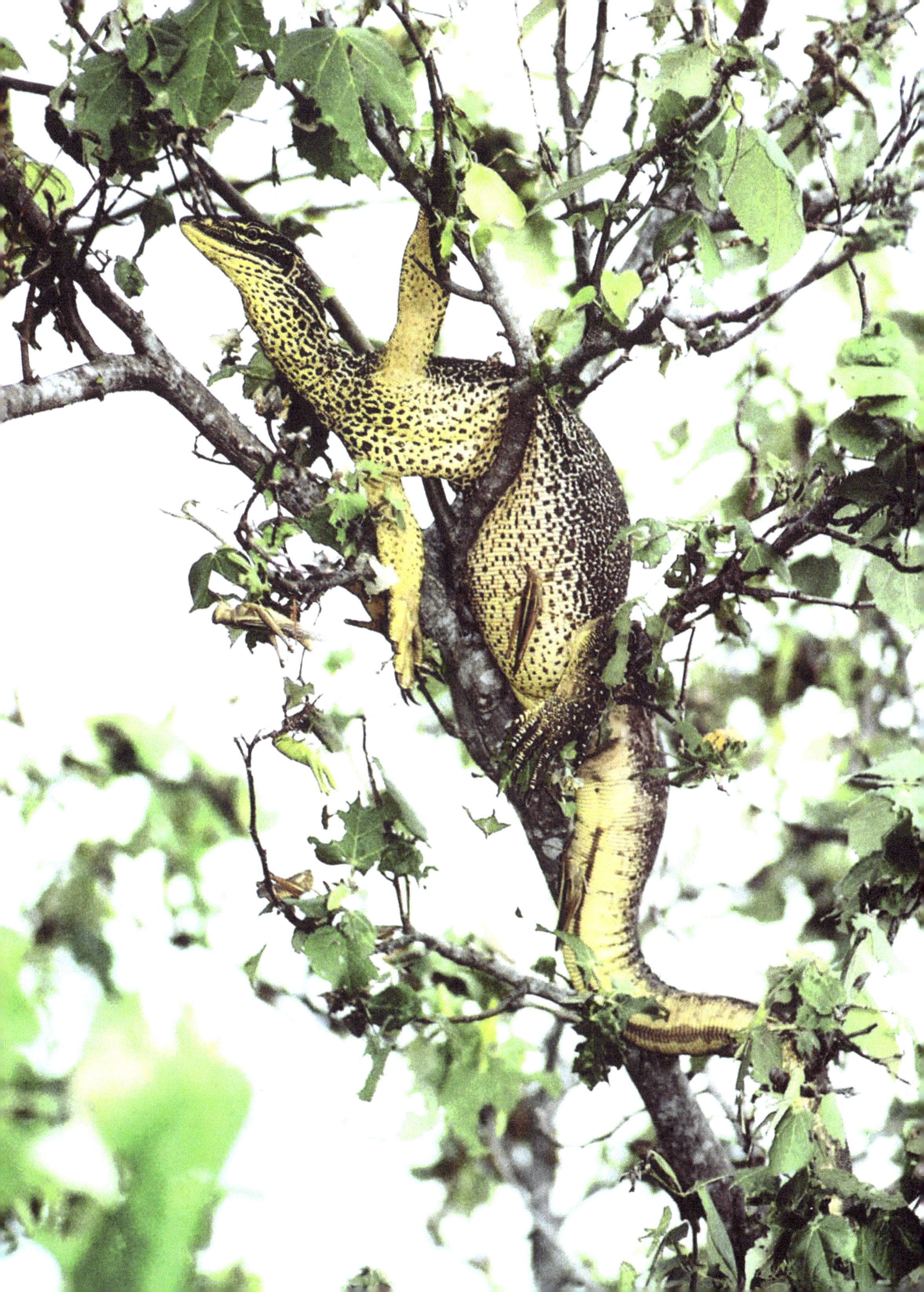

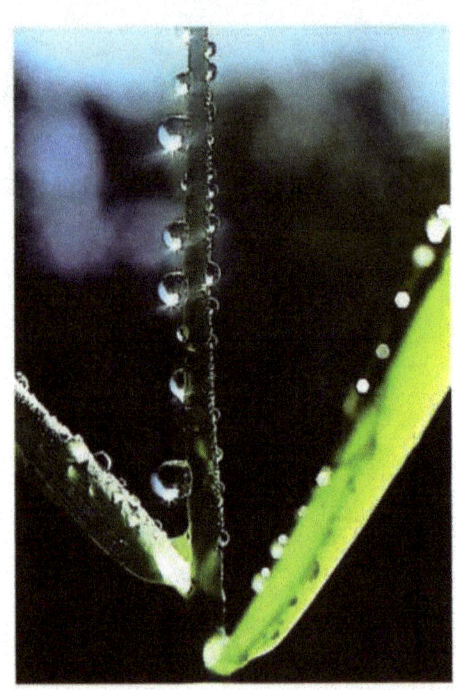

THE RAINS

Freely our praise comes to you, O God,
   worshipping in response to your faithfulness.

You visit the earth and water it,
   you come among us with refreshment.
You soften the hills with rains,
   and quench their thirst with storms.
The rivers of God are overflowing,
   the soil is prepared for new growth.
Creeks and swamps are renewed,
   waterfalls thunder with joy!

You crown the year with gladness,
   all your footsteps drip with new life —
life for wilderness places,
   till the mountain slopes are green,
flocks gather on the plains,
   and flowers carpet the bushland.

UPPER LEFT *Dew on Flagallaria*
LOWER LEFT *Djabiluku area, Magela Creek*
UPPER RIGHT *Twin Falls*
LOWER RIGHT *Buyuck Goluy Billabong*

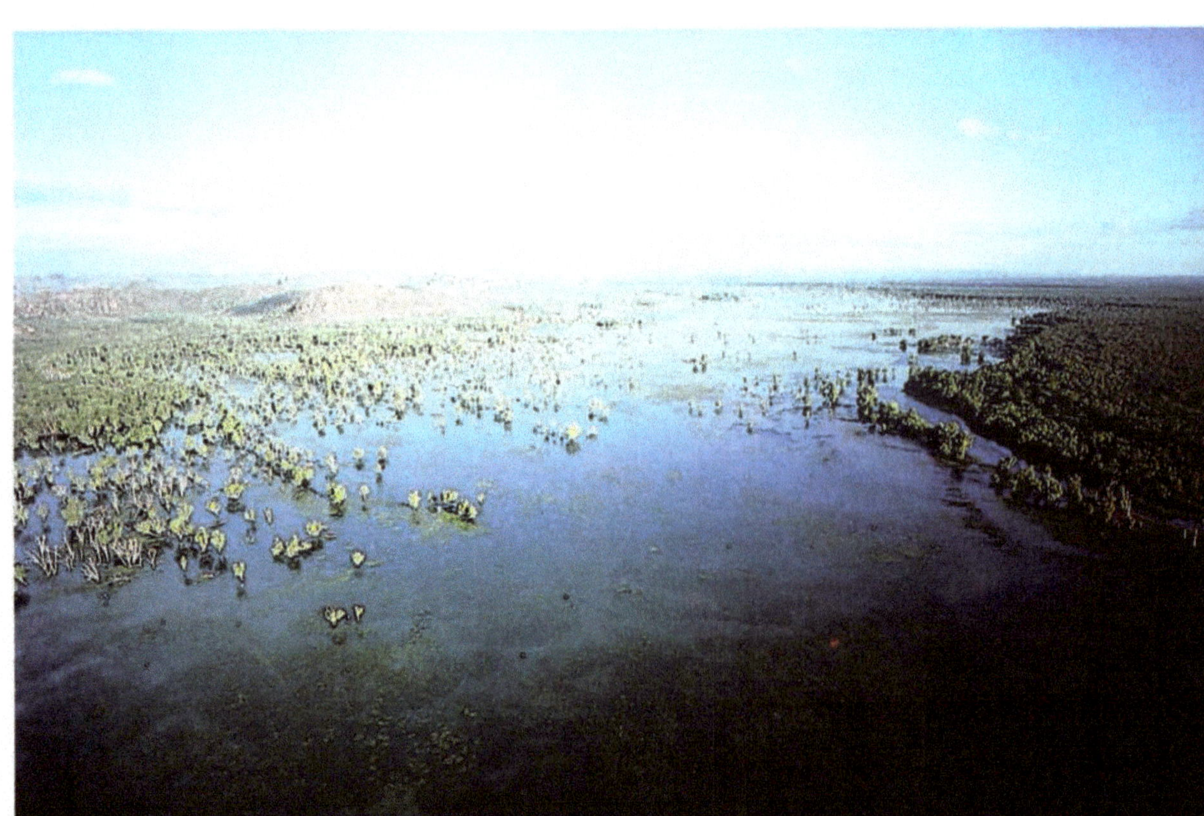

There is an ear that hears our prayers,
a love to whom all can turn.
You give us joy at the break of day,
and fill the evenings with happiness.
Everything declares its exaltation!
Everything is a song of highest praise!

(Echoing Psalm 65)

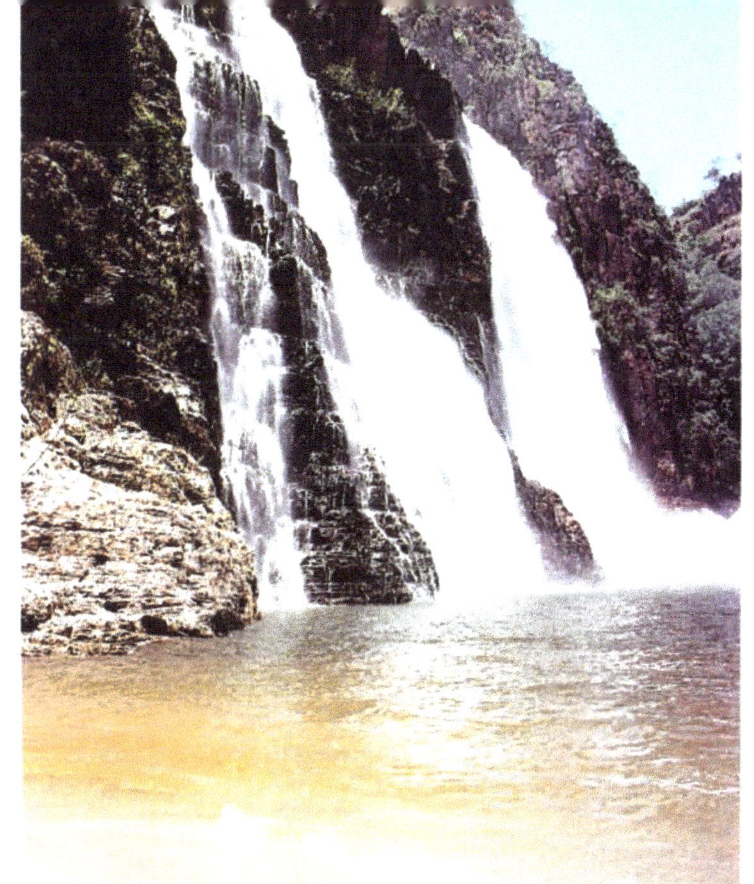

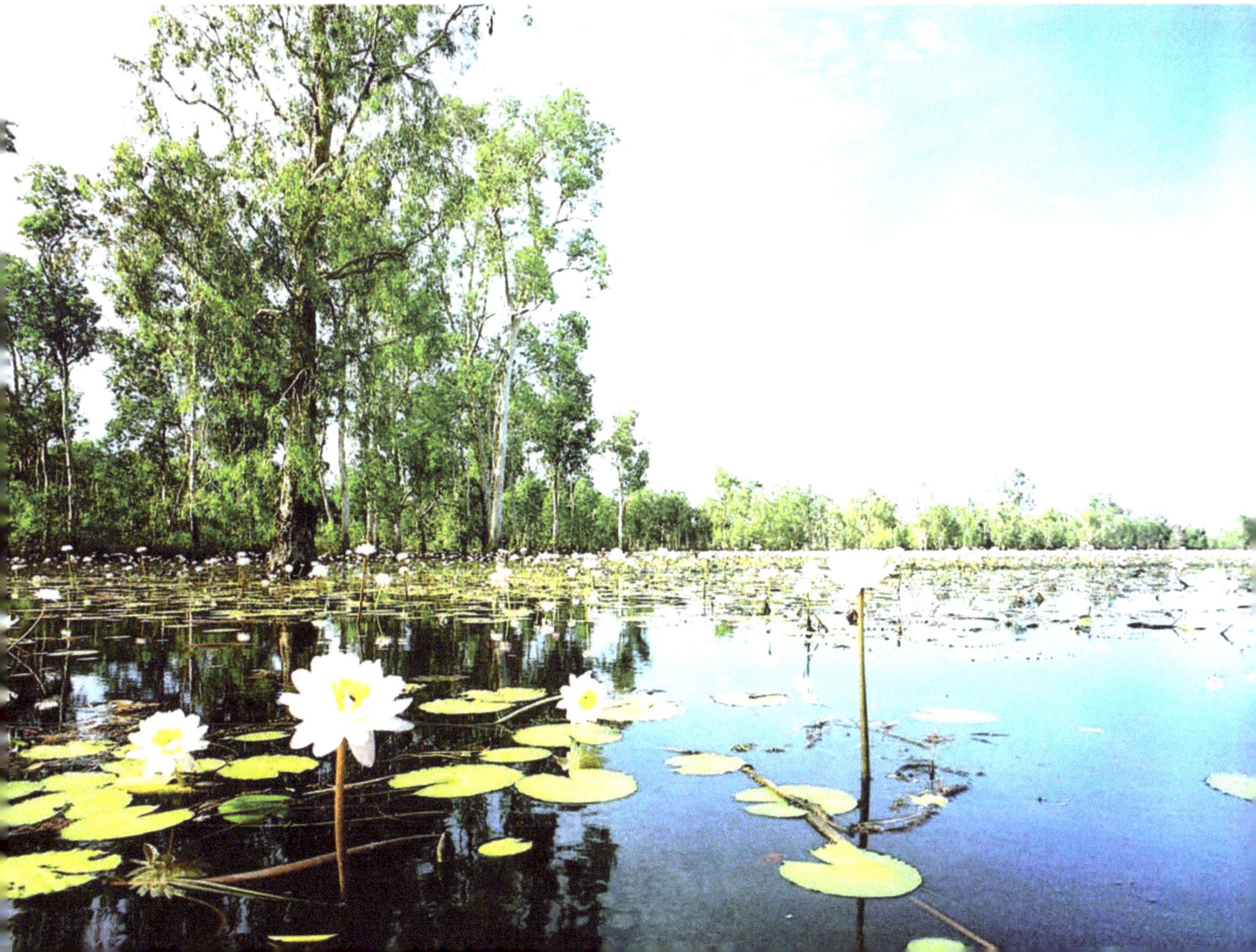

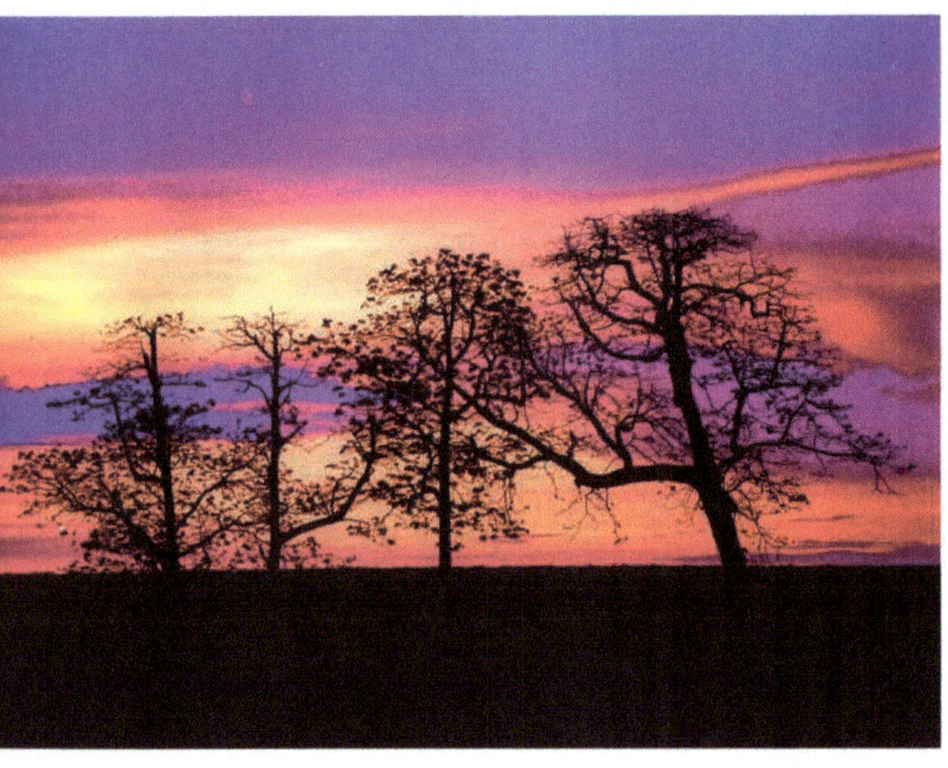

ROOTS

Your people, Lord,
and my people:
from the same dust
of Australian soil
you have fashioned us
to be one family.

Your people, Lord,
and my true people:
in their insights
and long, long story
in this timeless land
are found my true roots.

Their ancestors,
enjoying rock and creek,
reptile and bird,
sunrise and sunset,
ages before we came,
are my story.

My every rejection
or denigration
even to the least of these,
any paternalistic phrase,
severs me, maimed,
from deep-down springs.

Lord, have mercy.
Save your new Australians
from myopic madness.
Give us the humility
to allow them
to teach us many things.

LEFT: *Bombax trees on South Alligator River*
UPPER RIGHT: *Nipper Gabirriki at Djuwarr Gallery*
LOWER RIGHT: *Magela catchment*
OVERLEAF: *Upper East Alligator River*

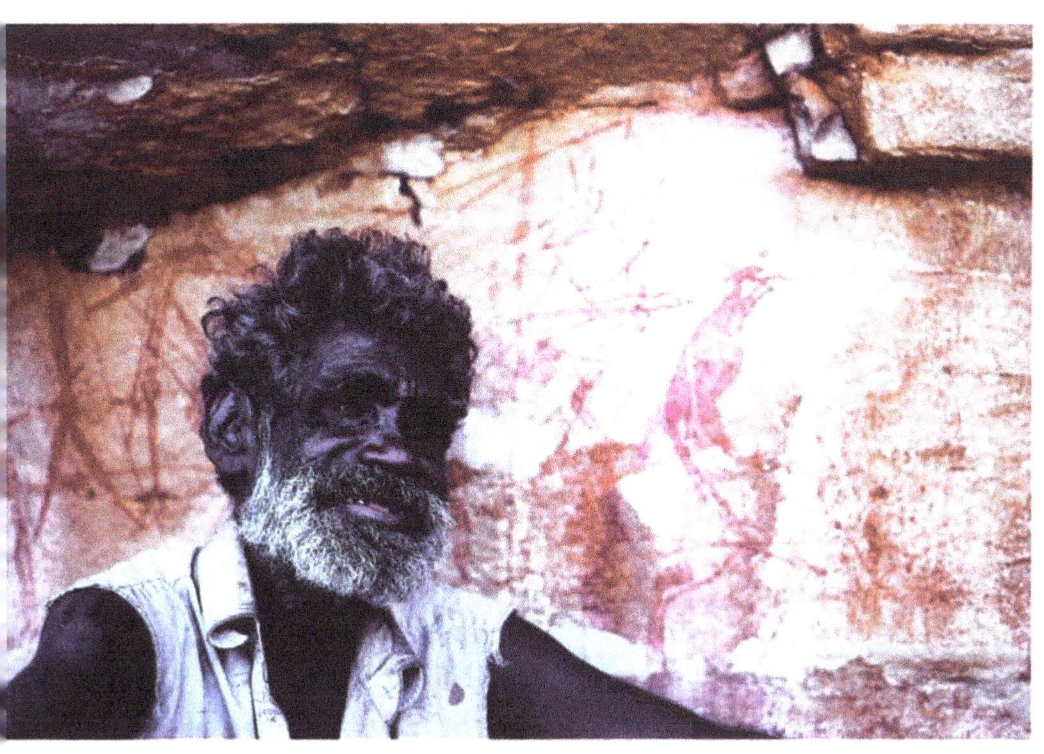

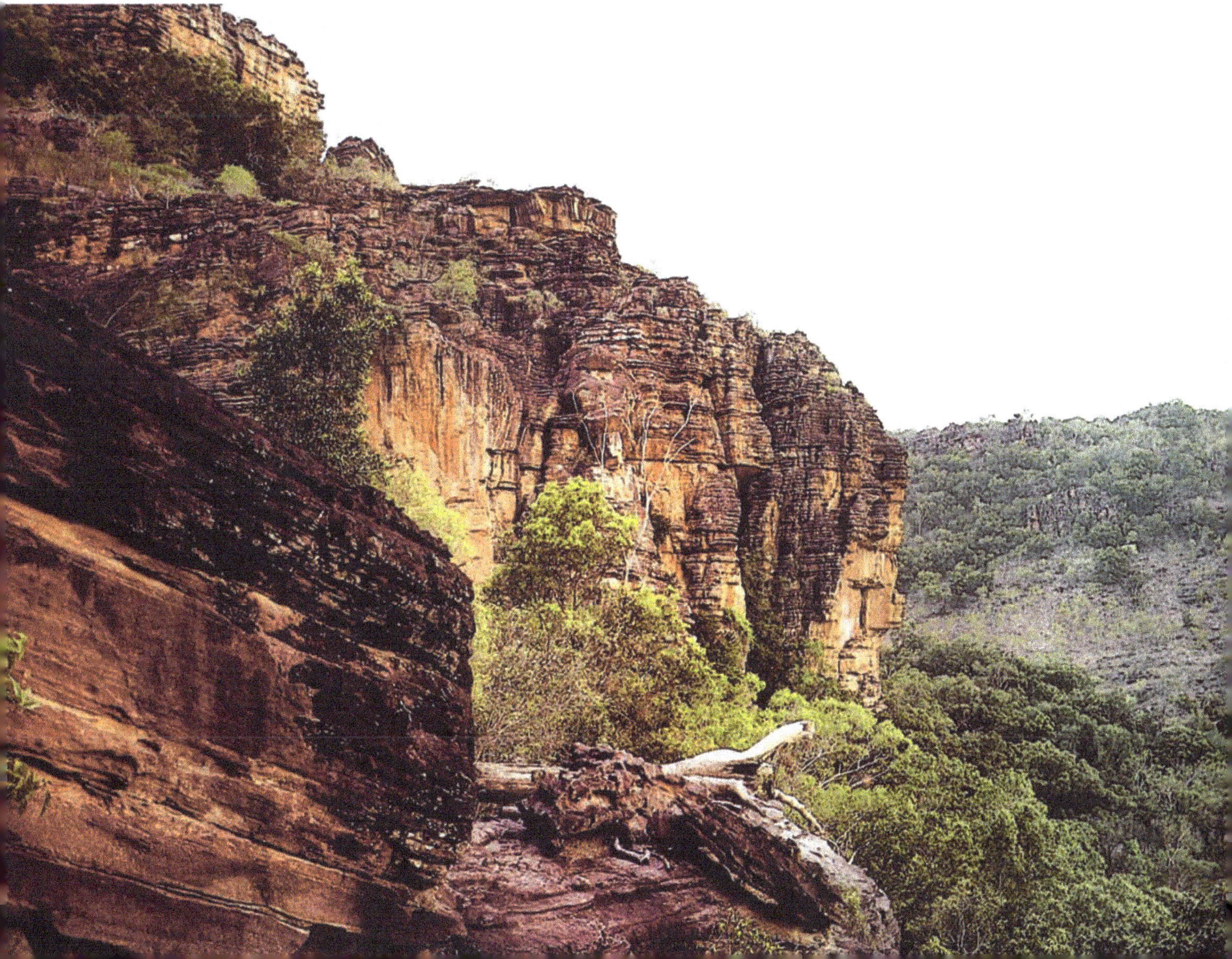

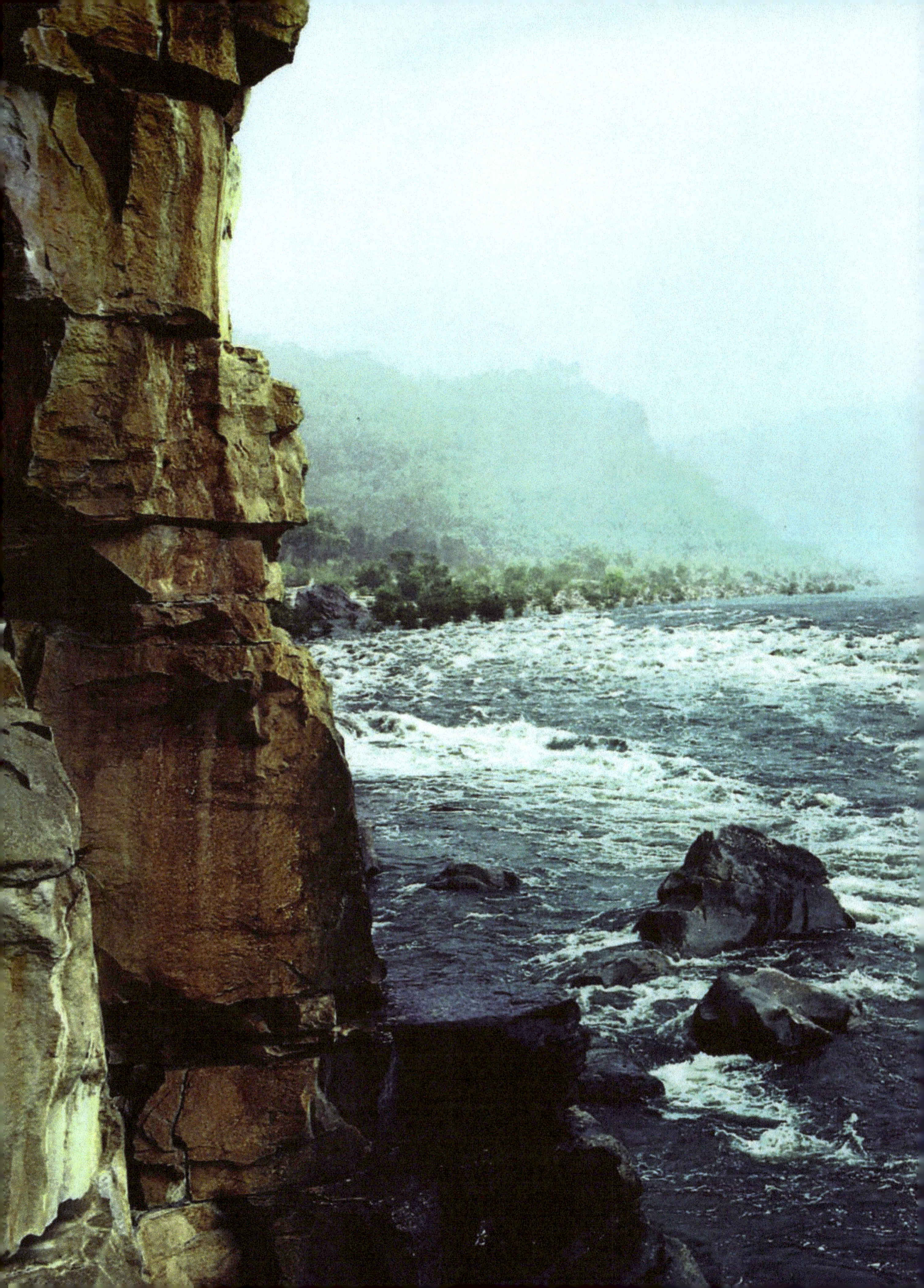

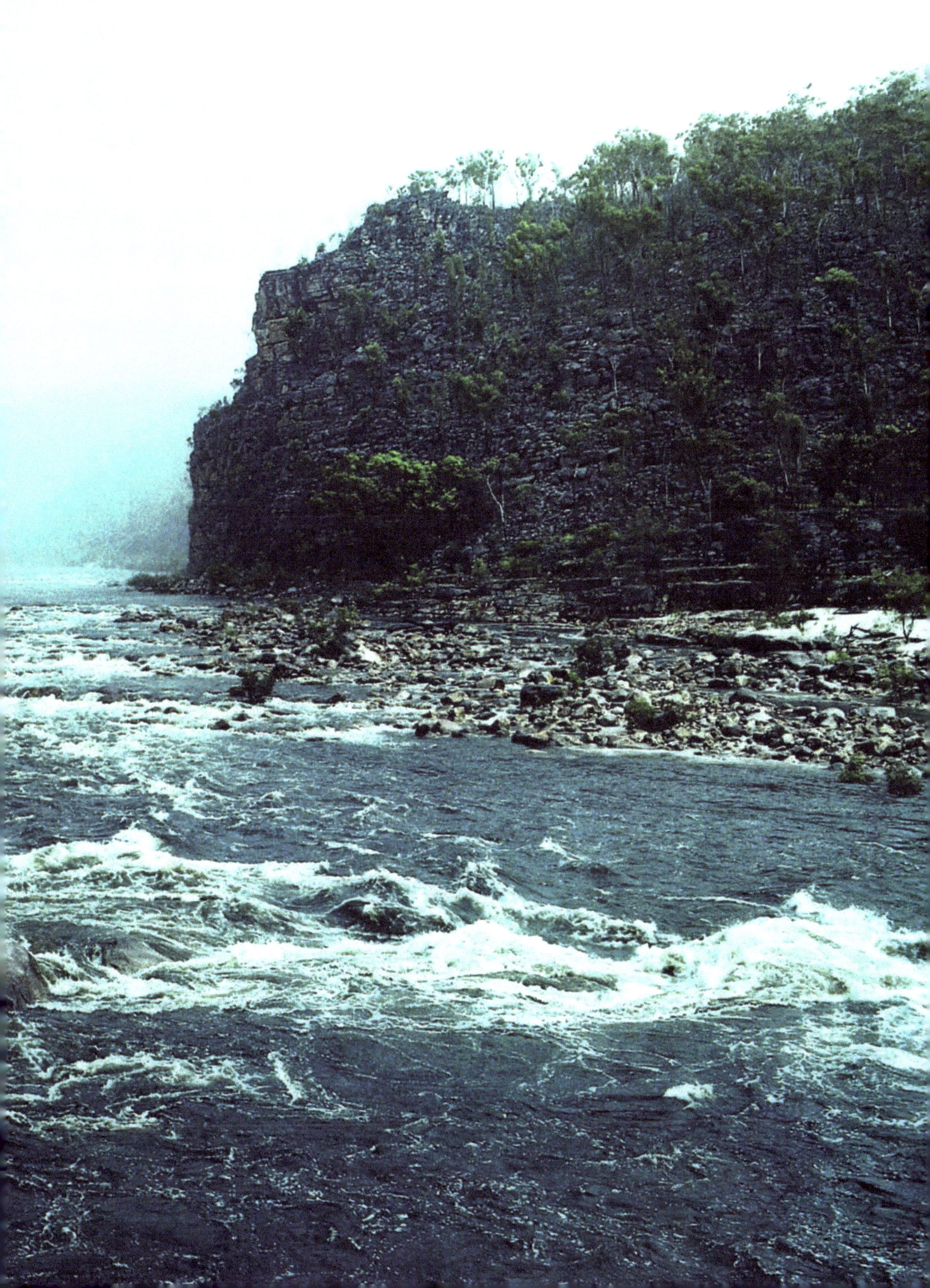

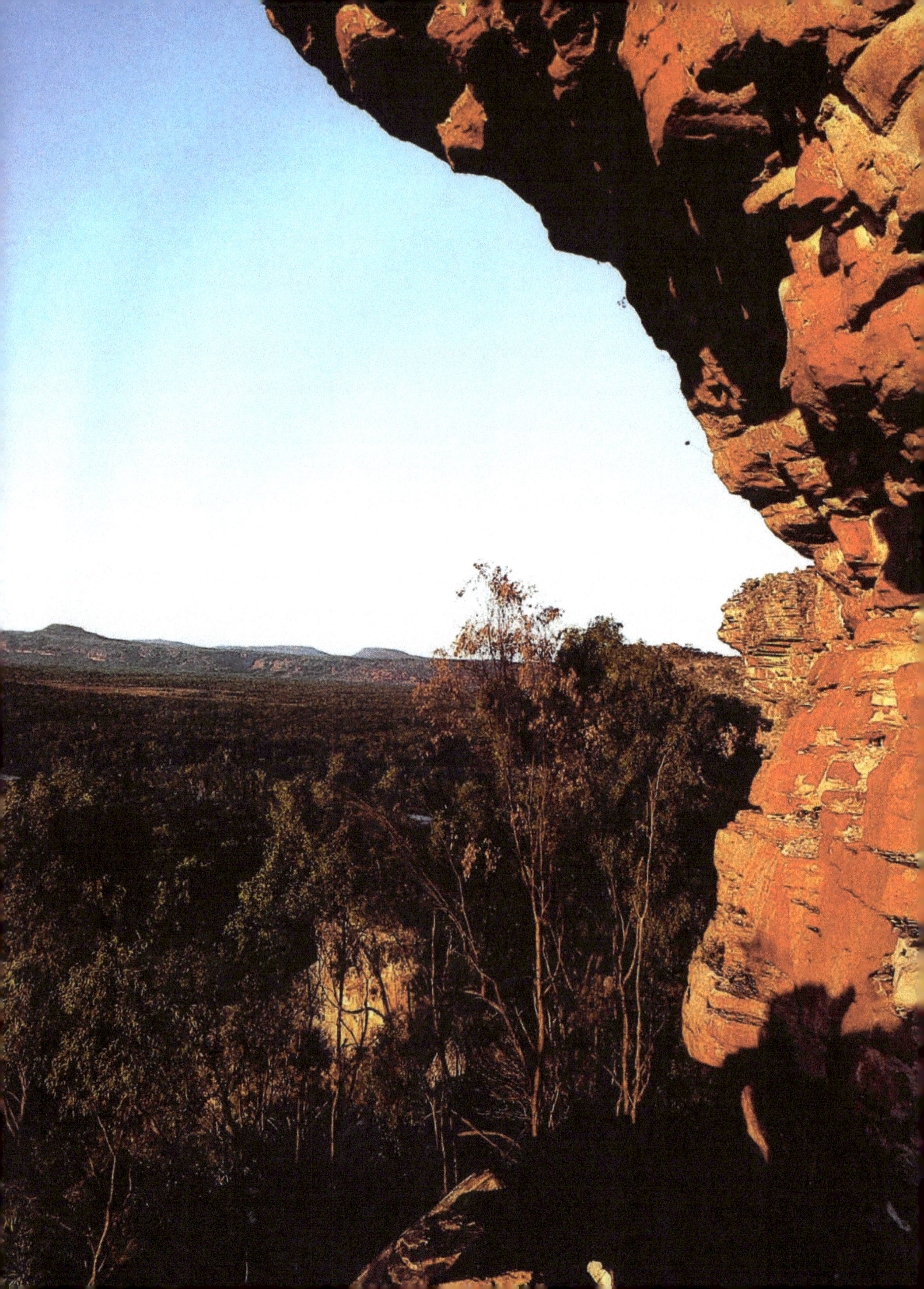

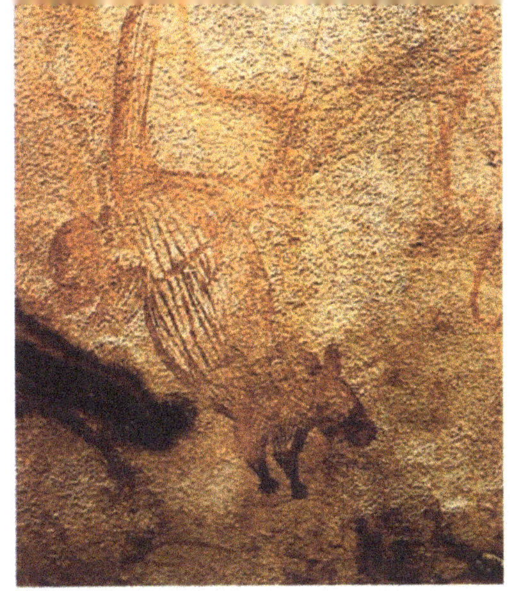

TRIBAL SITE

This is a joyful
and wonder-full thing:
to stand hushed
where a great people
lived continuously
from ancient days.

To be a brief part
of a noble stream,
generations onflowing
of precious
communal life
in this place.

How many
campfire meals?
How many happy tales
of a day's hunt?
Or the mighty deeds
of ancestors?

What wounds
of body or spirit
have been tended here?
What loving looks
silently exchanged,
or babies suckled?

Now we come, unworthy,
yet inheritors,
if we are willing
to humbly approach
and deeply respect
this stone cathedral.

Surely the Lord
is in this place,
yet we, in blindness,
knew it not. Now
how great the awe!
Lord, how great the awe!

LEFT *Djuwarr, Deaf Adder Valley*
UPPER RIGHT *Speared Kangaroo, Mangolin Gallery*
LOWER RIGHT *Banama Gallery (Djirringbal)*

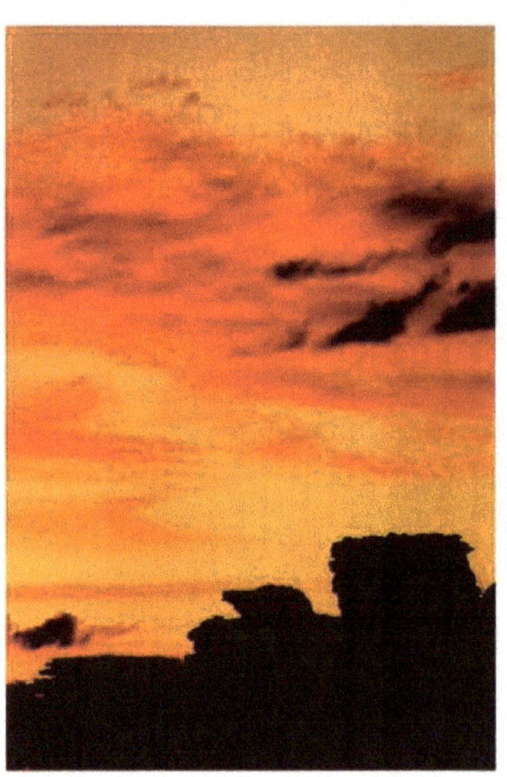

JESUS WEPT

I found him sobbing,
   Jesus, the one called Christ,
sitting on a stone ledge
in the large empty space
under a sloping overhang
   at Burrungguy.

He did not heed me,
   Jesus, the one called Christ,
but kept staring at walls,
fingering grinding holes,
brooding over the vacancy
   at Burrungguy.

He knew as a brother,
   Jesus, the one called Christ,
the inner meaning of this place
where once camp-fires glowed
for thousands of years
   at Burrungguy.

Never again, he knew,
   Jesus, the one called Christ,
never again the fires and soft chatter,
food, love, and laughter,
nor the songs of Namarrkurn
   at Burrungguy.

I left him weeping,
   Jesus, the one called Christ;
unable to watch with him
beyond a while in such grief —
or with such fierce love —
   at Burrungguy.

LEFT *Malangangerr*
RIGHT *Joseph Giradbul, Inyalak Gallery*

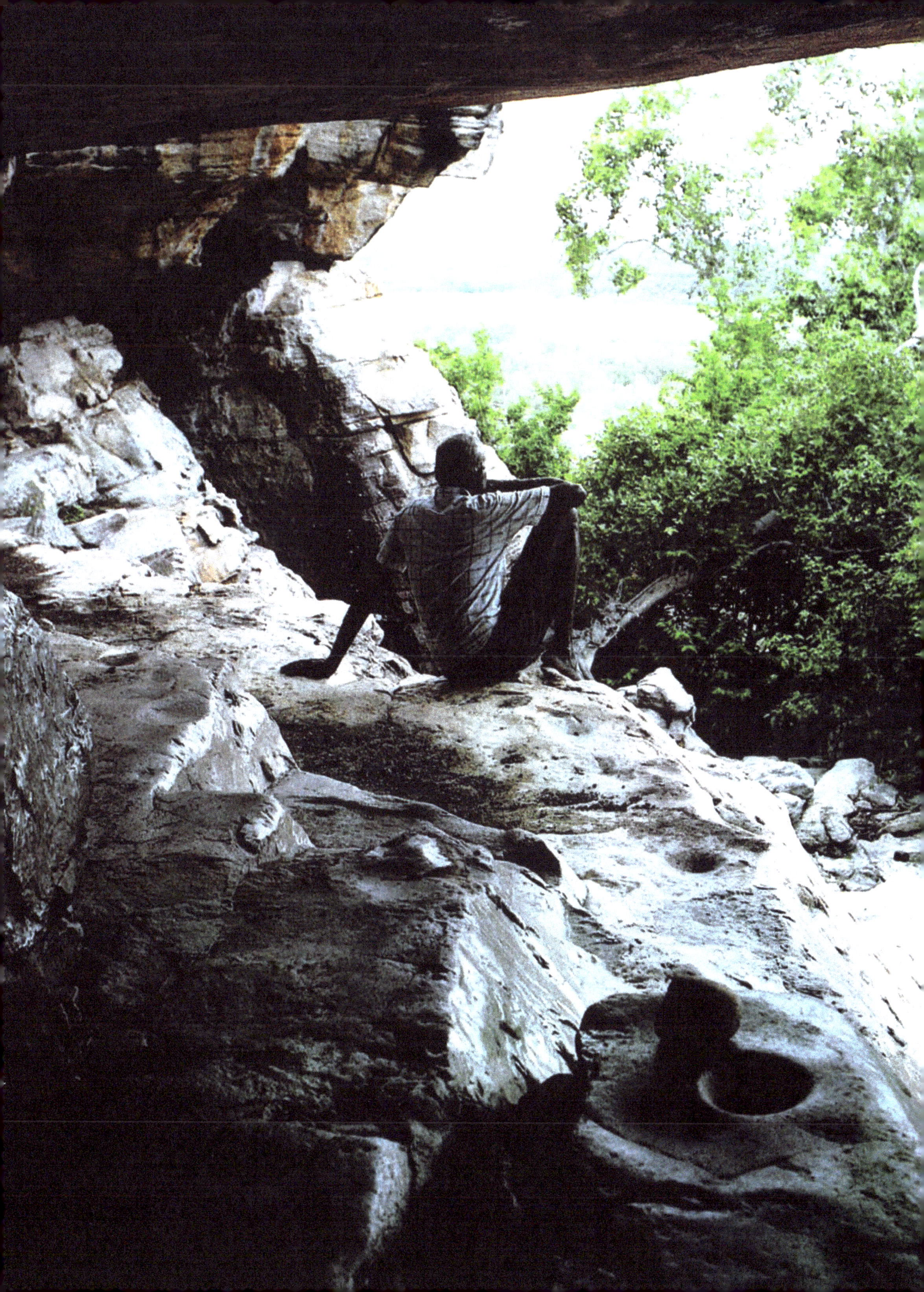

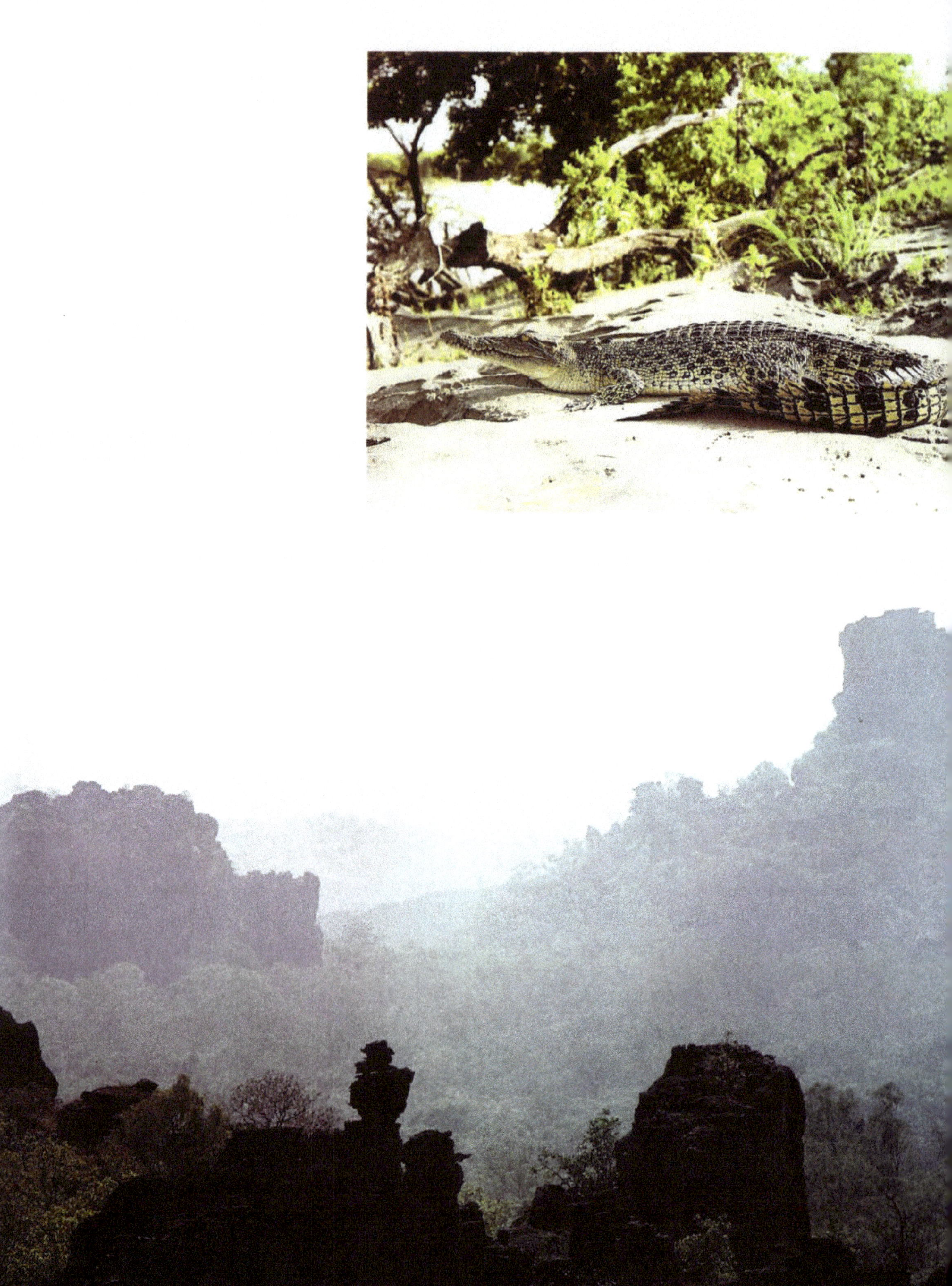

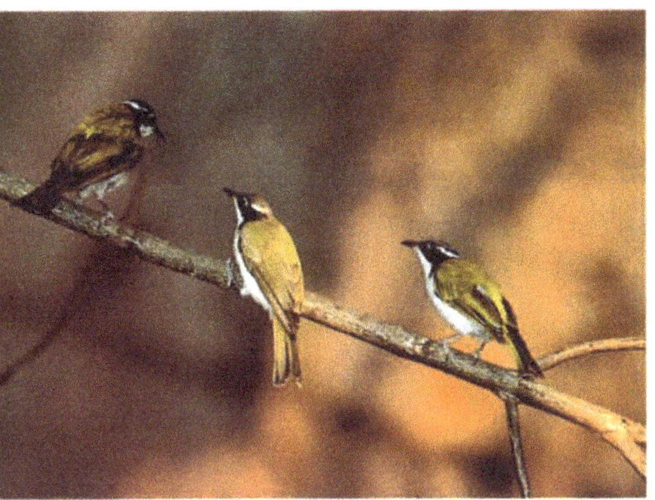

FOR EVERYTHING A PLACE

In the sandstone country
I hear the song
of the white-lined honeyeater,
and know
it belongs.

At the river's edge
I see the crocodile
basking in sunshine,
and know
it belongs.

Across the lowlands
I see a flock of pelicans
in thick formation,
and know
they belong.

Watching from the peak
of an ancient rock
we wait for Sunday's dawn,
and know
we belong.

UPPER LEFT *Crocodile*
LOWER LEFT *East Alligator Valley area*
RIGHT *White-throated Honeyeaters*

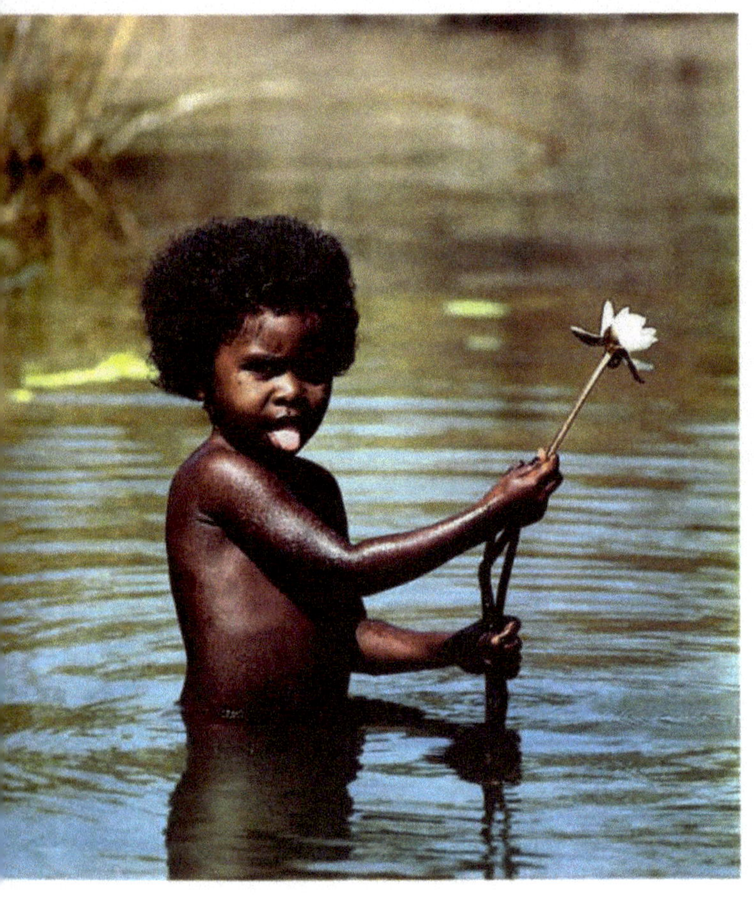

FOR THE MEEK

Wonderful is our humble Lord,
  friend of all the earth.
The whole world is his own,
  filled with unquenchable light.
He upholds the poor of the land,
and saves the children of the needy.

He comes like living water,
  like rains renewing the dusty earth.
Goodness fills his days,
  peace flows by without limit.
Low places provide fruit in plenty,
  even rocky places grow sweet fruits.

Then shall the lonely outback
  gladly bow before him.
Leaders not yet born
  shall freely serve him.
Precious shall his blood be
  in the hearts of all his people.

Longer than the sun shall rule
  across land and sea by day,
longer than the moon shall shine
  across the bushland by night,
the meek shall sing his name,
  and trust his utter love.

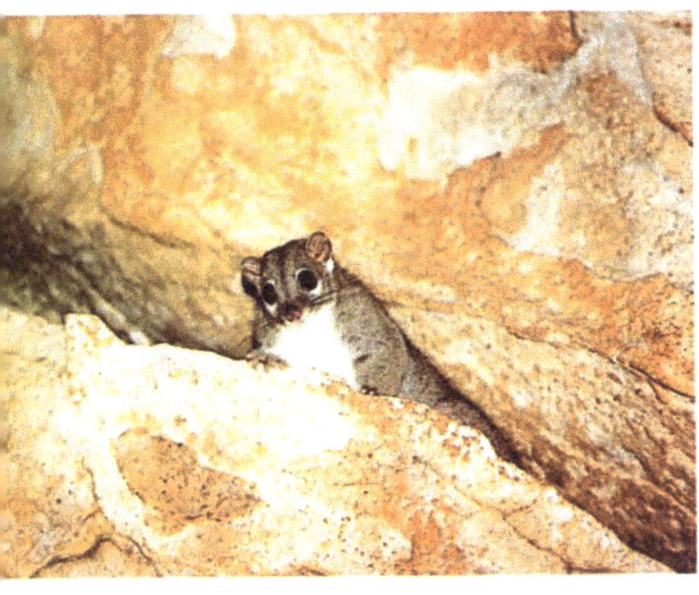

LEFT Cindi Cooper, Wildman River
UPPER RIGHT Rock Possum, Little Nawulandja Rock
LOWER RIGHT Djarrdjarr Billabong, Magela Creek

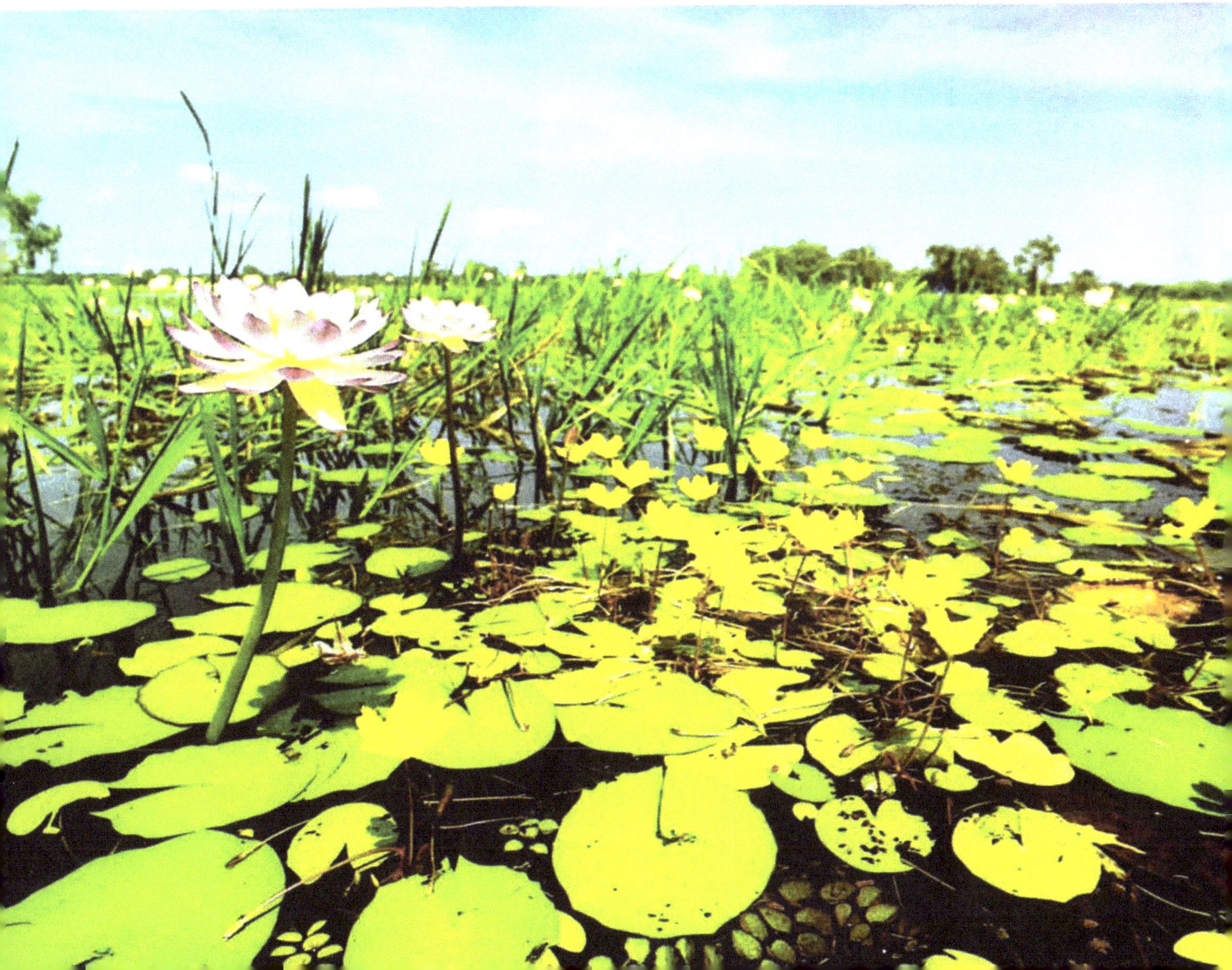

THE BLUES

Lord, I have bad days
when I pray without hearing,
and nights of grave disquiet
when my hand reaches into darkness.
I try to meditate,
but it makes things worse.
I complain and protest
without relieving my discontent.

On such overcast days I wonder:
Has God withdrawn his love?
I say to myself:
Was my faith ever real?
Were the sacred promises an illusion?
Is the Spirit a fiction?

Then, Lord, you bring me to my senses:
I refuse to bow to my feelings.
I say: The Lord is God
whether I feel him or not;
I am surely baptized,
no matter what oppresses me.
I am God's child,
and Christ has died to prove it!

(Inspired by Psalm 77:1–12)

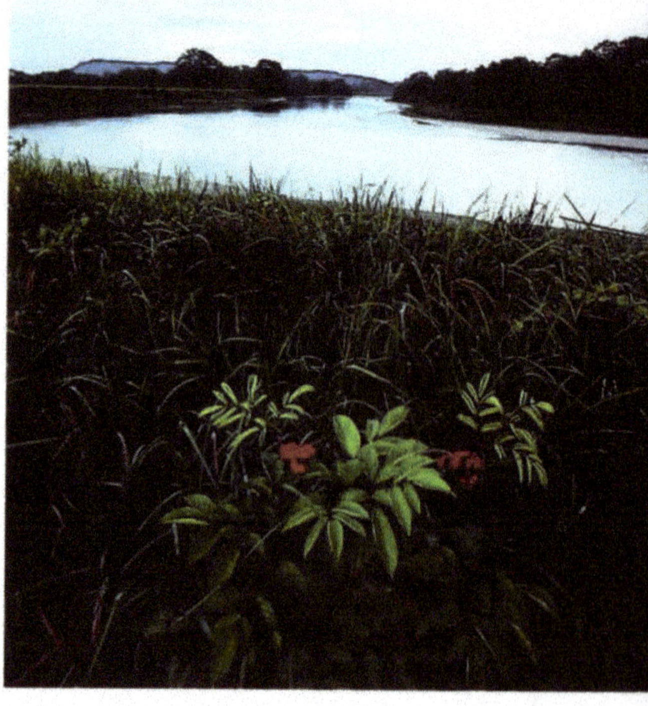

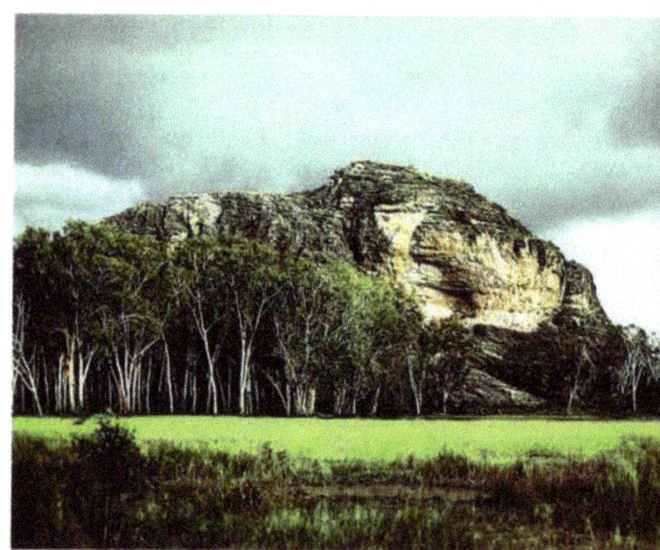

UPPER LEFT: *East Alligator Floodplain (Nardab)*
LOWER LEFT: *Jabiru Dreaming (Djagarna)*
RIGHT: *Riflefish Dreaming (Nyarlgan)*

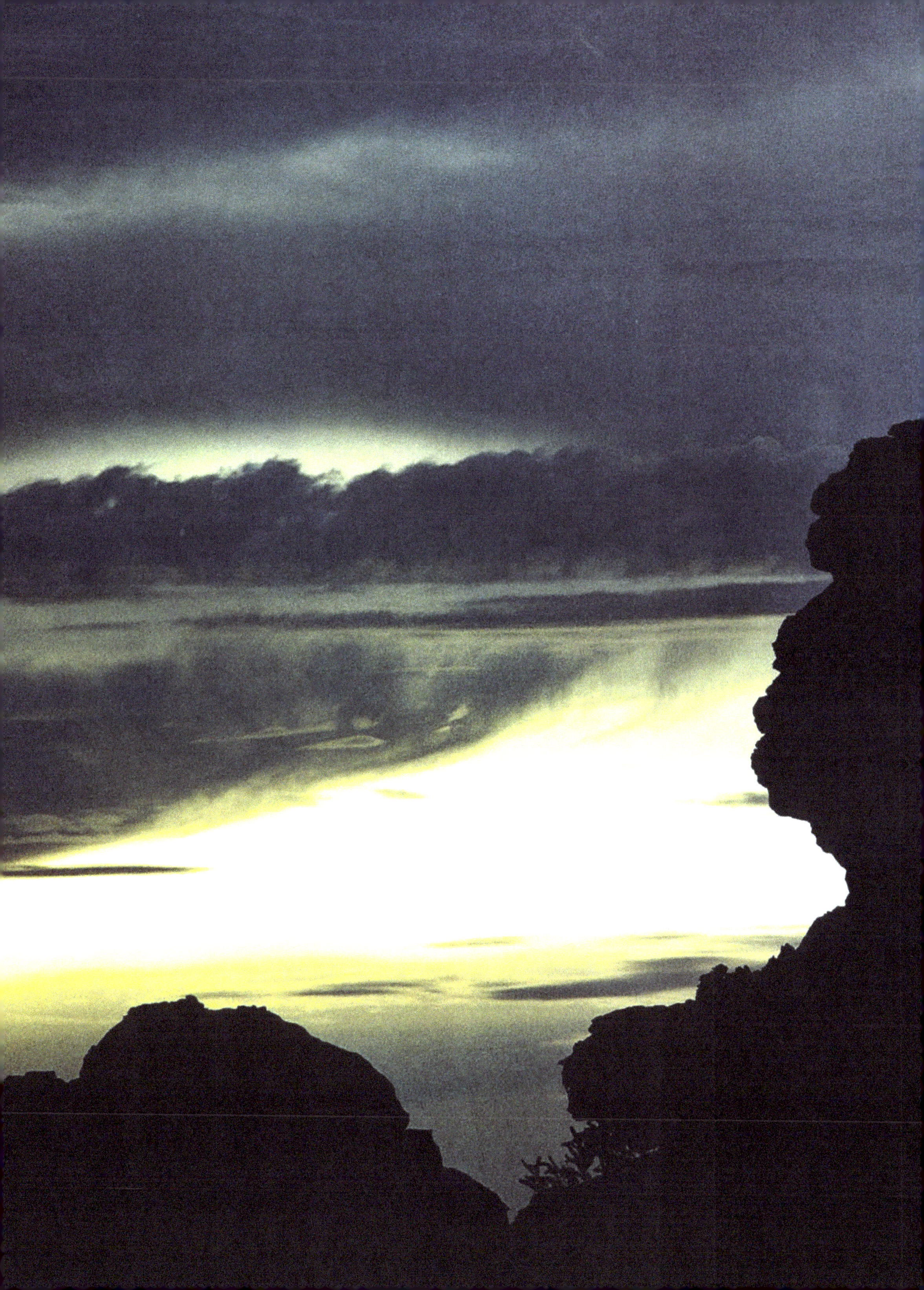

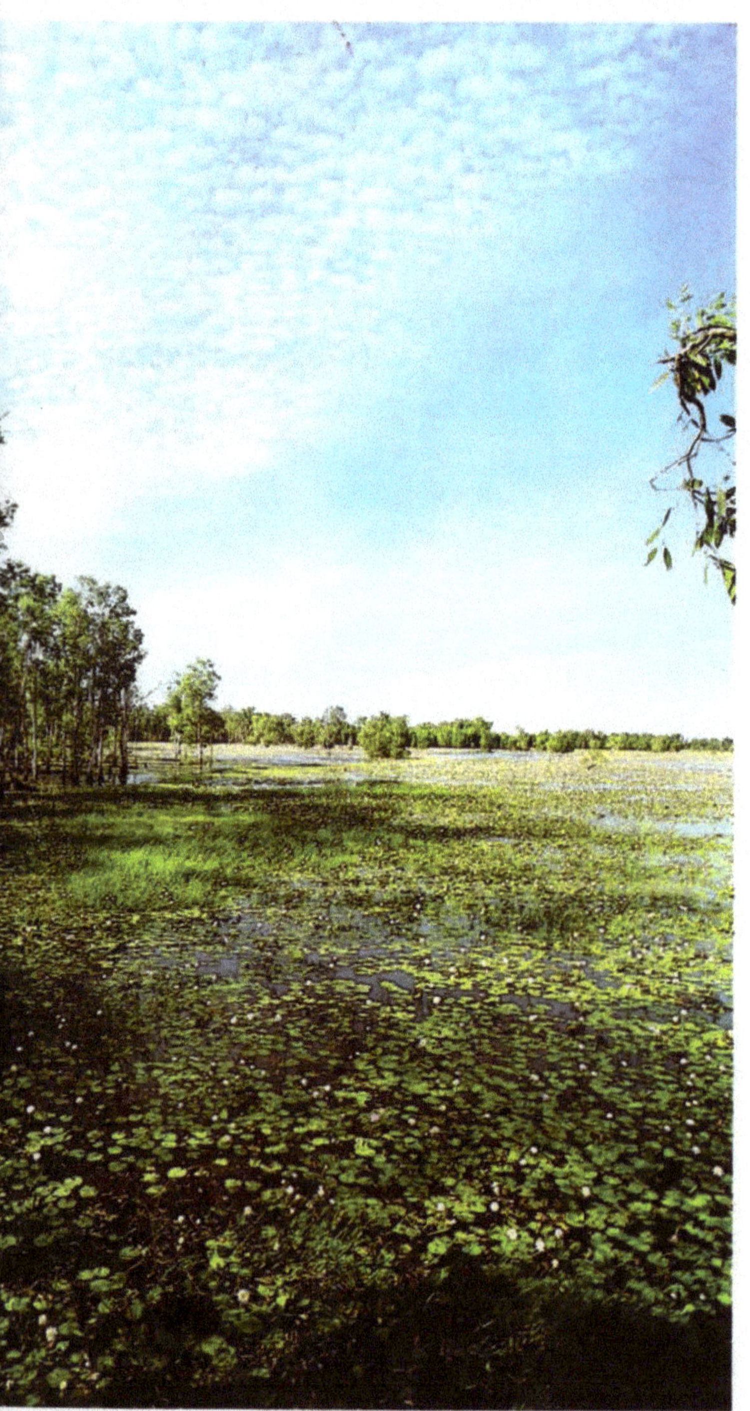

GLORY

Glory be to you, Lord,
for you have given us creation
with its colours and shapes,
sounds and tastes.

Glory be to you, Lord,
for you have given the human family
with its many tongues and cultures.

Glory be to you, Lord,
for you have given us Christ Jesus,
brother of each, and redeemer of all.

Therefore, with all loving people,
near or far off,
remembered or forgotten,
we join to praise you:

Holy, holy, holy Lord of joy,
the earth and the heavens are full
of the radiance of your glory.
Glory be to you,
friend most lovable,
Lord most wonderful!

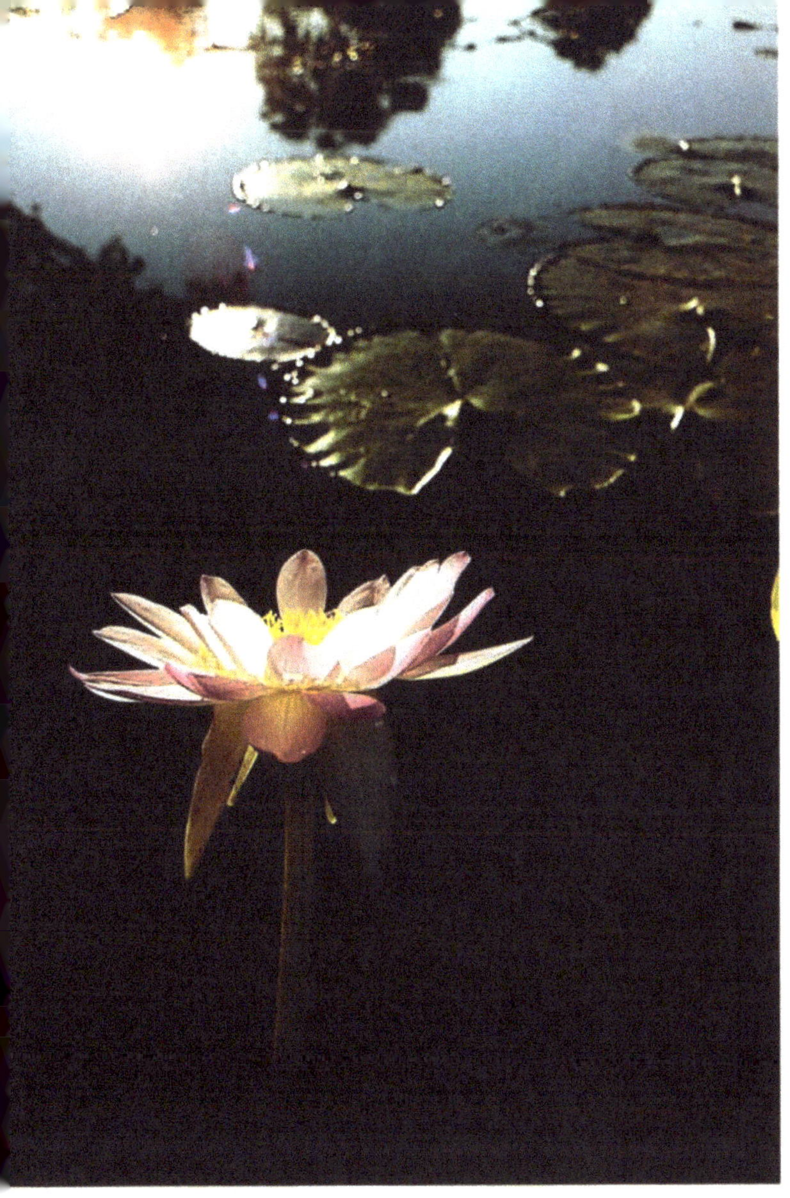

THE PRESENCE

Lord,
sometimes the air
seems charged
with your Presence,
saturated,
pulsing,
like a music
composed of
pure love.

Then it is
that the panting soul
is wondrously quietened,
for our dearest self
can breathe well
on even a little
of this atmosphere.

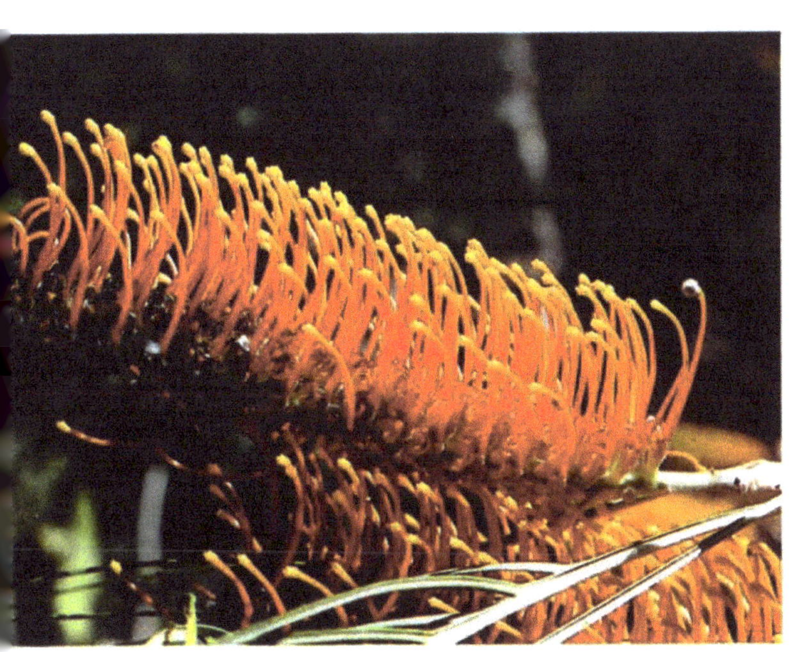

LEFT *Lilies, post-wet season, Buyuck Goluy Billabong*
UPPER RIGHT *Magela Creek Lily*
LOWER RIGHT *Grevillea pteridifolia*
OVERLEAF *Main escarpment (Namarrkurn)*

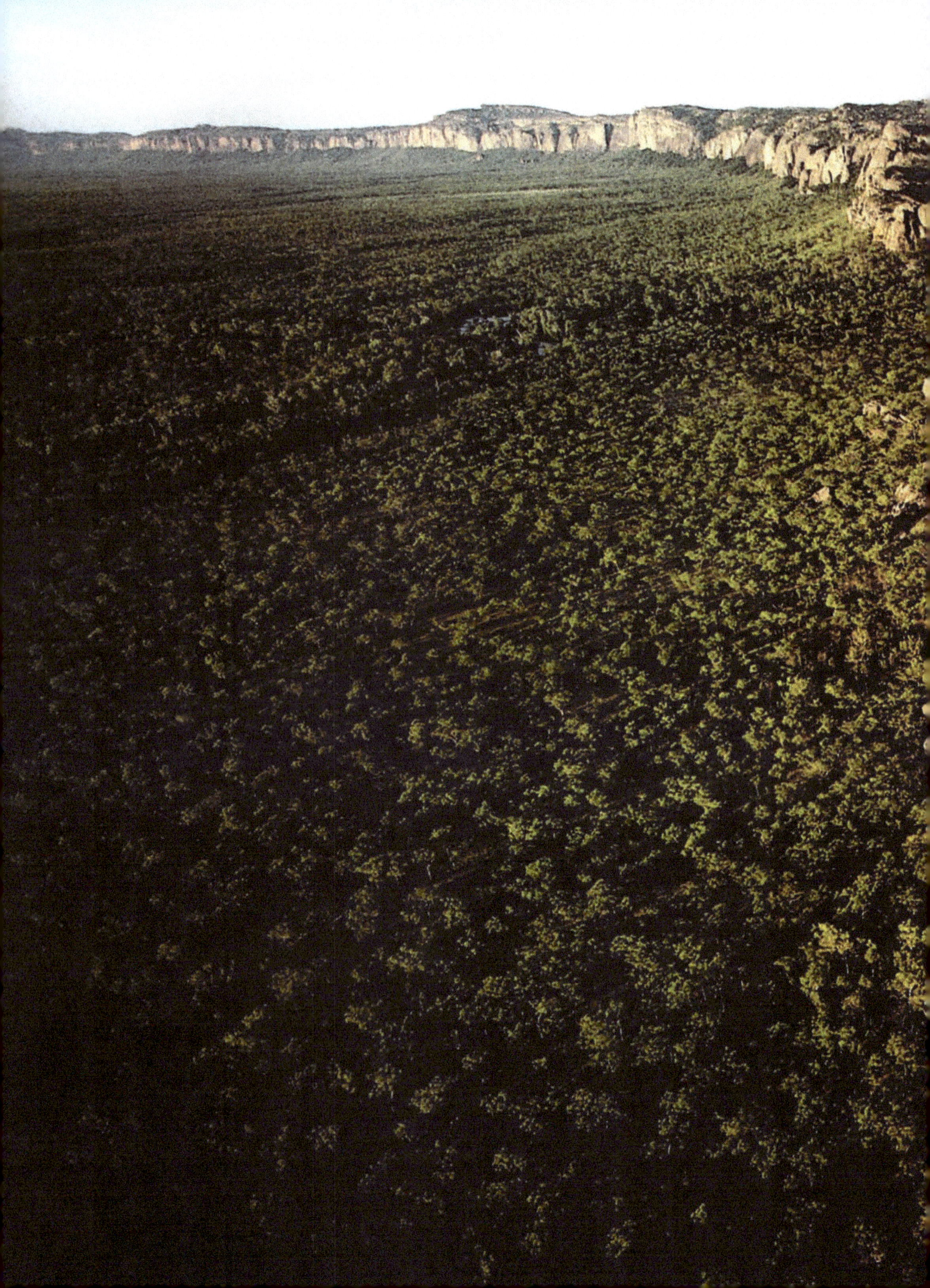

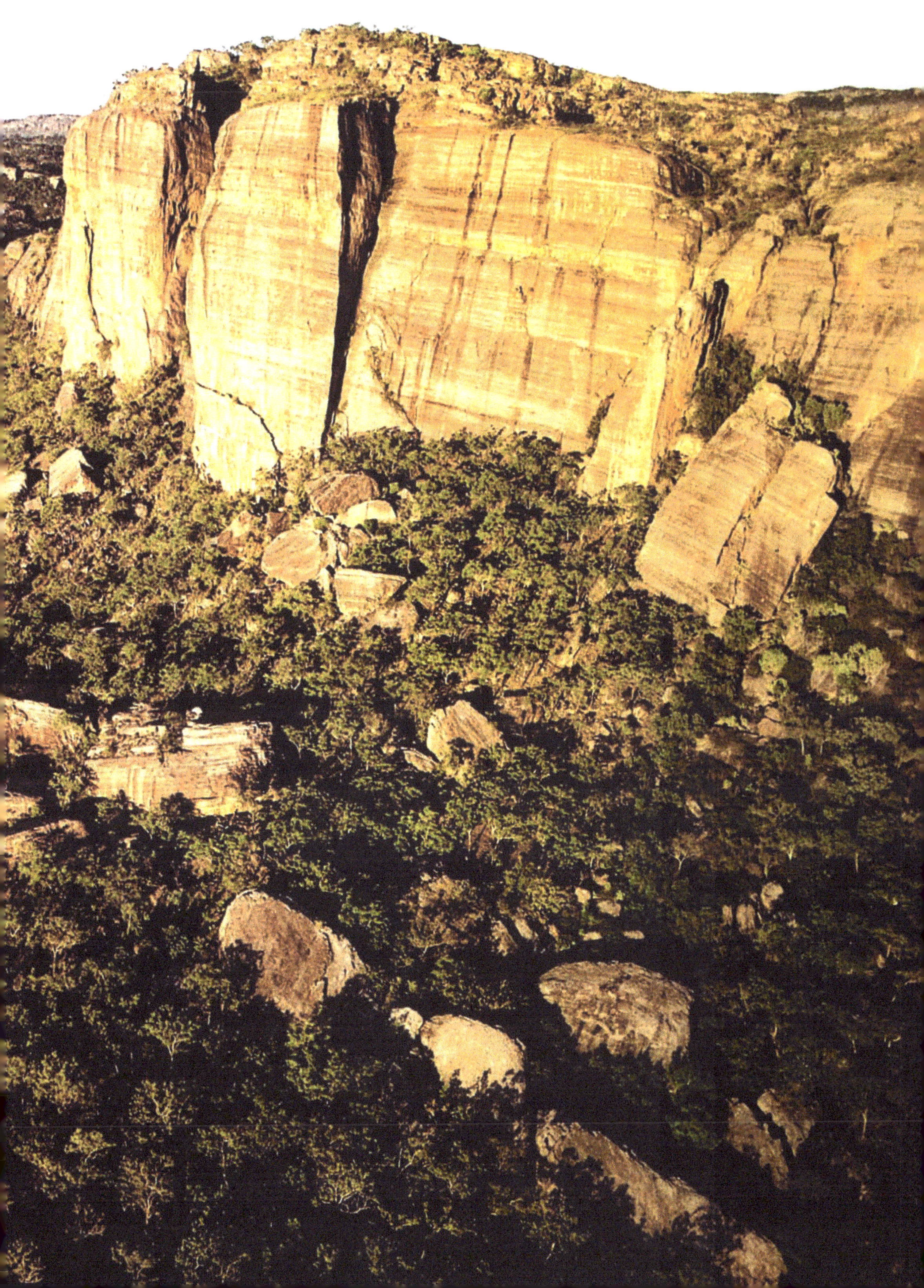

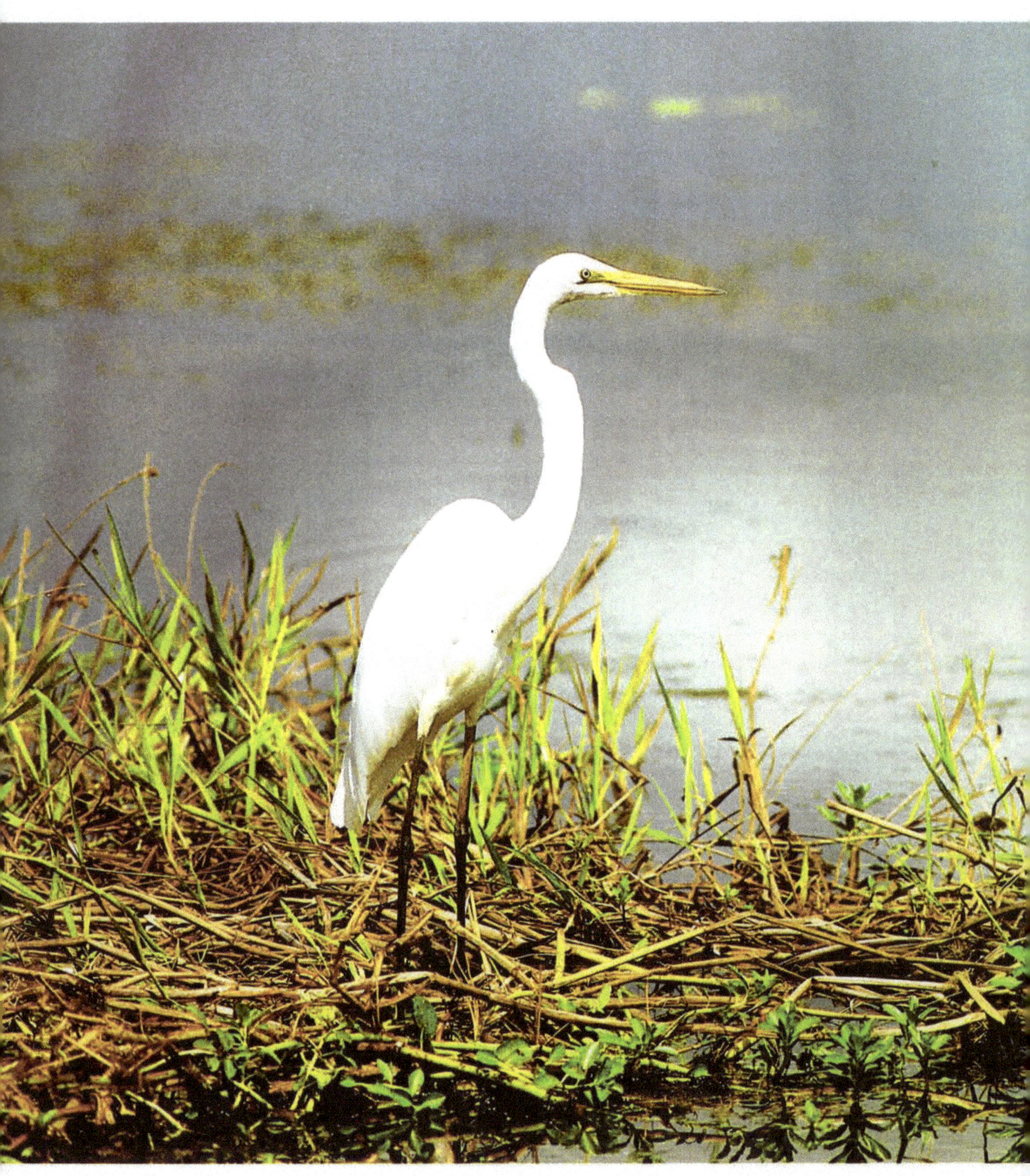

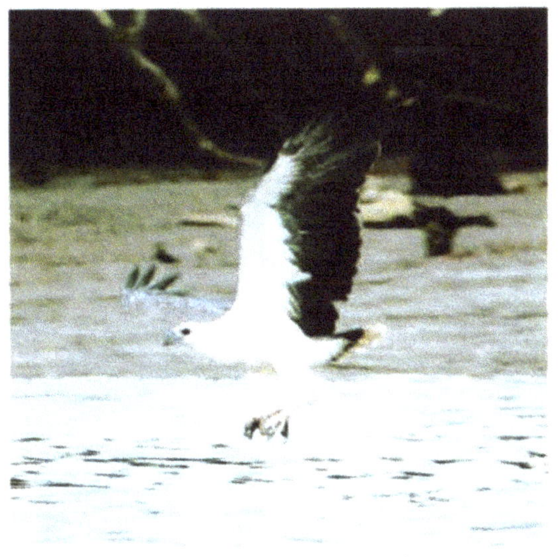

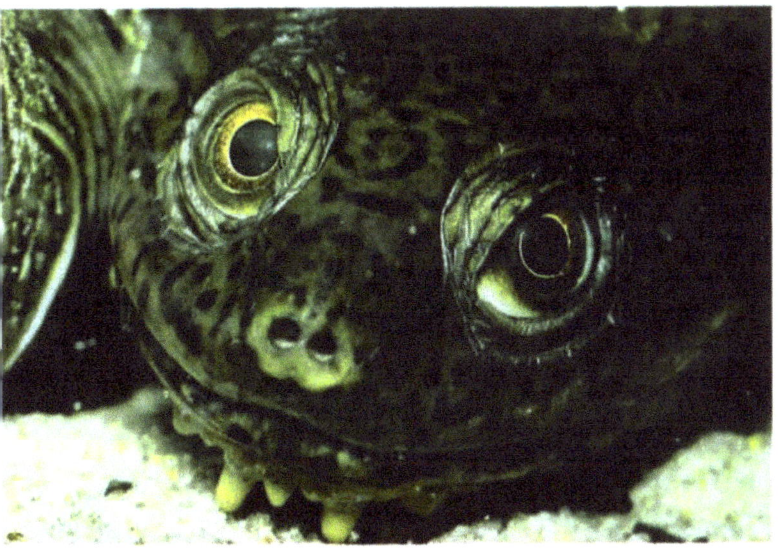

IF YOU HAVE BREATH

Let everyone praise the Lord of life.
Let all things praise the Lord of love.

Give praise in your churches,
sound your praise in open places:
with the grace of the great egret,
with the ease of the eagle,
with the tenacity of the turtle,
with the courage of the crocodile.

Sound your happiness, bugling brolga.
Give praise, chirping crimson finch.
Come all who have ears to hear.
Come all who have songs to sing:
Let everything that draws breath,
praise our most wonderful God!

(Inspired by Psalm 146)

LEFT *Great Egret, Wetlands*
UPPER RIGHT *White-breasted Sea Eagle*
LOWER RIGHT *Snake-necked Turtle*

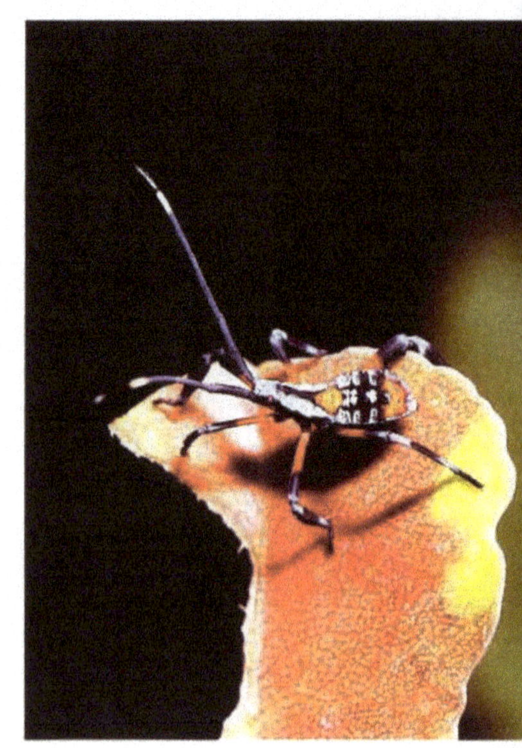

UPPER LEFT: *Assassin Bug*
LOWER LEFT: *Sandstone-dwelling tree frog*
UPPER RIGHT: *Morning Glory* (Ipomoea abrupta)
LOWER RIGHT: *Monsoon Forest Fly*

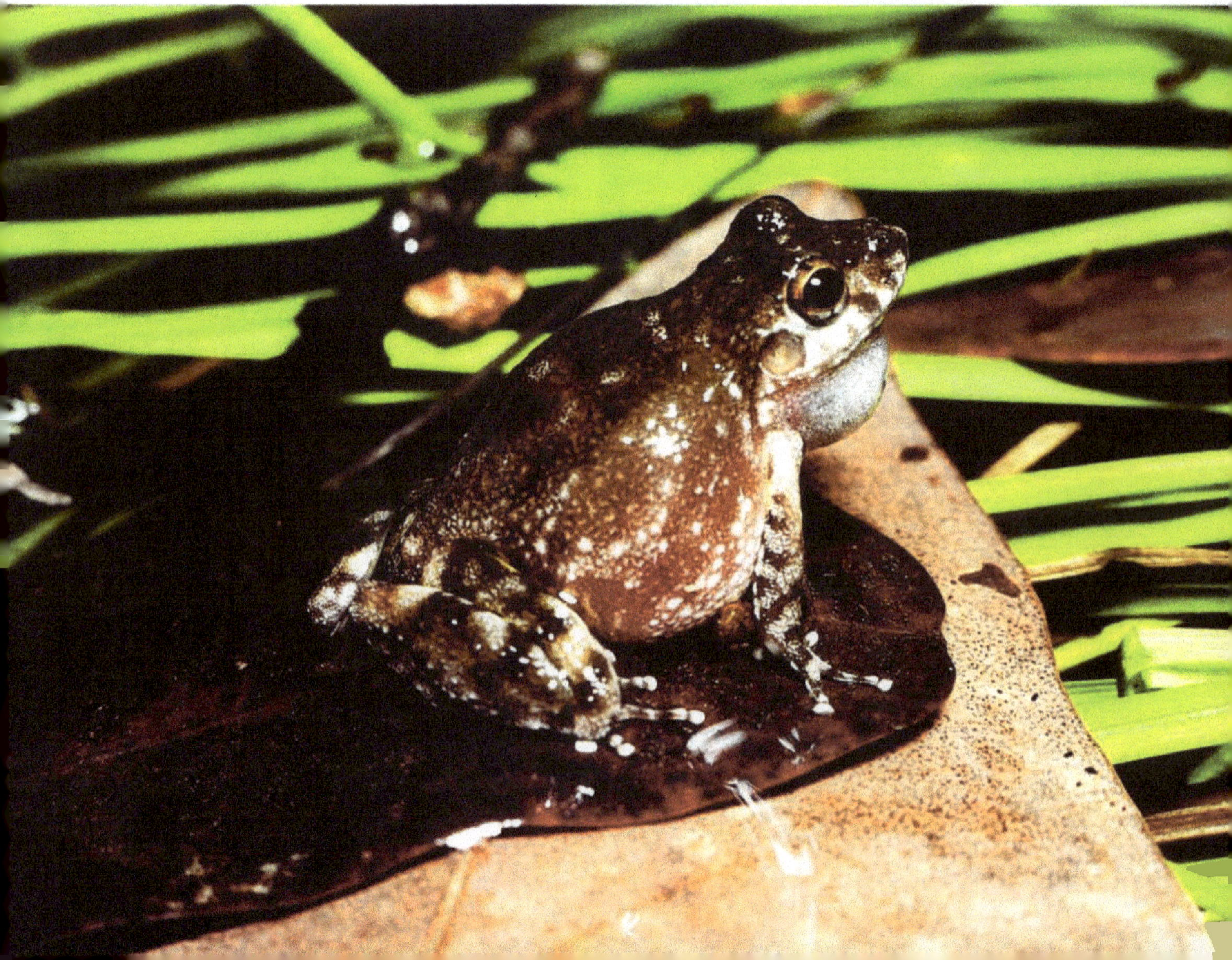

FROM BUSYNESS

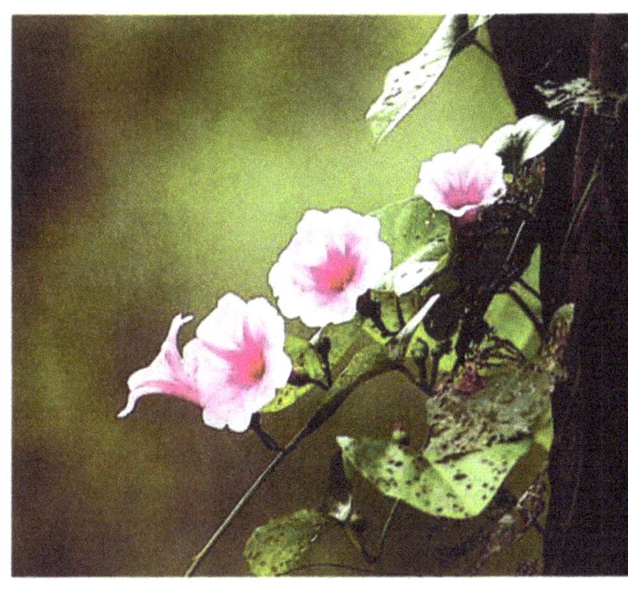

Lord, save me
from the busyness
that fails to see

your beauty
in every bush and tree,

your power
in every plant and flower,

your love
in all the things
that live and move,
including me.

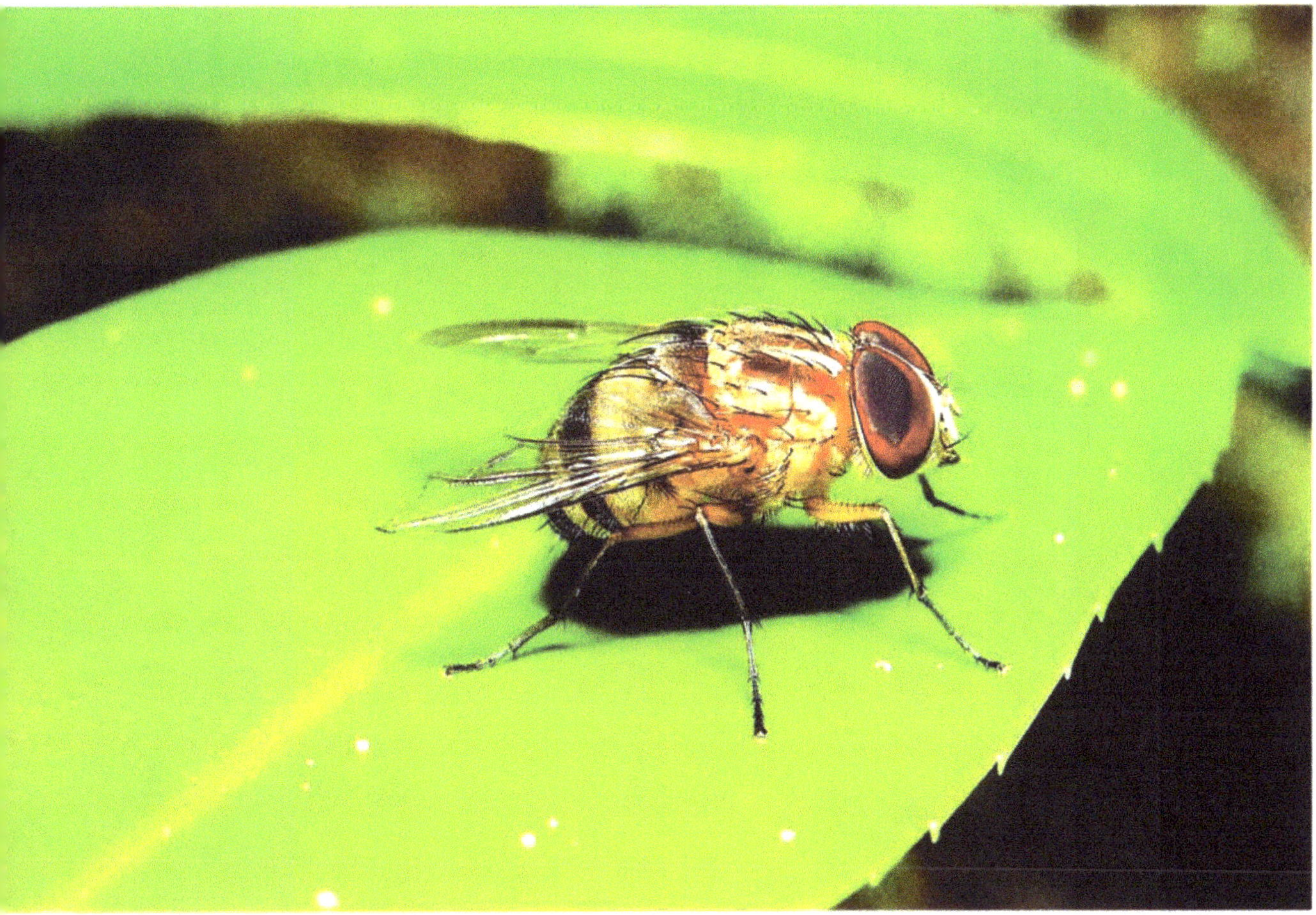

THE UNSPEAKABLE

There is a Truth
about which I cannot speak
without mistelling it.
Its treasure I cannot share
without shortselling it.

Its secret
seems less than a mustard seed,
yet shakes the mountains.
Its light
seems less than a moonbeam,
yet fills the world.

This Truth
cannot be grasped
by the greedy and proud.
The humble who live it
will truly know it.

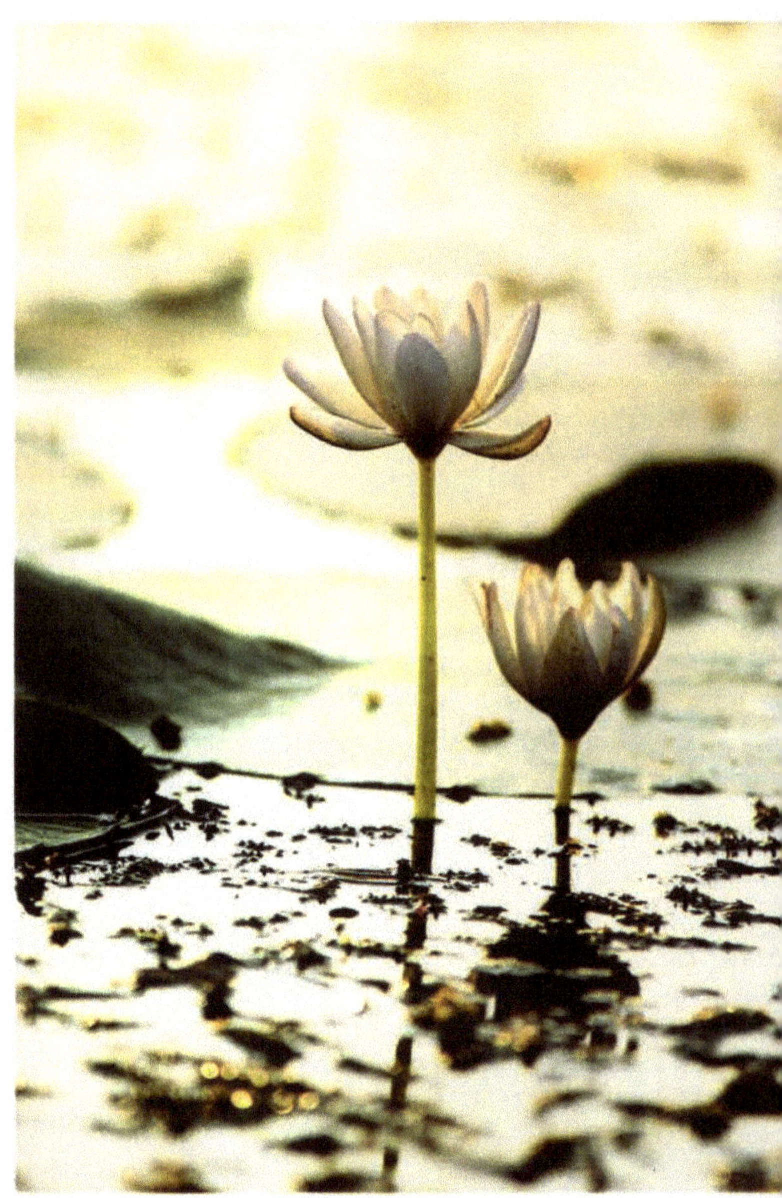

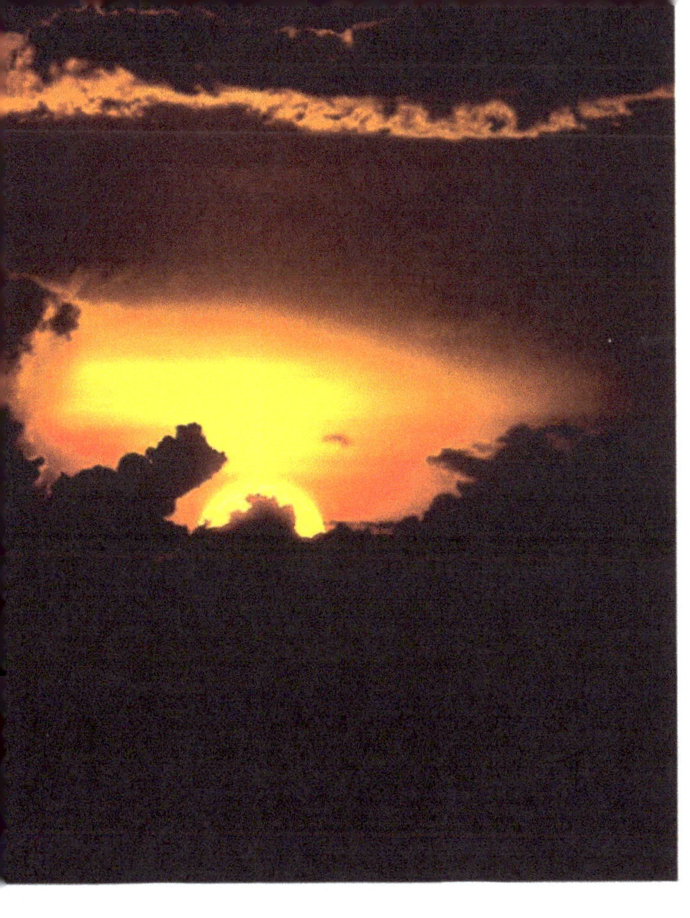

LEFT *Water Lily* (Nymphaea violacea)
UPPER RIGHT *Sunset over Magela Creek*
LOWER RIGHT *View from Nawurrkpil*

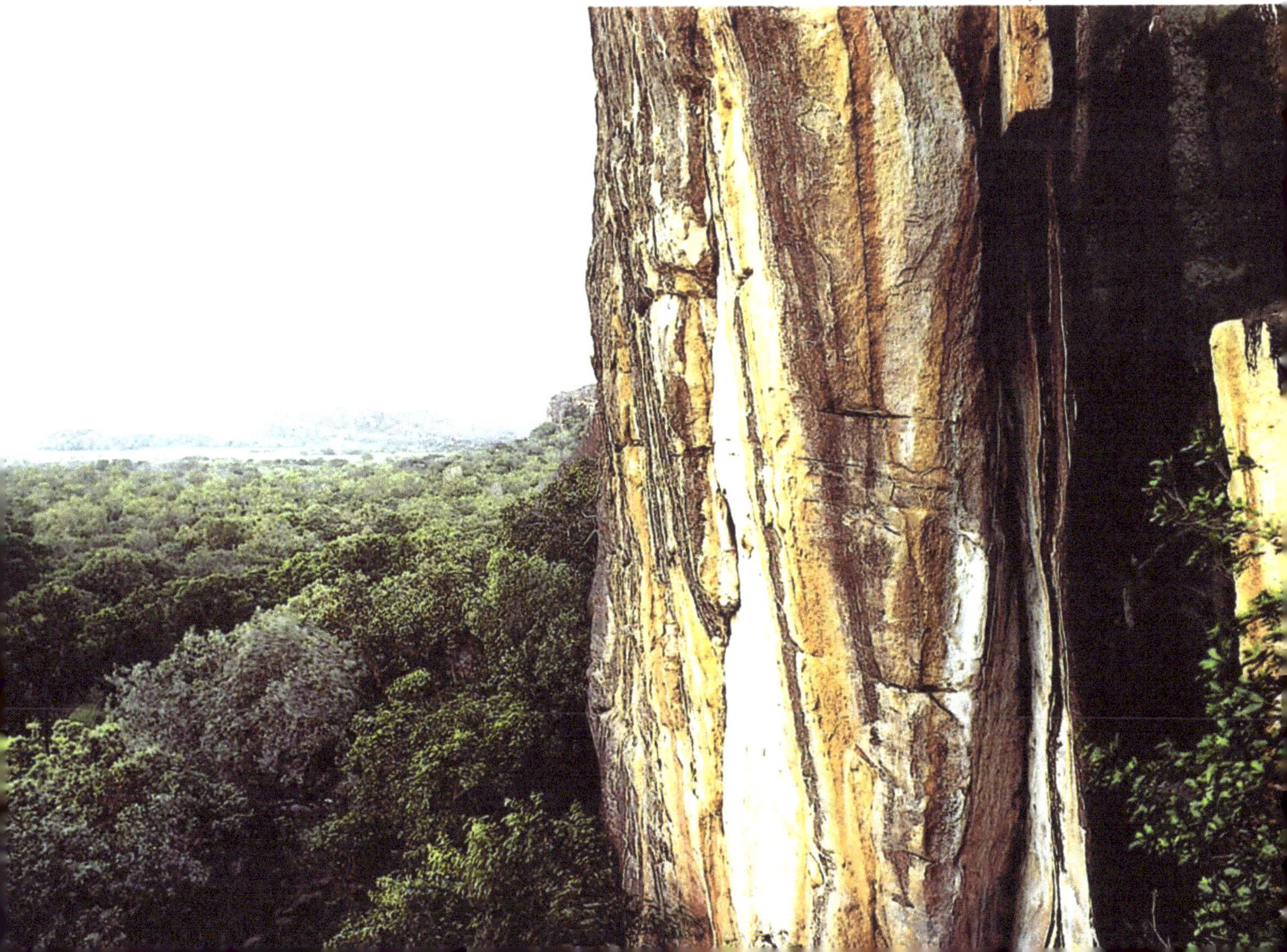

WHERE WERE YOU?

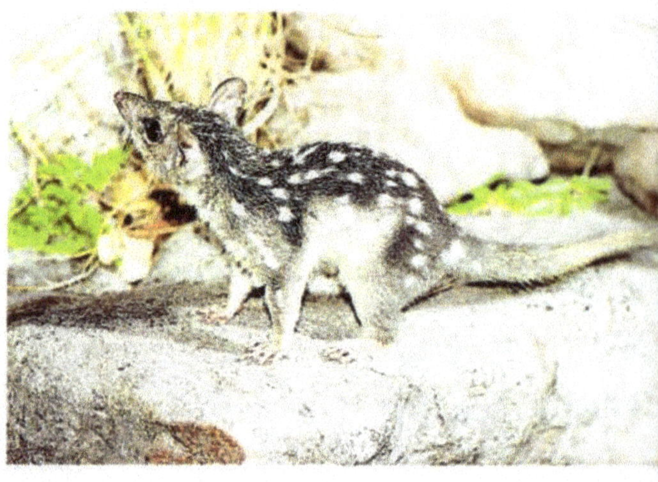

Where were you, mere human,
  when living creatures were formed?
What did you amount to
  when bird and beast took shape?
Did you play with the first native cat
  or feed the shy sugar glider?
Where were you when the python arrived,
  or when the butcher bird first sang?

You had no part in constructing the crocodile,
  you were not needed to draw the plans.
Watch it there on the reedy mudbank,
  see it basking in the sun.
What massive strength is in its body,
  what power is in its great muscles!
The tail is as sturdy as a gum tree,
  it fells animals like lightning.
Its bones are like steel pipes,
  its legs are as pile-drivers.
On its back there is a row of shields,
  an armour hard to pierce.
The jaws are lined with daggers;
  they close like an iron vice.
Its nostrils blow forth steam,
  its eyes gleam like the dawn.

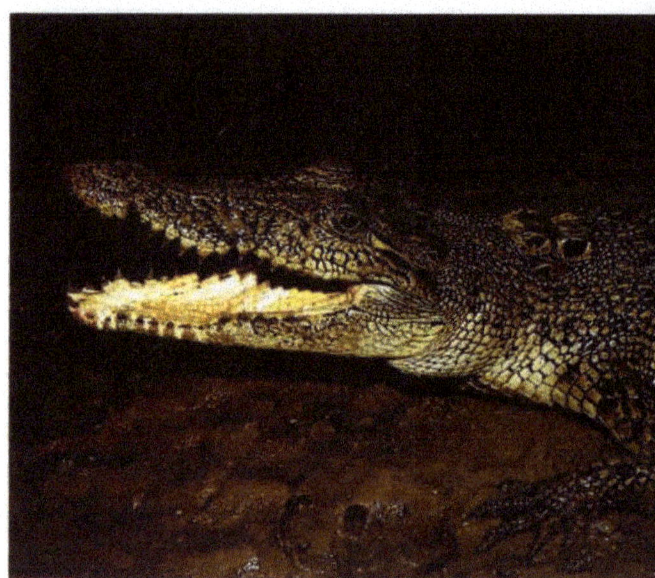

Where were you, mere human,
  when living creatures were formed?
You had no thought in their designing,
  you had no hand in their nurturing.
Be humbled, and consider the Purpose that planned,
  the Power that devised and sustains.
O worship the Lord in the midst of creation!
  Serve him as you treasure his handiwork!

(*Echoing Job* 38 – 40)

UPPER LEFT: *Little Northern Quoll*
LOWER LEFT: *Saltwater Crocodile*
RIGHT: *Northern Sugar Glider*

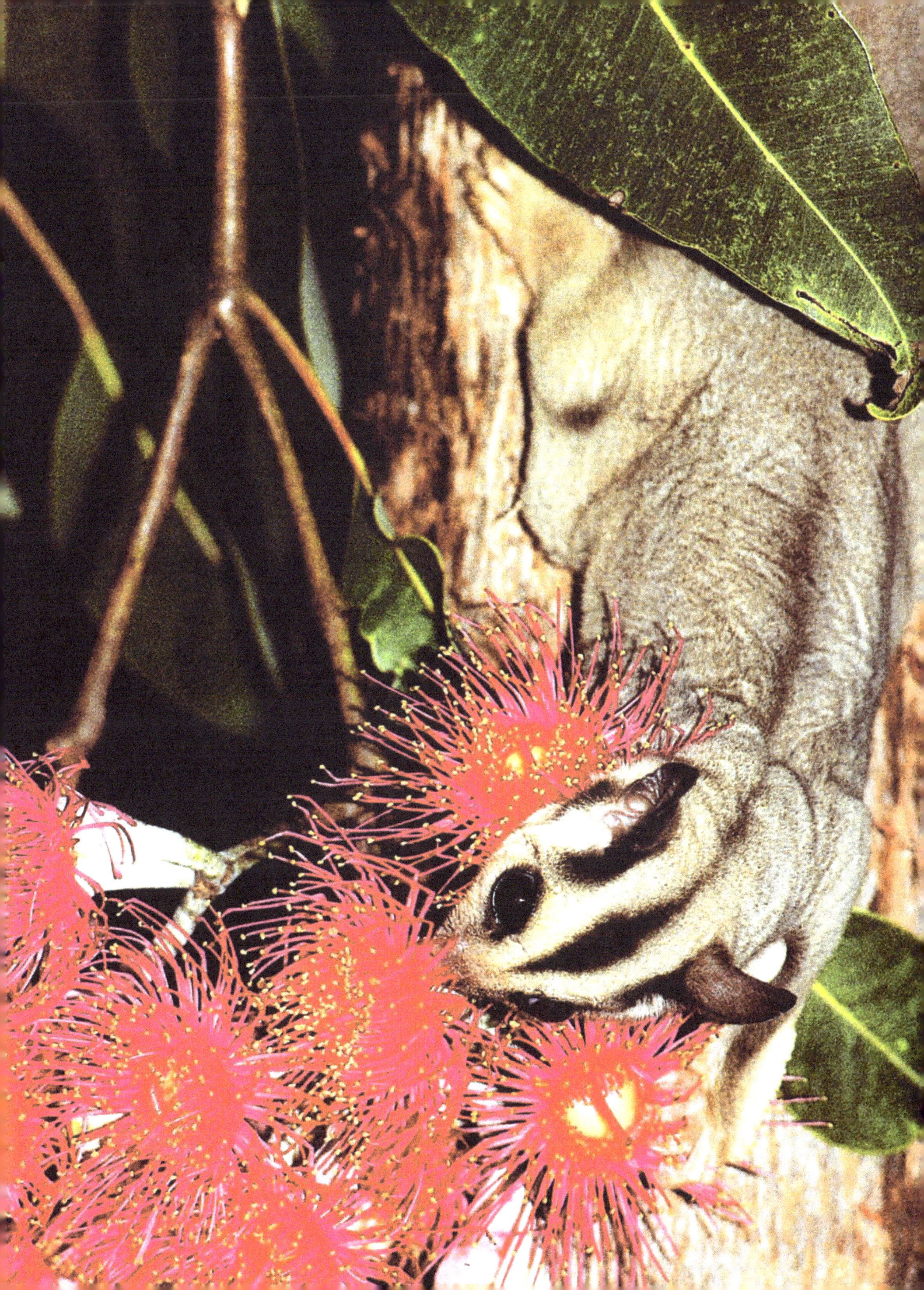

SIMPLE PSALM

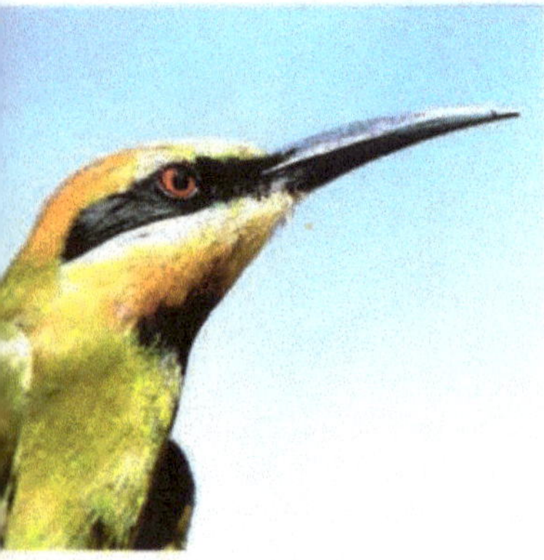

The sun shines freely on all things,
the craft of God is displayed.

How complete are all creatures,
how delightful to the seeing eye.
They go their way each morning,
each fulfilling a simple destiny.
They move in pairs or flocks,
each complementing the other.

Who can grow bored with such a world,
who can tire of its many patterns?
Who can grow weary of discerning
the fingerprints of a greater Glory?

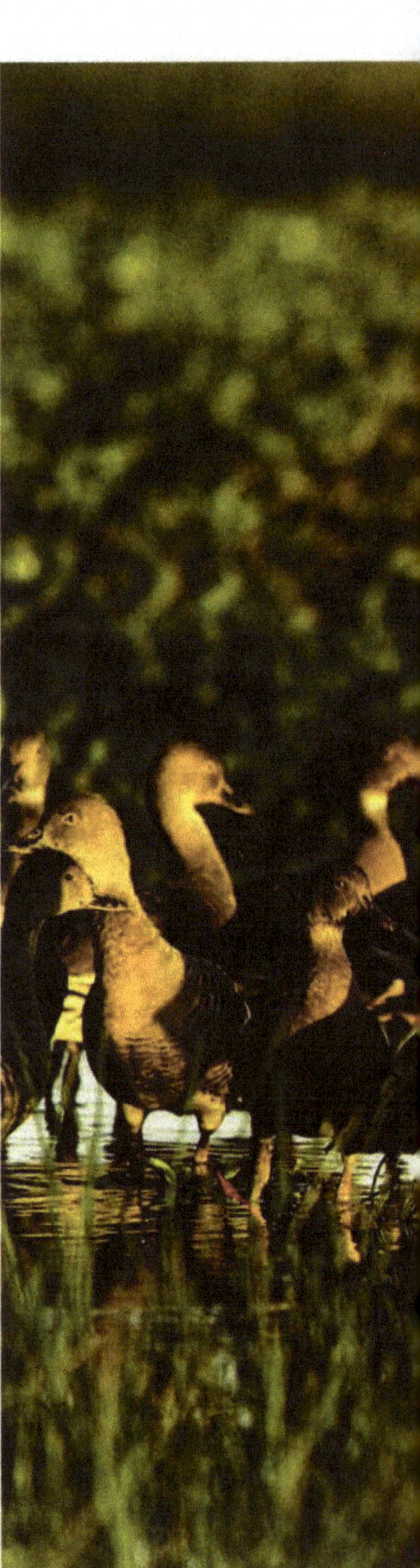

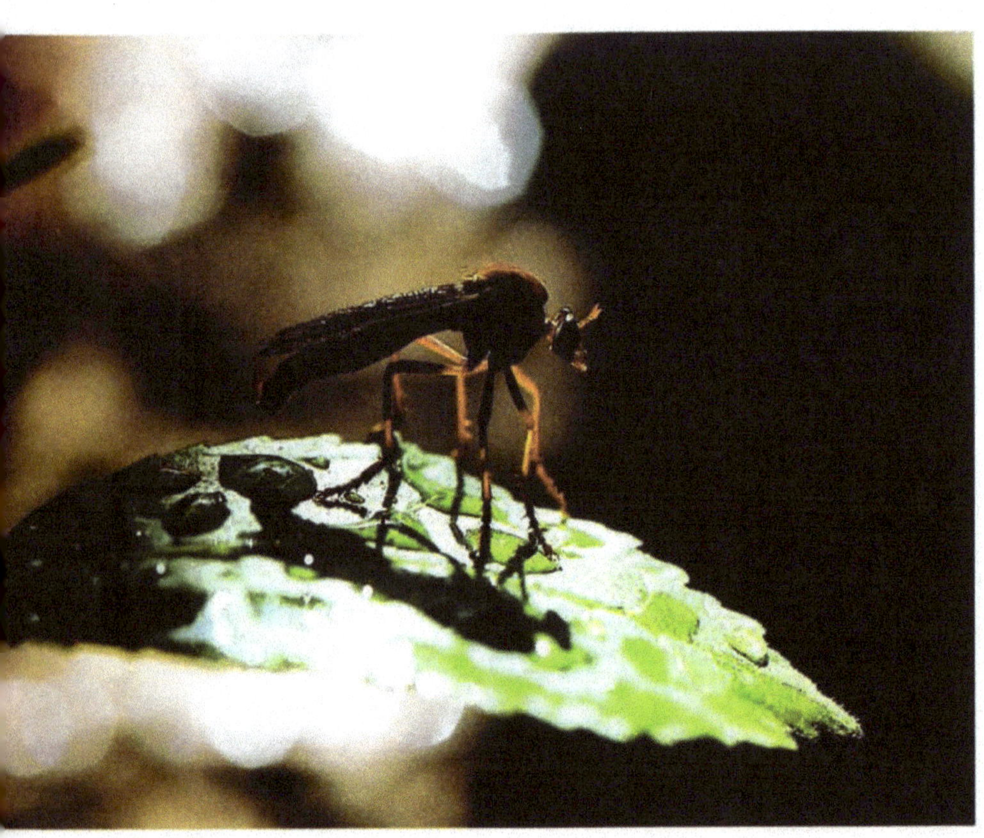

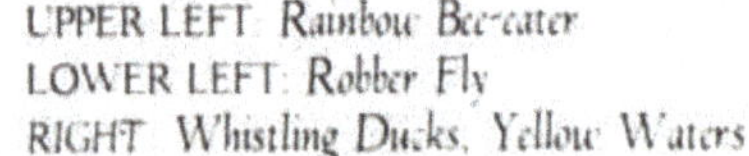

UPPER LEFT: *Rainbow Bee-eater*
LOWER LEFT: *Robber Fly*
RIGHT: *Whistling Ducks, Yellow Waters*

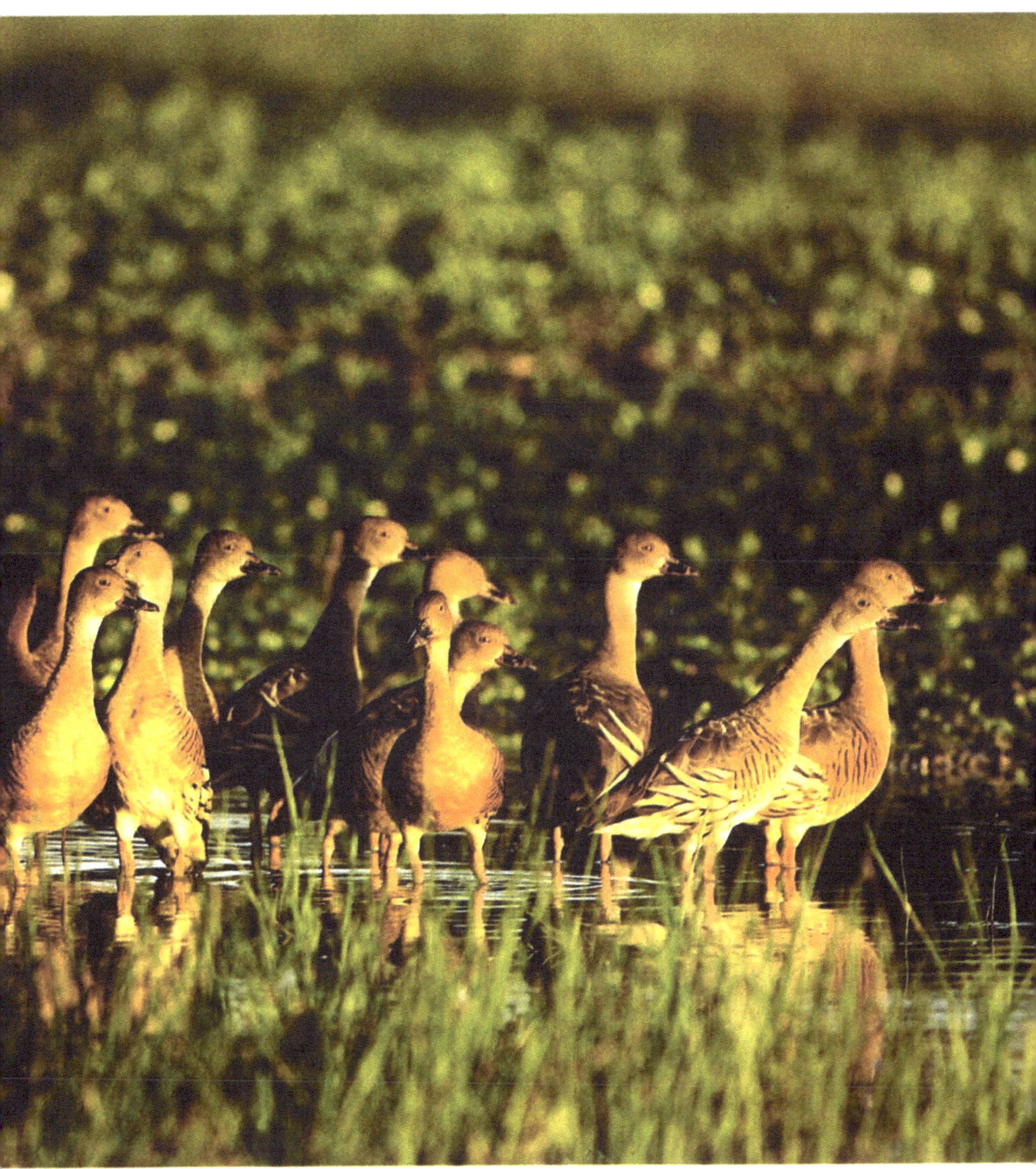

EPHPHATHA

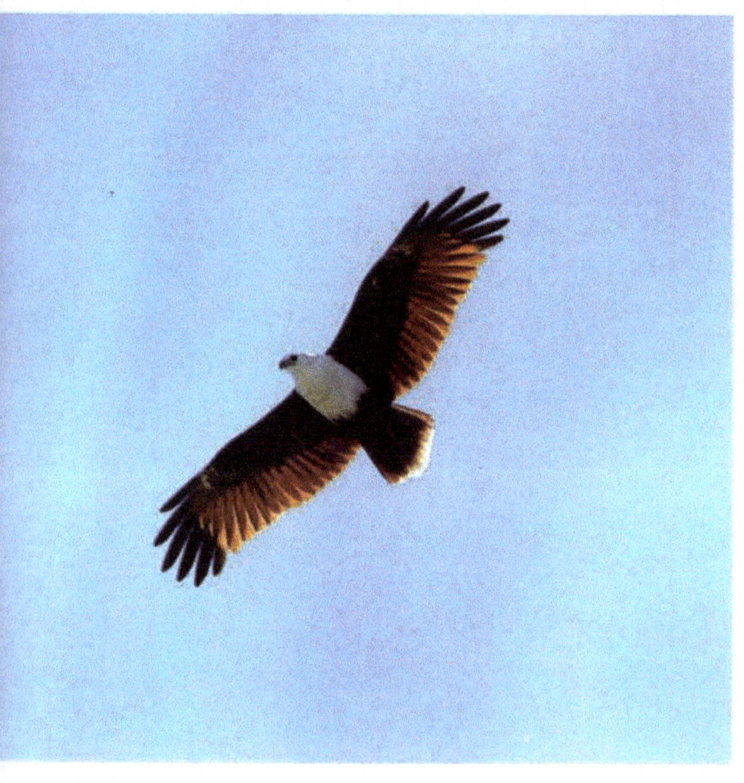

I begged a word.
But the whistling kite
and the cuckoo shrike
were all I heard.

I craved a sign.
But a swamp hen's nest
and a spoonbill's crest
were only mine.

I asked God why?
In the silence that came
he whispered my name
as the wind went by.

I knew it then:
In eyes that are clear,
in ears that hear,
he is present again.

LEFT: *Brahminy Kite*
UPPER RIGHT: *Habernaria Orchid*
LOWER RIGHT: *Red-collared Lorikeet*
OVERLEAF: *Mt Brockman (Djidbidjidbi)*

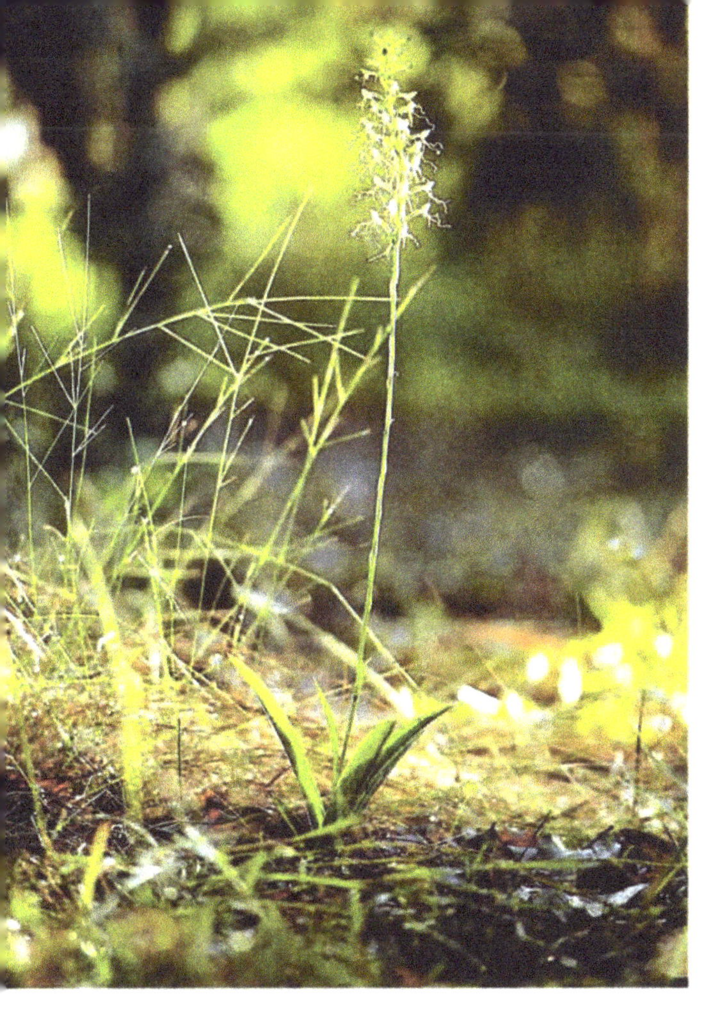

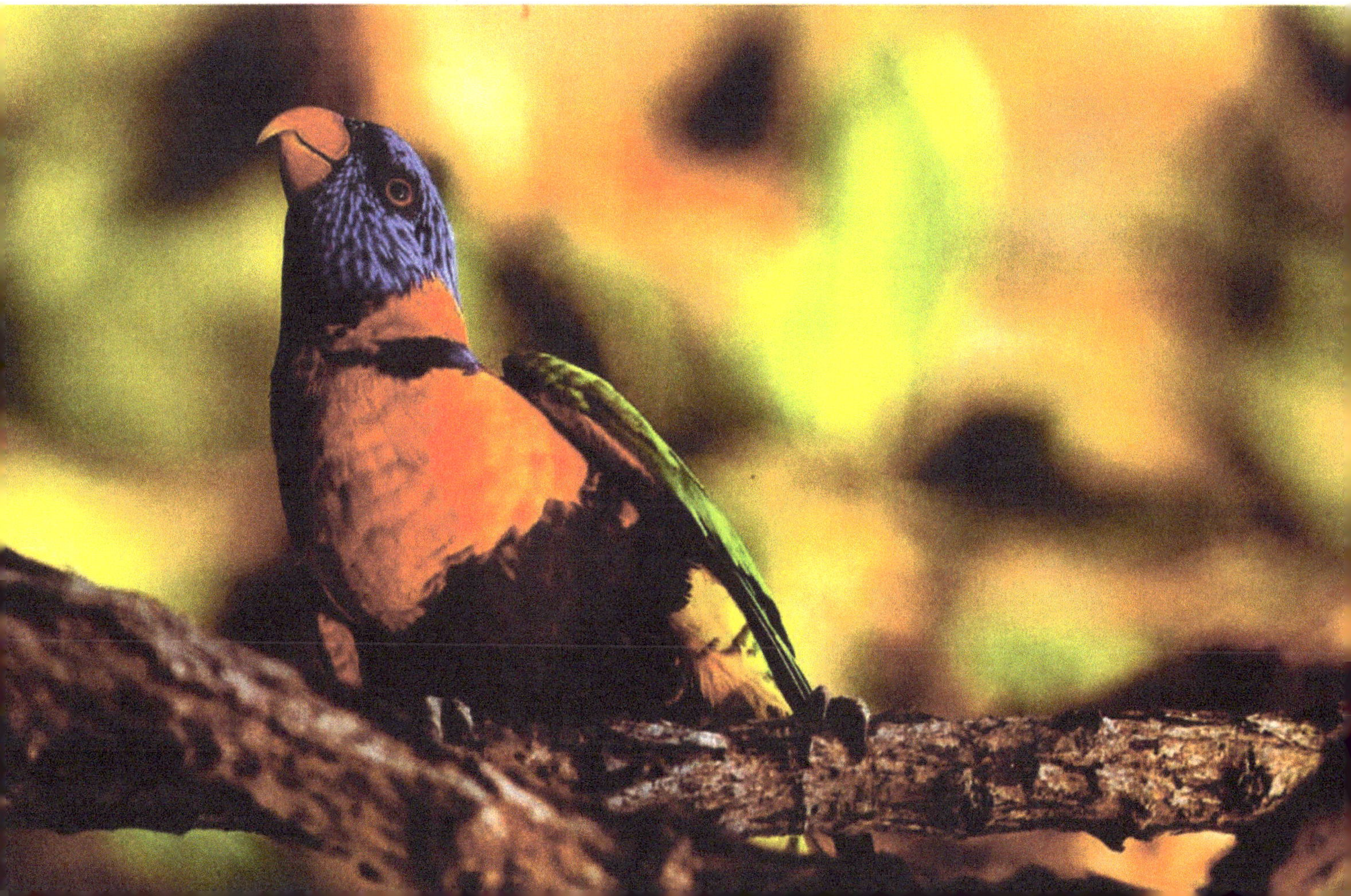

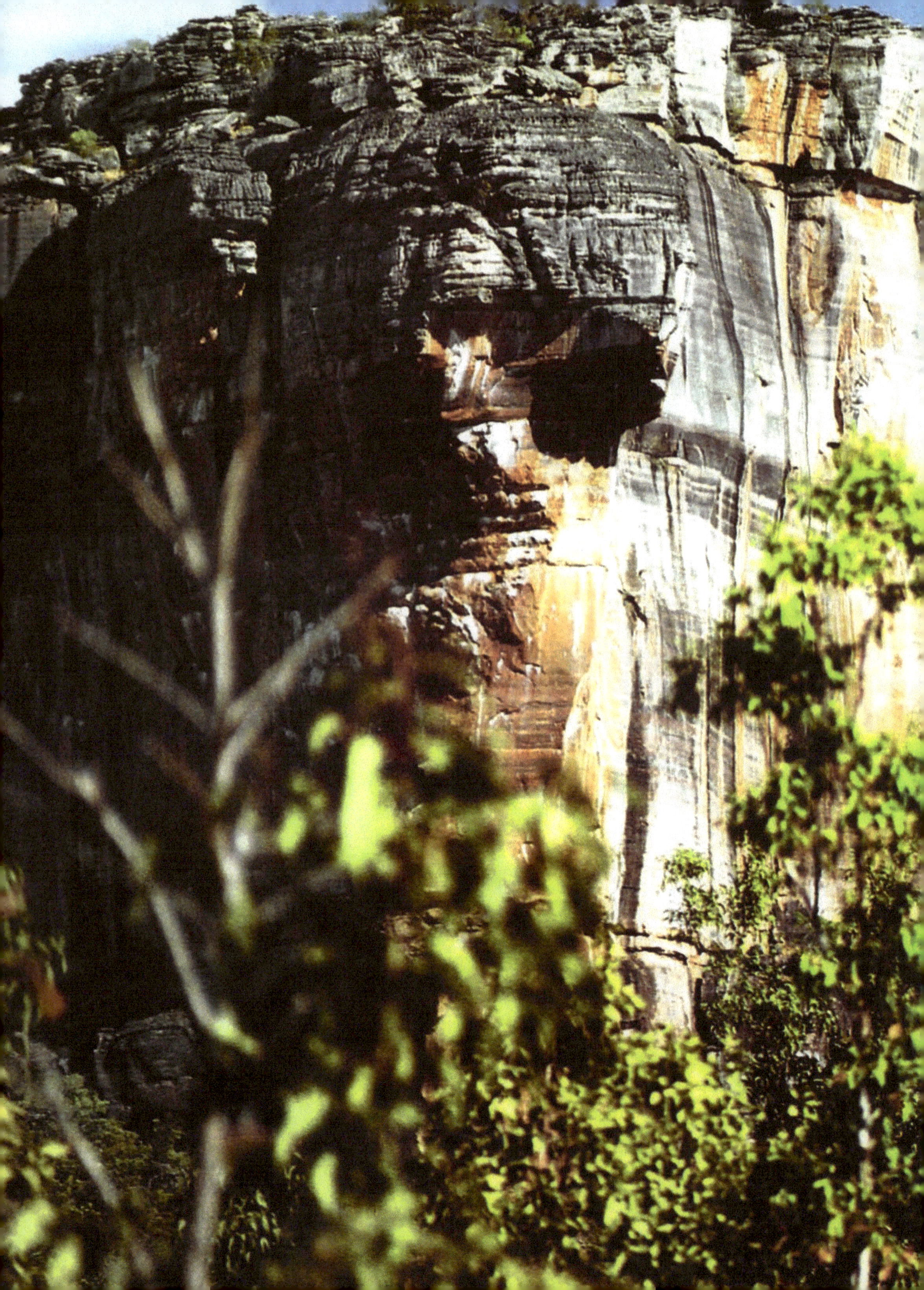

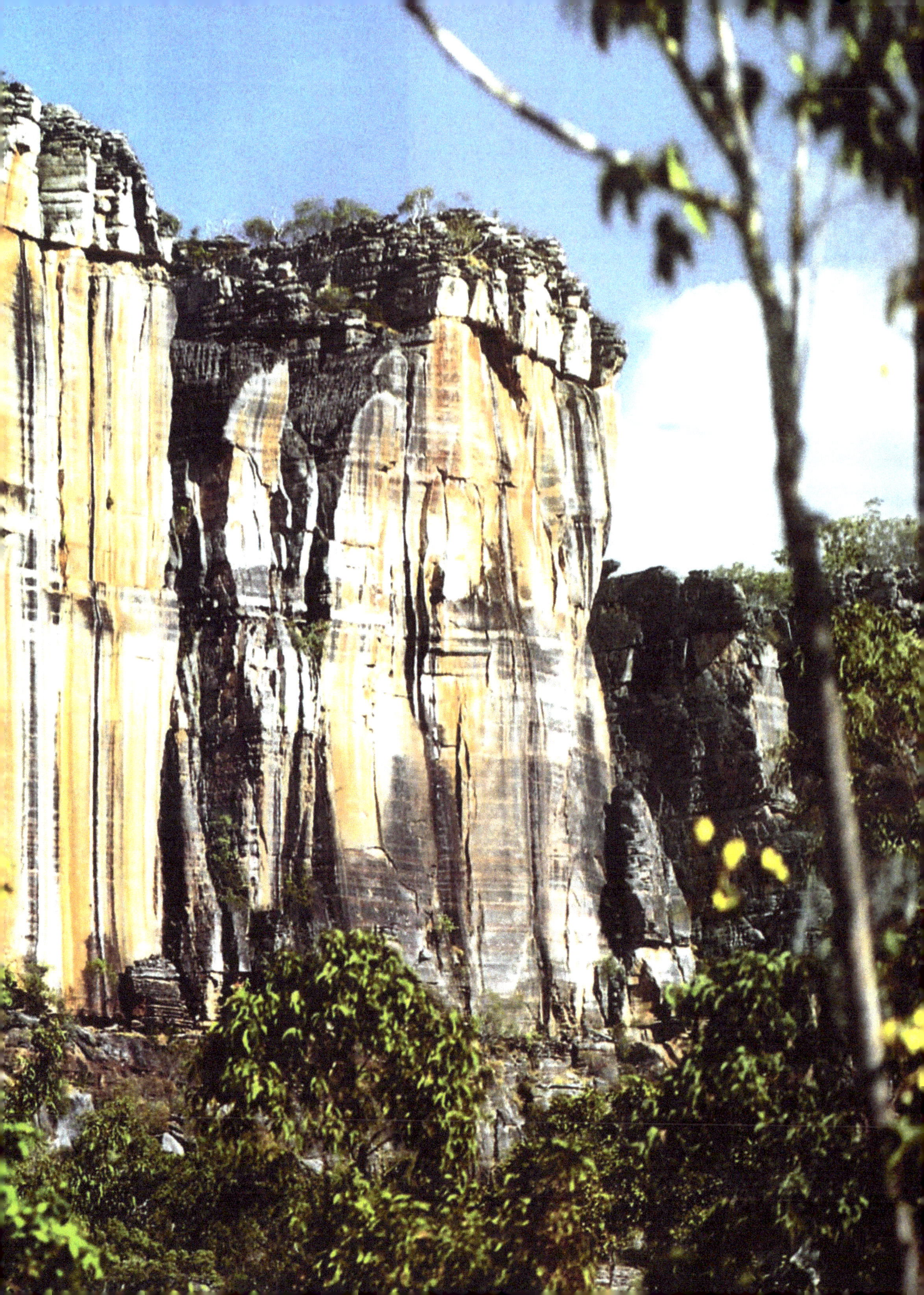

THIS TEMPLE

How lovely is your living place,
Joy of all creation!
My body and mind praise you,
all that I am delights in you!

Like the woodswallow I have a home,
a nest in dependable rock:
among these open chapels,
these altars under the sun
shaped by your loving hands,
my friend and my God.

Happy are those who recognize this temple;
joyful shall be their worship.
Happy are those who know your strength;
they shall love your ways.

Even in a valley of tears
they shall find hope.
Threatening storms
will bring new life.
Your friends grow in strength,
securely grounded in you.

God of the universe, you hear each prayer,
God of my forebears, you turn your ear.
One day walking with you
is better than a thousand alone.

I would rather be your poorest child
than a rebel living in luxury.
Your love shines brighter than sunlight,
transfiguring all things.
O God of the universe, and our joy,
happy are all who trust you.

(Inspired by Psalm 84)

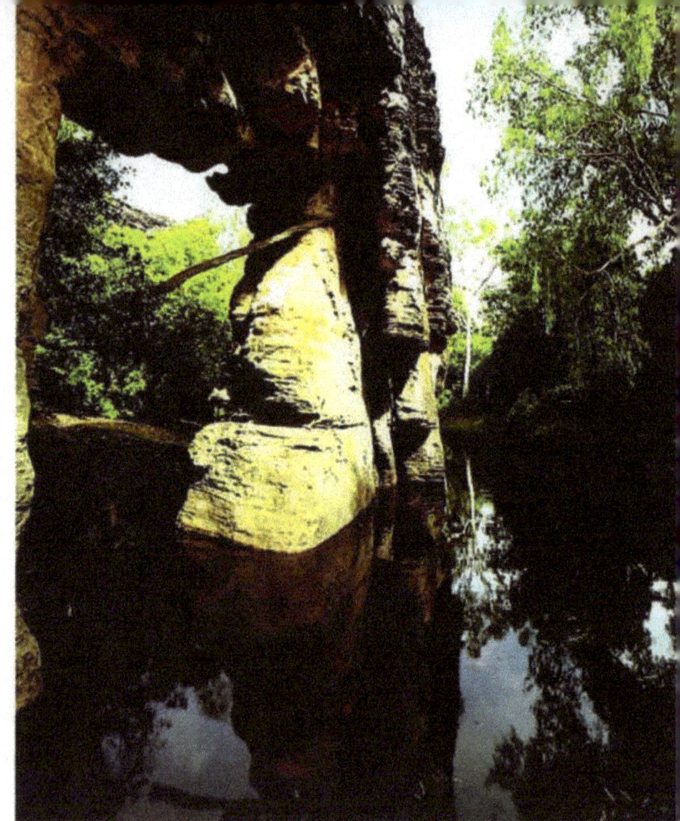

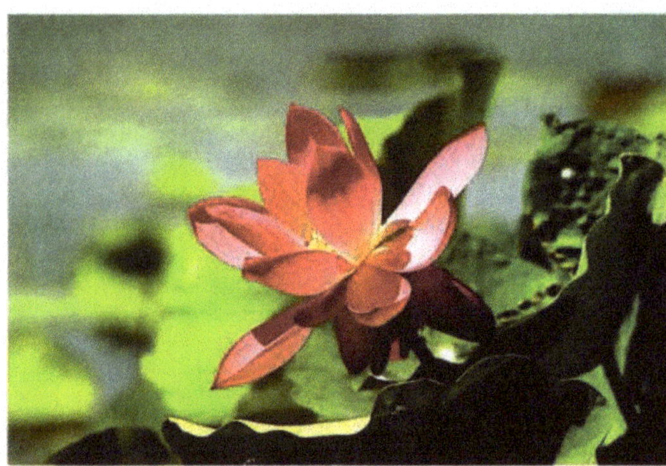

UPPER LEFT: *Side Billabong, East Alligator Valley*
LOWER LEFT: *Lotus Lily beside Walkarr Billabong*
RIGHT: *Magela Creek Lilies*

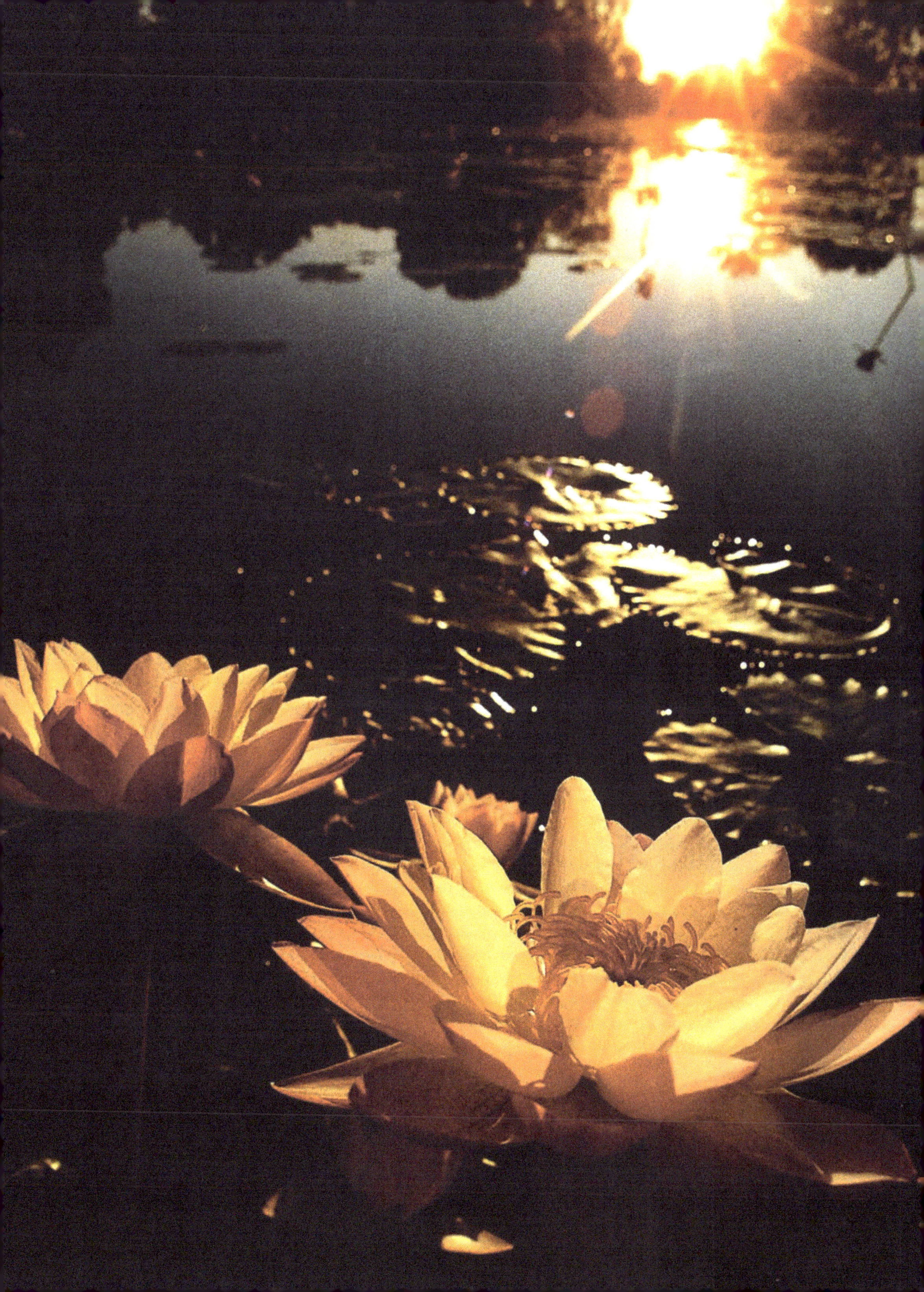

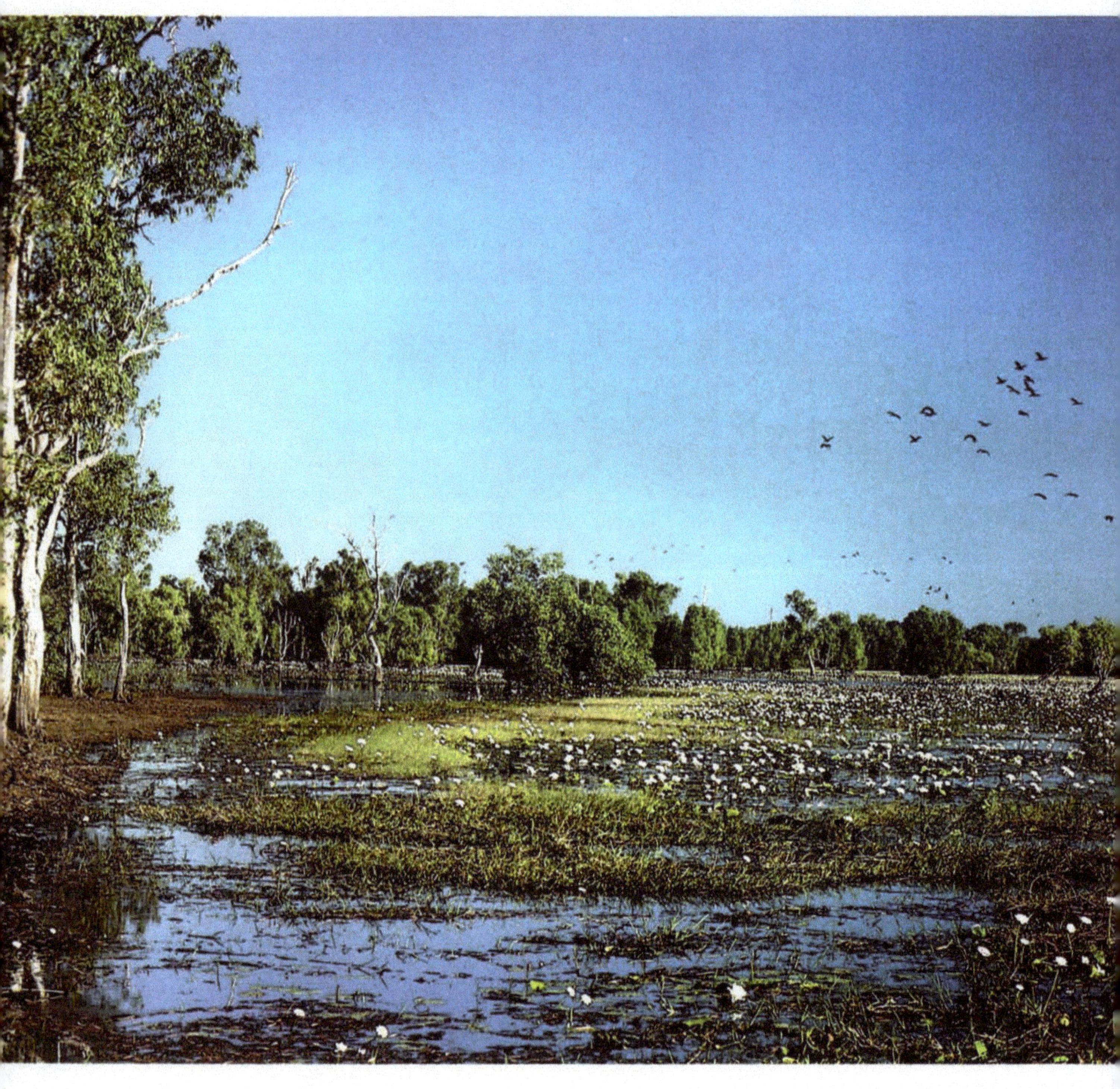

LEFT: *Lilies, post-wet season, Buywek Goluy Billabon*
RIGHT: *Twin Falls (Gungurdul*

MANY WITNESSES

O give thanks to the Lord
for he is good,

His love endures for ever!

Let the beauties of Yellow Waters
bear witness,
let the reflections of the South Alligator
portray it:

His love endures for ever!

Come, bushland around Jabiru,
tell your secret.
Come, wind through pandanus forest,
whisper your joy.
Water streamers of Jim Jim,
insist on it.
Roaring voice of Twin Falls,
declare it:

His love endures for ever!

Storms over the peaks of Koongarra,
thunder it.
Lightning over Mt Brockman,
signal it.
Spread the good news, Magela
in wide flood.
Woo us with the beautiful truth,
billabongs of Cannon Hill:

His love endures for ever!

Let every tourist and ranger,
fisherman and hiker,
let traditional owner
and visiting schoolchildren,
join in a flood of gratitude
and sing for joy:

His love endures for ever!

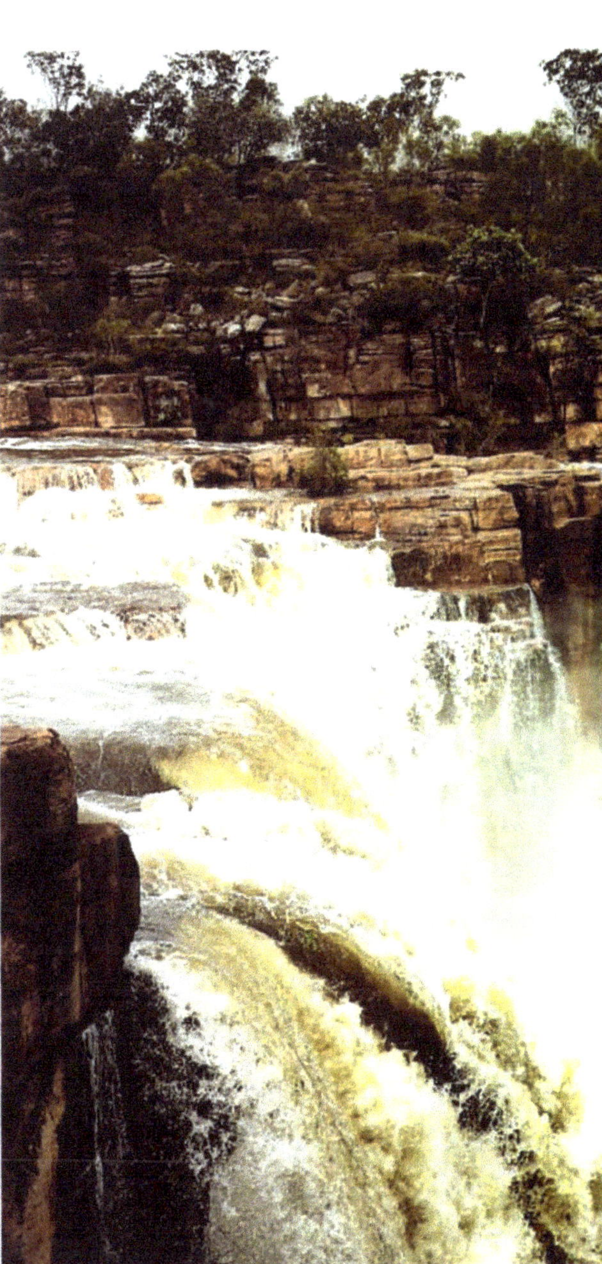

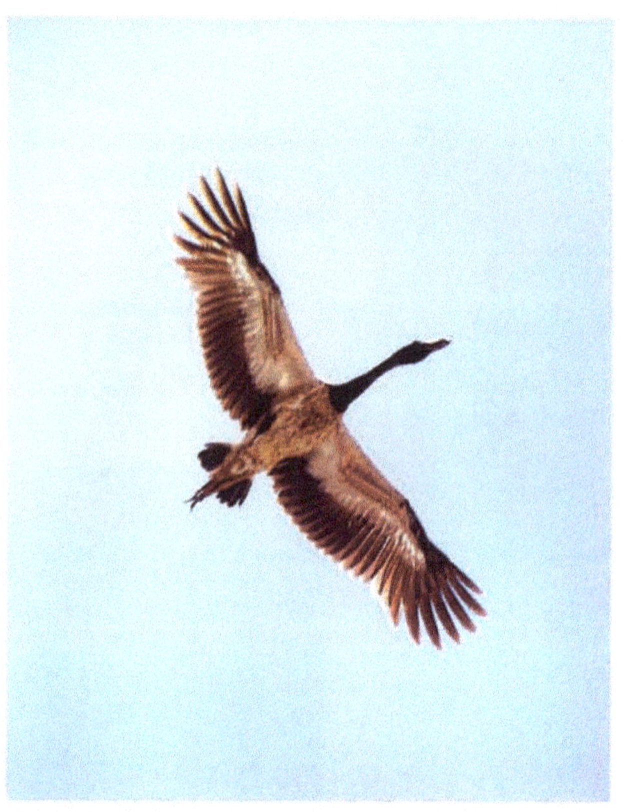

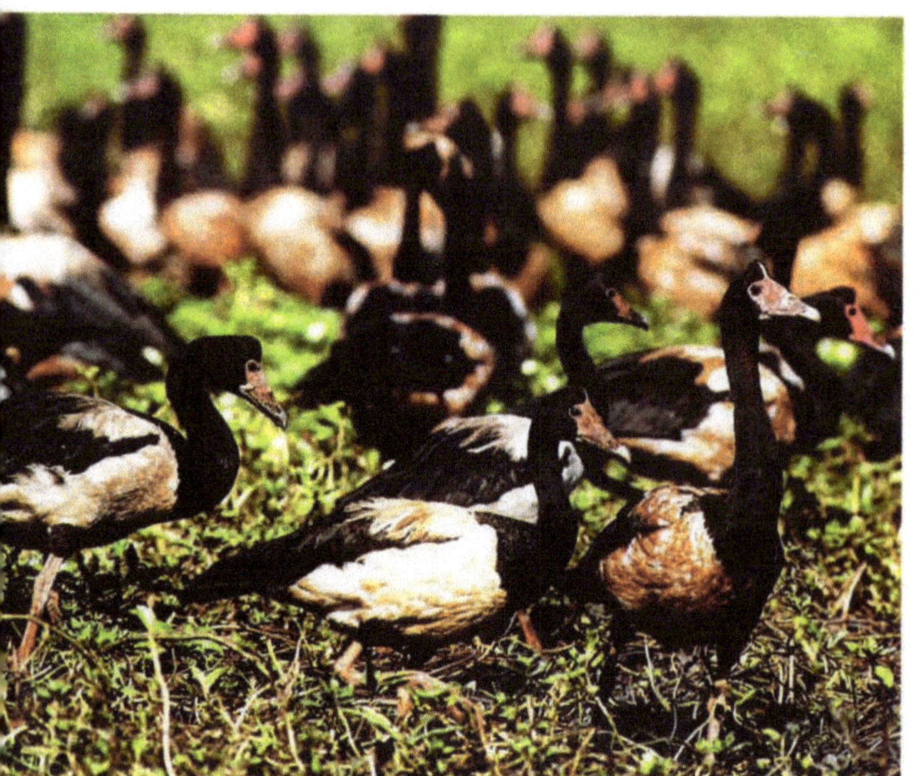

NOURLANGIE SUNSET

It was a simple evening meal —
just sandwiches and soft drink.
But under the paper barks
beside Anbangbang Billabong
it was something else.

We looked across watery lily fields
with an occasional white flower.
A family of wild geese
flew off in a flurry.
Two brown ducks
and some stately egrets
watched us warily,
but fed on.

Over the lone mangrove clump
rose great Nourlangie Rock;
when the setting sun
broke briefly through
funereal clouds,
it bathed the old rock face
of many dreamings
with glorious red ochre.

It was a simple meal
under the paper barks.
But it tasted
like sacrament.

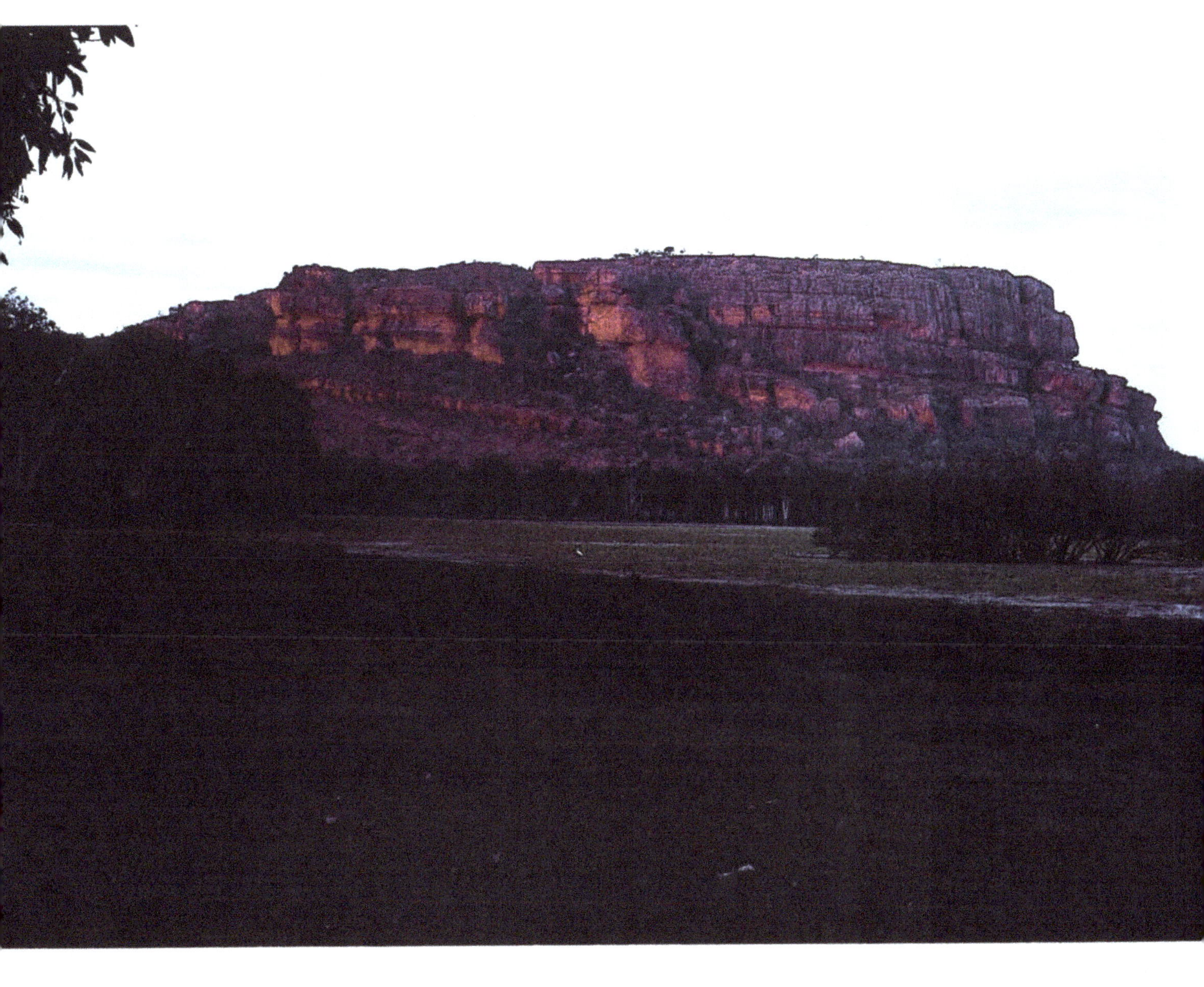

UPPER LEFT: Magpie Goose in flight
LOWER LEFT: Magpie Geese, late dry season
RIGHT: Nourlangie Rock (Burrunguy) from Anbangbang Billabong

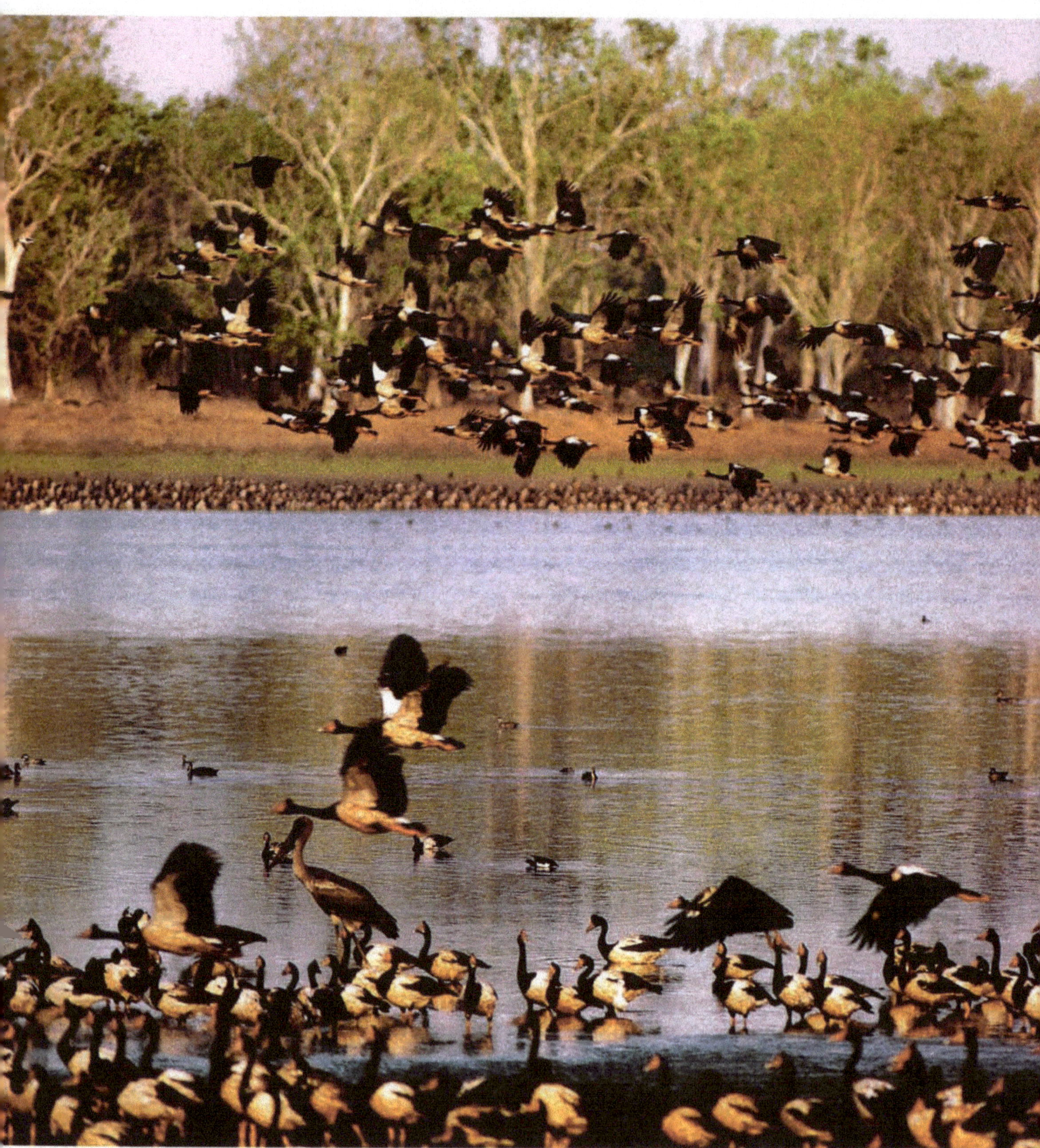

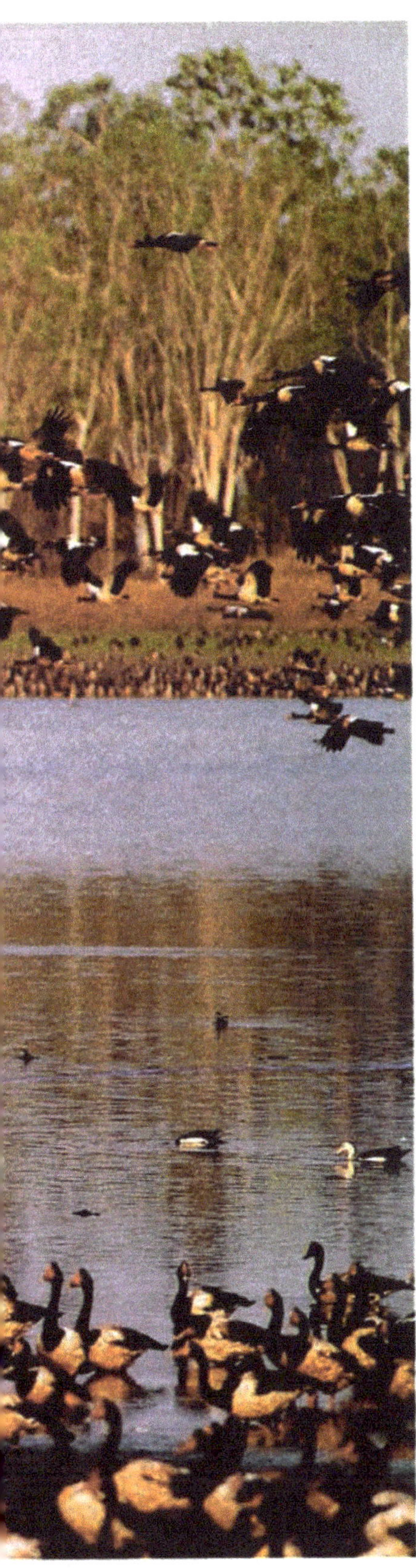

LIKE MANNA

Entranced
at sweet-sour dusk,
we watch the west
where wild geese fly
in restless quest.

Briefly
we savour a joy
which cannot be stored,
but, like true manna,
its Source adored.

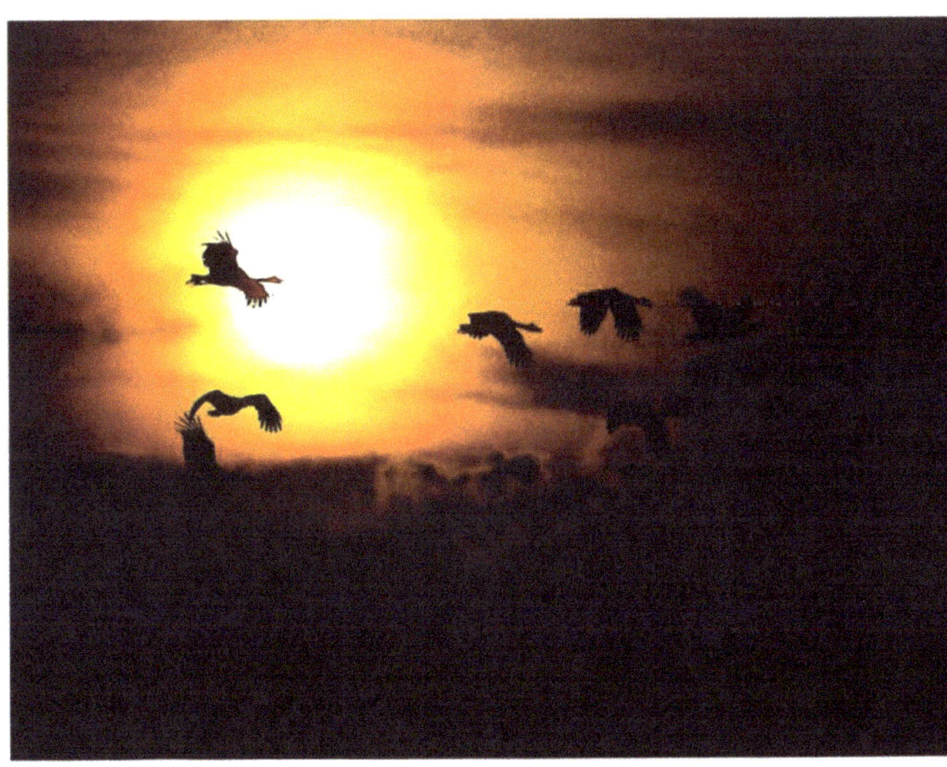

LEFT *Magpie Geese and Jabiru*
RIGHT *Geese of Umuual, East Alligator River*

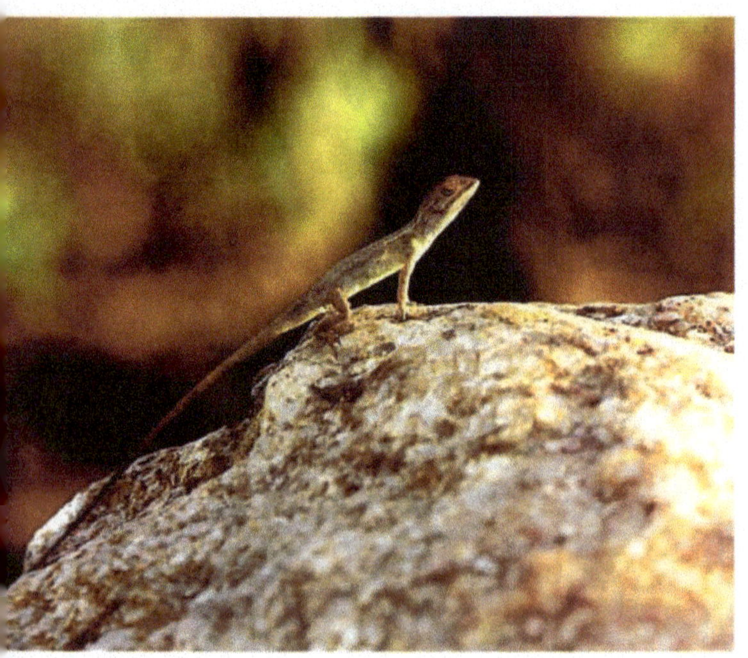

SHIFTING CAMP

When I leave
this life, Lord,
as a traveller shifting camp,
I will trust your word:
   Eye has not seen
   nor ear heard
   what you have yet
   in store.
But of one thing
I am sure:
   Trailing clouds of glory
   will I come
   from this world,
   my first, fair home.

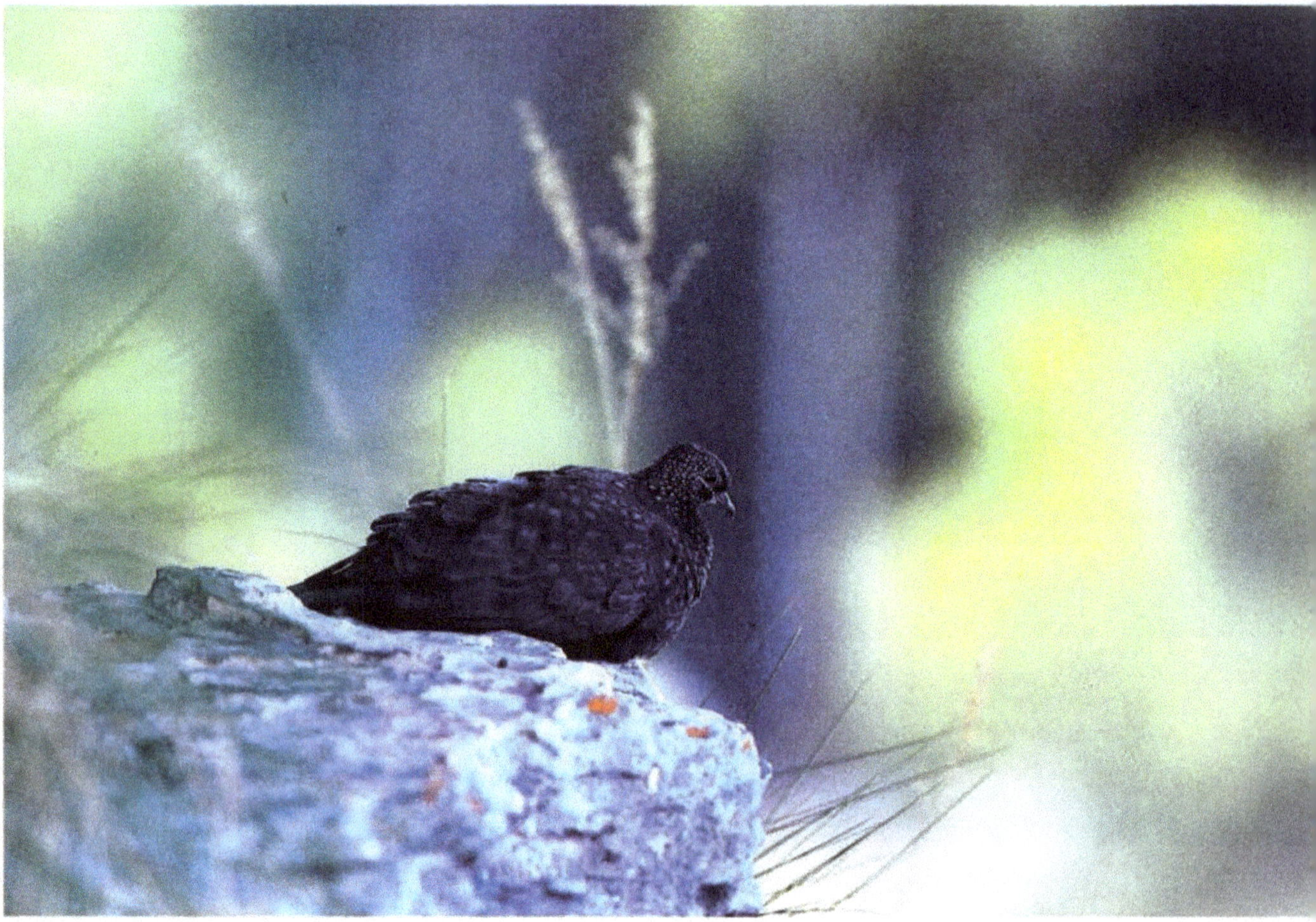

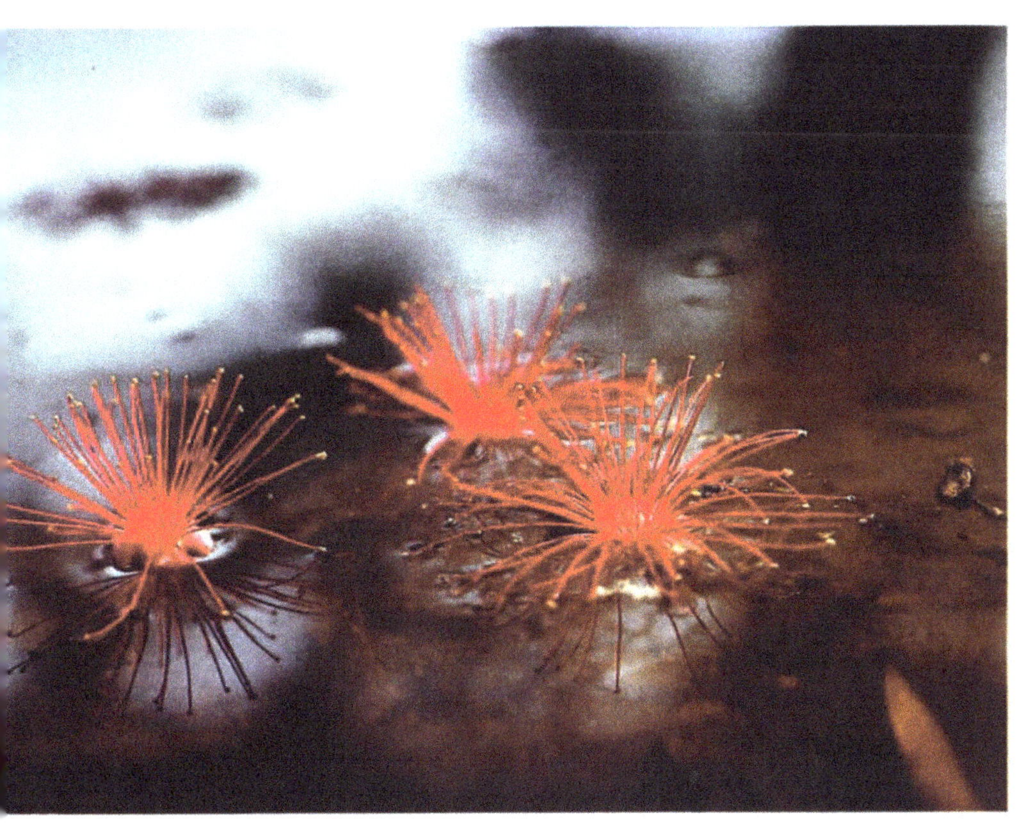

UPPER LEFT *Two-lined Dragon*
LOWER LEFT *Chestnut-quilled Rock-Pigeon (Gurrbelak)*
UPPER RIGHT *Barringtonia flowers, East Alligator Floodplain*
LOWER RIGHT *Lightning Dreaming (Namarrkurn)*

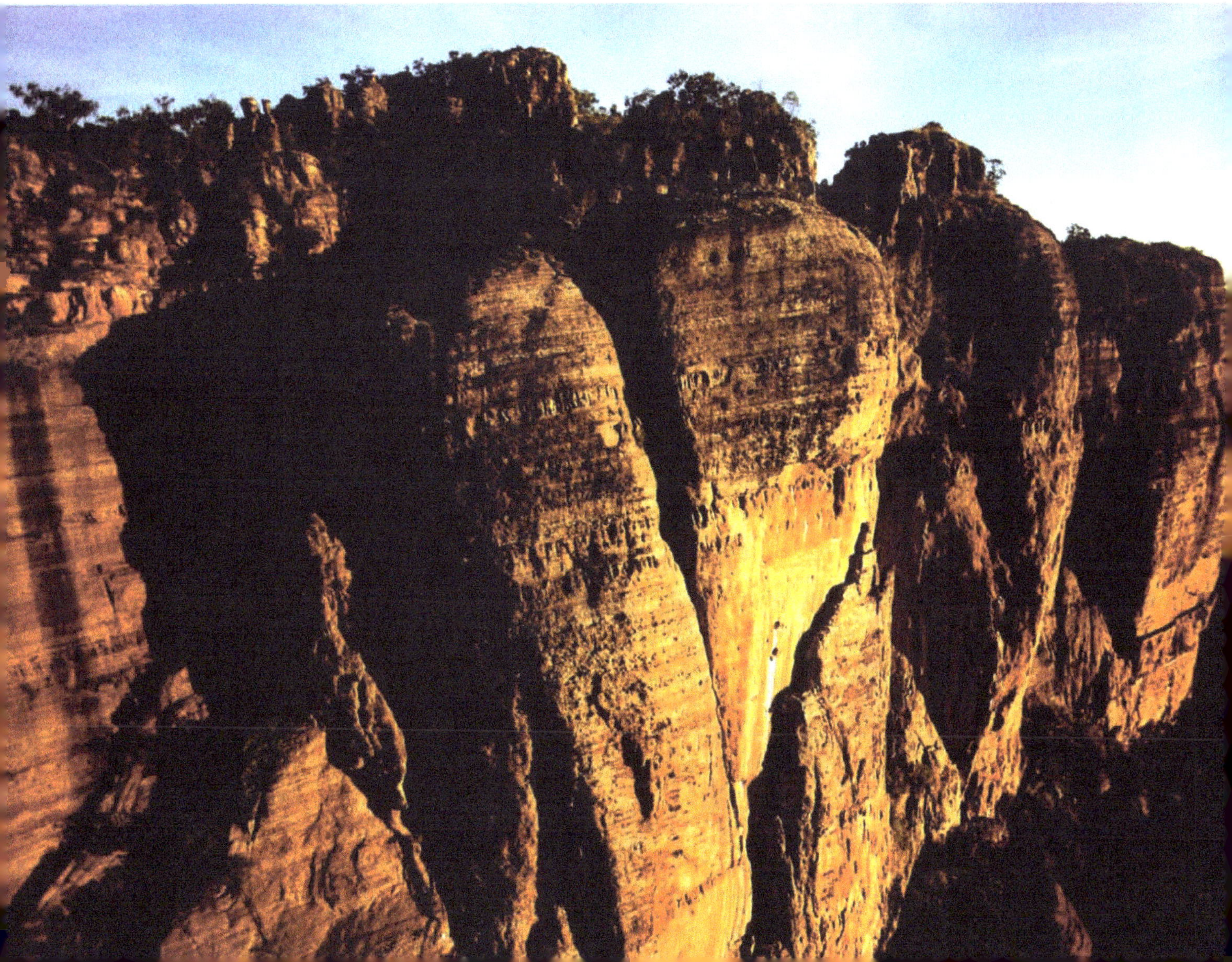

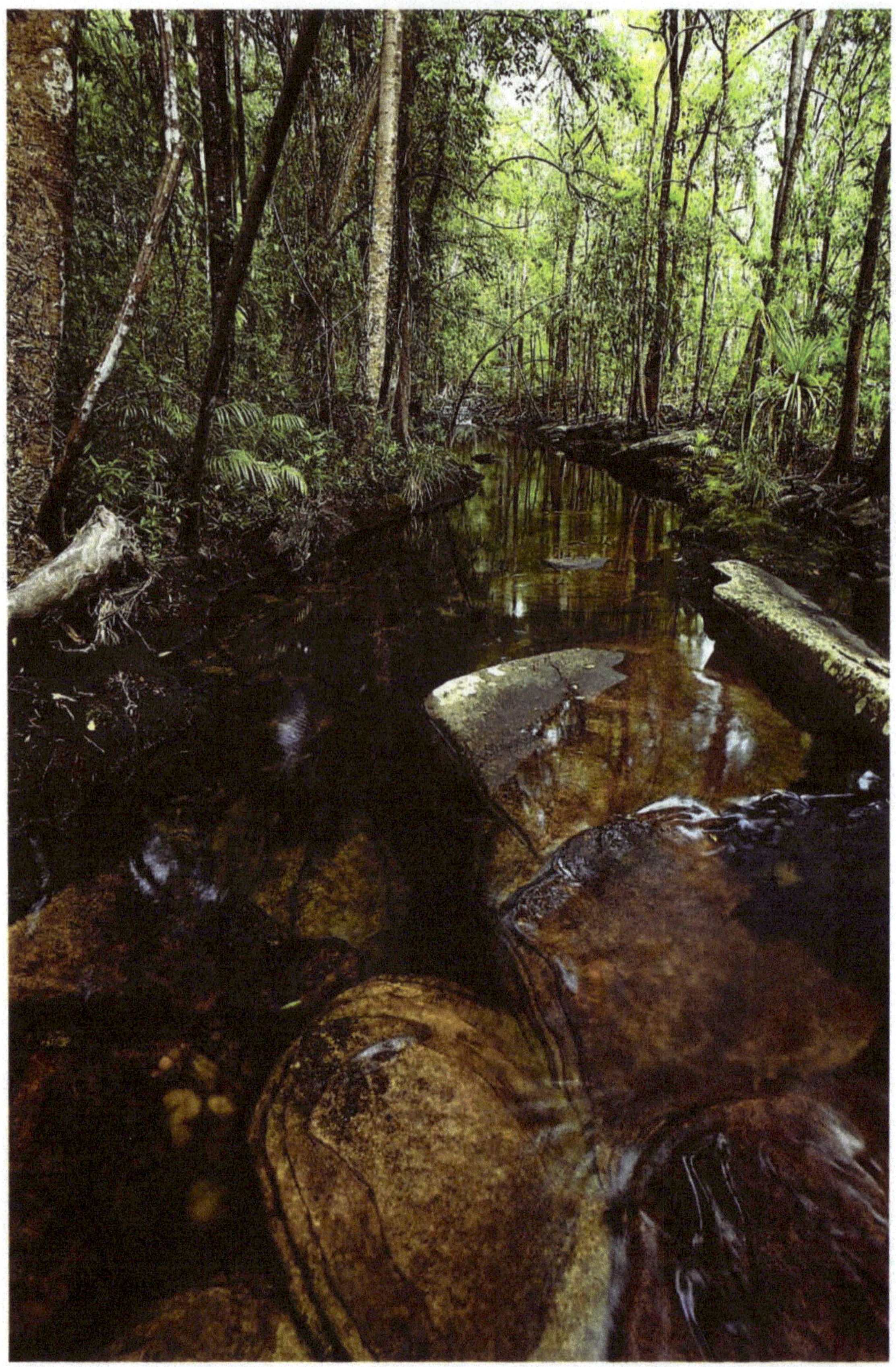

Gulungul Creek

Kakadu National Park is a rare natural jewel, renowned for its scenery and wildlife, its heritage and history, its timelessness. Here well known author Bruce Prewer and highly regarded photographer Ian Morris have captured the essence of Kakadu in one special volume. Prewer's inspiring poetry and the spectacular photography truly reflect the awesome beauty and spiritual treasure that is Kakadu.

From the tidal flats and floodplains, with their rivers and billabongs, to the rugged sandstone buttresses and pillars of the stunning Arnhem Land escarpment, Kakadu is a place of many faces and many moods, of which tourists see but a few.

Here to enjoy are large flocks of magpie geese and whistling ducks ... trees so covered with fleets of parrots that they seem in full blossom ... 6000 Aboriginal rock art sites (their styles spanning a period of about 20,000 years) ... the radiant colours of sunset and peaceful waterways ... the sights and sounds of a multitude of bird, butterfly, and reptile species —all co-existing in harmony, in a microcosm unadulterated by European settlement.

Kakadu National Park is an experience. Whether you have been there or not, this unique book will be a profound and treasured reminder of the grace and power of our Creator — the One who gives us places like Kakadu.

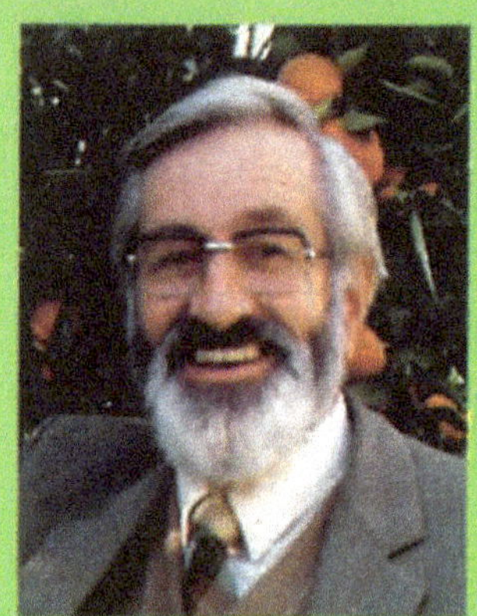

Bruce Prewer has become widely known in the past decade through his two published works: the immensely popular *Australian Psalms* and *Australian Prayers*. His literary skill, love for creation, and love for God, the gracious Creator-Redeemer, were instantly called forth again on his recent tour of Kakadu; the result is the poetry of this book.

An ordained minister of the Uniting Church, Bruce served parishes and the wider Church in Tasmania and Victoria for over 25 years before joining the collegiate ministry at Pilgrim Church, Adelaide's city parish, in the early 1980s.

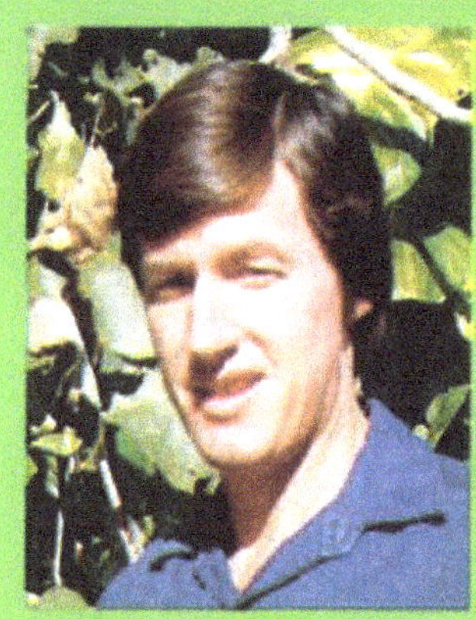

For Ian Morris, the ultimate experience is 'being in the bush with a camera'. After brief periods in wildlife research (marsupials) and teaching environmental education in Aboriginal communities, Ian Morris joined the Aboriginal ranger training program in the Kakadu area in 1978. Much of his environmental knowledge has come from his Aboriginal friends, and he now enjoys sharing this with others, particularly through photography.

Apart from significant initial guidance from Douglas Baglin, Ian Morris the photographer is self-taught. He enjoys a high reputation for his art, and his work has been featured in scientific journals, the popular press, and especially in wildlife and conservation-oriented books. Of special mention are: his collaboration with Bill Neidjie in *Kakadu Man*, the curriculum series *Discovering Aboriginal Culture*, Commonwealth Government materials on Kakadu National Park, and the National Geographic Society's recently-released film *Australia's Twilight of the Dreamtime*.

Ian Morris as a Christian is grateful that he can help to increase awareness of the plight of our natural ecosystems, and hopeful that Aboriginal and non-Aboriginal Australians will be drawn closer together through mutual appreciation of both the loving Creator and the unique, magnificent environment which is his creation.

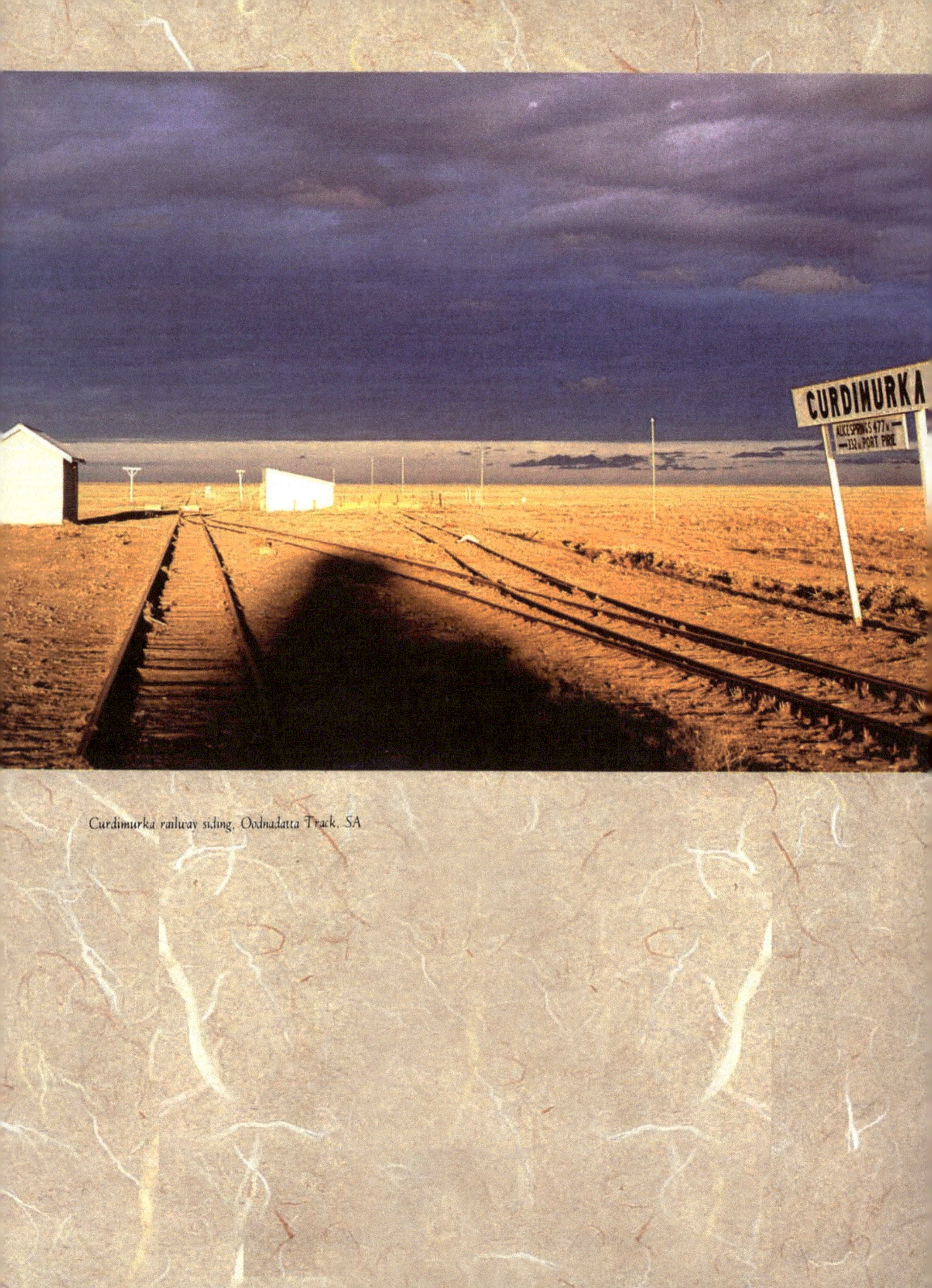

Curdimurka railway siding, Oodnadatta Track, SA

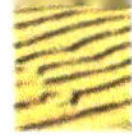

OUTBACK REFLECTIONS

AUB PODLICH
BRUCE PREWER

with photographs by
JOCELYN BURT

Additional photography by Aub Podlich, Ian Morris, and Bruce Prewer.
Photographs not credited in the captions are by Jocelyn Burt.

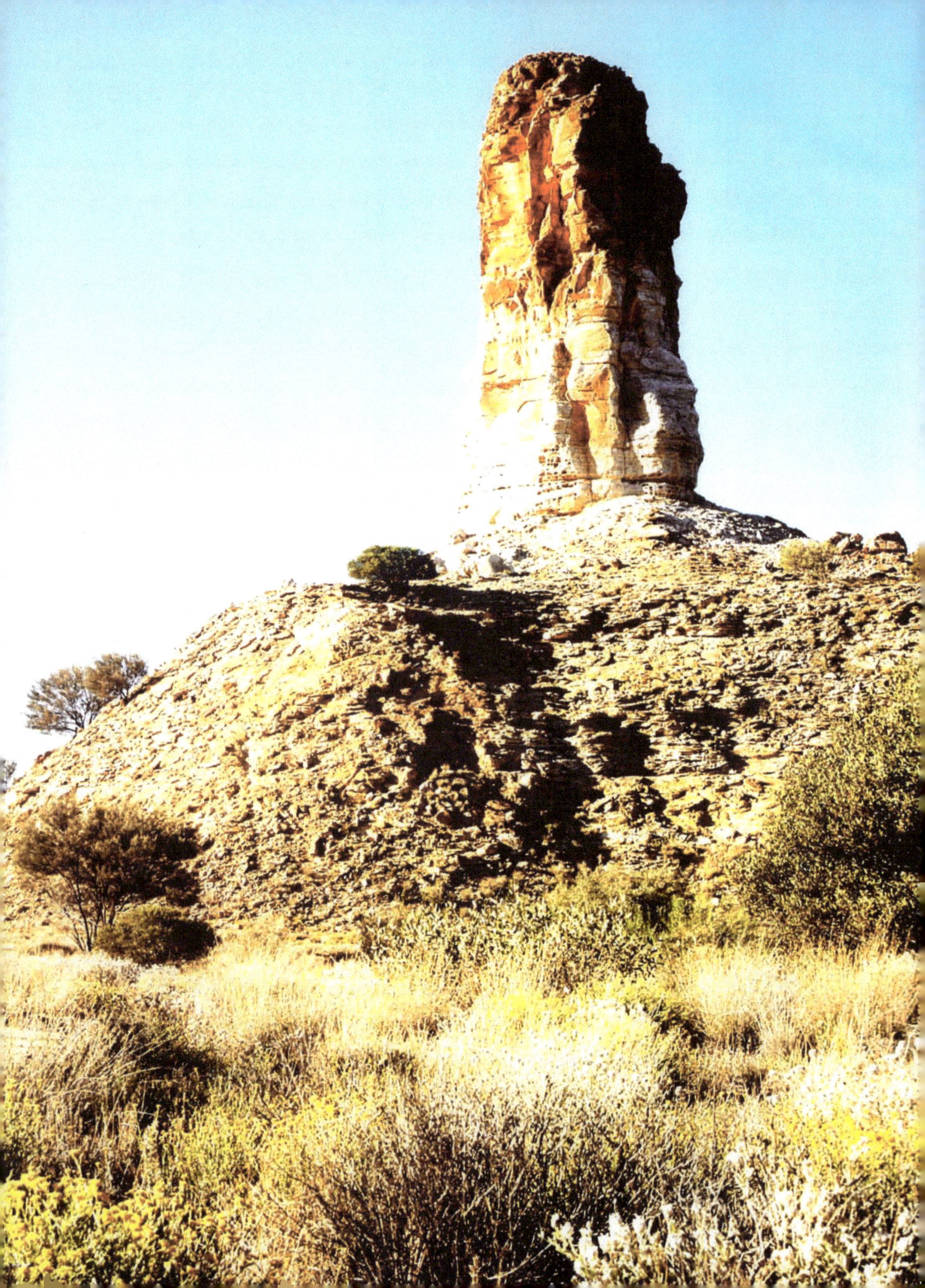

INTRODUCTION

He had few qualifications and little experience. To the establishment, his announced intention of finding an overland route from Queensland's Darling Downs to Port Essington in the Northern Territory, a distance of nearly 5000 kilometres, was nothing short of an impertinence. He wasn't even an Englishman! Major Thomas Mitchell, the establishment's official explorer, labelled the insatiably curious, fiercely determined Prussian Ludwig Leichhardt 'a damned foreign coaster!' Fifteen months after leaving Jimbour station, and long given up for dead, the Leichhardt party, having beaten all the incredible rigours of the bush and survived Aboriginal attack, stumbled into Port Essington. Leichhardt, returning to Sydney in time to hear his own funeral dirge being sung, became a colony's hero.

However, on his third expedition, in 1848, there was to be no resurrection. Leichhardt set out again on a most ambitious attempt to cross Australia from the very margins of white settlement at Mount Abundance near Roma in Queensland, to present-day Perth in Western Australia. The land opened its mouth and swallowed him, his six companions, their eight horses, 50 bullocks, 20 mules, and all their provisions. No trace of that entire party has ever been found, its ultimate fate remaining one of the most closely guarded secrets of the Australian outback.

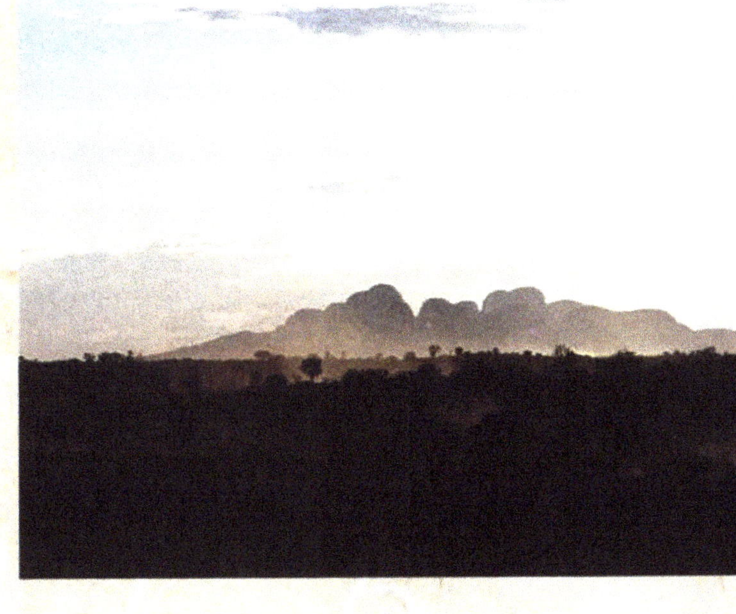

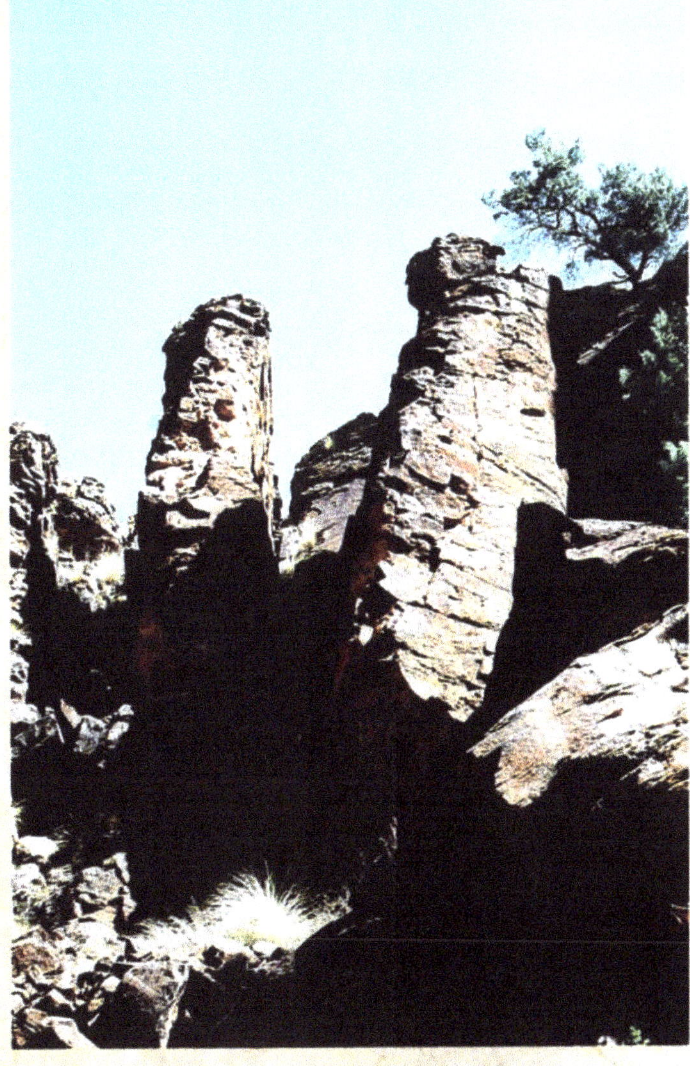

LEFT: *Spring Wildflowers, Chambers Pillar, NT*
UPPER RIGHT: *Distant view of the Olgas, Uluru National Park, NT*
LOWER RIGHT: *N'Dhala Gorge, NT*

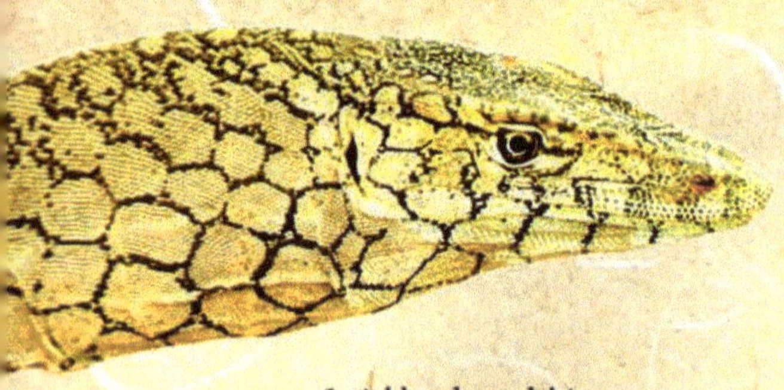

UPPER LEFT: *Kangaroo jawbone* PODLICH
LOWER LEFT: *Sand-dunes, Eucla, WA*
UPPER RIGHT: *Old wagon, and ruins of the Warrina railway siding, Oodnadatta Track, SA*
LOWER RIGHT: *The Channel Country in drought, near Birdsville, Qld*

Leichhardt and his men were not the first curious and determined 'damned foreign coasters' to be swallowed by the Australian outback, nor would they be the last. Australia's arid interior has drawn people to itself for untold thousands of generations. Many whom the land clasped to herself never returned, an ominous reminder that this vast area of God's harsher Eden was never to be underestimated or taken for granted. The outback, as a recent tragic news story about the deaths of four stranded Aboriginal travellers

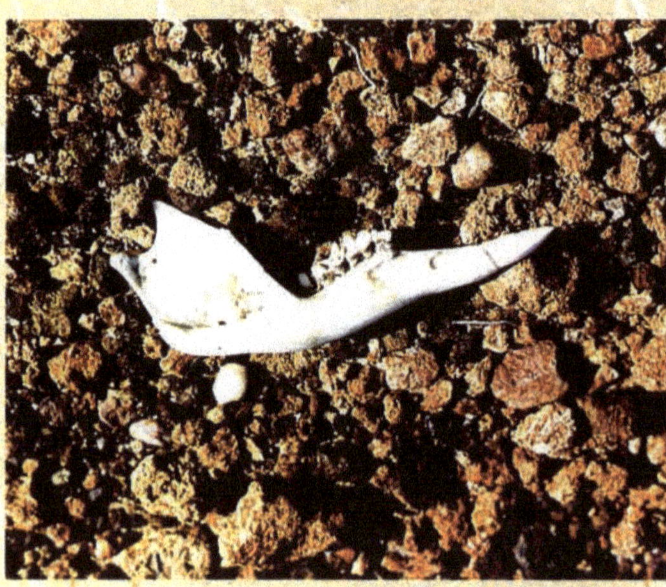

grimly illustrates, can be relentlessly unforgiving. Yet for all that — perhaps partly because of it — the Australian outback has a lure and a fascination for Australians which touches familiar chords in the mind of this nation of coast-huggers and city-dwellers. Looming large among all the myths which describe us as a people is the outback, dreaded, mysterious, and fascinating.

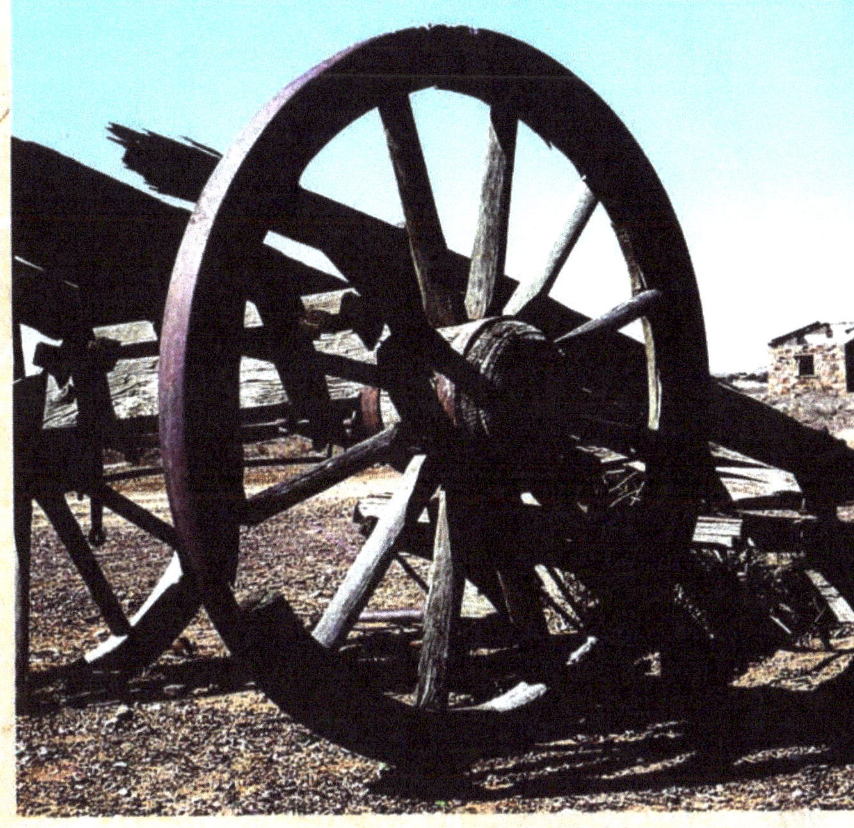

At the heart of that myth is a lively song about a sheep thief who committed suicide by drowning in an outback waterhole:

> Once a jolly swagman camped
> by a billabong,
> Under the shade of a coolibah
> tree.

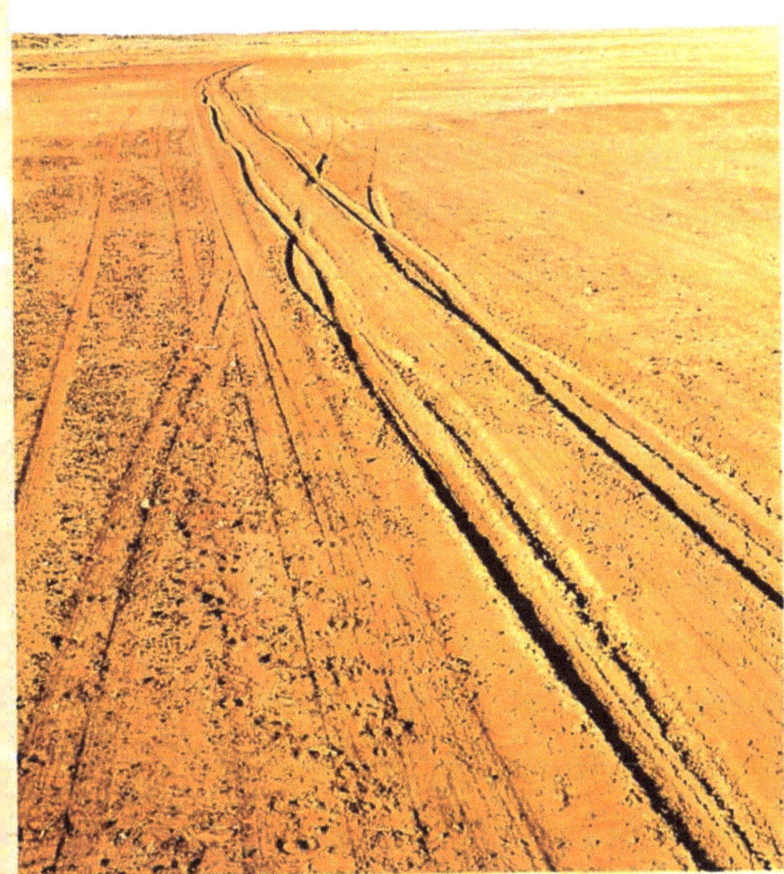

Never mind that most Australians wouldn't know a coolibah if they did camp under it, couldn't distinguish a billabong from a bilby, and will never see a genuine swagman — 'Waltzing Matilda' from Combo Waterhole has become *our* song!

Despite its importance in our national psyche, Australians have difficulty defining the boundaries of the outback. Some suggest that it begins and ends in our own minds! The very term 'outback' for the vast inland of Australia indicates that for most Australians there is a huge part of this land where they not only do not live and work, but where they could never feel at home. Words like 'remote', 'harsh', 'hostile', when applied to the outback, place that area in contrast to life in the settled, civilised, urbanised environments of the seaboards. Australia has few outback cities. We are indeed a whole nation of 'damned foreign coasters', to whom much of our own land will always remain that strange area 'out back' from our day-to-day existence.

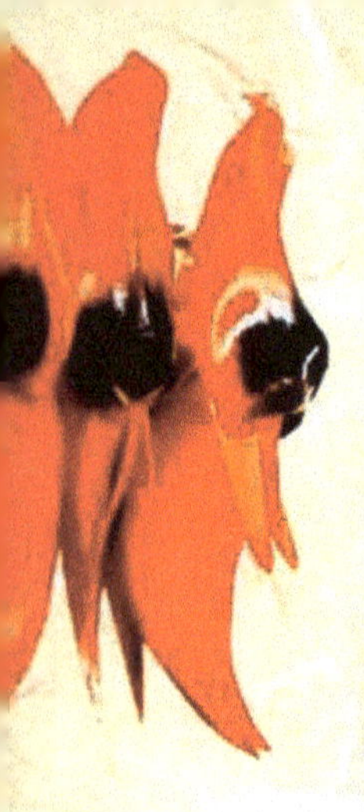

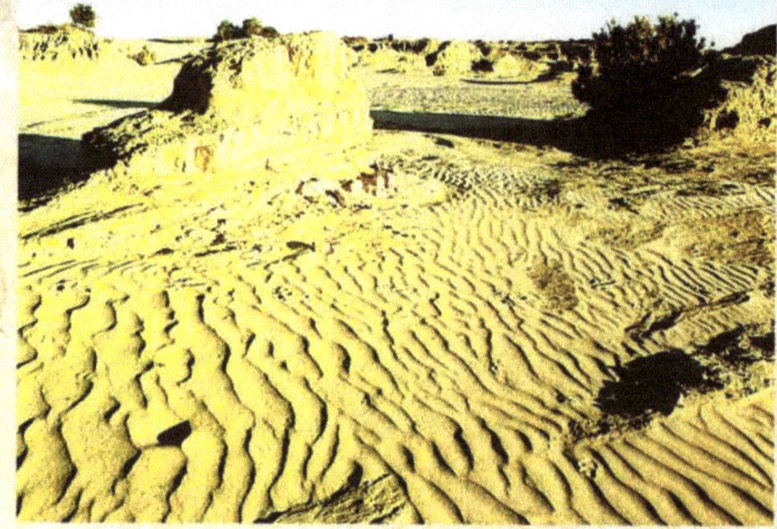

For most Australians then, the outback is no more than a tourist destination. More accurately, it is a seemingly endless plain of low unattractive scrub, bulldust, heat, flies, stones, and sometimes rough roads, which must be endured in long tiring days of driving en route to the marvellous places that make all the driving worthwhile, at least once in a lifetime: Uluru, the Olgas, the Flinders Ranges, Kings Canyon, Katherine Gorge, the Kimberleys, the Stockman's Hall of Fame . . .

There can be no denying, even by the most comfort-conscious city visitor, that the natural wonders of the well-known tourist route are magnificent. Bathed in early morning or late afternoon light, the rich colours of the inland are beyond compare, the cliffs and sandhills, folded ranges and snaking gorges burning with red, purple, yellow, and ochre flames. Landforms and rock sculptures surprise and delight, from the looming sleeping-animal shapes of Uluru and Katatjuta, to the giant beehives of the Bungle Bungles, the smooth sweeping walls of roseate

UPPER LEFT: *Mungo National Park, NSW*
LOWER LEFT: *Ayers Rock, Uluru National Park, NT*

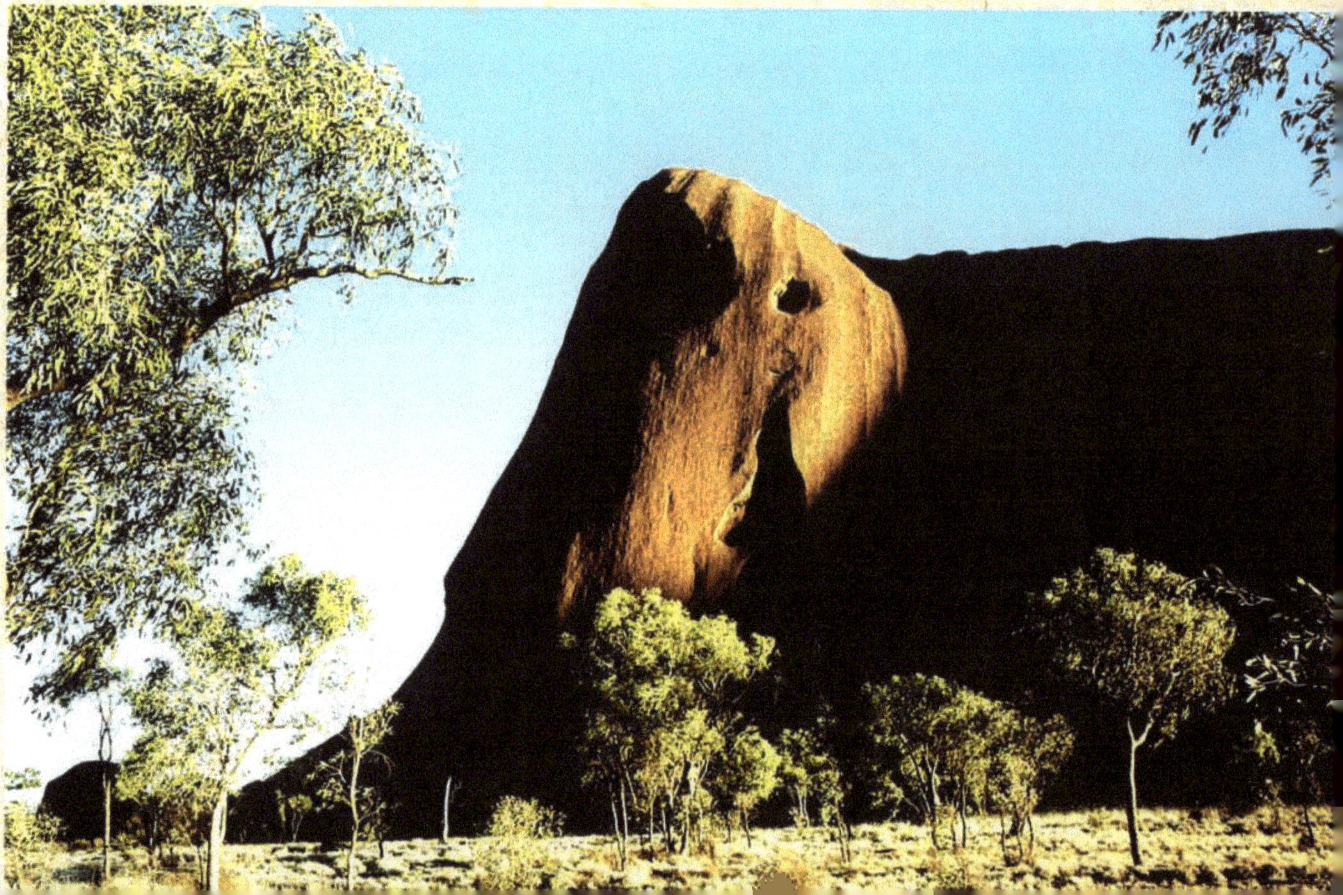

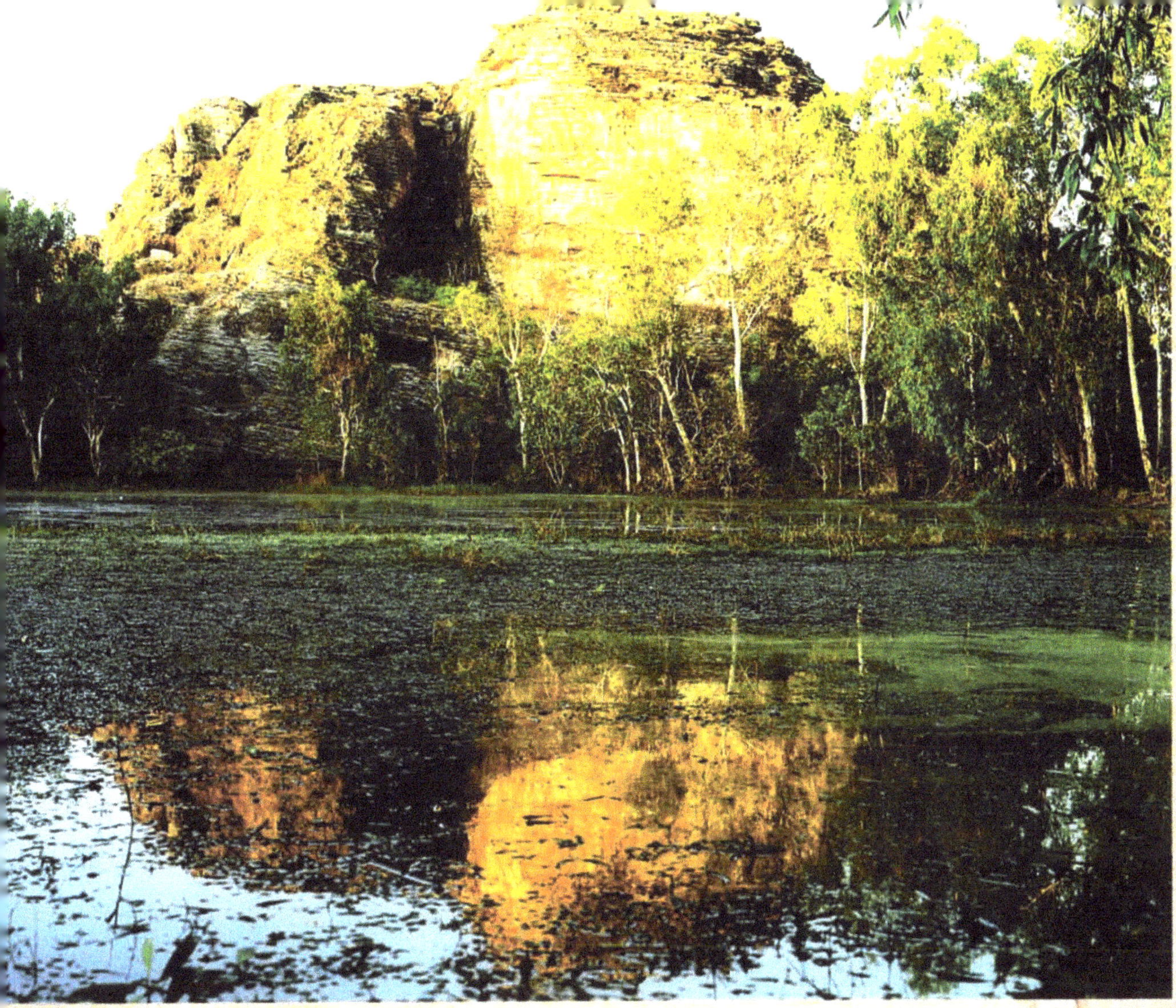

sandstone at Kings Canyon, the exquisitely rounded, delicately balanced Devil's Marbles, and the giant saucer of the Wolf Creek meteorite crater. Scientific oddities and visual delights go hand in hand: remnant rare Livistonia palms in Palm Valley, dinosaur prints at Winton, the lime-rich emerald green water of Lawn Hill Gorge, the legendary min min lights of Queensland's west, and the profusion of desert wildflowers after rain. Over all this brooding, eroding, and crumbling landscape hangs the impression of great age, and of a wonderful ancient beauty sculpted and painted by time and hardship. And who will ever forget the blaze of outback stars on a clear inland night?

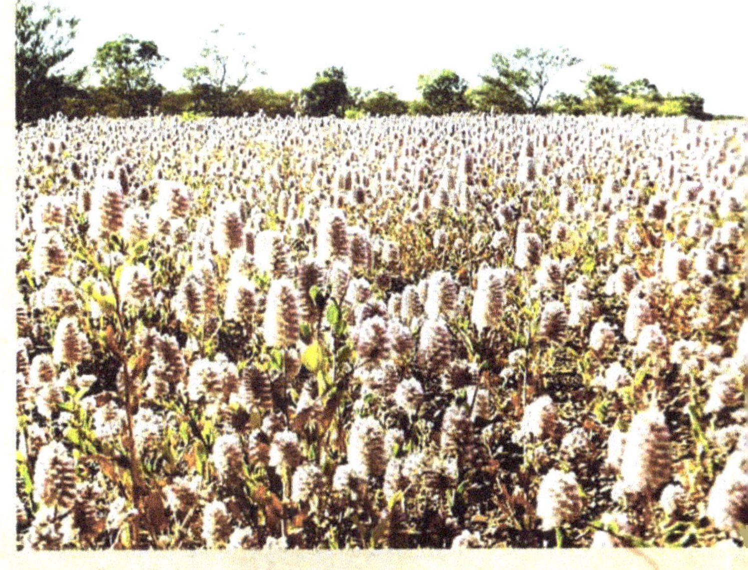

UPPER RIGHT: *Jabiru Dreaming, Kakadu National Park, NT*
LOWER RIGHT: *Mulla mullas in bloom, Pilbara, WA*

For those prepared to observe and understand, there are many surprises arising directly from the struggle to live and thrive in an environment where the norm is extremes of both temperature and rainfall. The tough desert acacias — mulga, gidgee, boree, myall, and the expressively named 'dead-finish' — with their fine grey foliage and pleasant form, swarm over vast areas. In other places, graceful casuarinas called desert oaks, clothed in weeping emu-feather plumes, cast welcome shade in an ocean of golden-crowned, sand-stabilising spinifex. Few trees are as starkly beautiful as the gnarled ghost gums which cling to the red cliffs and top-rock country. Along nature's highways, the mostly dry watercourses where phantom rivers run deep underground, thousands of cockatoos, parrots, and honeyeaters ransack the twisting avenues of river red gums and coolibahs for nectar and nesting hollows. The unusual and often showy flowers of grevillea, hakea, emu bush and desert rose grace areas of red sand and rocky outcrops, while few wildflower displays could out-miracle the miracle of previously bare desert plains in bloom after convenient rain. Around Uluru and in all the deep slashes of gorges, the snaking latticework of the roots of Ilyi, the rock fig, is often the first clue to the presence of a harvest of yellow and brown fruit.

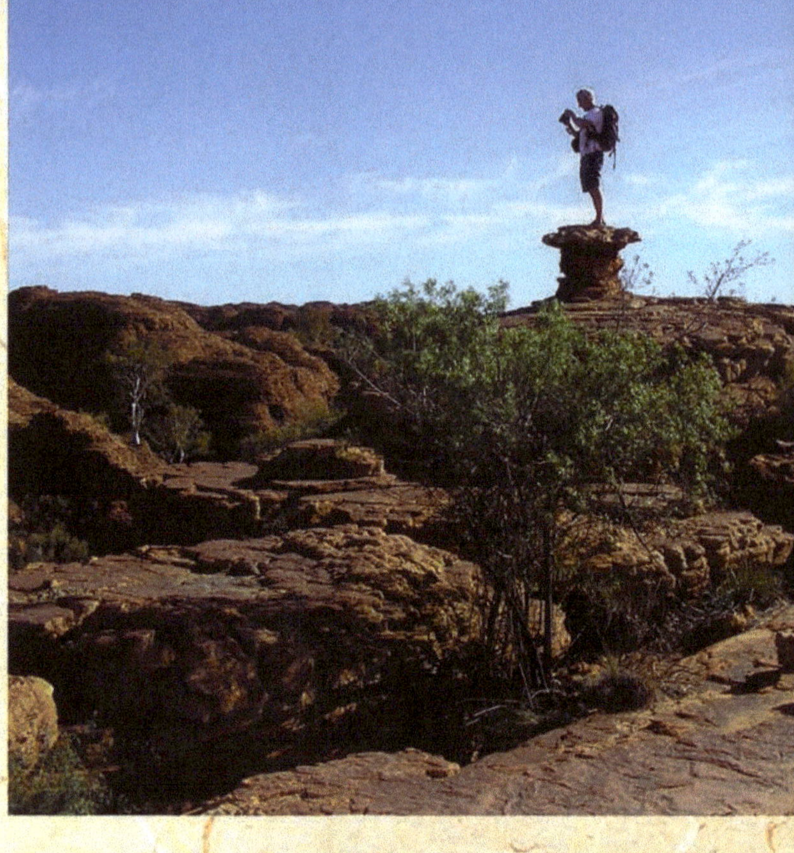

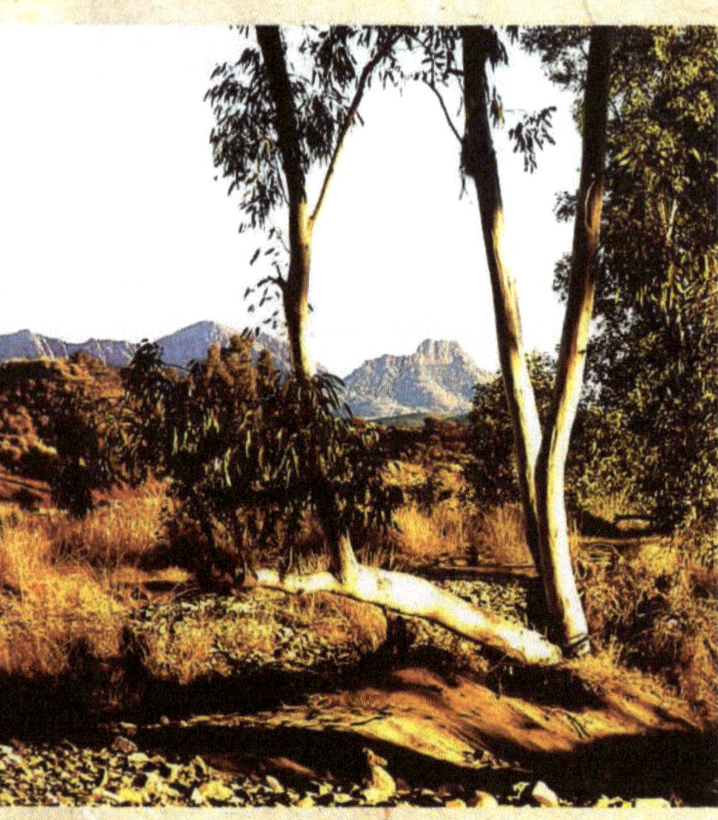

UPPER LEFT: *The view from on high,* PREWER
LOWER LEFT: *Finke River and Mount Sonder,* NT

Even the most unobservant tourist cannot fail to notice, from the comfort of a moving vehicle, the commonest outback wildlife: red kangaroo and emu, wallaroo in rocky areas, plains turkey and wedge-tailed eagle, little flocks of finches, galahs, and budgies, and

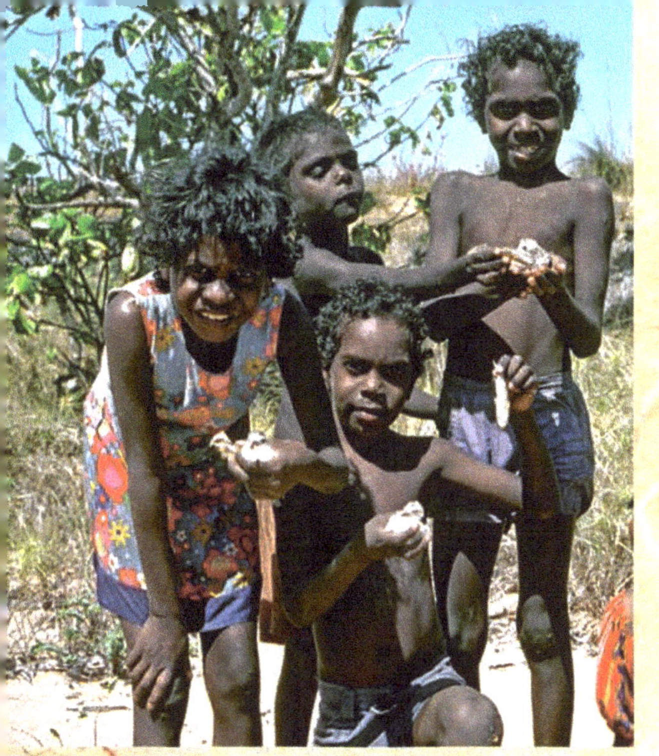

even an occasional curious dingo. But for the dedicated and persistent, there are even greater rewards: the remarkable shield shrimps in ephemeral rock pools on top of Uluru, the blind marsupial mole which 'swims' along underground in the sandhills, the etchings of a thousand footprints on the sands, of nocturnal creatures such as hopping mice, bilby, dunnart, gecko, and mulgara. Deep under the ground, safe in their cavities, lie those amazing living reservoirs, the honey-pot ants, and the water-storing frogs.

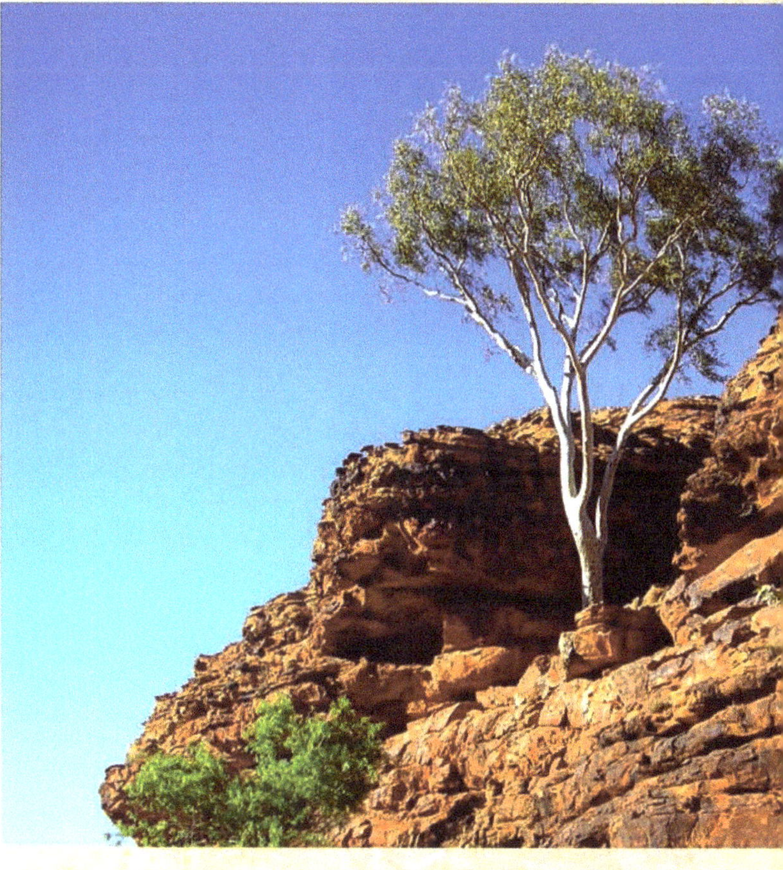

Evocative as it is of large, classical themes, it is perhaps fitting that the outback should embrace the very heart of Australia. Here the struggle between life and death is always apparent. The vastness of the land reduces human beings to a wholesome humility. In places like this we are recalled to the value of simple things: the priceless nature of water, of shade, of life, and of death, on which all life feeds. Here there is always more to life than meets the eye, always so much going on under the surface. Here the vast flat wilderness draws to our surfaces the simultaneous emotions of ecstasy and terror. The long straight roads remind us that life is a journey through ordinary, but ever more surprising places, via the few spectacular memories dotted along the way. The beautiful, the special, the holy, must be found in the ordinary, if they are to be found at all. And everywhere, and over everything, hovers this sense of something, someone, greater.

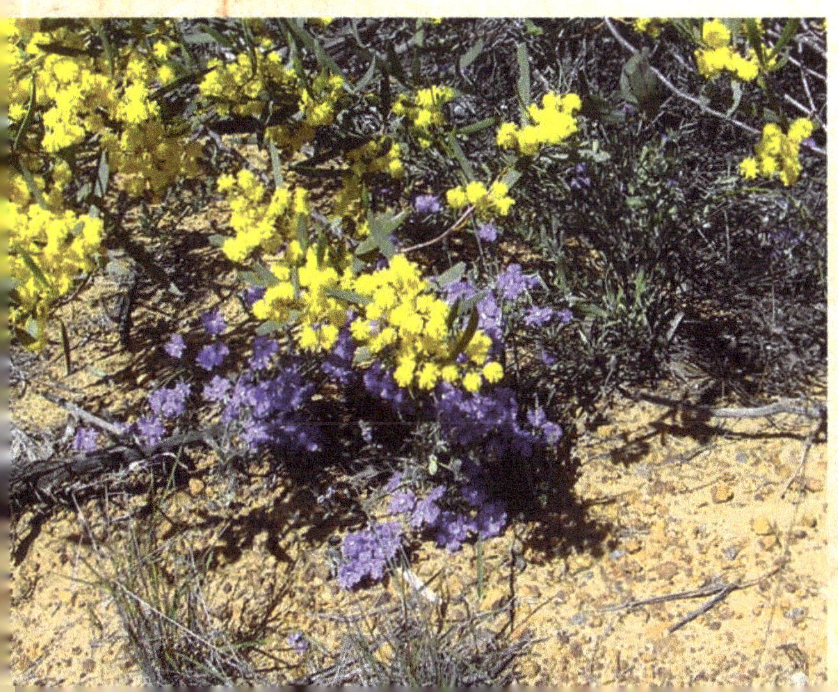

UPPER RIGHT *Dakurra, August '77,* MORRIS
FAR RIGHT *Kings Canyon, NT,* PREWER
LOWER RIGHT *Wild Flowers, Outback WA,* PREWER

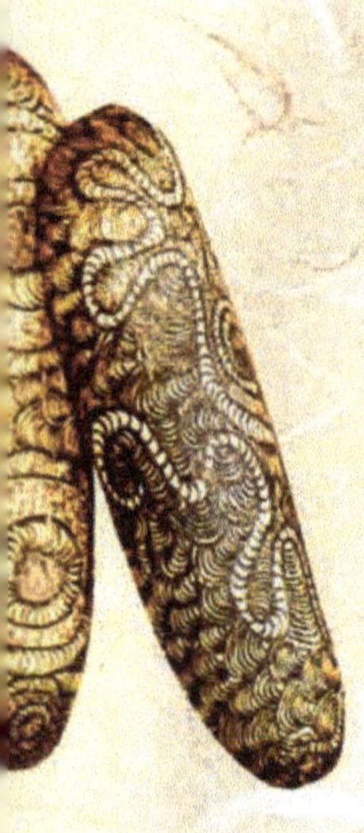

Nor can we ever forget that what for most Australians is remote and somewhere 'out back', is for many others 'home', a home treasured and loved and part of their very lifeblood. White Australians, thinking of people in the outback, recall the history, myths, and exploits of explorers, shearers, drovers, and pastoralists. Our tradition abounds with stories of courageous men and women pioneers who pushed their mobs deeper and deeper along the inland waterholes in search of Australia's most economically valuable plants, the grasses. The modern equivalents of those people still harvest the grass with flocks and herds, mustering their stock with horses and dogs, helicopters and motorbikes.

There are outback towns where people live in incongruous lawned oases of suburbia in the desert, mining camps and missions, outstations and tourist resorts. To many of these more recent arrivals the outback has become their permanent home, and they in turn have incarnated the Australian spirit of gameness, endurance, and easy-going mateship. This is the land of remarkable people and remarkable achievements: Flynn of the Inland, the Flying Doctor, Qantas, Traeger's pedal wireless, the Overland Telegraph, School of the Air, giant road trains, epic cattle drives, windmills, hot gushing artesian water, and solar-powered telephones. It is also the source of the nation's 'soul', some of our most famous art and literature.

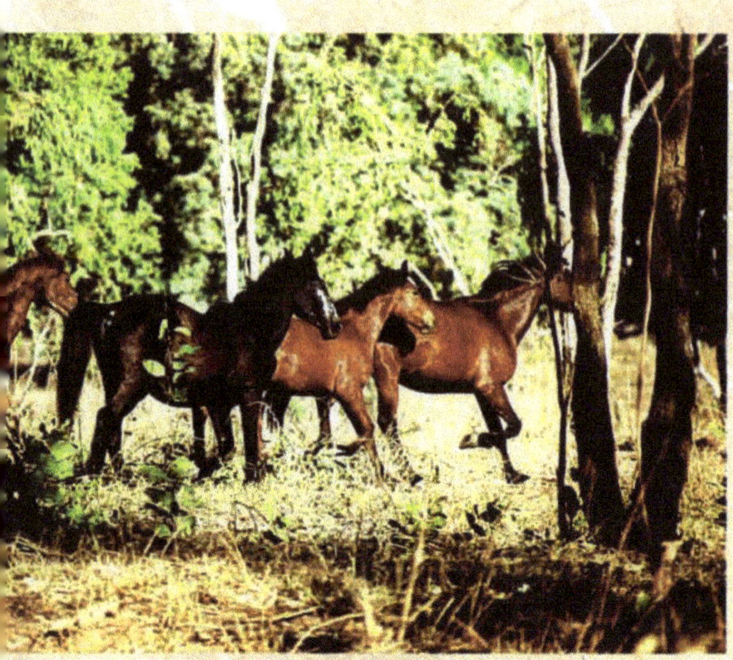

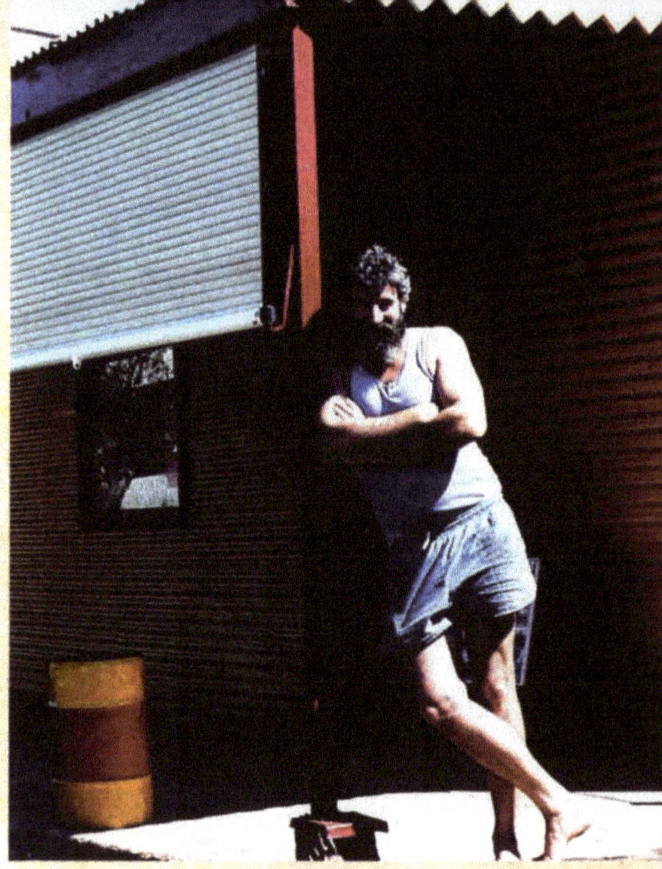

Sometimes omitted in the scripting of the history of the outback are its first inhabitants, the many different Australian Aboriginal peoples. These other outback people possess a wealth of accumulated knowledge and wisdom of living in the outback for untold generations, and this lies often untouched by white society. While we recall the struggles and failures of our early white explorers of the outback: Bourke and Wills, Sturt, Leichhardt, Gosse, Lasseter, and the

UPPER LEFT At Wyndham, WA
LOWER LEFT Brumbies on the run, NT
UPPER RIGHT Road trains, Oodnadatta, SA
LOWER RIGHT Old Friends, PREWER

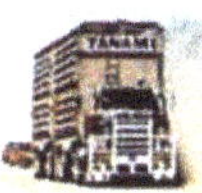

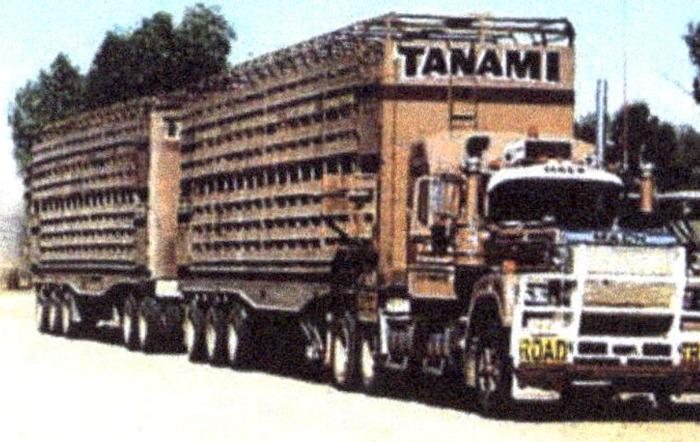

hardship suffered by white pioneers 'beyond the never-never', we forget what wonderful skills were possessed by these remarkable and resilient original inhabitants of the land. They lived in all this apparent harshness as we live in suburbia. Theirs were the secrets of the water places, the sources of bush food, the fire-farming of the vegetation, and the different emphases of the turning seasons. They were our first artists, singers, and poets, and our first and finest bushmen, explorers, and pioneers. Their 'song-lines' or 'Dreaming-tracks', the routes invisible to white people, which dwarfed the famous Birdsville and Strzelecki Tracks, or the Canning Stock Route, sang them step by step right across the arid inland, through the territories of neighbours whose languages were as foreign to them as English is to Chinese. Their contribution to the modern pastoral industry remains largely undocumented and unrecognised in the 'official' records of that industry. These people who left no imposing monuments, built no roads, no massive cities, buildings, or military bases, who husbanded a most fragile environment, have much to teach all Australians about the basics and priorities of life on earth. We would do well to listen, and learn.

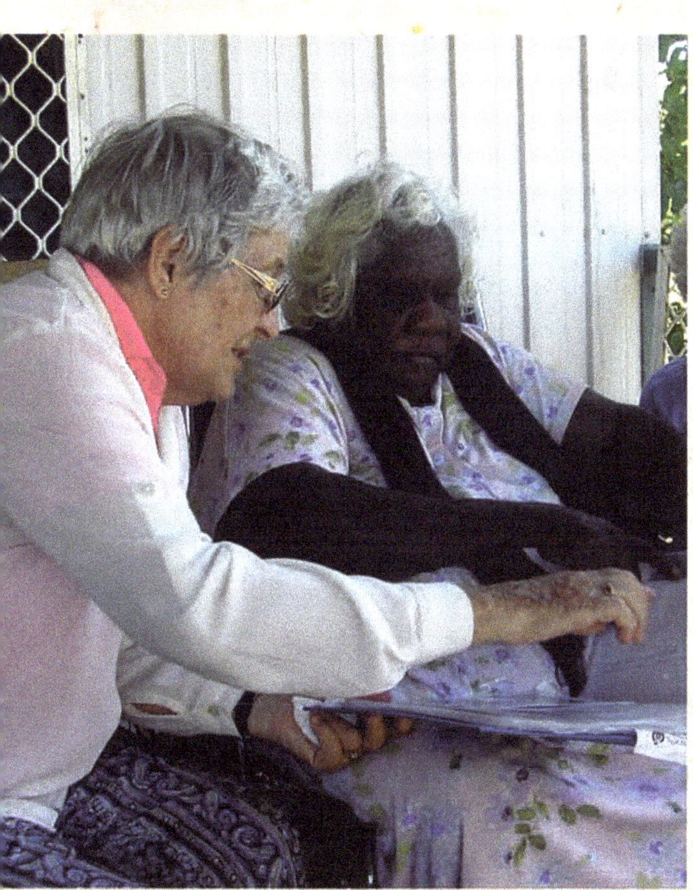

The outback ultimately does not belong to us. The very nature of the land itself ought to be testimony enough to that. This fragile ecosystem belongs to the Lord, and, as part of that ecosystem, we are honoured with the responsibility of living in it in such a way that the land itself benefits from our presence. This is the challenge to which every Australian is called, whether we are a once-in-a-lifetime visitor — 'a damned foreign coaster' — or whether we are among those fortunate enough to call the Australian outback our home.

March 1991

Aub Podlich

THE COLOUR OF SILENCE

It is said that silence
is golden,
but around here
it is red.

Red as serrated mountains,
like Dreamtime dinosaurs
slumbering in the sun.

Red as the warm sand
among the emu bushes
and between one's toes.

Red as a desert sunrise
kissing the ghost gums
and transfusing the sky.

Red as the blood of the Friend
who comes with us
to the end of the world.

PREWER

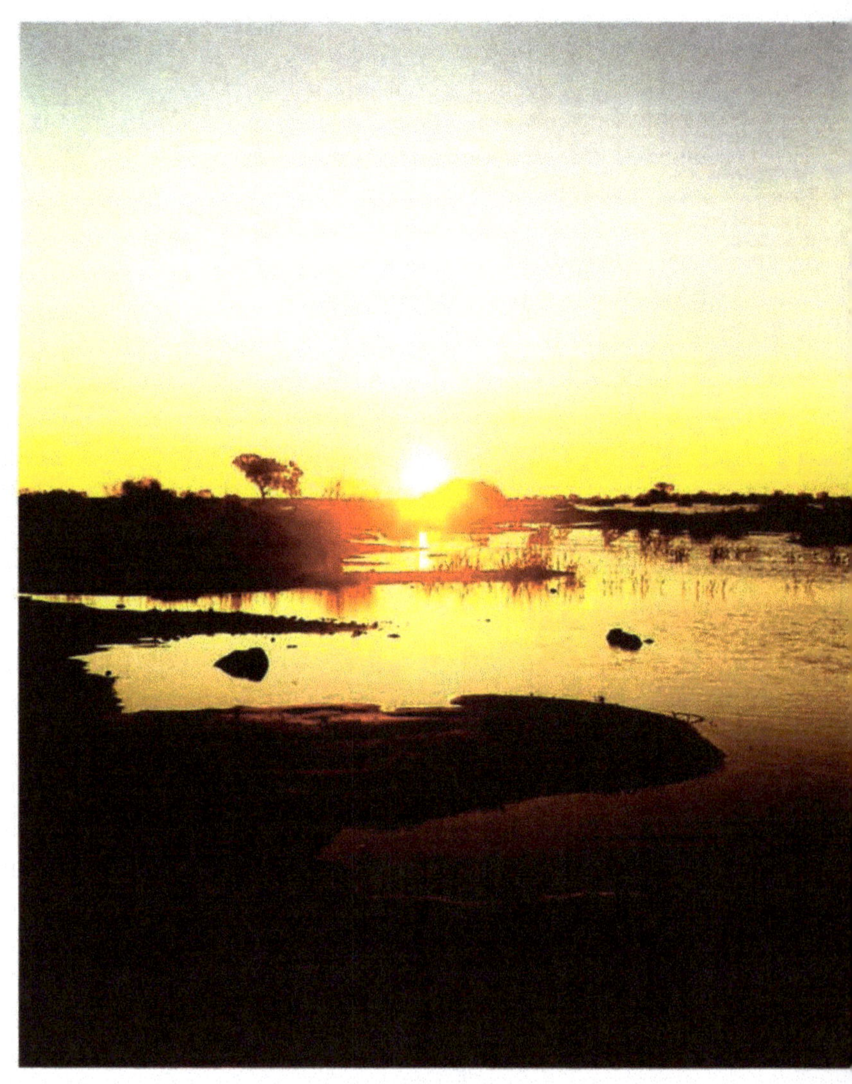

LEFT: *Cooper Creek in flood, near Etadunna, at sunset, SA*
UPPER RIGHT: *Yampire Gorge, Hamersley Range National Park, WA*
LOWER RIGHT: *Chambers Pillar at sunset*

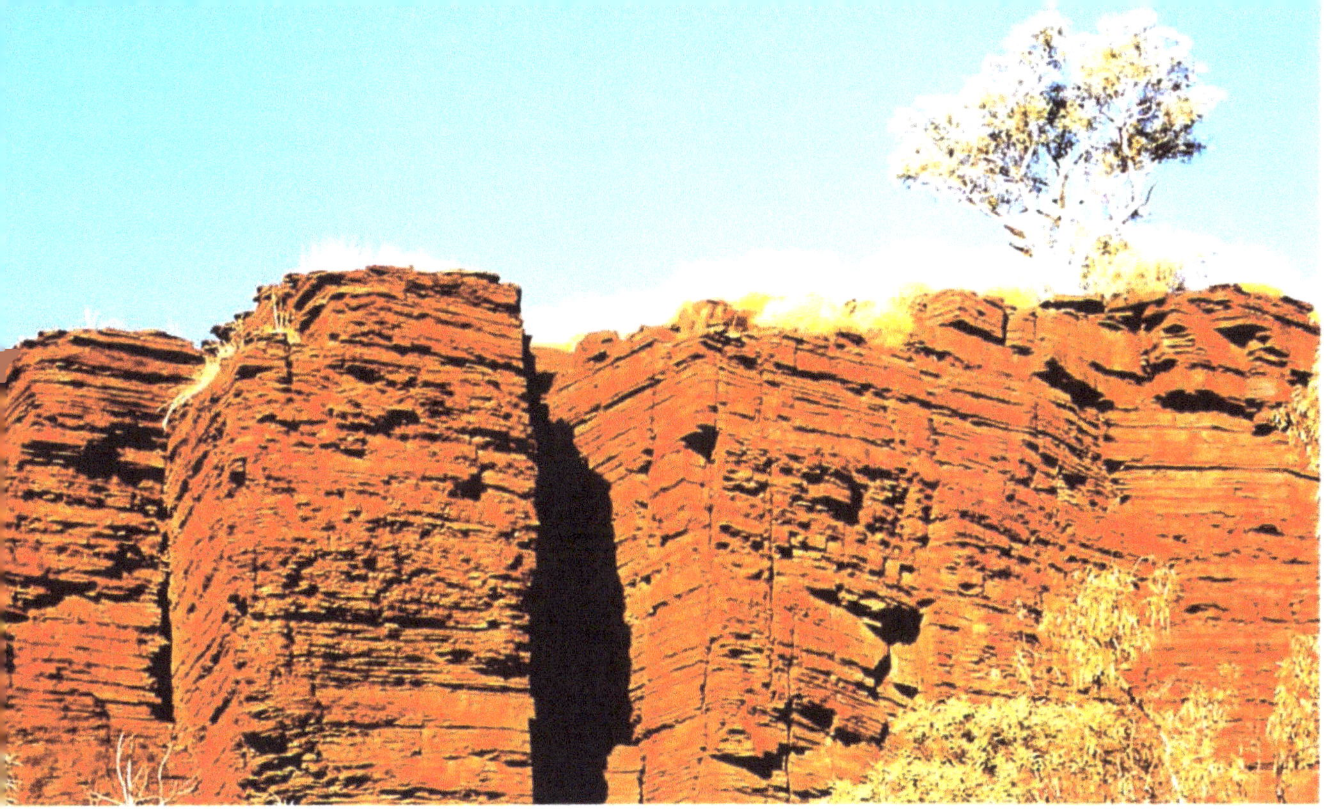

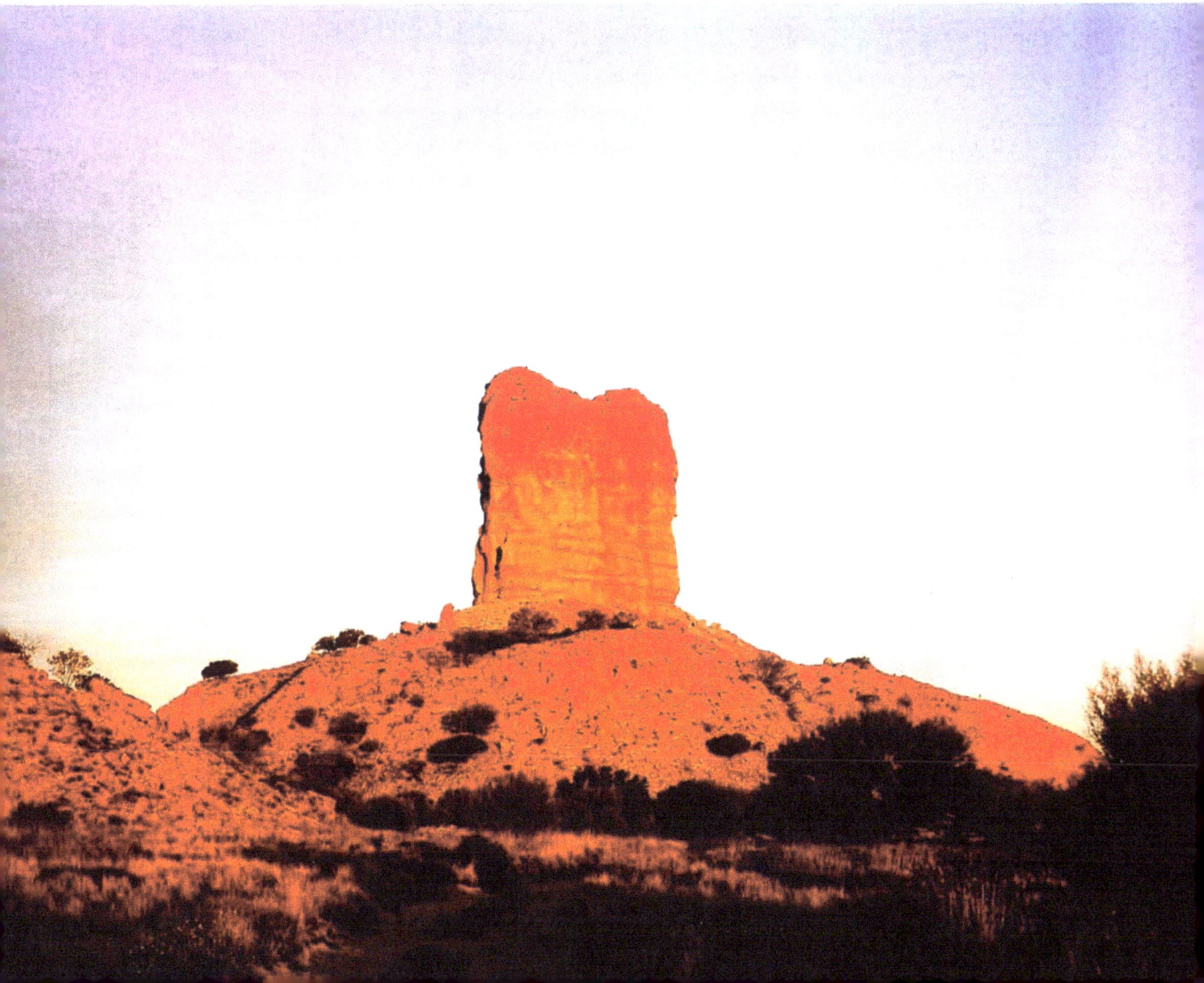

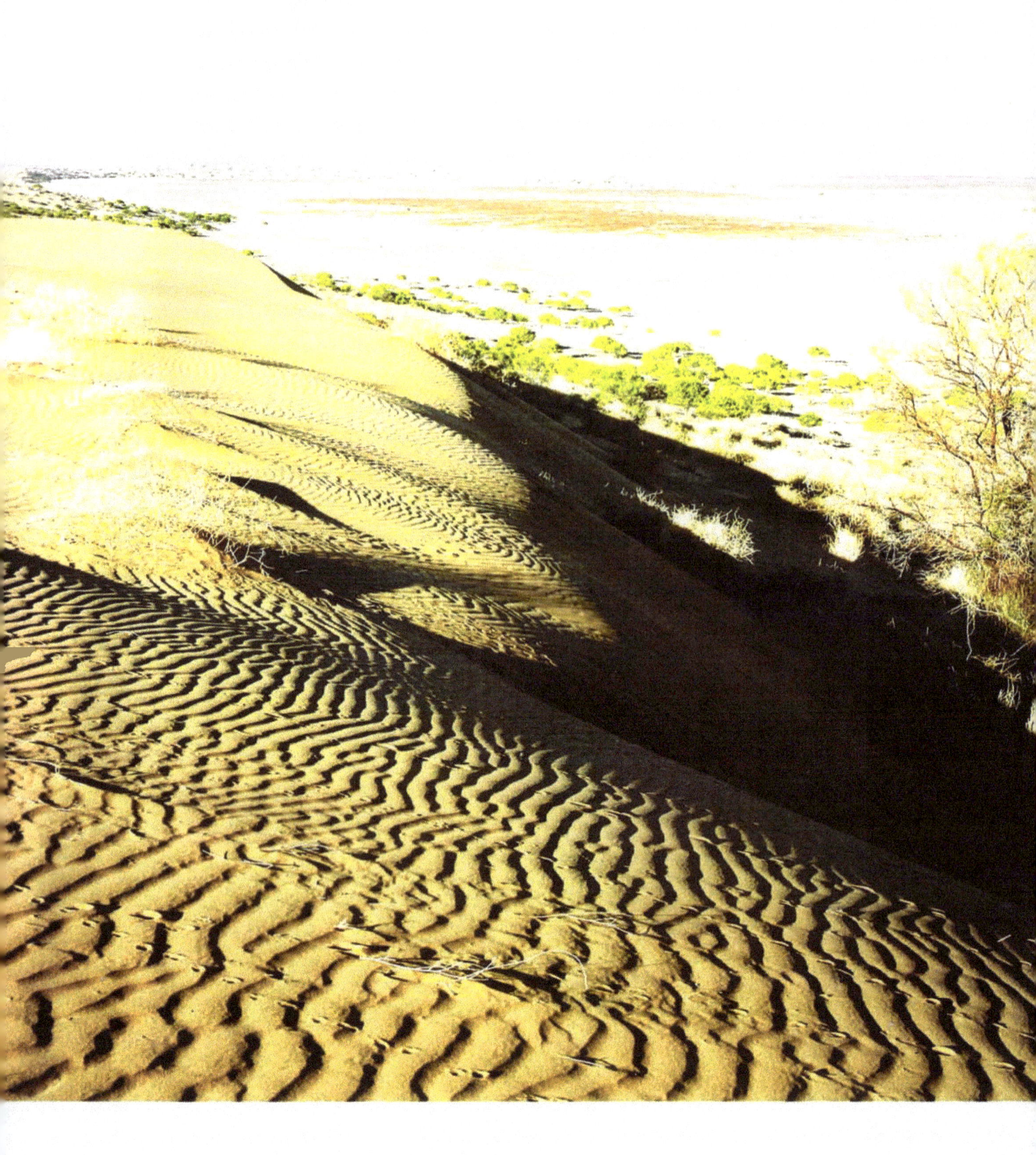

WISDOM

'And he sees the vision splendid
of the sunlit plains extended,
And at night the wondrous glory
of the everlasting stars.' *

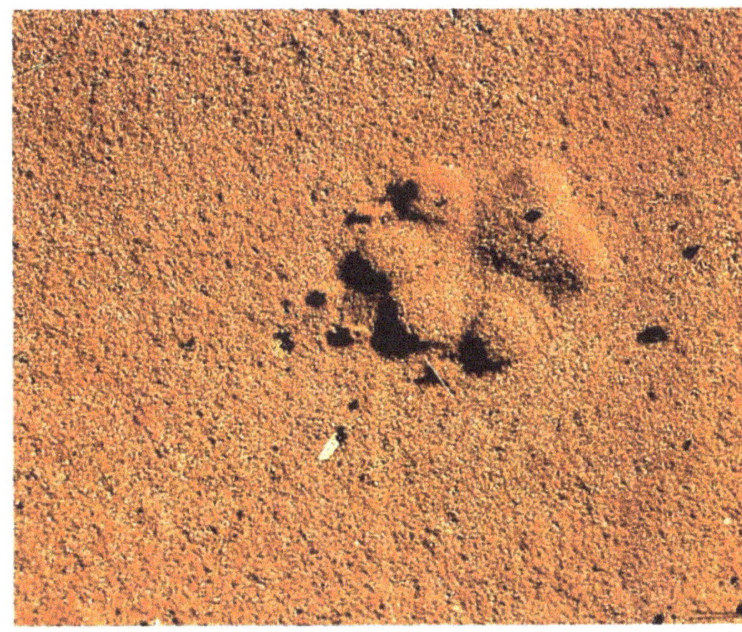

Little children,
do not banish
your sense of mystery,
nor stifle
your sense of wonder,
lest you become as boring
as the world of the bored.

Do not close out
the possibilities
by assuming this
an empty place,
a wasteland.

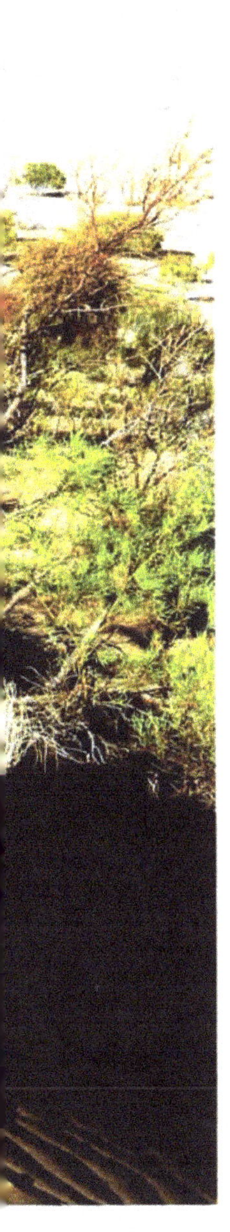

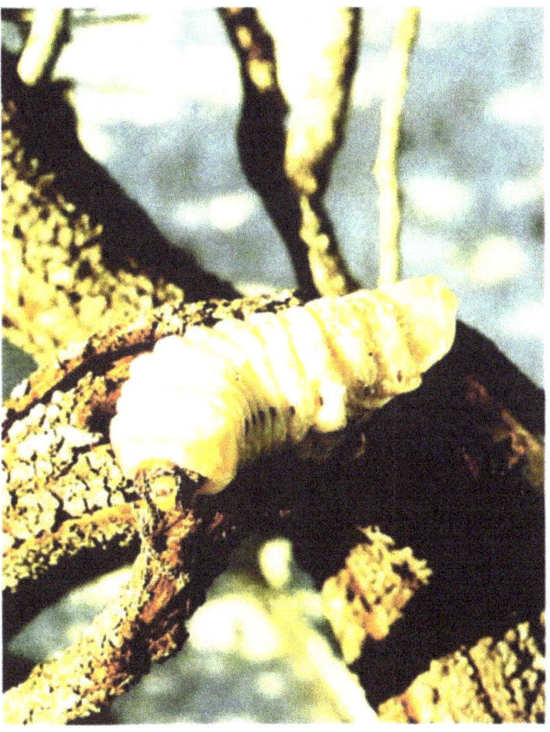

Lest you miss the surprises
in every landscape
and the mysterious pointers
to ever greater visions,
welcome every opportunity
as a chance to grow
in every way.

* *Banjo Paterson,*
'Clancy of the Overflow'

PODLICH

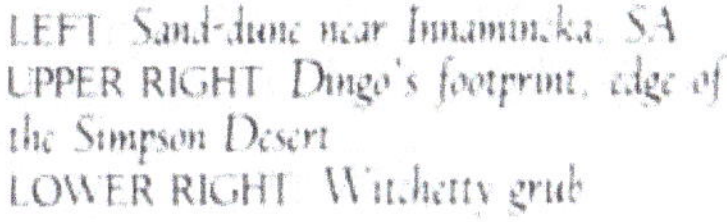

LEFT *Sand-dune near Innamincka, SA*
UPPER RIGHT *Dingo's footprint, edge of the Simpson Desert*
LOWER RIGHT *Witchetty grub*

I WANT TO SEE

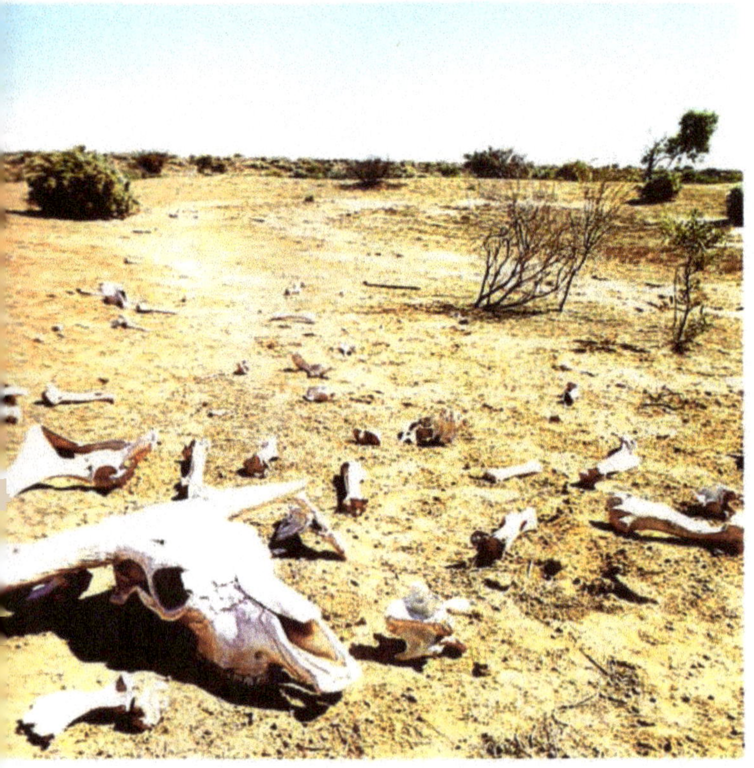

'Jesus asked him,
"What do you want me to do for you?"
"Lord, I want to see", he replied.' *

It's a hard land.
Crows gouge the eyes
from the sheep
bogged in the dams.
In the mulga fringe,
wild pigs wait
for descending dark
to rip the sightless sheep apart.

Blind,
in a dangerous land,
is a terrible state to be.

Good Shepherd,
take pity on me.
I want to see.

* *Luke 18:41 NIV*

PODLICH

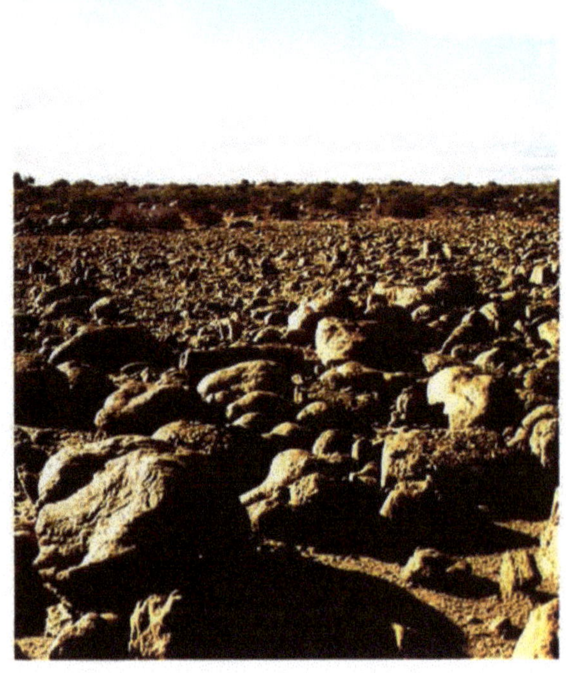

UPPER LEFT: *Sun-bleached cattle bones near a dry waterhole*
LOWER LEFT: *A stony plain, near Pimba, SA*
UPPER RIGHT: *A lone dead tree at sunset, Kimberley, WA*
LOWER RIGHT: *Ormiston Gorge, MacDonnell Ranges, NT*

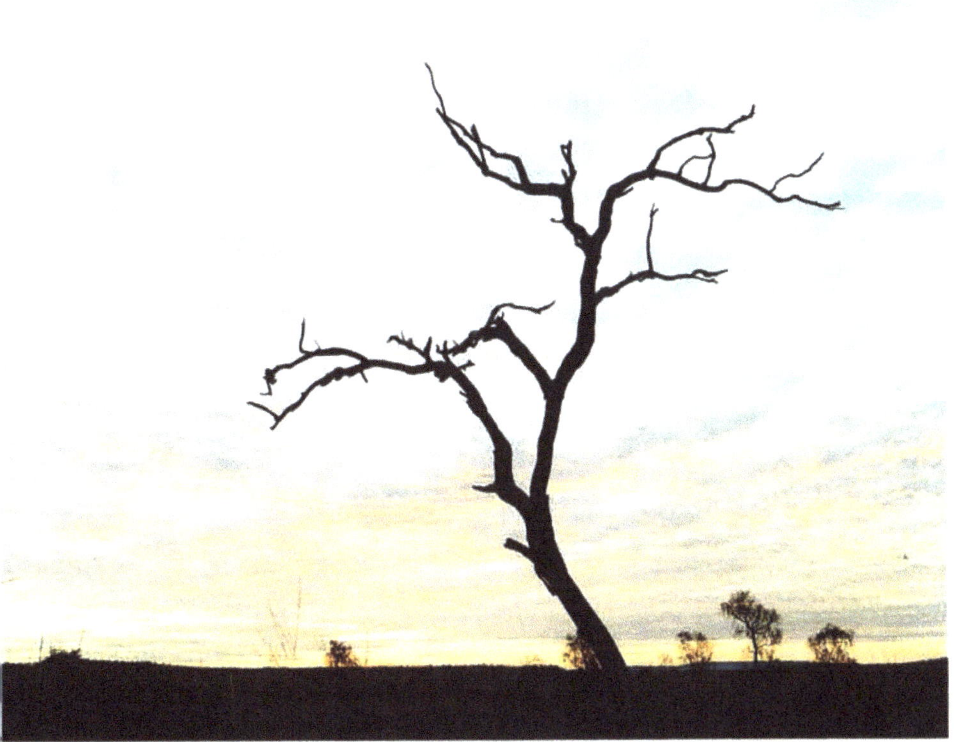

WHICH ANGELS?

Some find only the alien
in these wildernesses;
a place for the Enemy
and his angels of chaos.

Some see only the beauties,
censoring the ugly
realities of life's struggle
and death's nearness.

The son of Mary,
who defied deceits,
wrestled the devil here
and was fed by angels of light.

PREWER

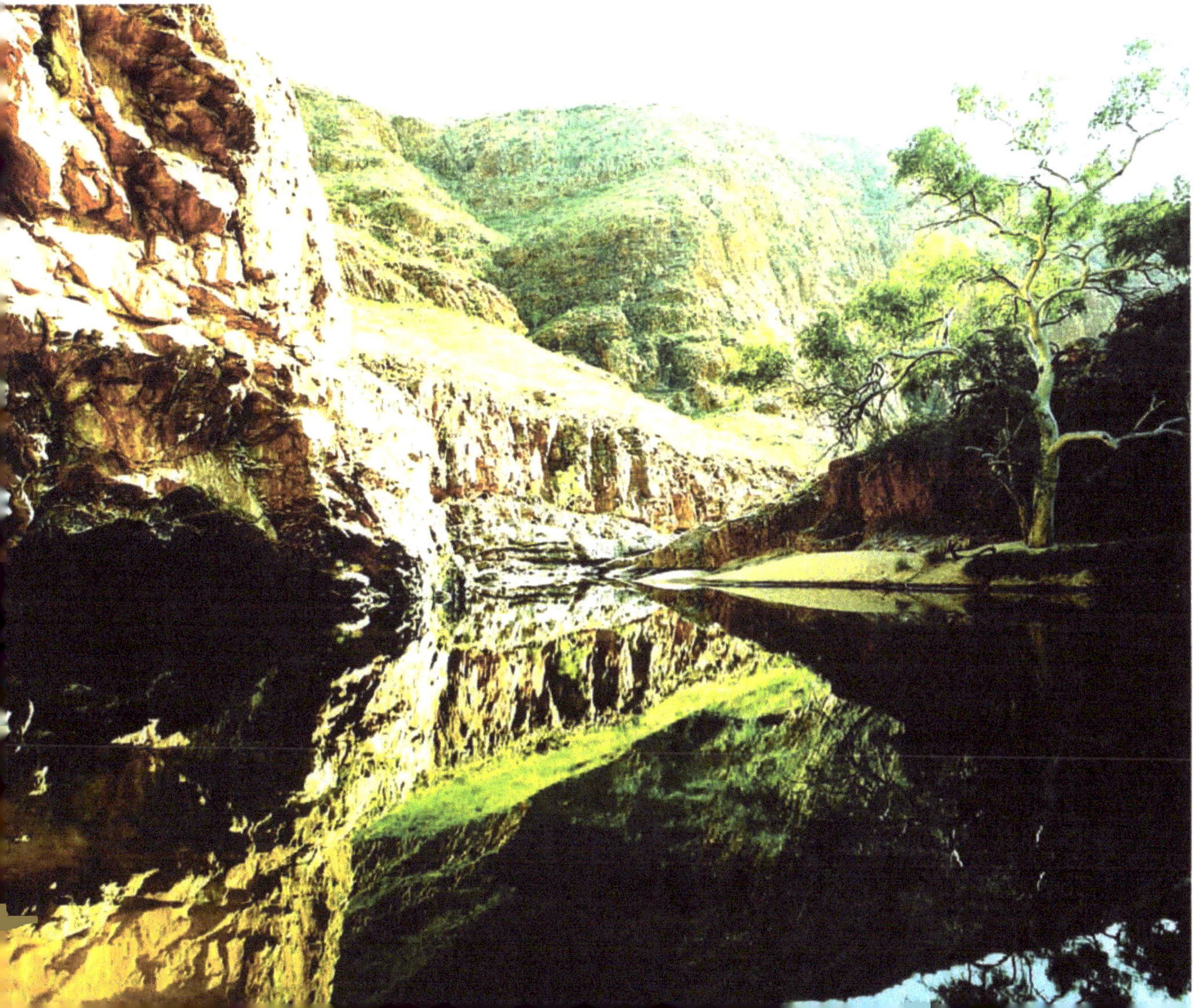

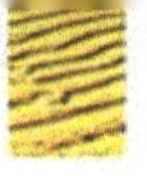

GOD OF SHORT-LIVED THINGS

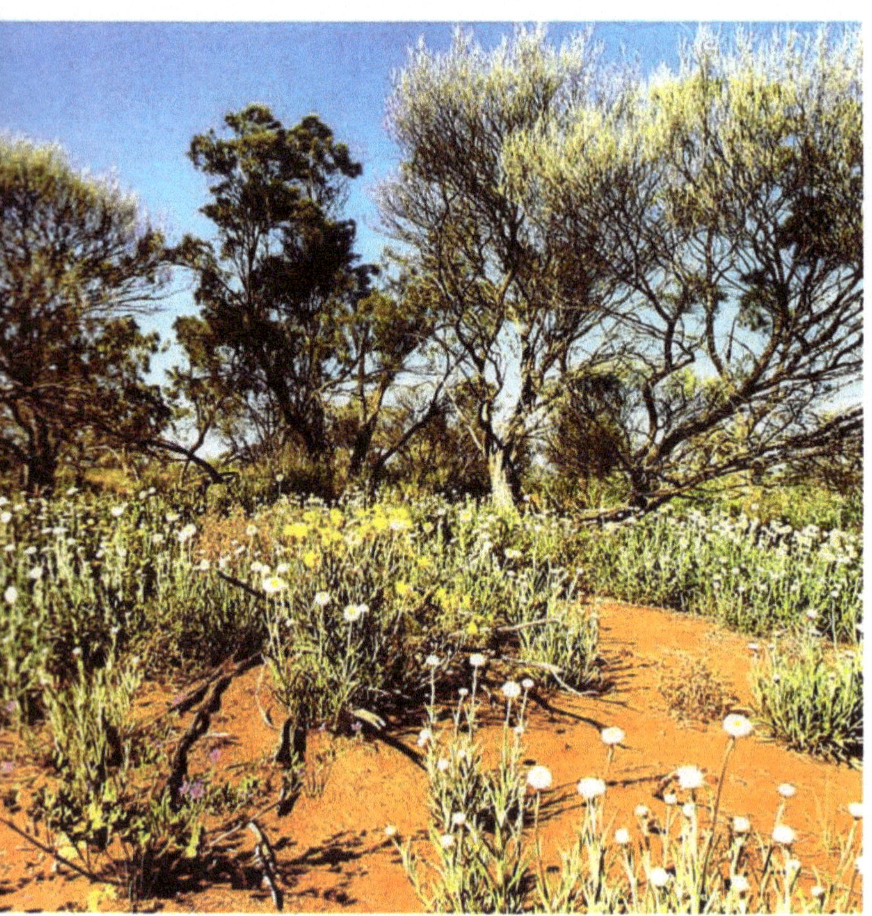

God of short-lived things:
When you bless the earth with rain,
flowers explode like fireworks
all over the desert plains.
But when you fan the fire of your sun,
they fizzle and fade
like fireworks spent and done.

But their seeds
are sparks
already sown.

Jesus,
when you promised your followers
homes, families, fields —
and persecutions as well, *
I hear you say:
'When I shower you with flowers
and then take them all away,
in both the giving
and the taking,
I am still loving you,
still sowing you with seed
for the life that never dies'.

And I practise my reply:
'The Lord gave
and the Lord has taken away;
may the name of the Lord be praised'. *

* *Mark* 10:3C
** *Job* 1:21 NIV

PODLICH

LEFT: *Spring wildflowers, near Lake Harry, SA*
RIGHT: *Sand-dune, near Erldunda, NT*

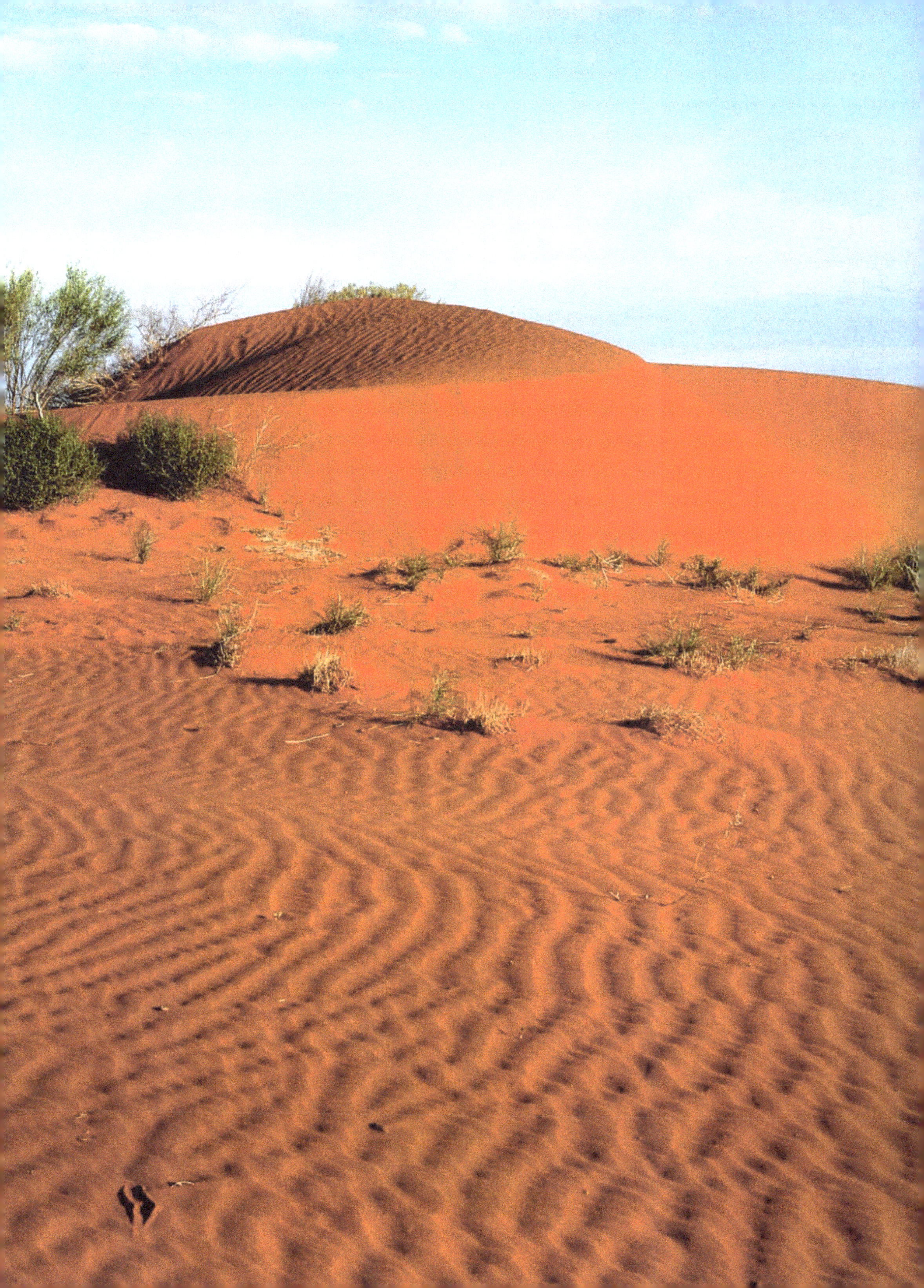

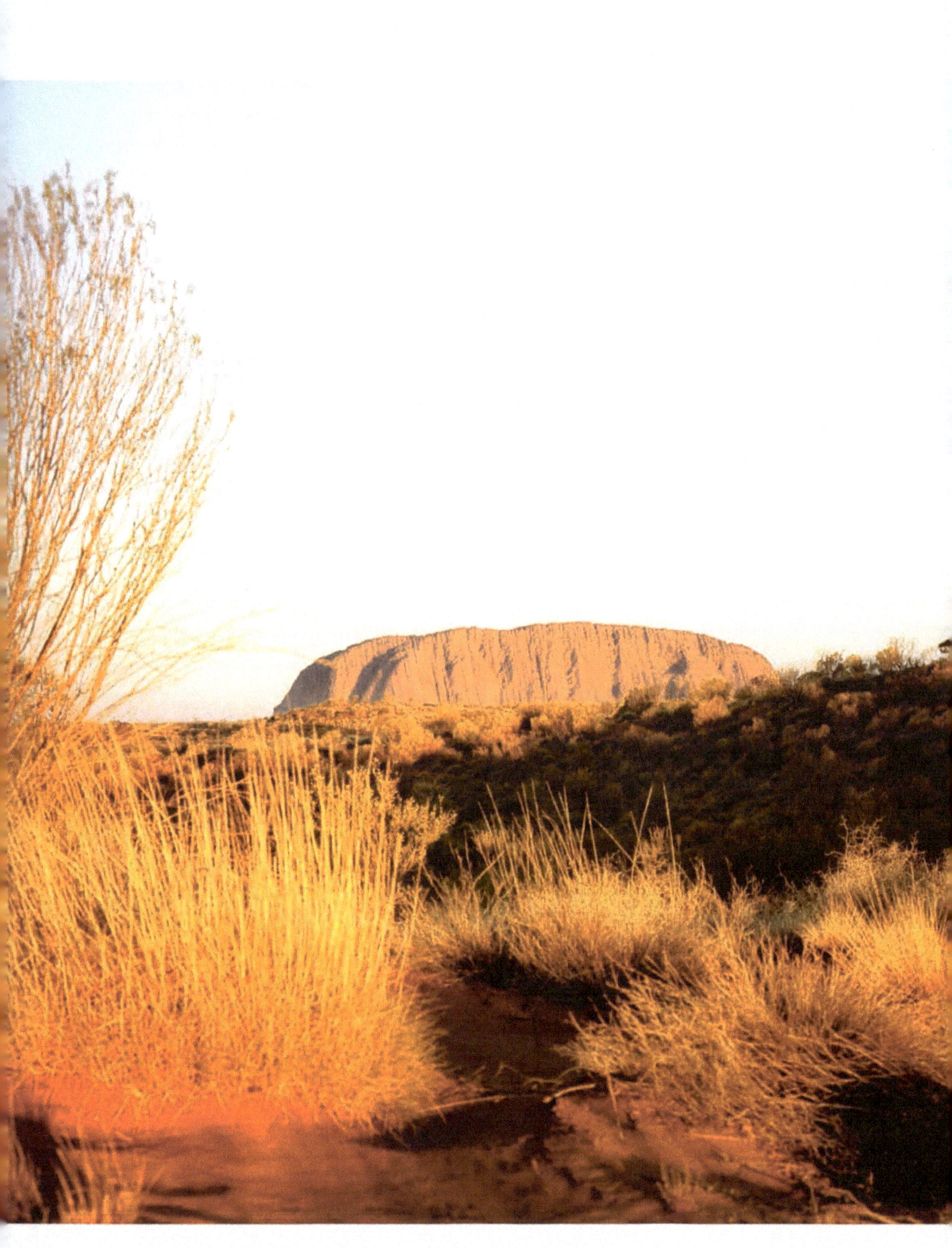

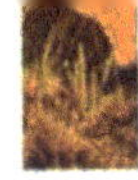

ULURU

LEFT *Ayers Rock, Uluru National Park, NT*
RIGHT *Climbing Ayers Rock*
OVERLEAF *Devil's Marbles, NT*

Ant people, ant people,
up and down the rock;
ant people, ant people,
climbing by the clock.

Up and down, up and down,
some with ease, some with pain;
the day ends, another dawns,
up and down they stream again.

From air-conditioned buses,
they have not come to stay;
into cars and off to Alice,
hurrying to get away.

White illusion: see and conquer,
mount it and stand tall;
photographs to prove they did it,
but no print upon the soul.

Great icon from the Dreaming
hides its secret worth;
only the pure in heart and meek
shall inherit this earth.

Ant people, ant people,
up and down the rock;
ant people, ant people,
climbing by the clock.

PREWER

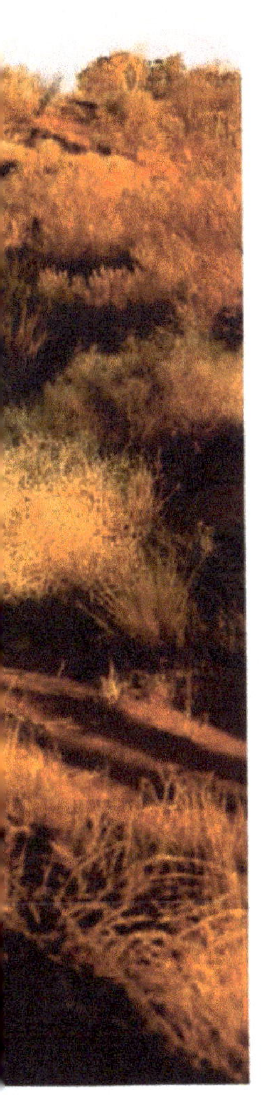

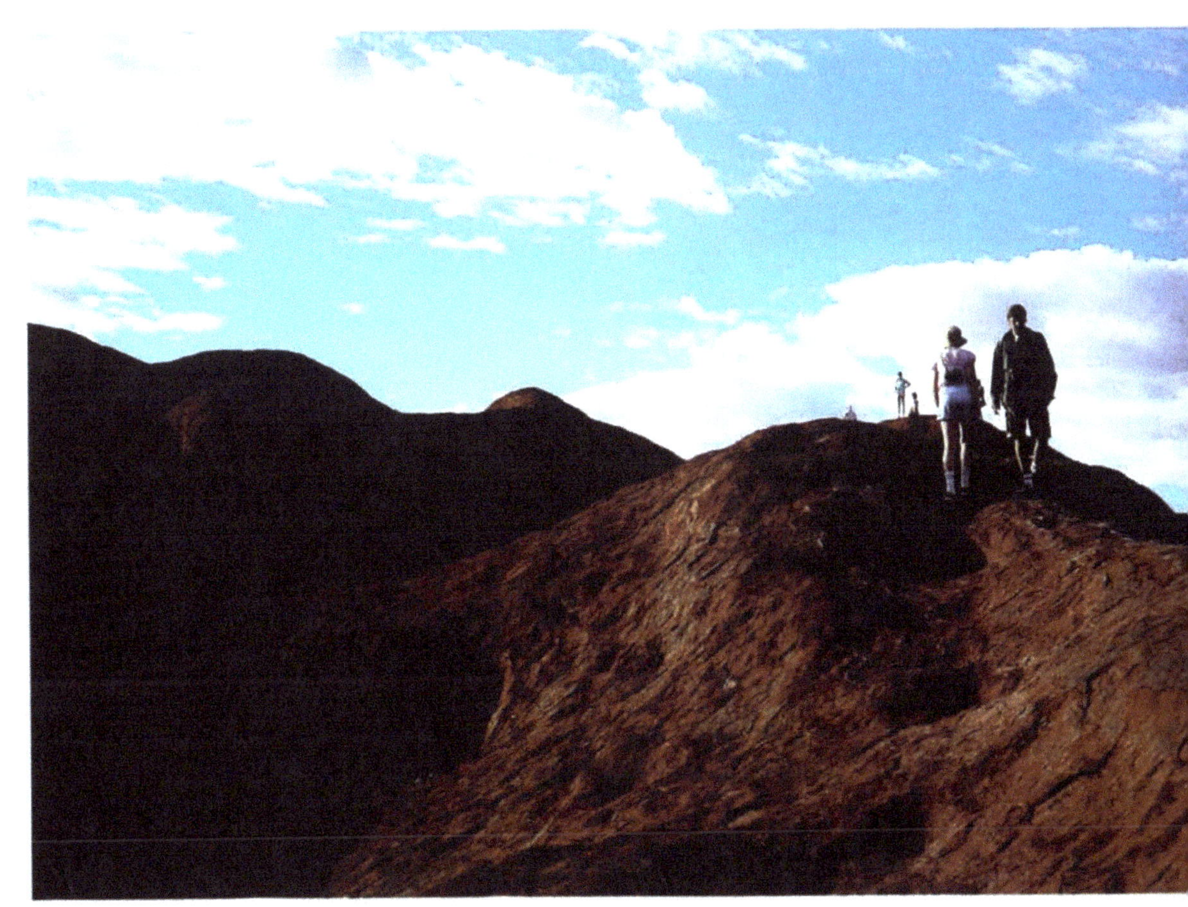

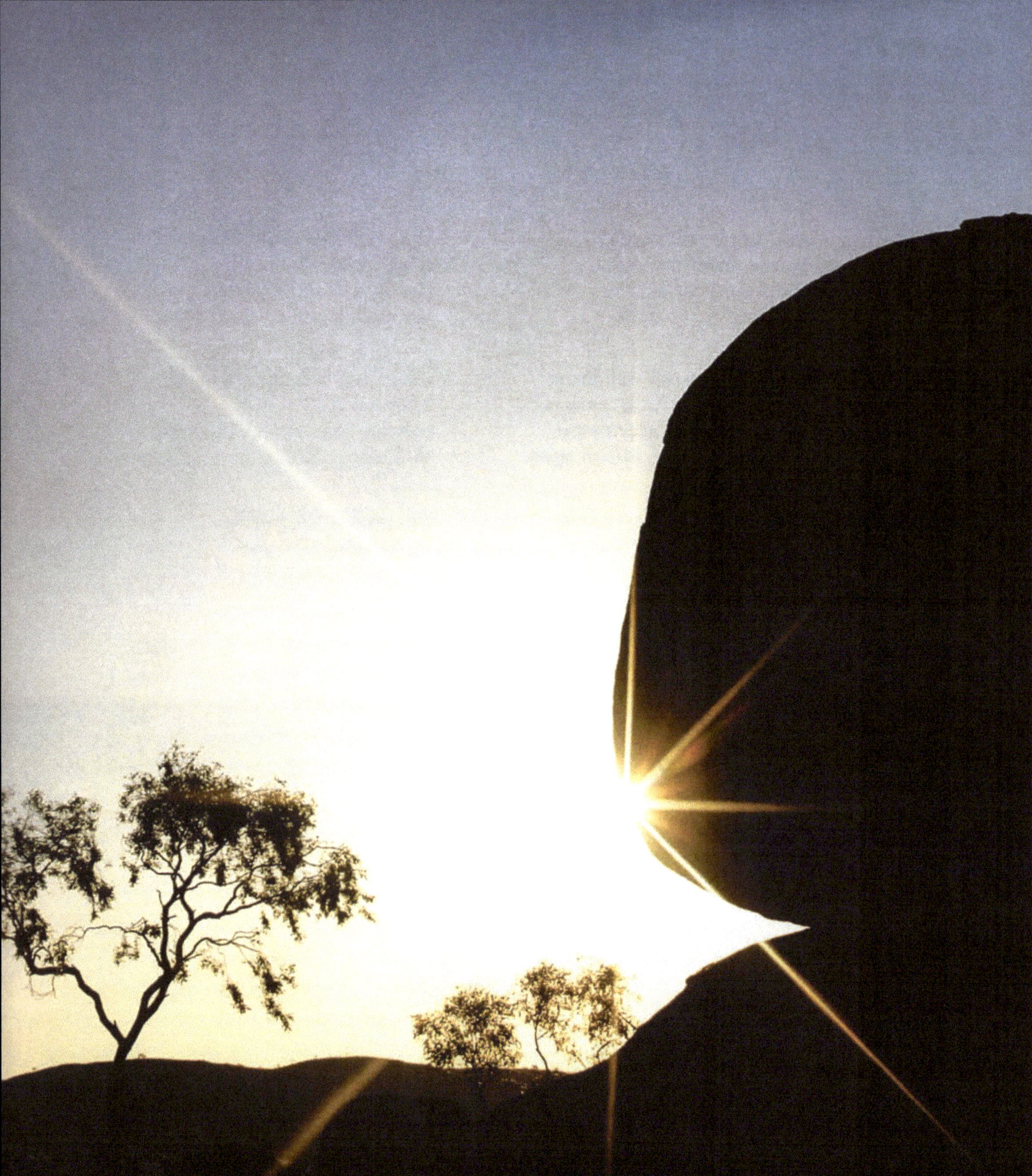

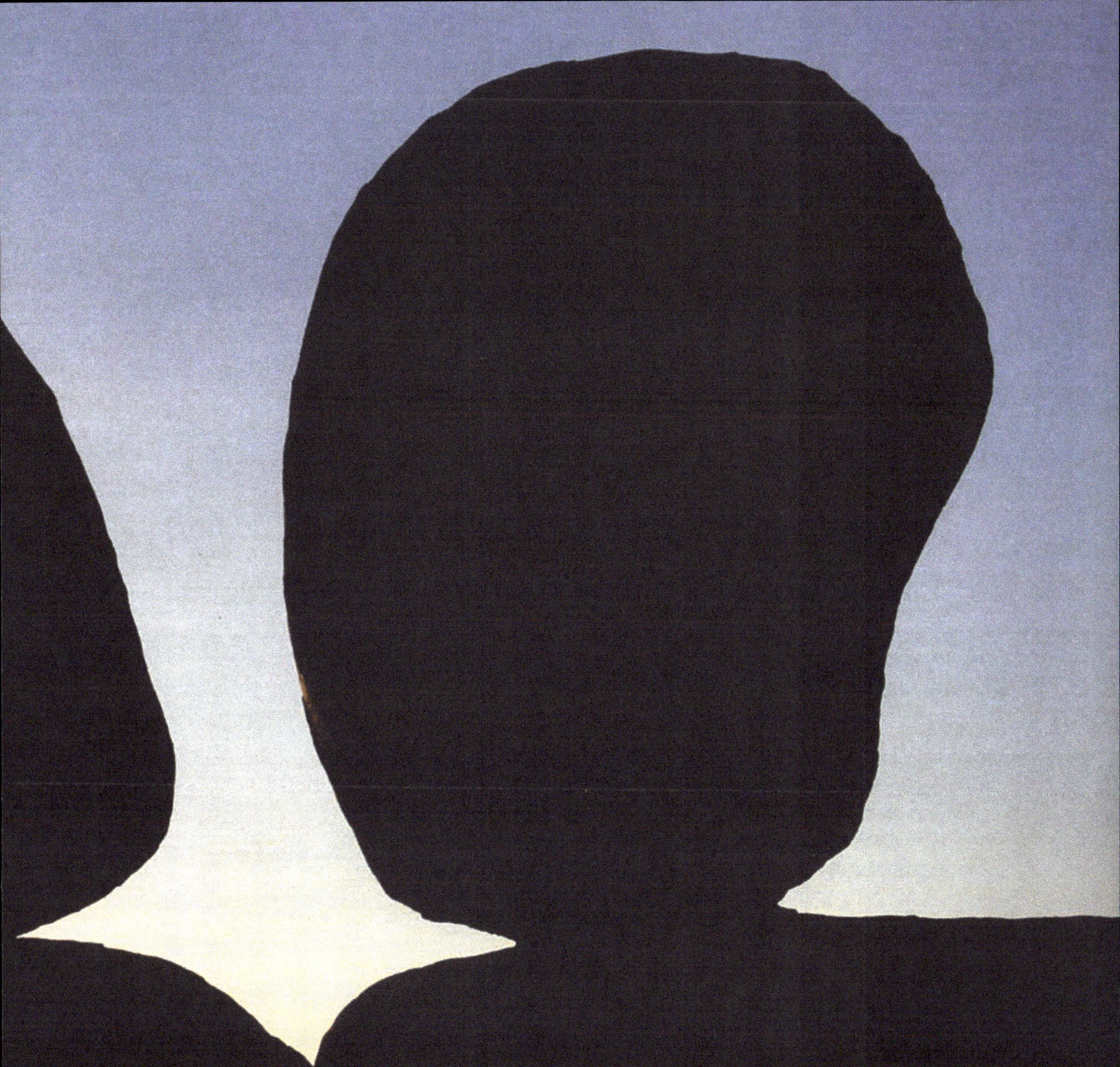

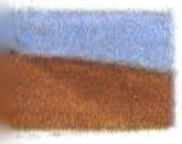

BEFORE YOU

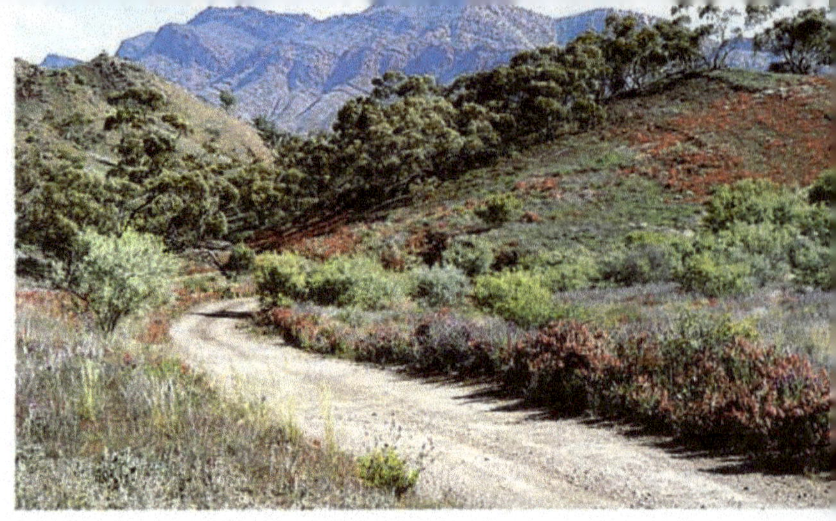

Let me stand before you,
God whom I fear,
like these ancient hills,
all my pretensions
eroded away.

Let me kneel before you,
God whom I love,
like these sandy streams,
all my own fullness
drained away.

Let me rest before you,
God whom I trust,
like these ruined homesteads,
all my sufficiency
blown away.

Let me live before you,
God whom I need,
like this barren plainland,
all my profusion
withered away.

PODLICH

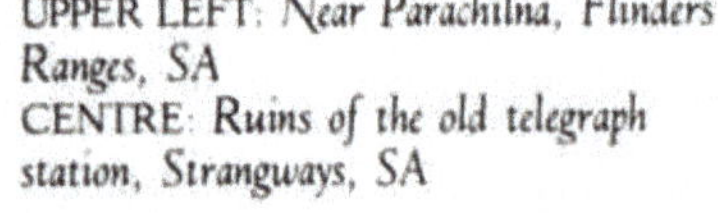

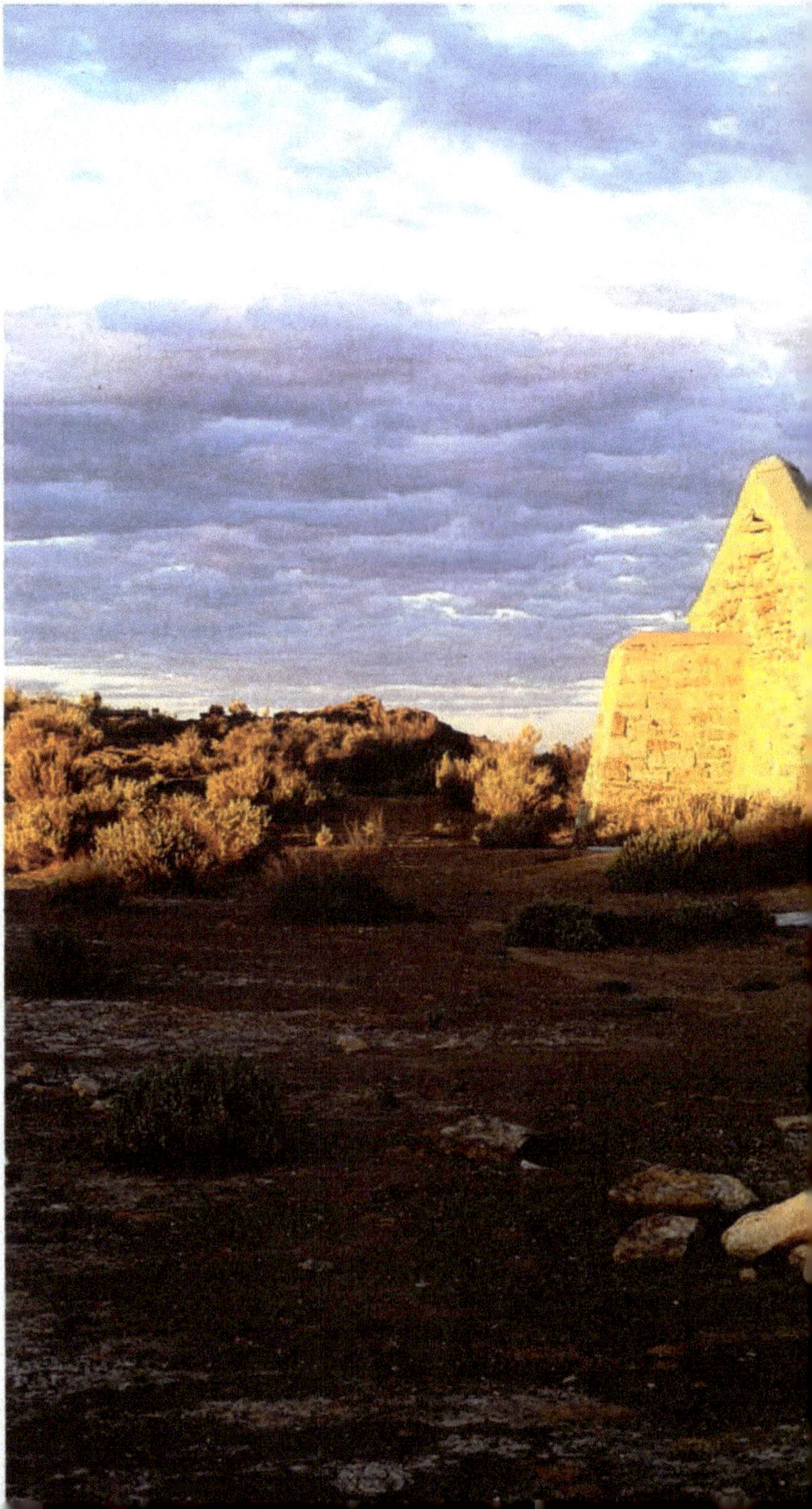

UPPER LEFT: *Near Parachilna, Flinders Ranges, SA*
CENTRE: *Ruins of the old telegraph station, Strangways, SA*

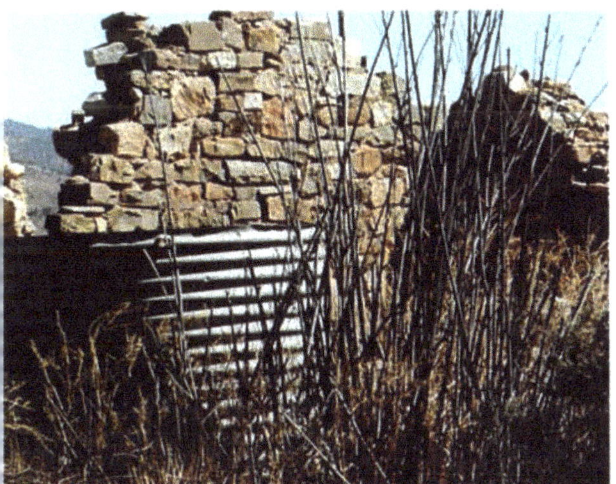

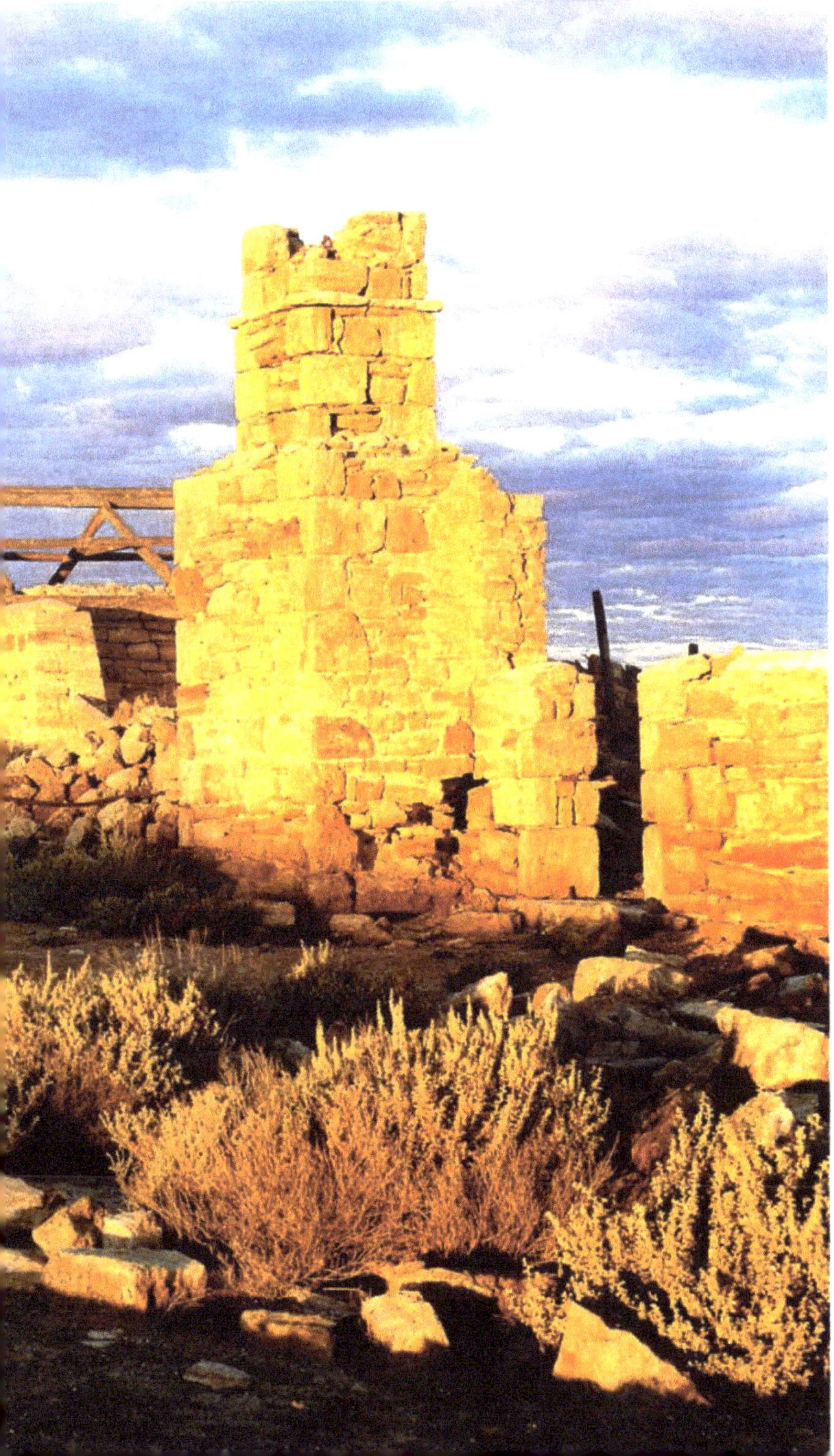

BROKEN DREAM

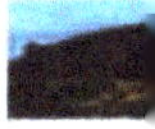

Exploring
in the Flinders Ranges,
we come across
a broken dream.

A little stone cottage,
beautifully constructed
one spring last century,
when the grass was very green.

Sited carefully,
on a small rise
overlooking a creek
that rarely runs.

It is dry now,
as it usually is,
and although it's spring
the land around is dust.

Many are such dreams
that are built carefully
on mistaken ground,
to become ruins.

Dismayed, we turn
to finger again
that other Stone
which builders rejected.

PREWER

UPPER RIGHT: *Ruins of the Gordon Hotel, Flinders Ranges, SA*

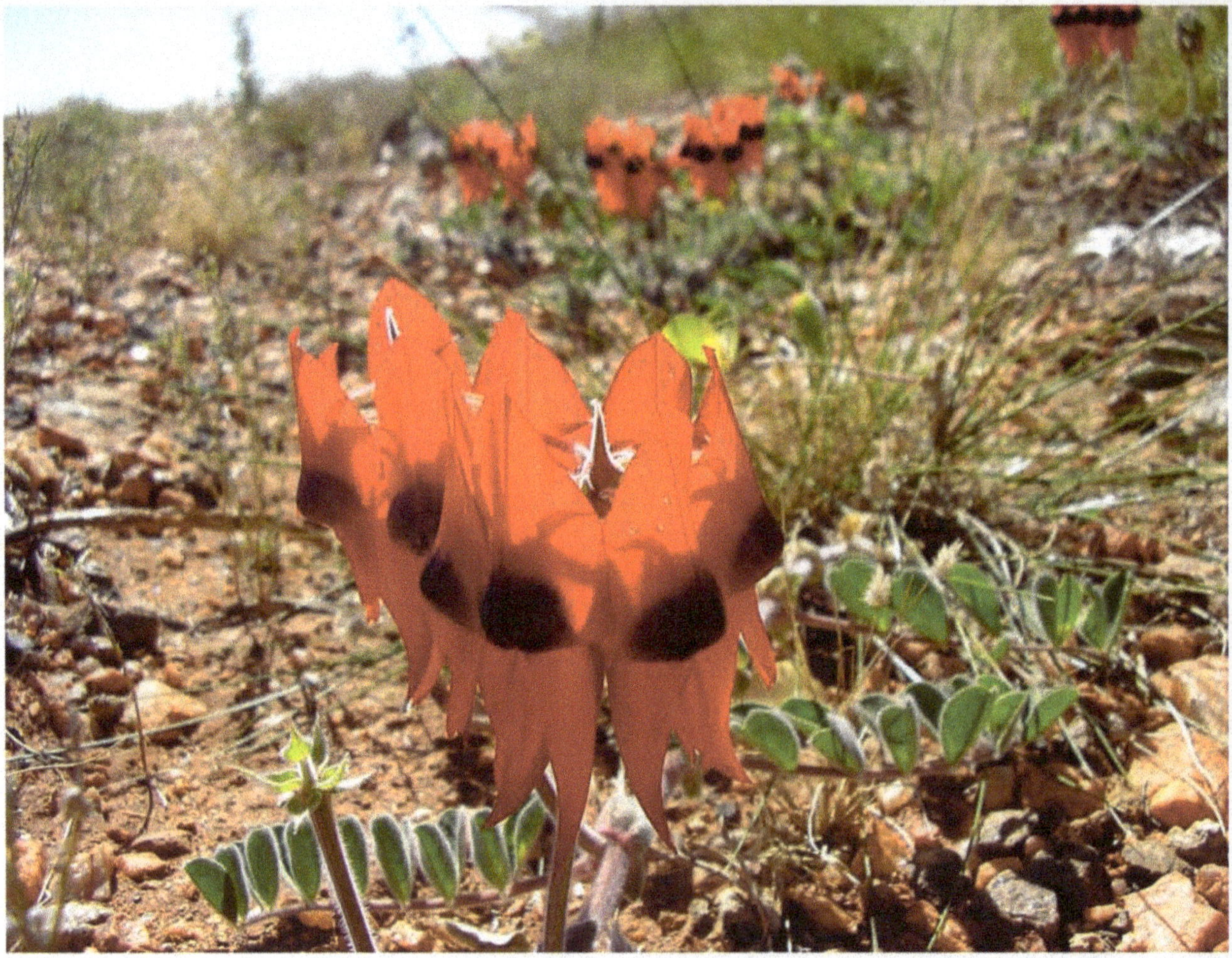

PARADOX

It takes
a million wheeling budgies
to blot the light
from the sun,
but only a single desert flower
to unmask the splendour
of the Mighty One,
who outshines
even the sun.

PODLICH

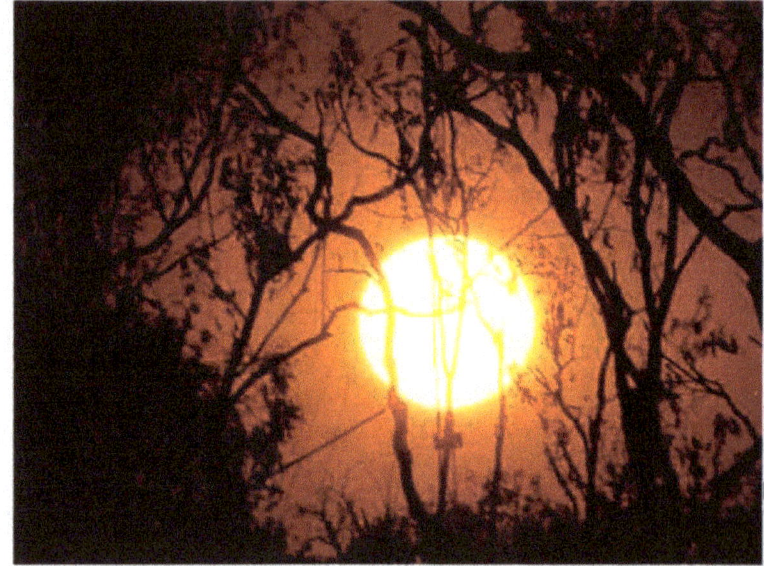

UPPER LEFT: *Sturts Desert Pea, Outback WA,* PREWER
LOWER LEFT: *Sunrise, tropical top of the Northern Territory*

GHOST GUM

You call them ghost gums,
but such majesty
will always be
the Holy Ghost's gums
to the likes of me.

PODLICH

LOWER RIGHT *The Twin Ghost Gums, near Alice Springs, NT*

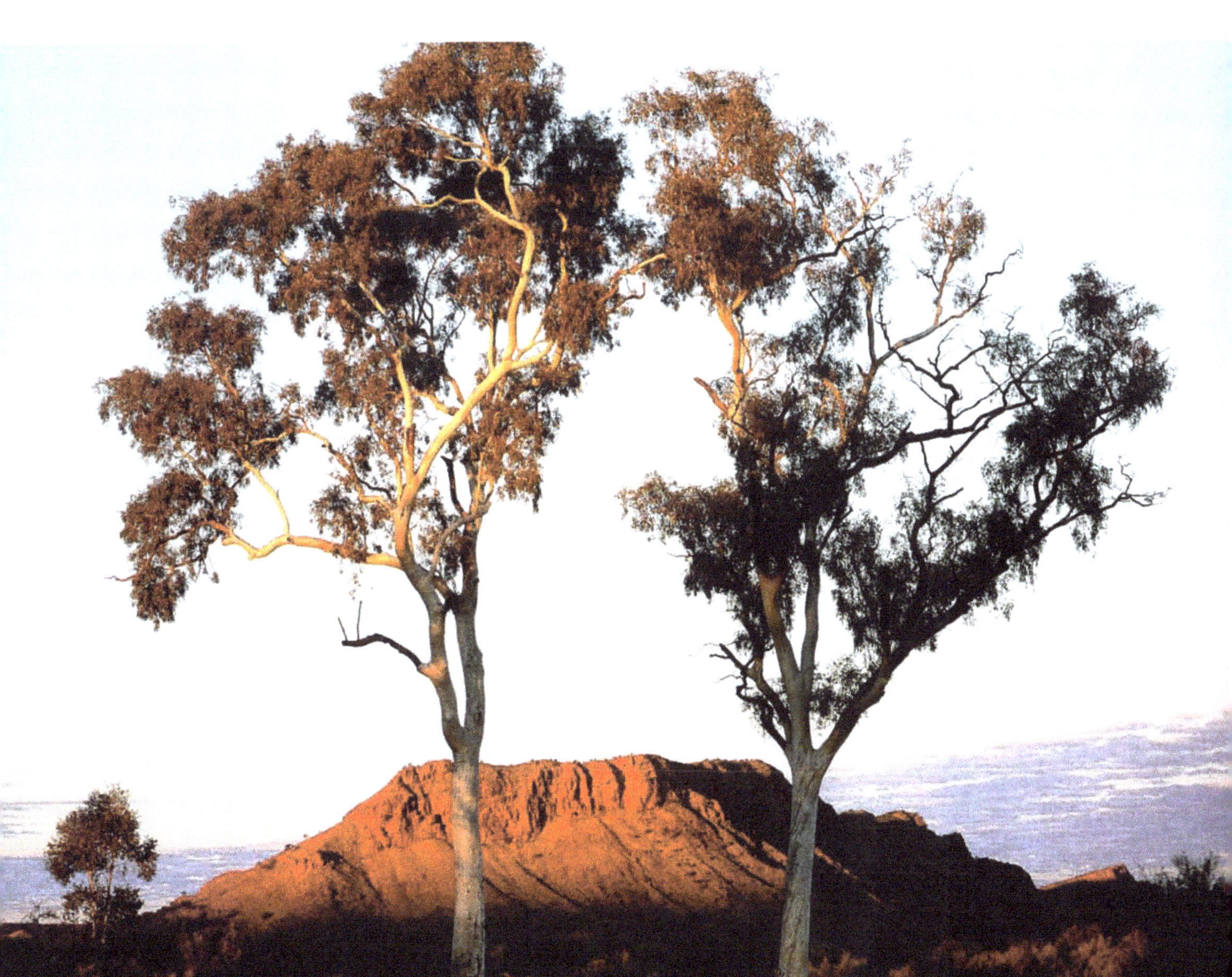

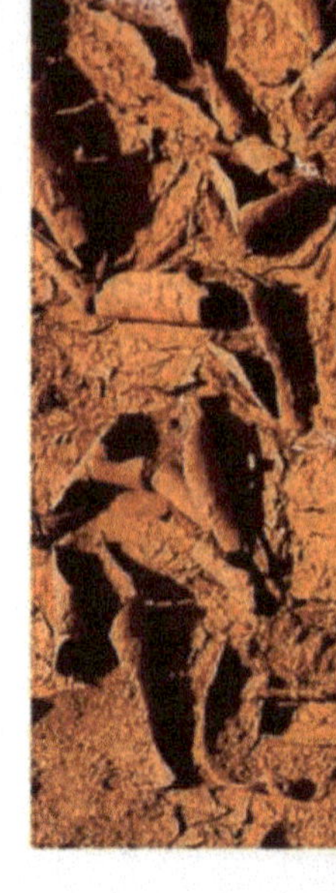

WAITING FOR RAIN

The red dusty land
longs for summer storms
to green the grass
and call emu, euro,
plains turkey, back again.

Life rolls in
on a wild wind.

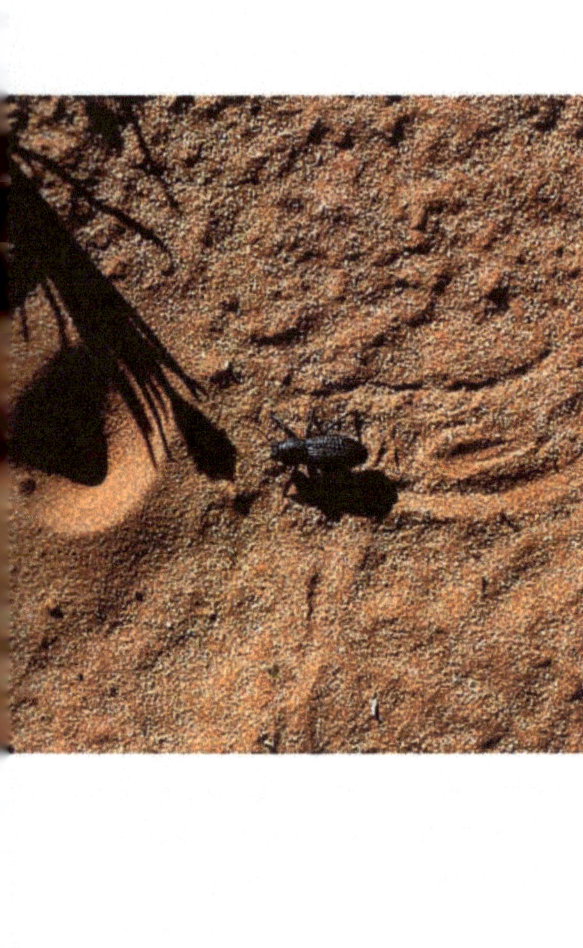

From earth as dry
and red as this,
the Lord shaped our kin
and greened them
with his own life-giving breath.

So grace us, Lord Jesus,
with your refreshing Spirit;
give us this red earth's resilience
when long suffering
drains our spirits
and dries up our joy
like the face of a parched dam.

We wait with hope
for your cool breath
to green us.

Make us live
and love
again.

PODLICH

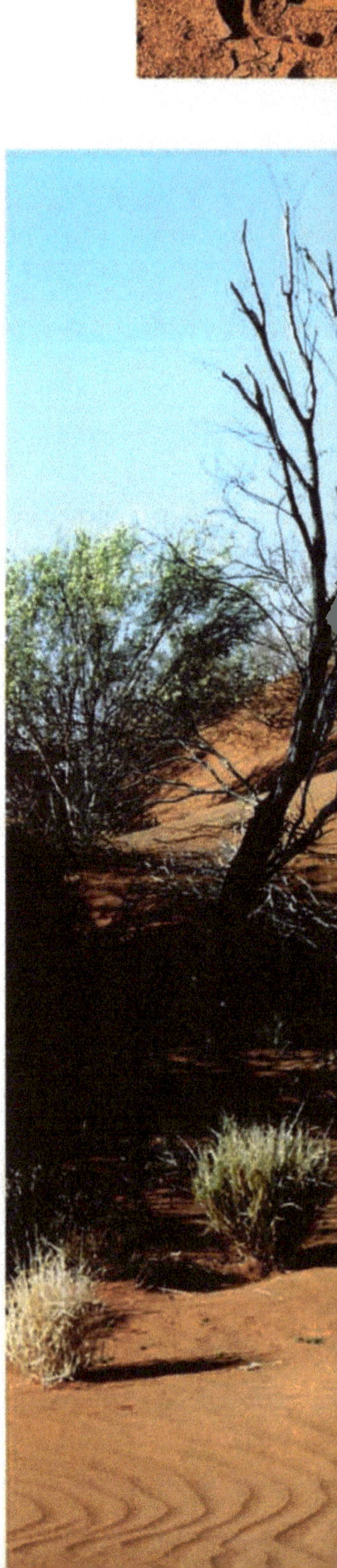

LEFT: *A beetle, Simpson Desert*
UPPER RIGHT: *Dried mud, Central Australia*
LOWER RIGHT: *Sand-dune, NT*

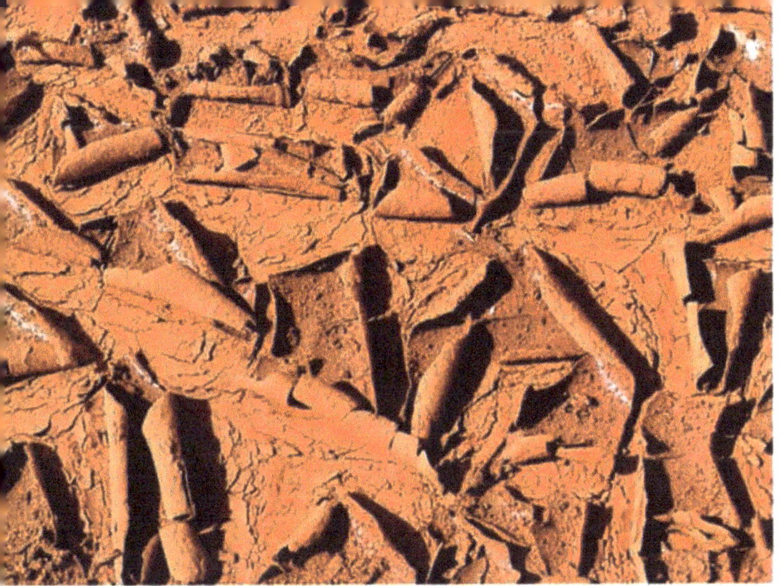

DUST

God,
if we're all dust,
and to dust we shall return,
there's sure a lot of us
already gone back
to the great outback!

PODLICH

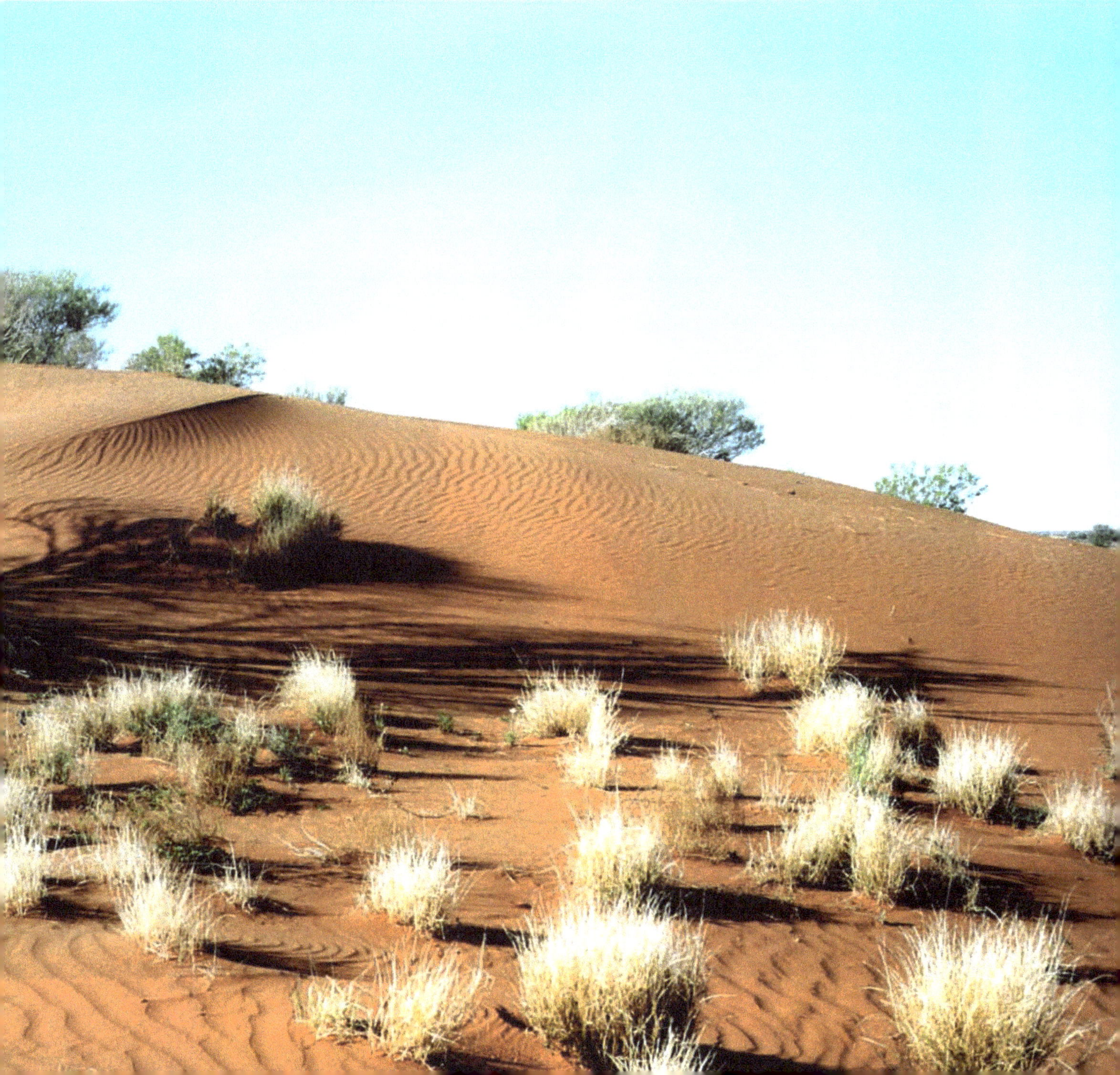

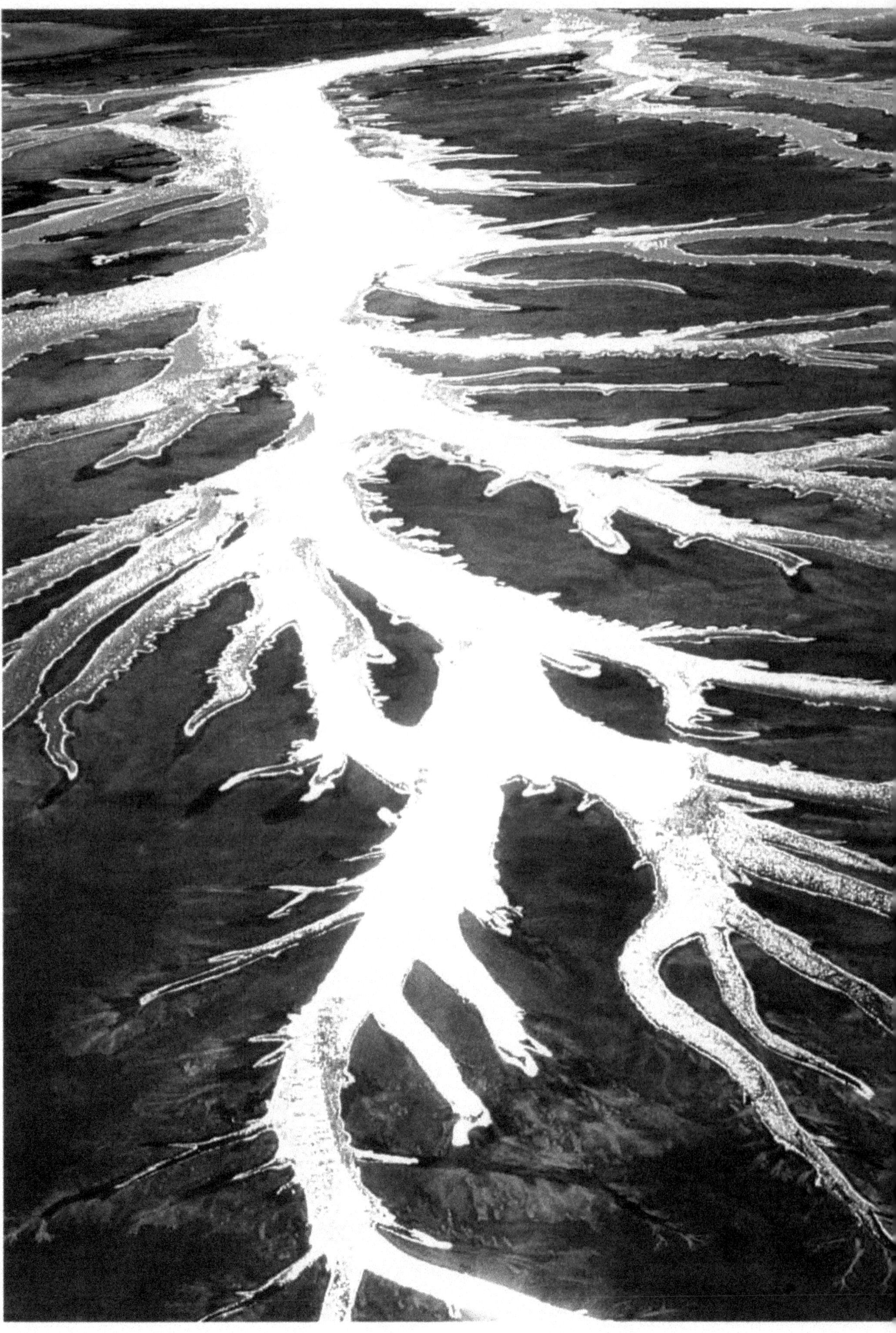

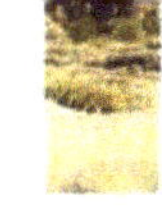

PROGRESS

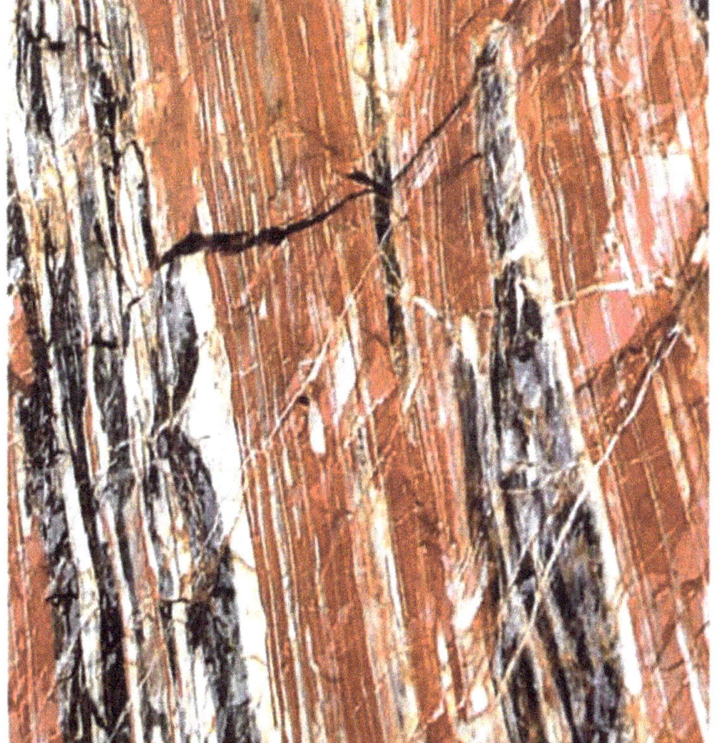

The land is a Pintubi painting
from the air,
all dots and circles.
The only straight lines
are raw slashes
of roads and fences,
railways and powerlines.

By contrast, nature's highways
are ribbons of trees,
coolibah, ghost gum, red gum,
that snake and twist and curve
around red and brown blotches,
on mosaics of yellow and grey.

Perhaps God's idea
of getting somewhere
is more circular than ours,
leisurely, and less direct,
in tune with the contours
of the land,
and at one with it.

PODLICH

RIGHT: *Jasper, Marble Bar, WA*
LEFT: *Tidal erosion patterns, from the air, Derby, WA*

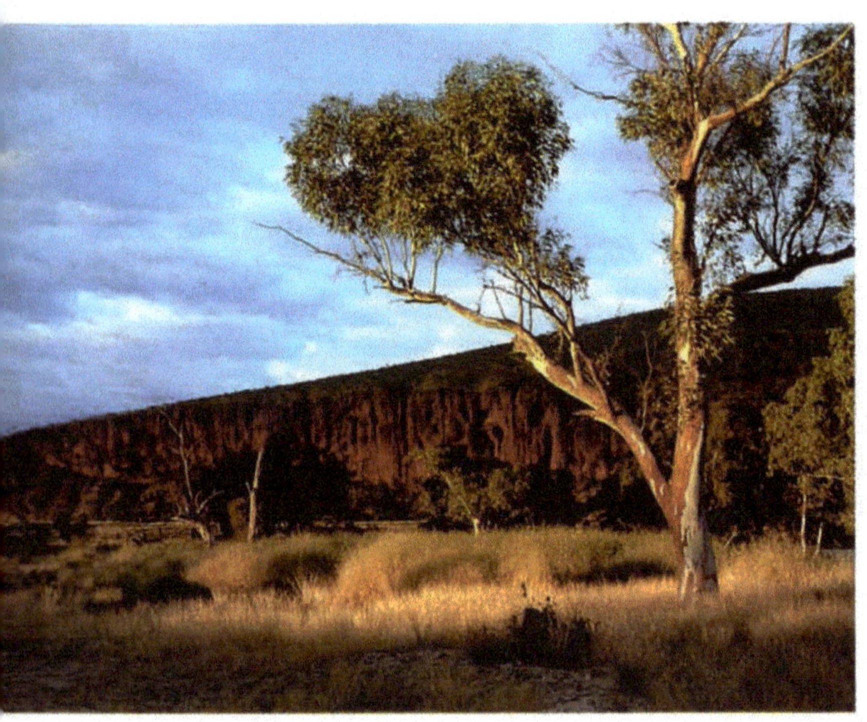

MORNING AFTER

How awesome is this place!
How strange the aura here!
The very cliff tops blaze
with a flood of pastel fire,
with a Presence unsuspected
when I blithely spread
my sleeping-bag
in last night's dark. *

A moving flush
creeps down to touch
the face of cliffs,
the tips of ghost gums,
the crowns of hillside spinifex,
and the alert ears
of a single wallaroo.
The very air is tinged
with roseate breath.

Who's there?
I mean to say,
but mouth instead
a quiet prayer,
like a child's tiny knock,
at the smallest crack
in a great king's door.

* *Derived from Genesis* 28:16,17

PODLICH

LEFT: *Glen Helen, west of Alice Springs, NT*
RIGHT: *Manning Gorge, Kimberley, WA*

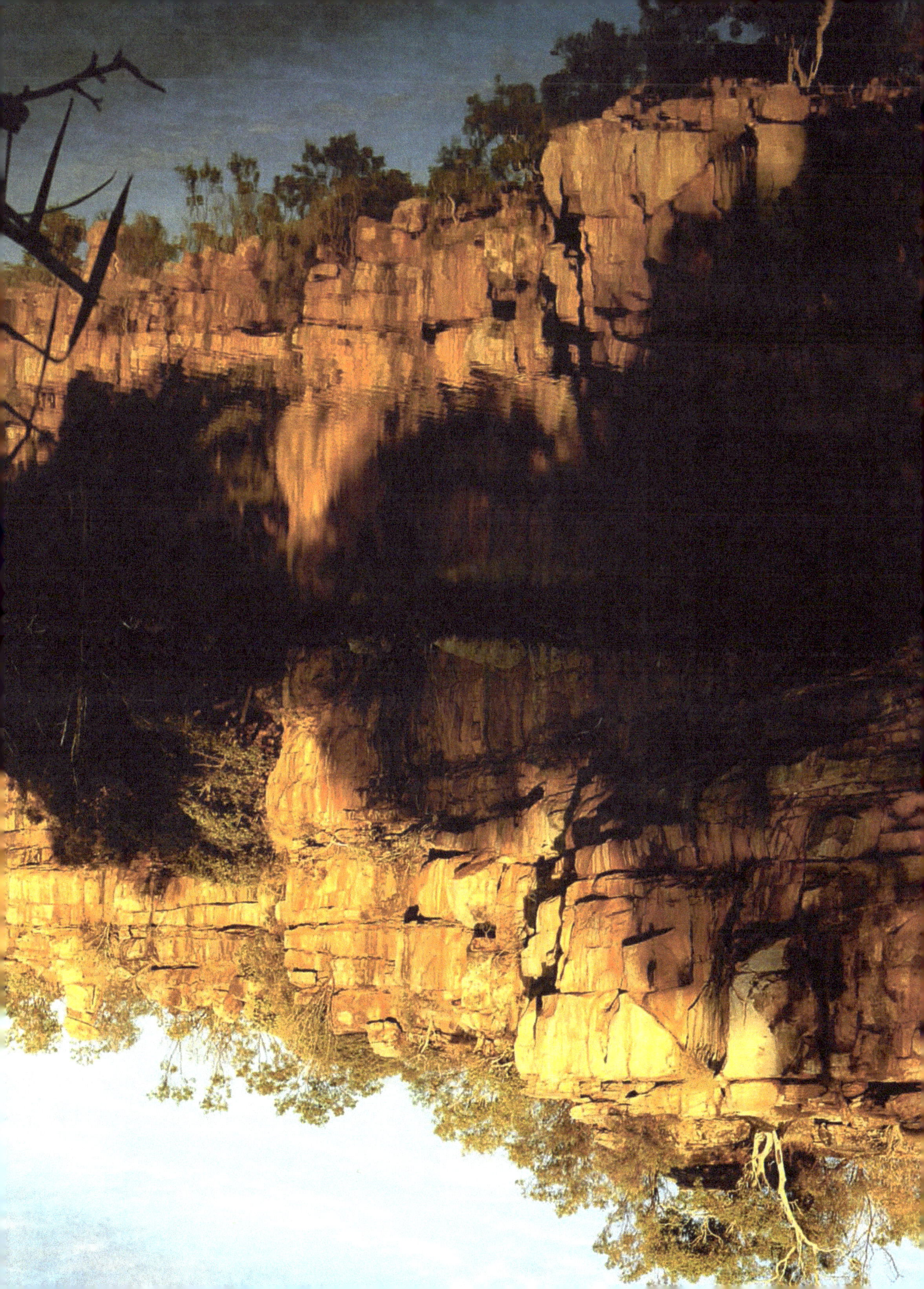

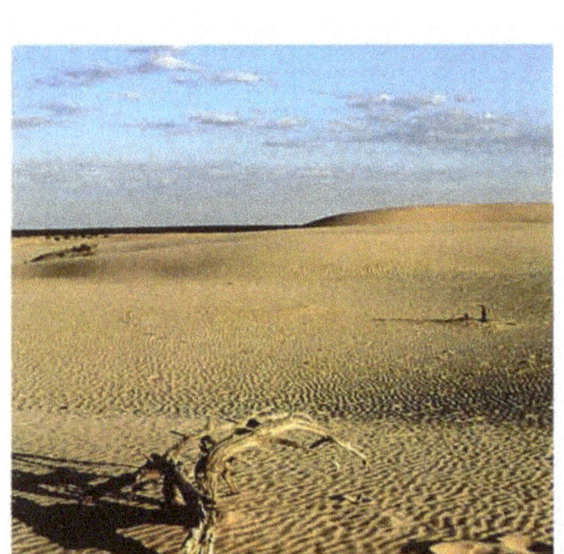

TAKE OFF YOUR SHOES

Like God, this land.
We don't meet the desert;
  it confronts us,
  uncompromising
  in rock and sand.

Arid plains, bare hills,
are not defined by our names;
  they won't submit,
  cannot be shaped
  by human wills.

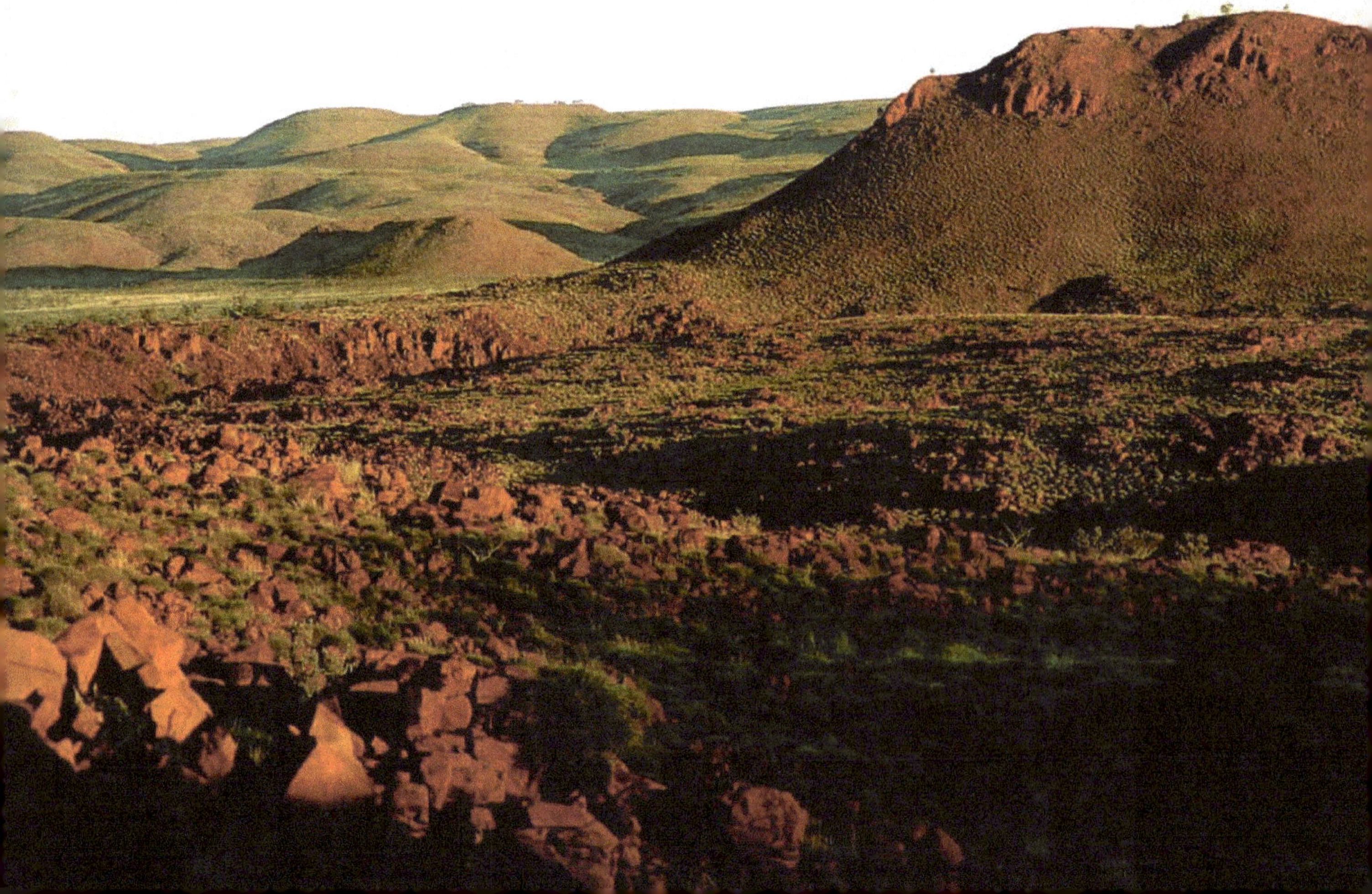

Fools err herein.
They work to overpower;
  to control,
  to mould and exploit
  this untameable thing.

Bare feet are better;
the humility to learn
  the desert's ways,
  its secret life,
  its hidden water.

The Lord of the prophets is near:
'I am who I am'.
  Moses and Elijah,
  the Baptist, and Jesus
  grew tall here.

PREWER

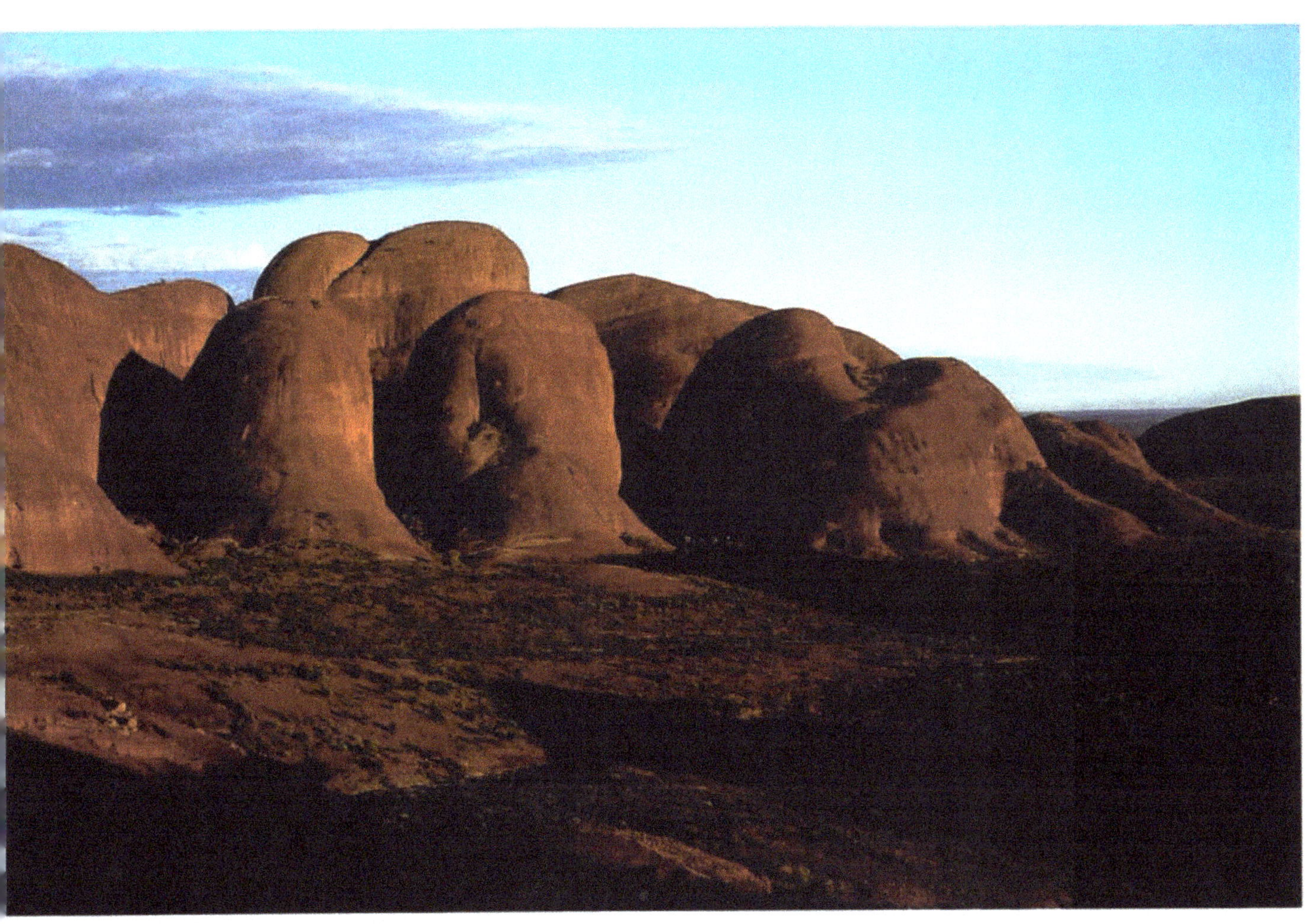

UPPER LEFT: *Sand-dune, south-west NSW*
LOWER LEFT: *Chichester Range, Pilbara, WA*
RIGHT: *The Olgas, Uluru National Park, NT*
OVERLEAF: *Sunrise, Yellow Water Lagoon, Kakadu National Park, NT*

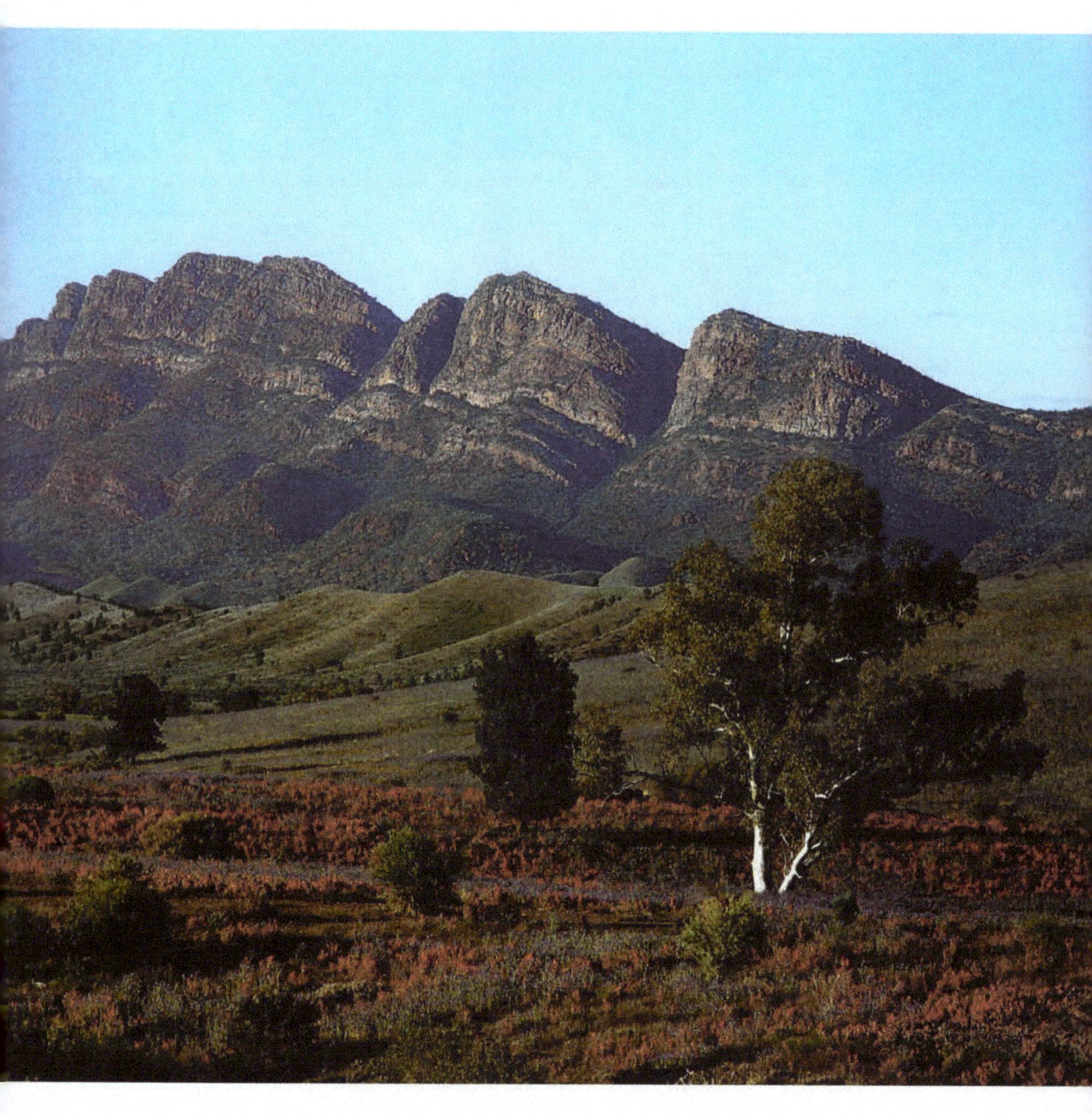

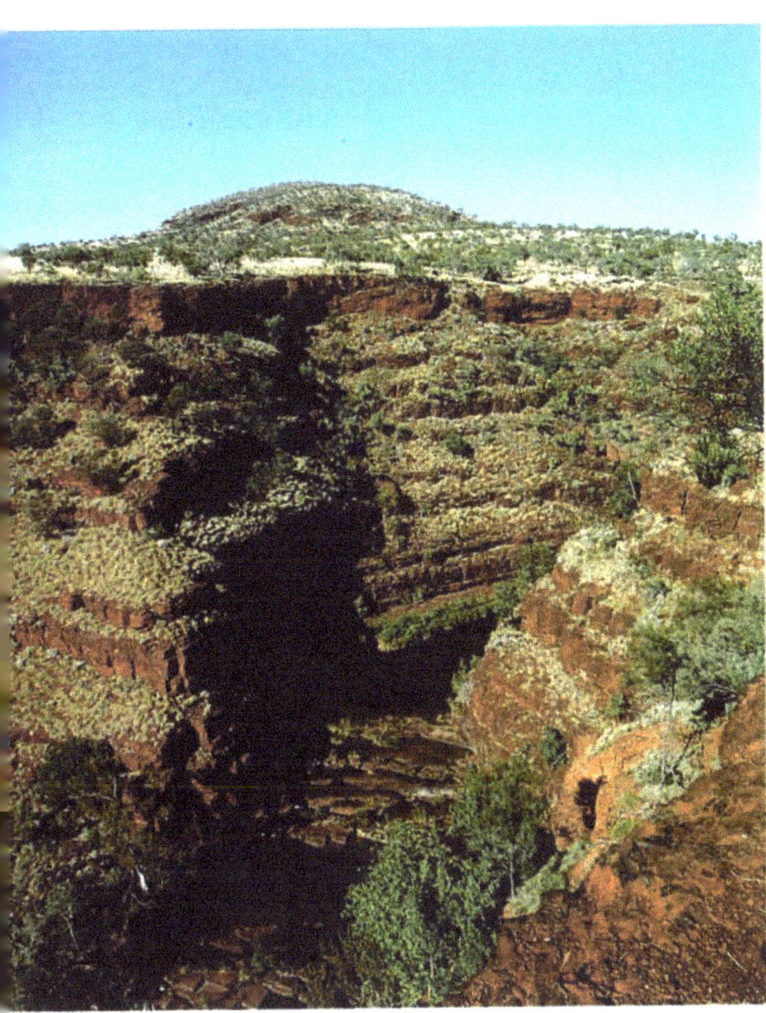

LEFT: *Elder Range, Flinders Ranges, SA*
RIGHT: *Dales Gorge, Hammersley Range National Park, WA*

THE NORTHERN FLINDERS

Great Creator,
Friend of the earth,
some have called these ranges
a tortured landscape,
ruptured and convoluted
as if by some alien power.

It is not so.
There is nothing tortured here;
just your ongoing creation
still showing the effects
of one of its more spectacular moments.

This rugged scene is natural;
as natural as native pines on slopes,
rock pools in shaded ravines,
the yellow-footed wallaby at dawn,
or the moonlight over the peaks.

Here is a site for worship:
you overawe us with the work
of your little finger;
you embrace our noisy lives
with your silences;
you startle us
with your stark beauty;
you quieten the fever of our worrying
with your immense patience.

This is a good place
to discard wristwatches
and take no thought
for tomorrow.

PREWER

RIVER RED GUMS

'The river reds drink prodigiously; their deep roots pump a tonne of water a day, and there is more plant tissue spread out below ground than above it.' *

Unseen God,
from whose hidden waters
I must drink deeply
if I am to flourish
like these magnificent trees,
majestic in beauty,
heavy with honey,
blossoming with screeching birds:

Sweep away the shallowness
of my purely surface concerns,
and grant me depth
which extends all the way
to life drawn from you.

So let me be,
like these trees,
'planted by streams of water',
a sign of hidden resources.

**John Vandenbeld,*
from Nature of Australia (Collins)

PODLICH

RIGHT: *Ormiston Gorge, MacDonnell Ranges, NT*

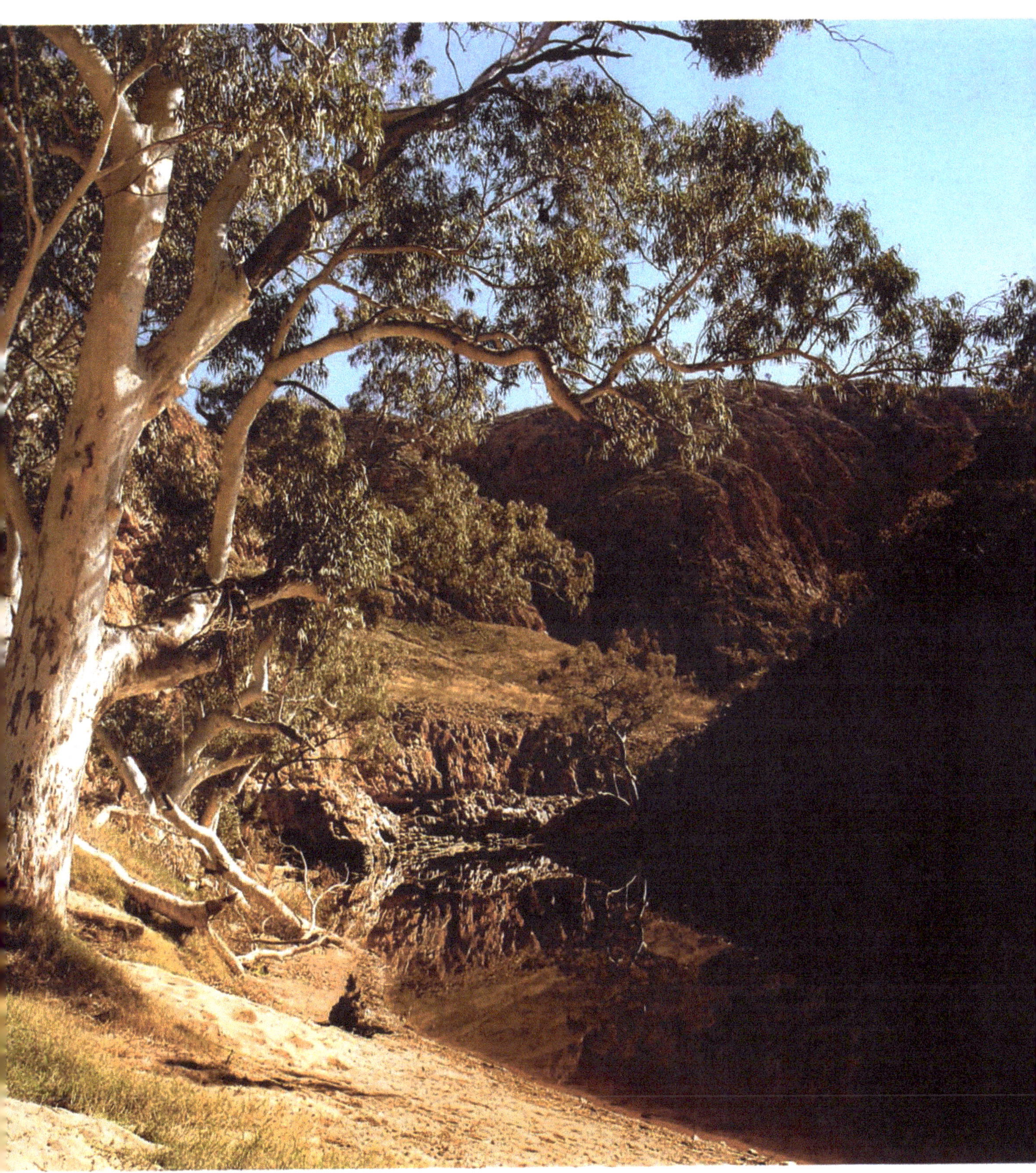

THE WILDERNESS YEARS

Against my inclinations,
against my will and prayer,
you took me to the desert
and left me wandering there.

You shunned my many protests,
ignored my plaintive pleading,
you left me in the desert
and denied me any leading.

Sometimes for lonely weeks,
sometimes for months or years,
you made me learn the desert
and taught me through my tears.

I longed for sweet communion,
I begged for easier days,
but you gave me only leanness
and forced me to learn new ways

It seemed my life was wasted,
faith nothing but a gloss,
but I found you in the desert
still carrying that cross.

PREWEF

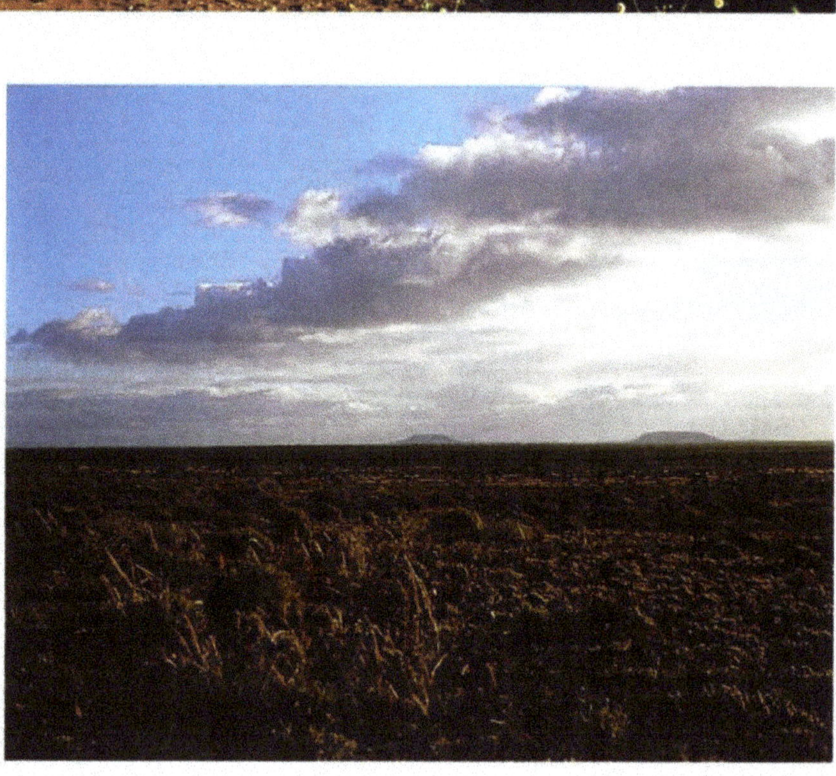

UPPER LEFT: *Sandhills near Cordillo Downs, SA*
LOWER LEFT: *Near Pimba, SA*
UPPER RIGHT: *The dry bed of the Hugh River, NT*
LOWER RIGHT: *Sunrise over Malu, the Olgas, Uluru National Park, NT*

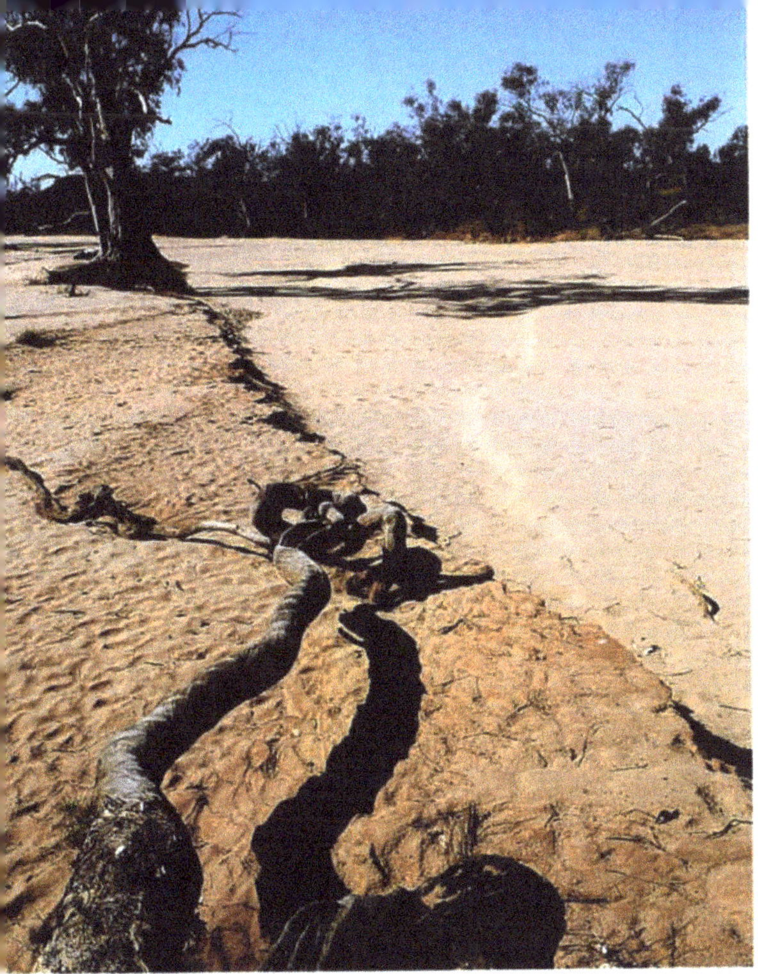

DESERT PARADOX

Here in the desert country,
   where shade is rare
   and even spinifex sporadic,
I experience exquisitely
   the absence of God.

Then I begin to know,
   in every dry creek bed
   and across sand ridges,
that paradoxical Presence
   whose loneliness cried aloud
   on a desolate Friday
when the world turned black.

PREWER

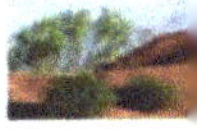

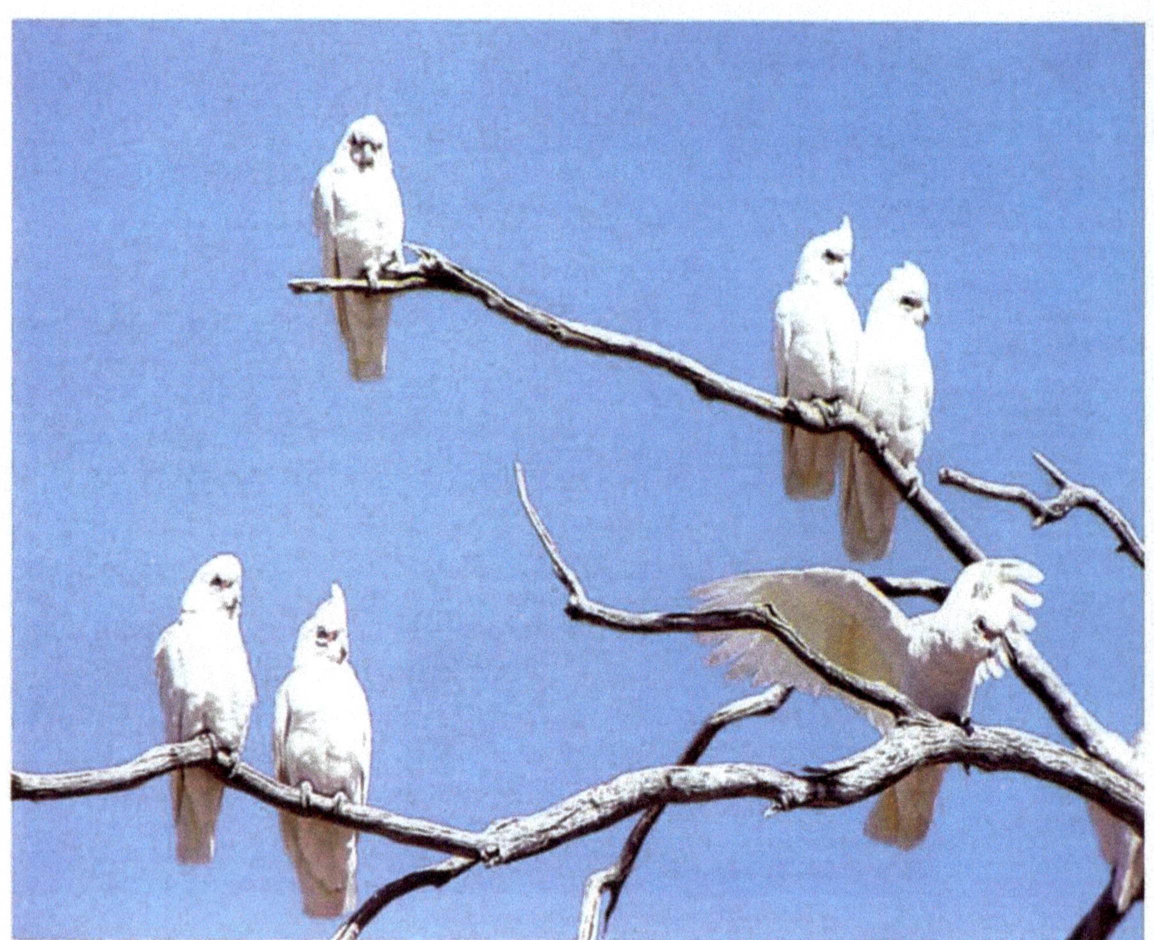

BIRDS

Budgies?
Just God's way
for the mulga to change
its suit of conservative grey
to extrovert green!

Galahs?
Now he's filling
the endless blue
with wheeling storm-clouds,
pink and grey!

Corellas?
Look! He's left his white washing
flapping
on that gidgee tree!

PODLICH

LEFT: *Corellas, near Birdsville*
RIGHT: ***Nyiknyik Class Baralmana,*** MORRIS

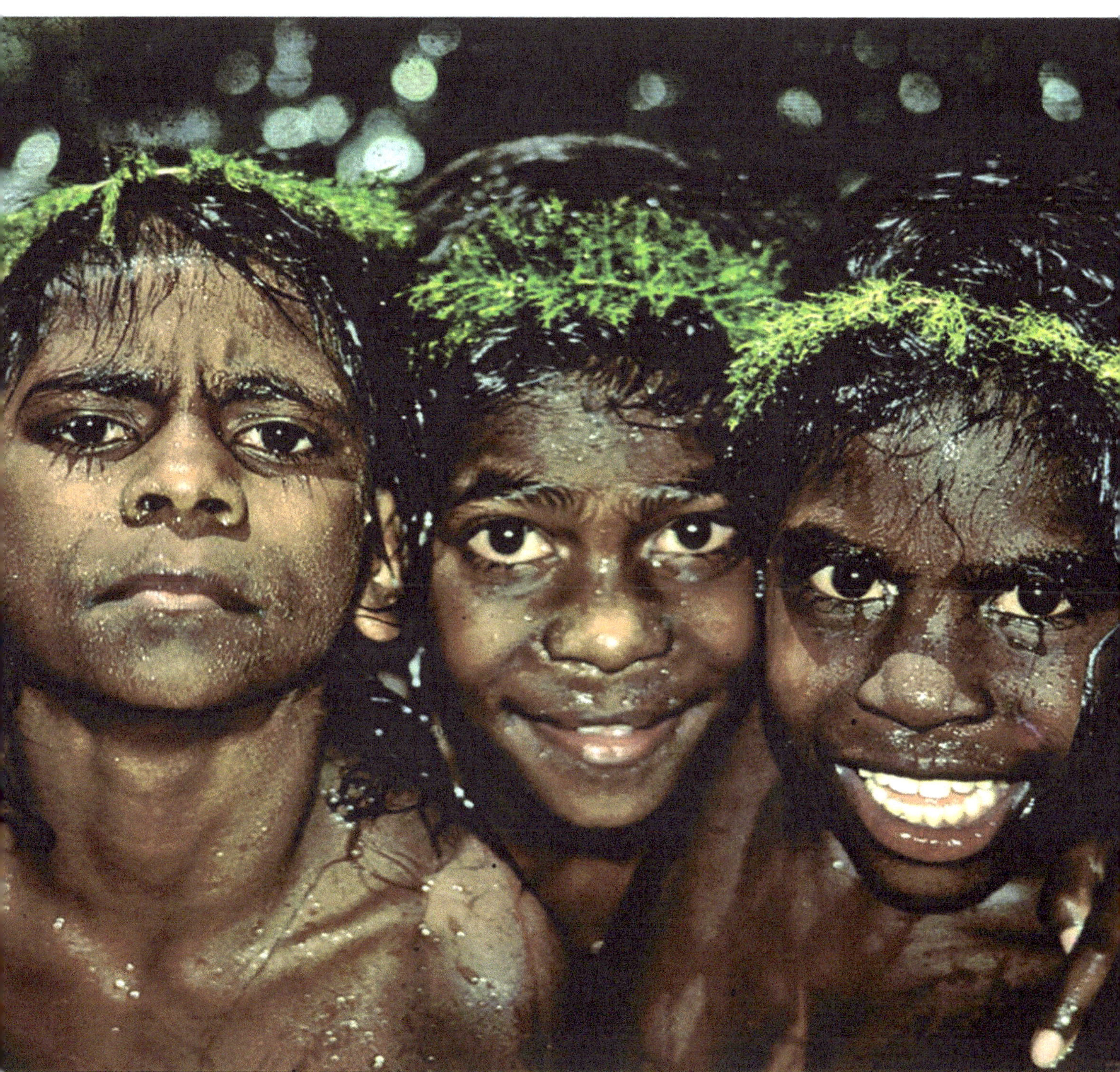

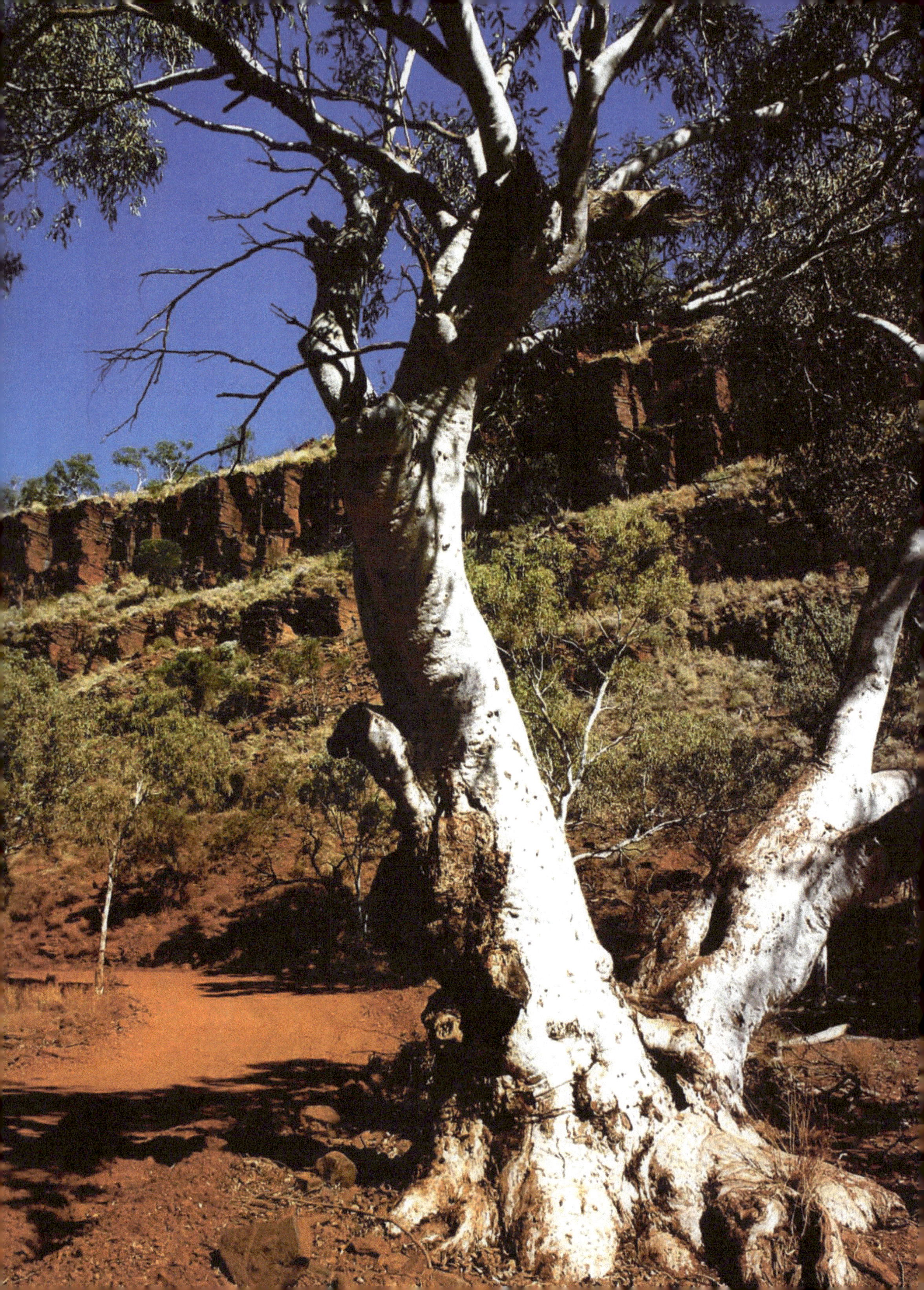

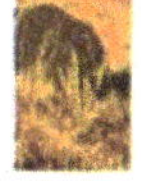

GHOST GUM ON CLIFF FACE

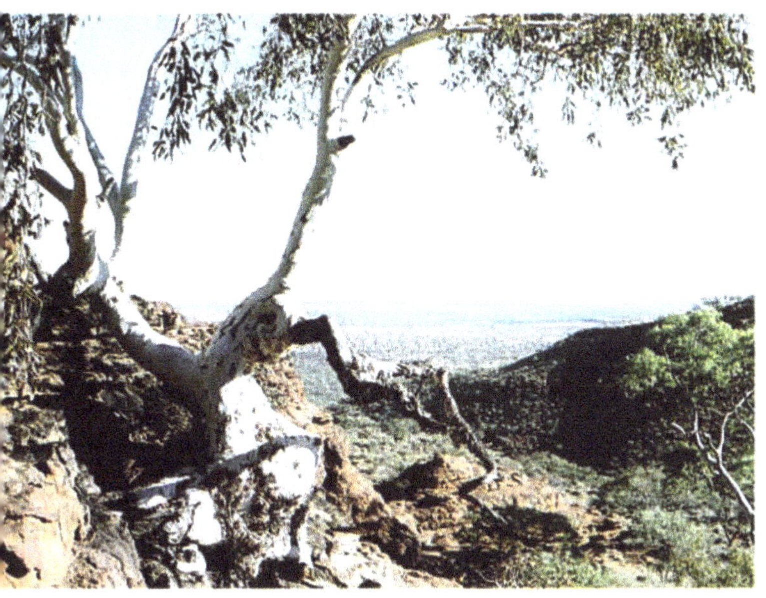

Look at the magnificence
of this struggling tree,
carved by adversity!
How tenaciously
she wraps arthritic knuckles
round the hard dry stone
where she flourishes
so beautifully!

God of suffering,
the mother of endurance;
of endurance;
the mother of character;
of character,
the mother of hope;
of hope,
the mother of beauty:

Grace me, in suffering,
with the artistry
of this faithful tree.

PODLICH

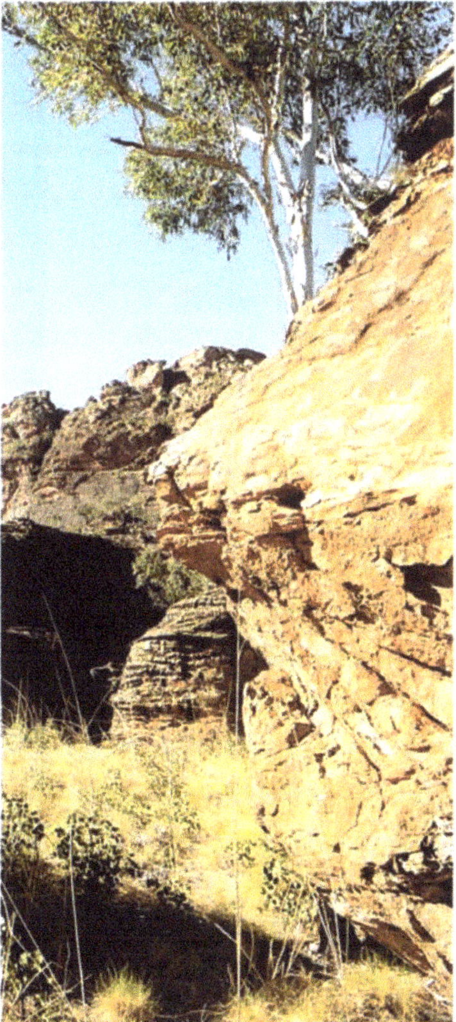

LEFT: *Yampire Gorge, Hamersley Range National Park, WA*
UPPER RIGHT: *Ghost gum* (Eucalyptus papuana), *Kings Canyon, NT* PODLICH
LOWER RIGHT: *Keep River National Park, NT*

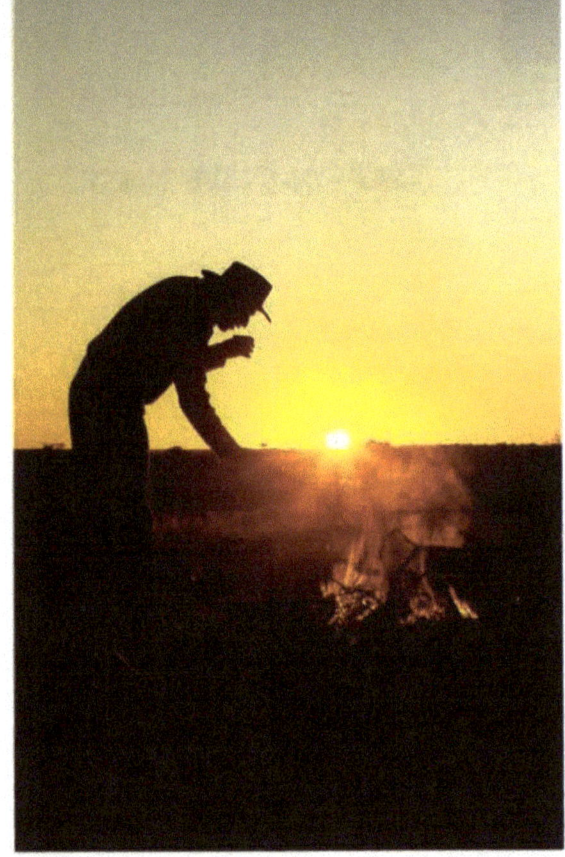

INLAND AT NIGHT

On my back
in the swag
no wind
cool night
stars almost touchable.
Elemental quietness
so quiet I can hear
my own thoughts
and know them
for what they are.
Last vestiges
of urban anxieties
like python skin
peel away.
Thoughts pause
raw contemplation
wells up
wordless
yet full of wisdom
and iridescent
as the sky.
It is good
to have camped
near Bethel.

PREWER

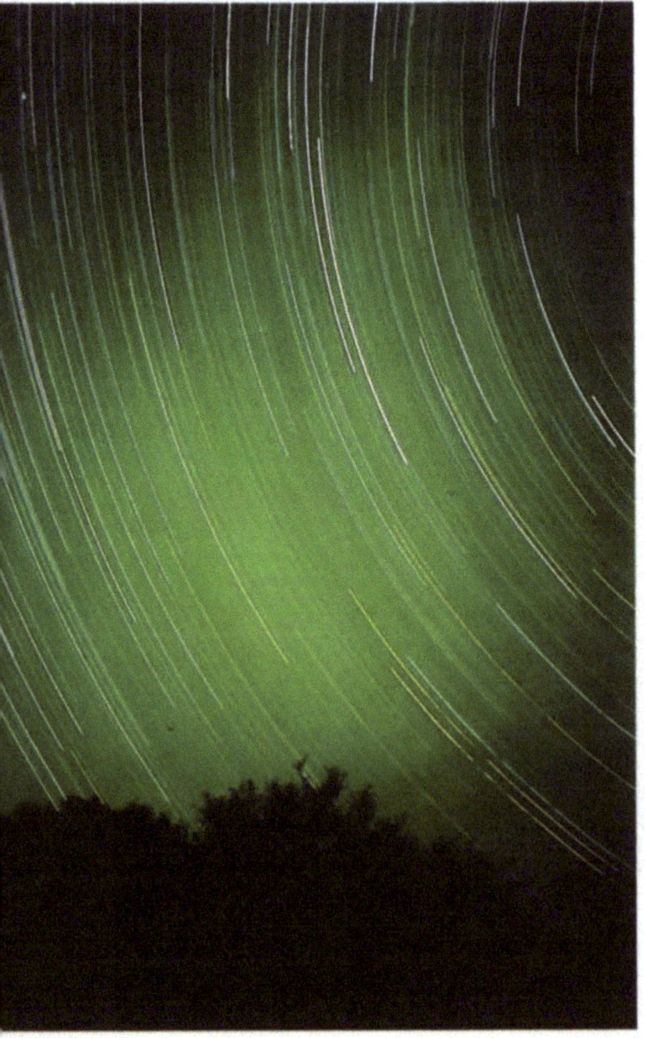

UPPER LEFT: *Camping*
LOWER LEFT: *Stars in a night sky, outback NSW*
RIGHT: *Moonrise over the Olgas, Uluru National Park, NT*
OVERLEAF: *The Pinnacles Desert, Nambung National Park, WA*

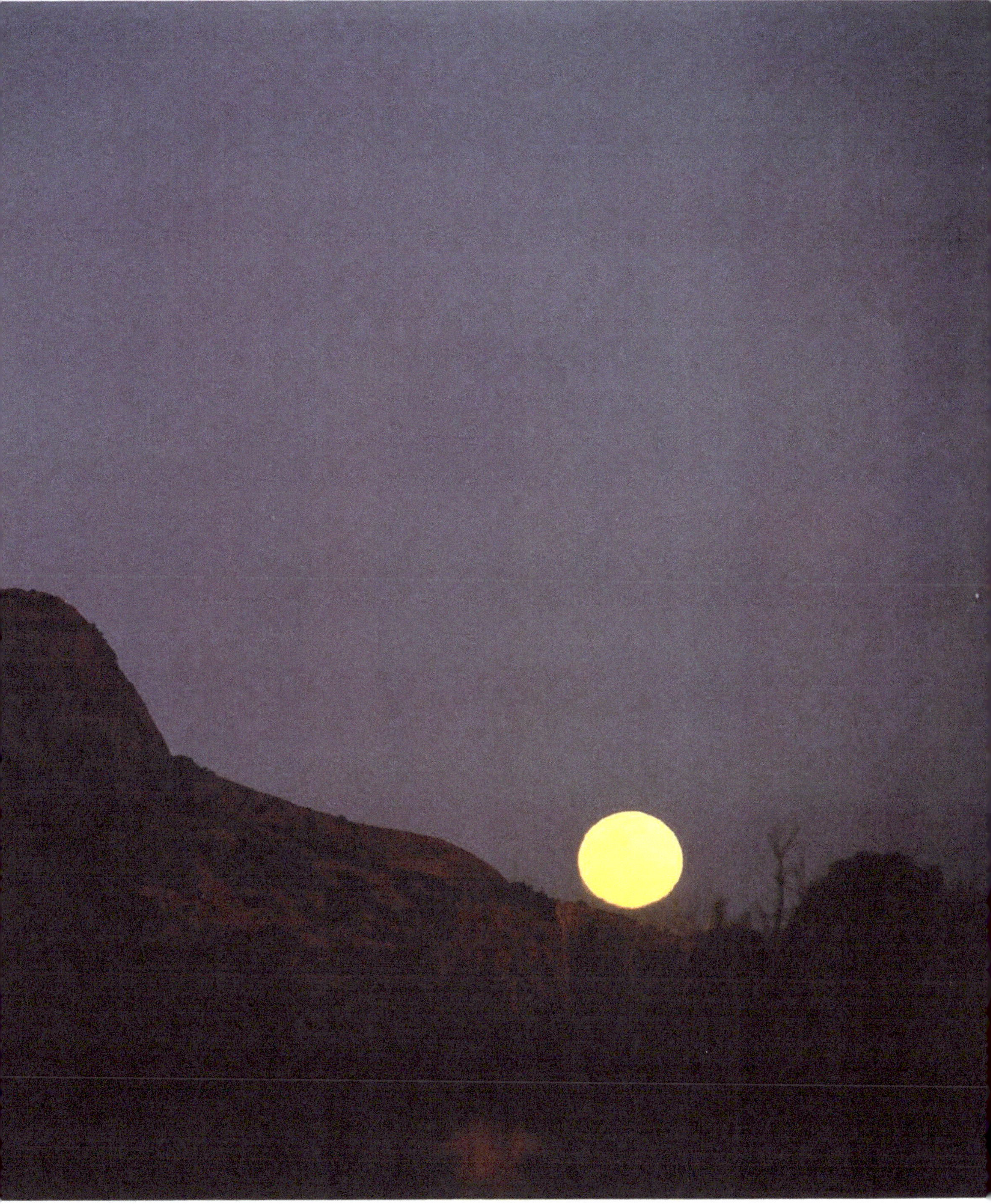

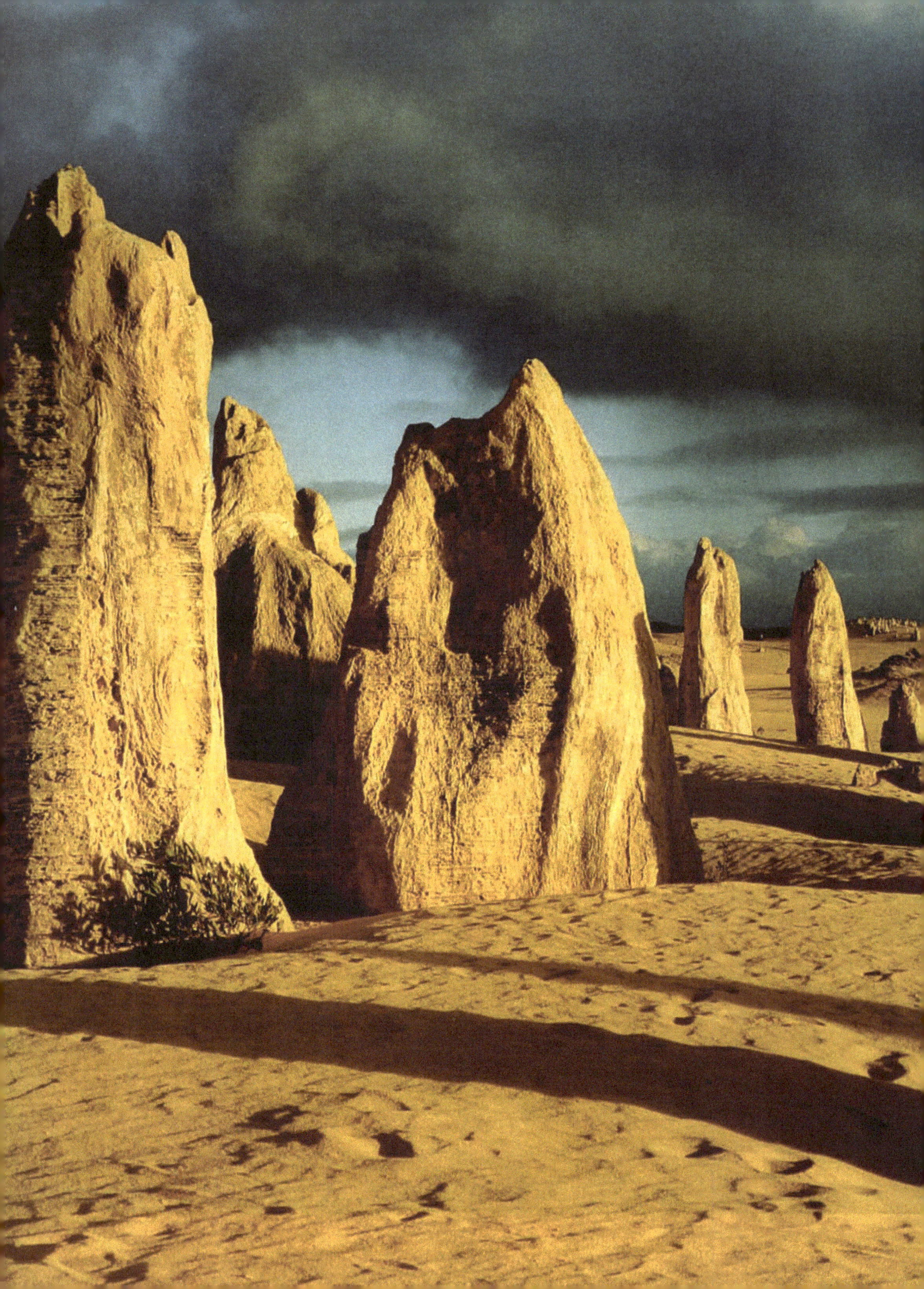

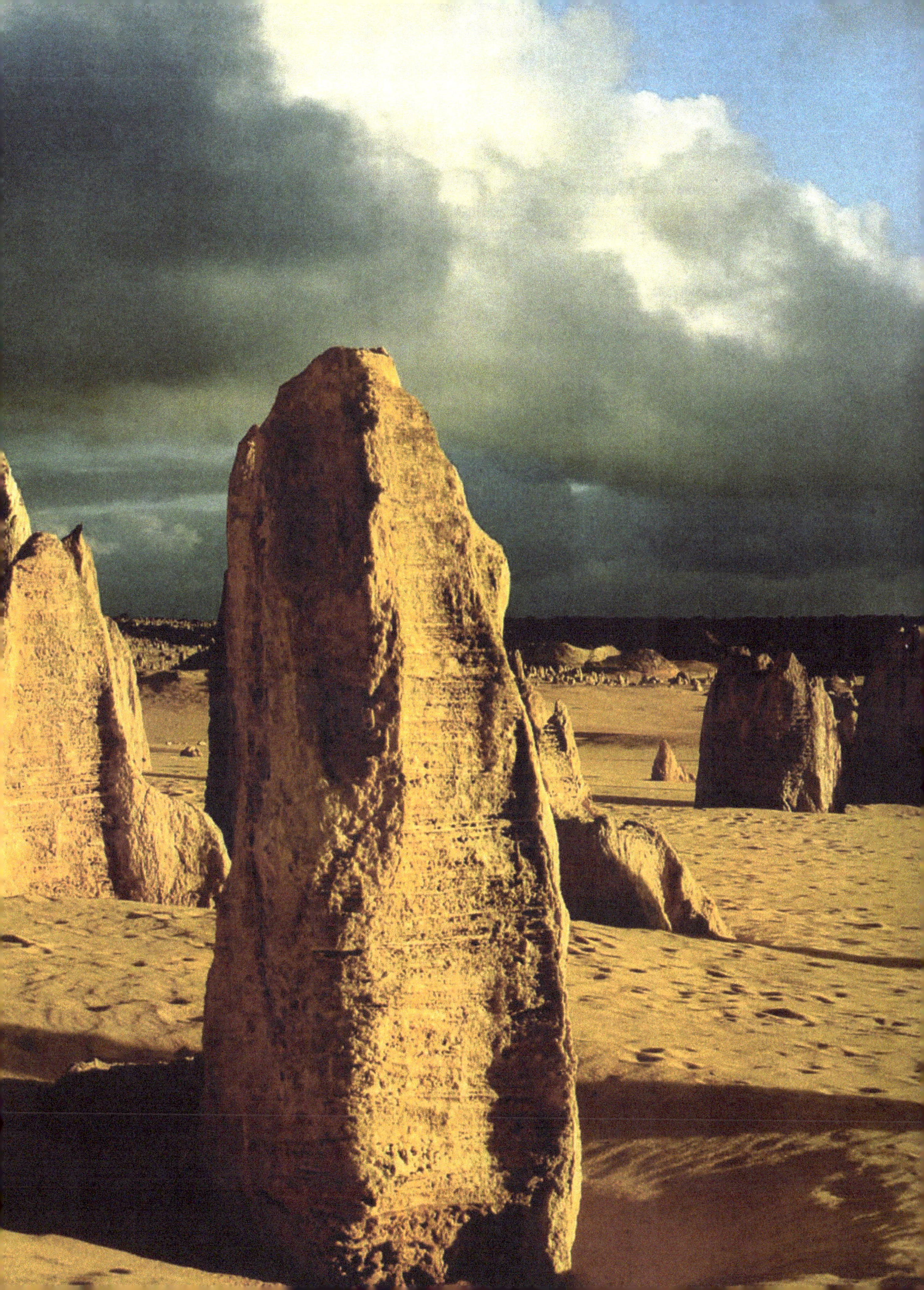

SILENCE

Not far from the Musgrave Ranges,
we stand on an outcrop of red rock,
and view all points of the compass.

It is all so quiet today
that one can hear the soft whispers
of a gentle breeze on face and hair.

How precious is this moment,
unprocurable back home;
yet here it is not rare.

PREWER

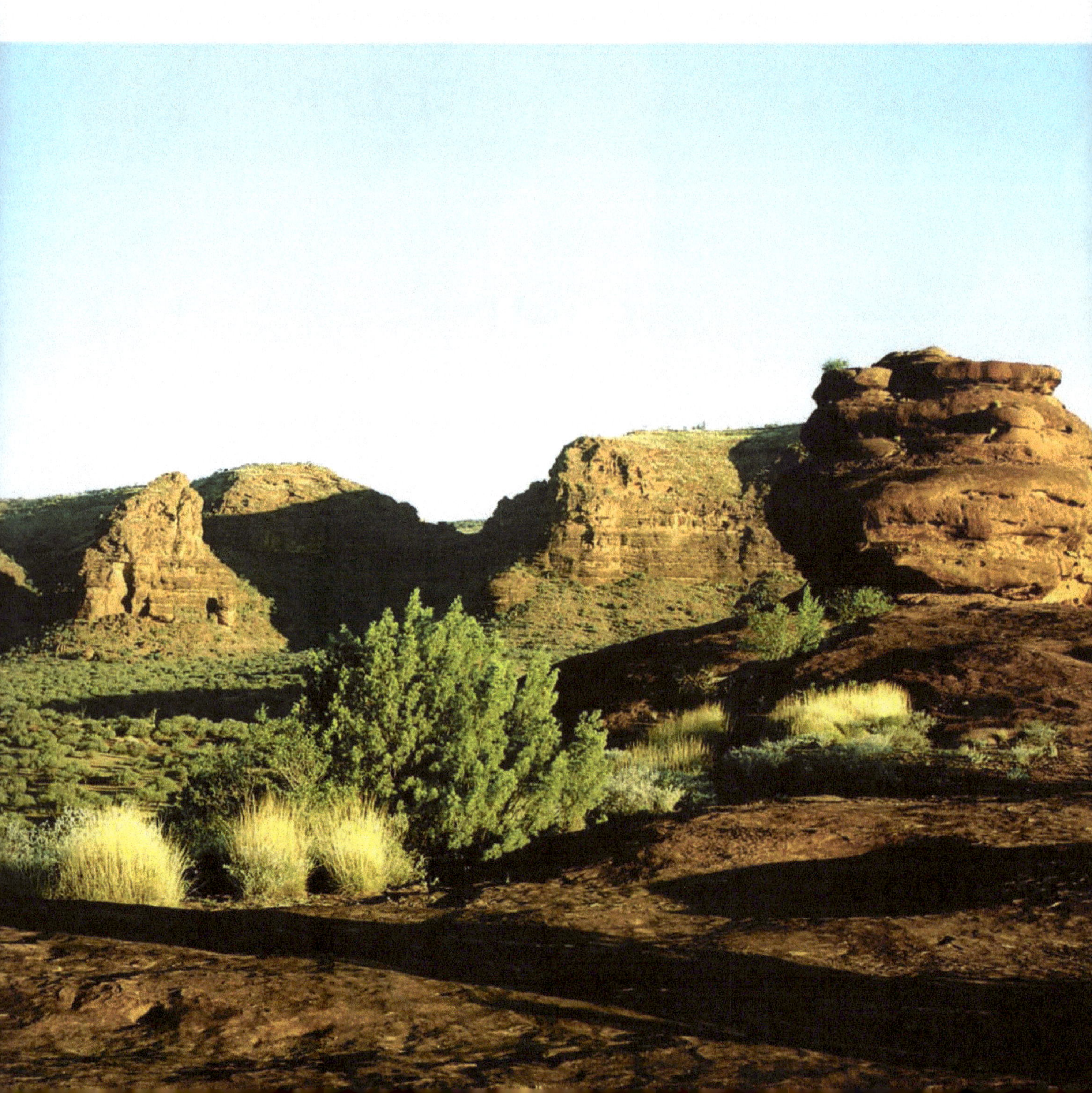

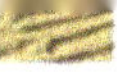

DESERT FLOWER

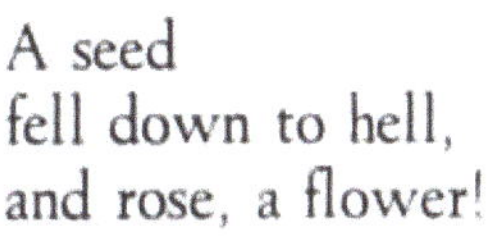

A seed
fell down to hell,
and rose, a flower!

Look! Here she comes,
walking Christlike
on that burning sea
of stones!

PODLICH

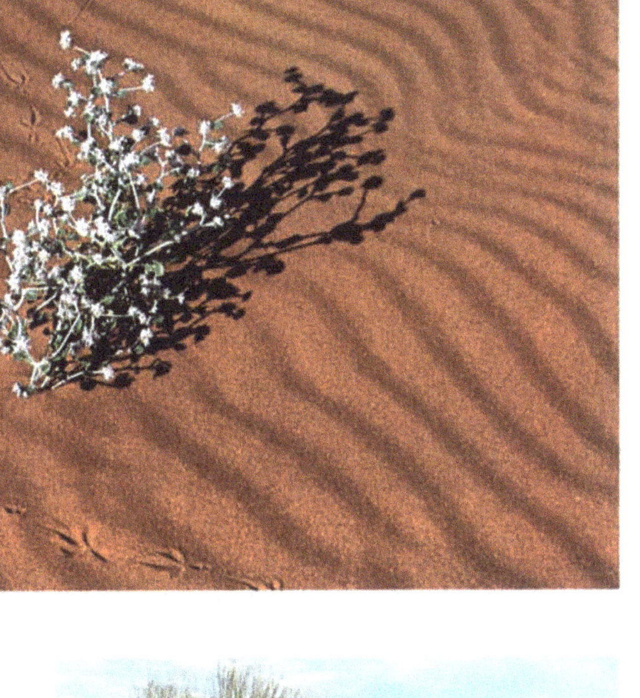

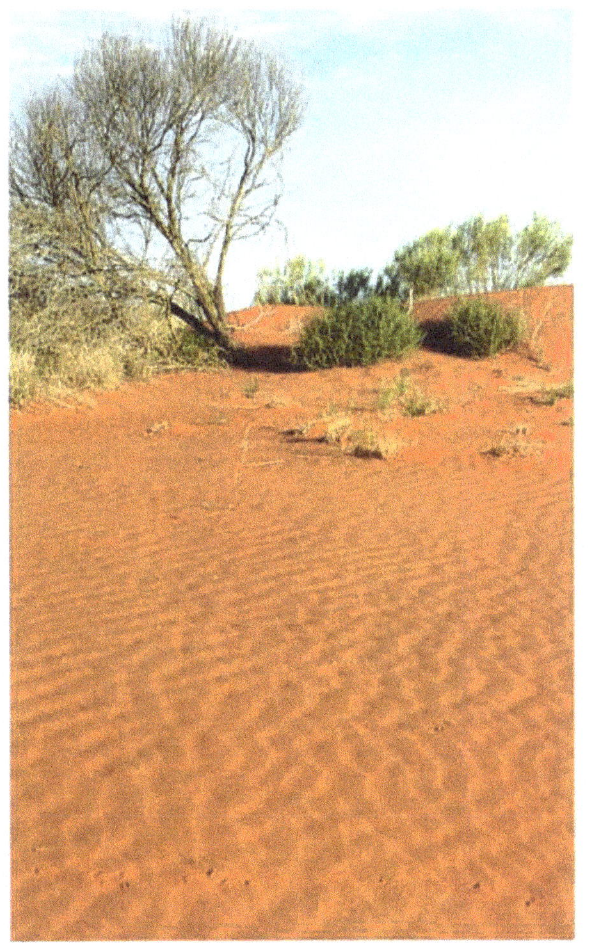

LEFT: *The Amphitheatre, Finke Gorge National Park, NT*
UPPER RIGHT: *Footprints and flowers, Birdsville Track* PODLICH
LOWER RIGHT: *Sand-dune, south of Alice Springs*

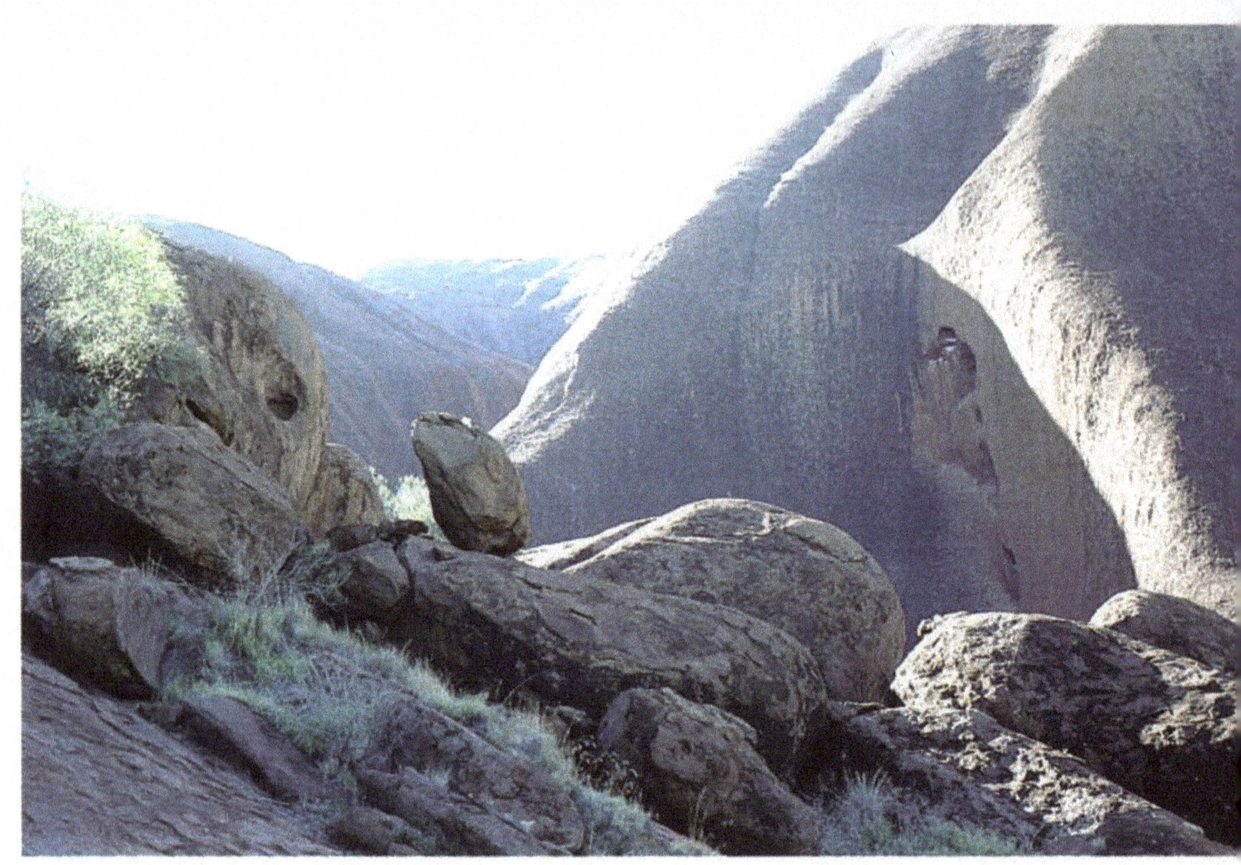

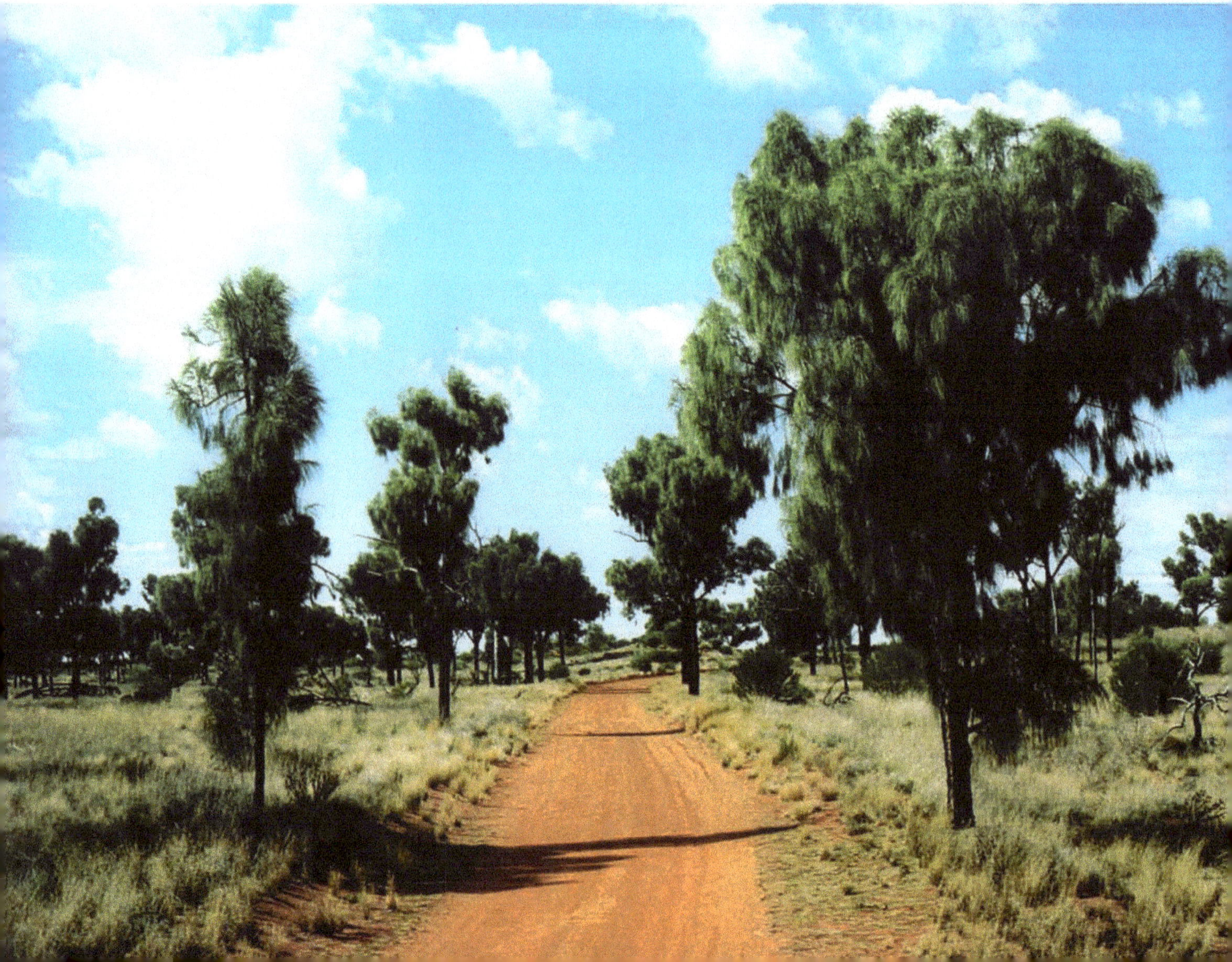

HEAT AND SAND

Fierce country,
strange hard beauty,
most of it not for postcards.
Like its Creator,
not to be taken lightly.

Yet some wise ones,
who seek to live with it
instead of against it,
with the desert creatures
find a homing place
and new prayers.

Sand on a hot wind,
sore eyes and dry tongues,
yet the desert oaks
make parables,
and from deep down
slake their thirst.

It's not for those
who itch to handle and control
even the thing they worship.
The Creator of all this
will be what he will be,
fierce untameable love,
sharing the crosses.

PREWER

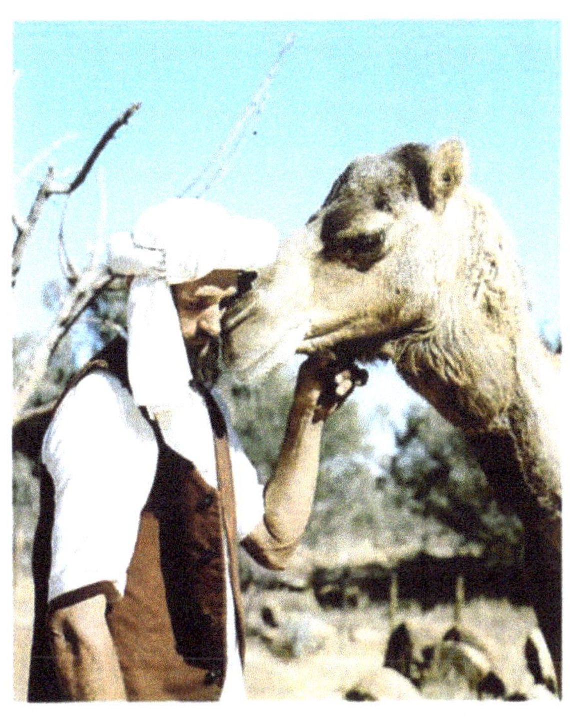

UPPER LEFT: *Ayers Rock, Uluru National Park, NT*
LOWER LEFT: *Desert oaks near Kings Canyon, NT*
RIGHT: *Man and his camel, Alice Springs, NT*

DRY WATERCOURSE

Don't judge the church
by its surface flow,
when God doesn't seem
to be there;
judge it by the love
its people show.

Under the dry watercourse,
a rich river, far below,
is tapped by flourishing trees.

Searching roots
will always find
the water of life.

The water itself
will draw them.

PODLICH

LEFT: *Glen Helen, west of Alice Springs, NT*
UPPER RIGHT: *Cooper Creek, near the Birdsville Track, SA*
LOWER RIGHT: *Palmer River, NT*

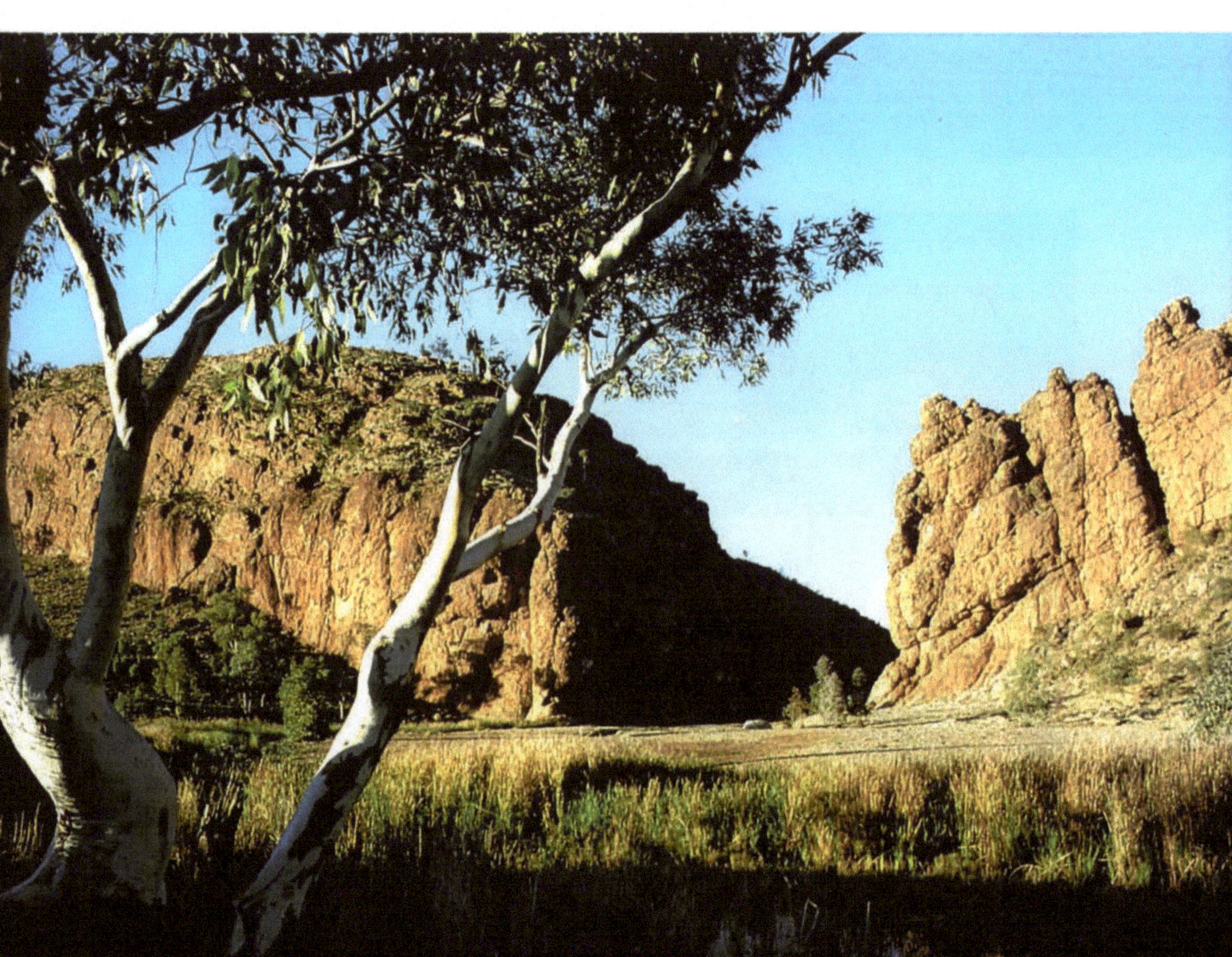

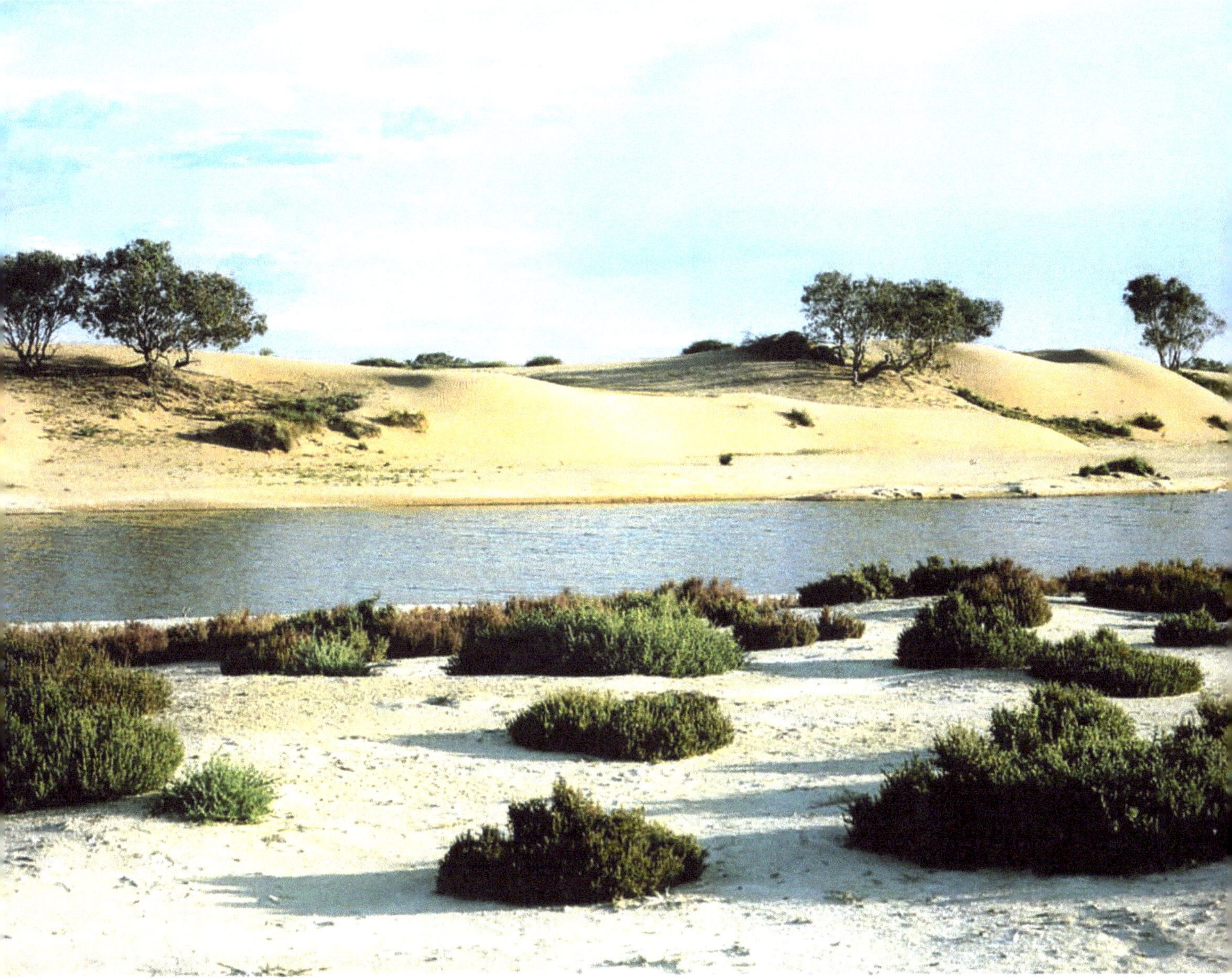

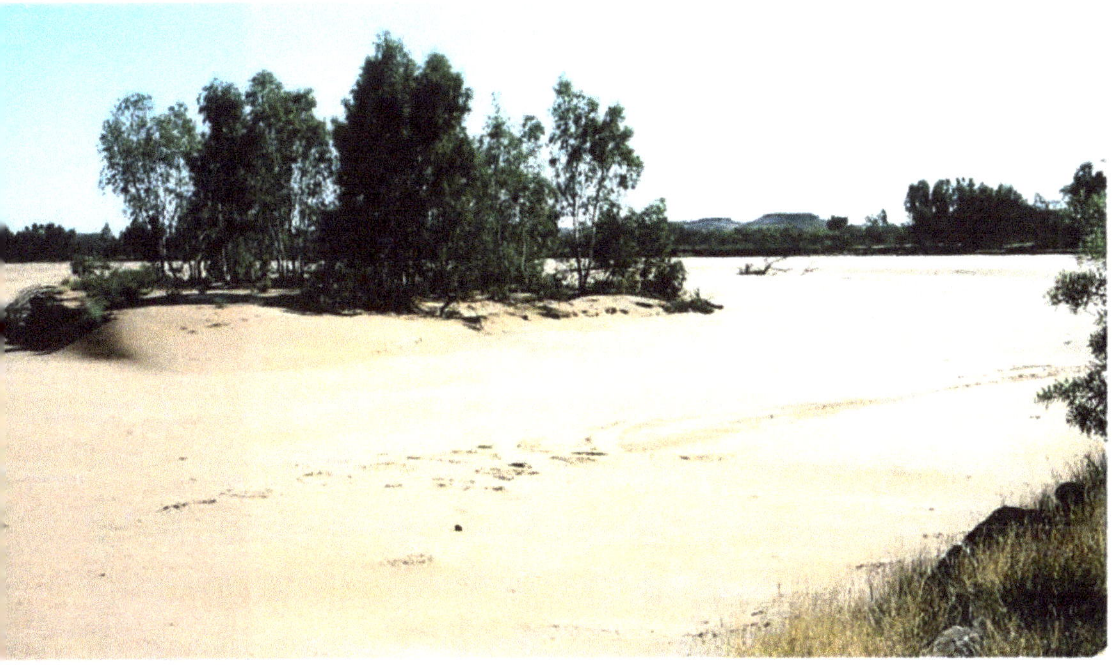

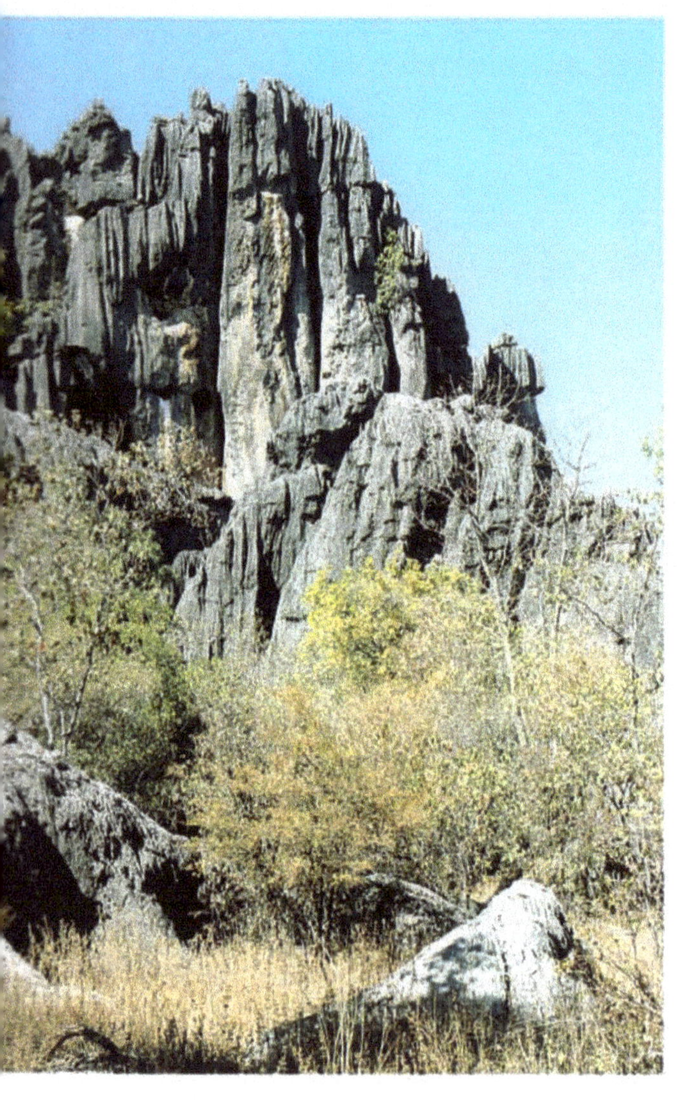

ERODED HILLS

Time
has eroded us
to remnants and relics
of distant, different days,
just as it has with you.

Wild dry winds at evening
sandblast our features now;
in the icy grip of midnight
our fault lines give way;
seared by the heat of noon,
we crumble and fall away.

But for all that,
there is beauty yet.
We are still sculpted
by the kinder hand of God,
and in his softer light
we still stand —
magnificent!

PODLICH

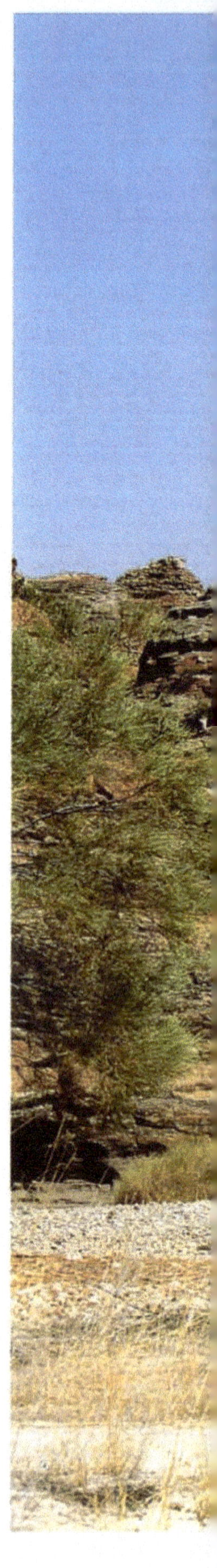

LEFT: *The Archways, Chillagoe National Park, Qld*
RIGHT: *Piccaninny Creek, in the Bungle Bungle Range National Park, WA*

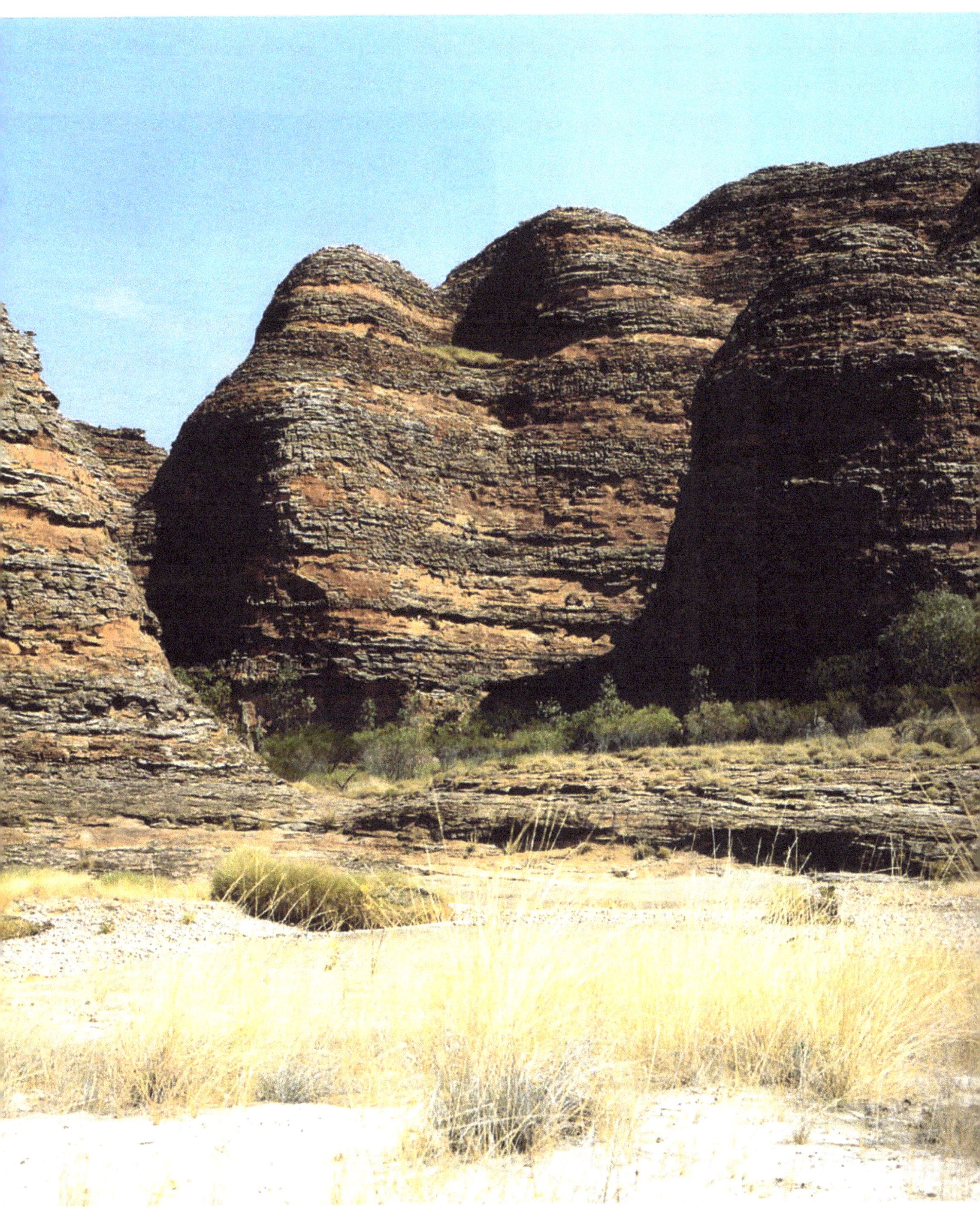

FOR TERMITES AND ANTS

'Go to the ant, you sluggard;
consider its ways and be wise!' *

Let us celebrate
the termite and the ant,
the uniqueness of their number,
and the part that God assigns them
in the life of the outback.

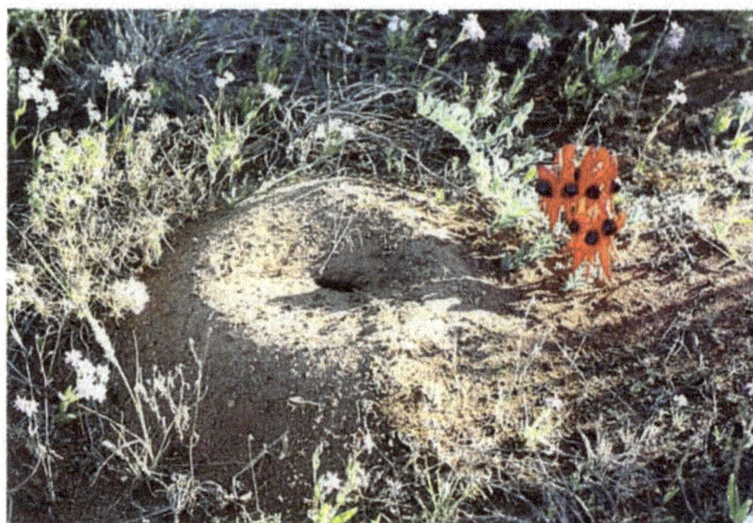

Let us celebrate
those sweepers and cleaners
of the bush — the termites,
by whose ceaseless cut and slice
the litter of the land
is born again as energy and fuel.
Let us marvel at their cities
that spear above the plain
like dog-tooth tombstone forests,
with air-conditioned bunkers
and communication maze.

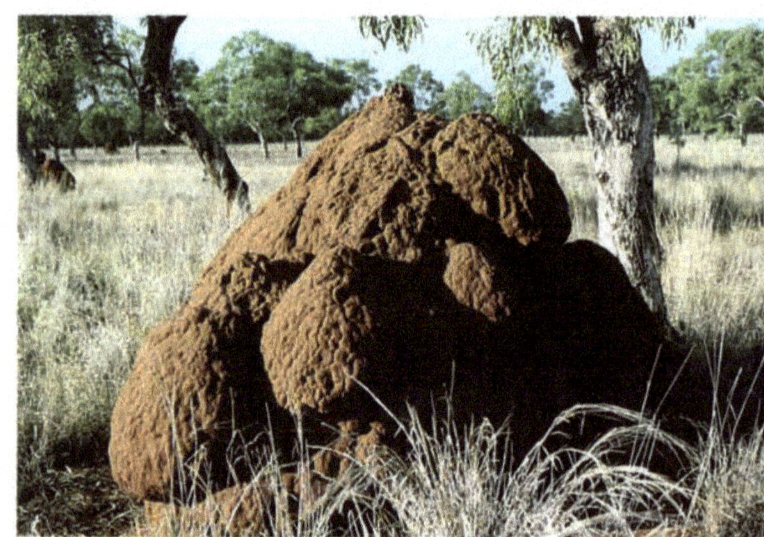

Let us celebrate
those sculptors and shapers
of the bush — the ants,
by whose gathering and tunnelling
the nutrients are cycled
through an aerated soil,
and seeds are spread.
Let us marvel at their nurture
of insects beneficial
to a host of plants,
and their relentless war
on predators.

Let us celebrate
the quiet usefulness and industry
of termites and ants,
cooperating in each colony
to the benefit of all,
and of their land.

* *Proverbs 6:6 NIV*

PODLICH

UPPER LEFT: *Ants' nest*
LOWER LEFT: *Termite mound, Kimberley, WA*
RIGHT: *Giant termite mound, near Pine Creek, NT*
OVERLEAF: *Ayers Rock and the Olgas, Uluru National Park, NT*

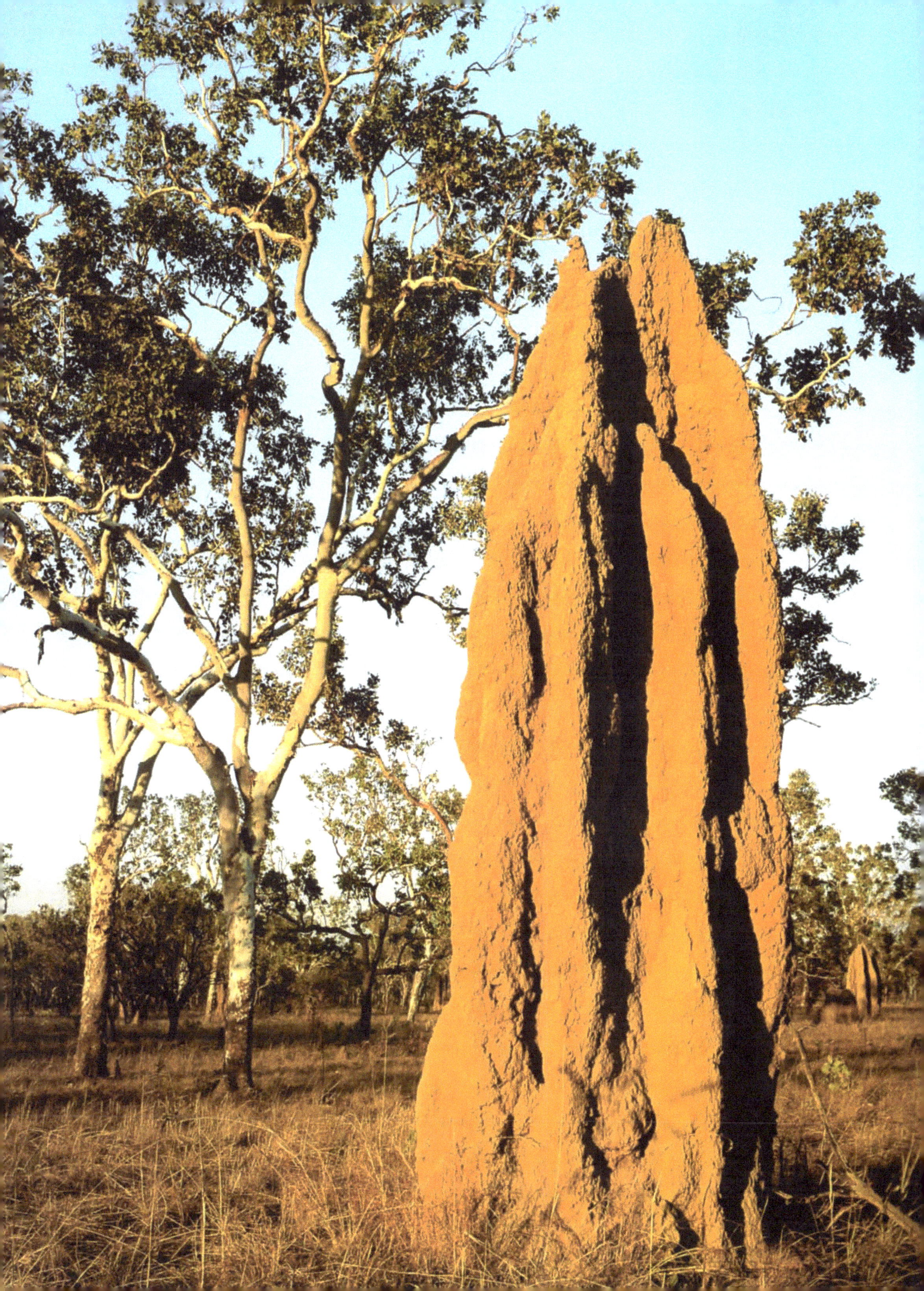

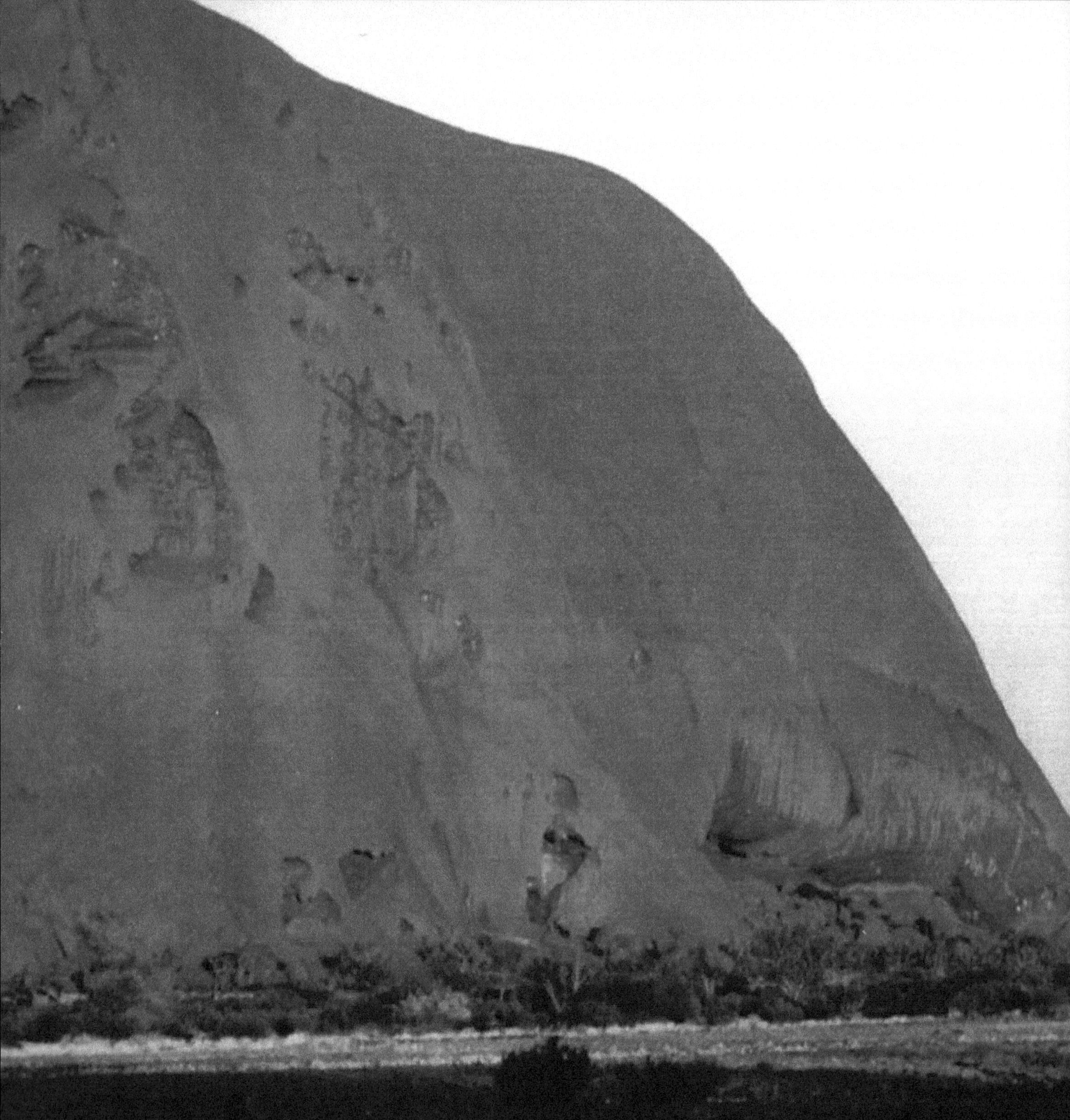

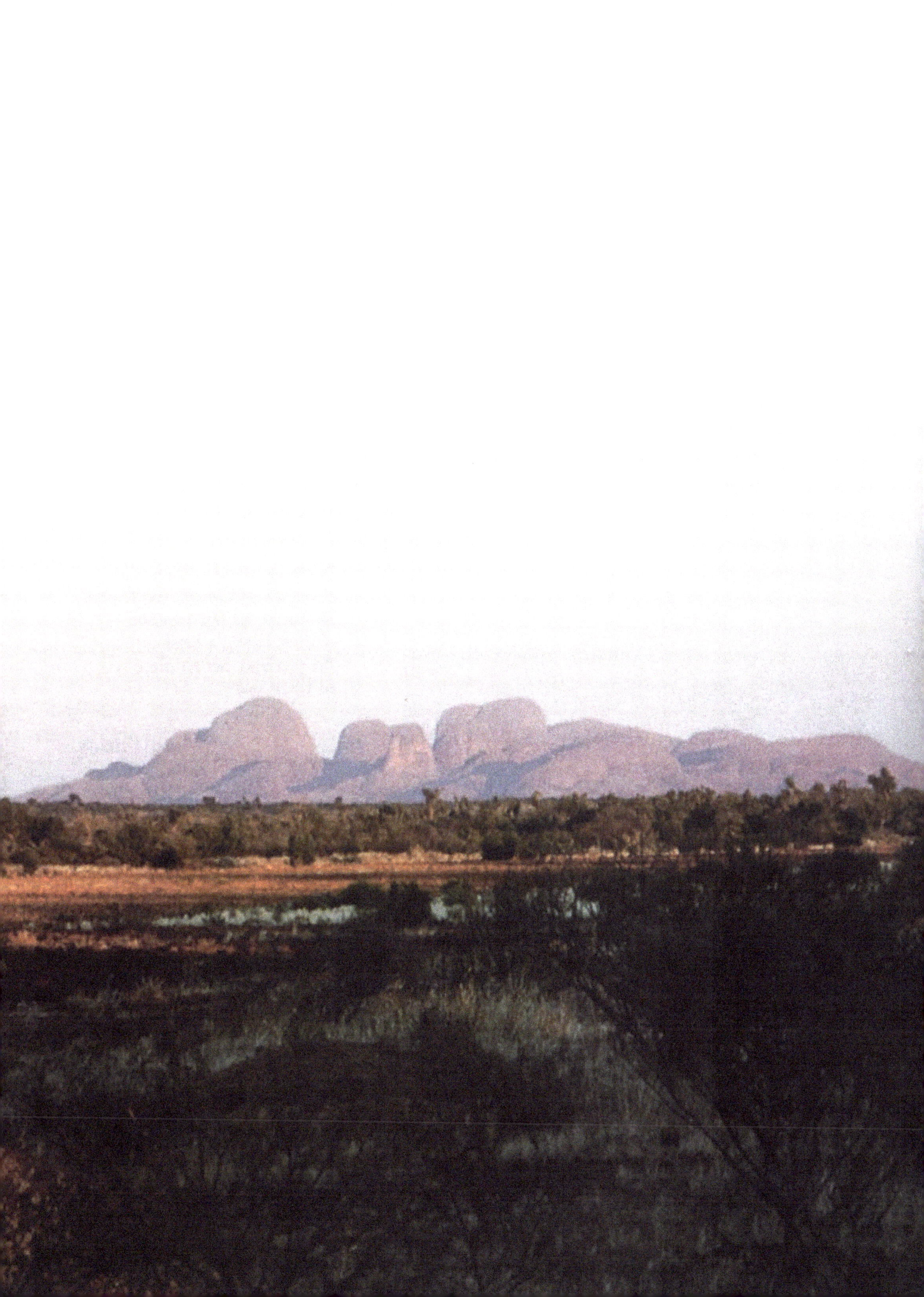

SALVATION

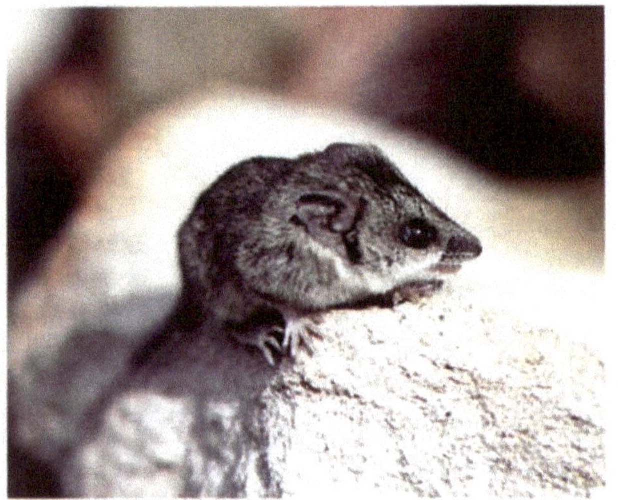

'He brought me out
into a spacious place;
he rescued me
because he delighted in me.' *

A single thin-ribbed dingo
picks its way at noon
across an inland sea
of shimmering stones
as wide as the fiery sky.

We saw him
when to our dull eyes
he was only a moving dot.

Hopping mouse and dunnart,
planigale and bilby, you're safe!
In this broad flat expanse
of your Father's hand,
the predator has no place
to lie in wait.

* *Psalm 18:19 NIV*

PODLICH

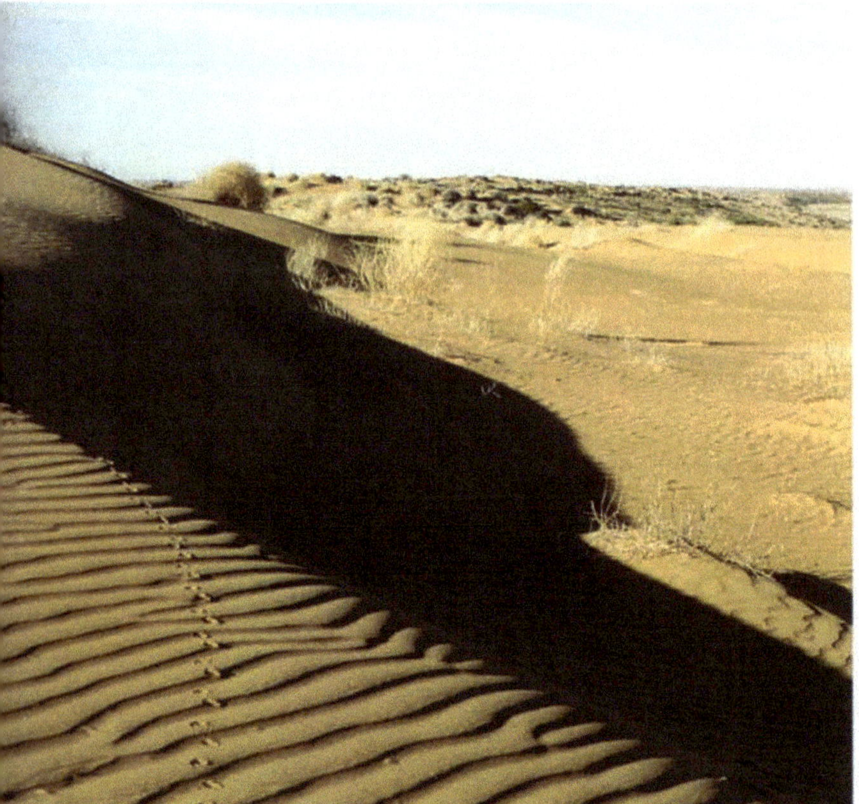

UPPER LEFT: *Dunnart* PODLICH
LOWER LEFT: *Sand-dune near Birdsville*
RIGHT: *Dingo, near Alice Springs*

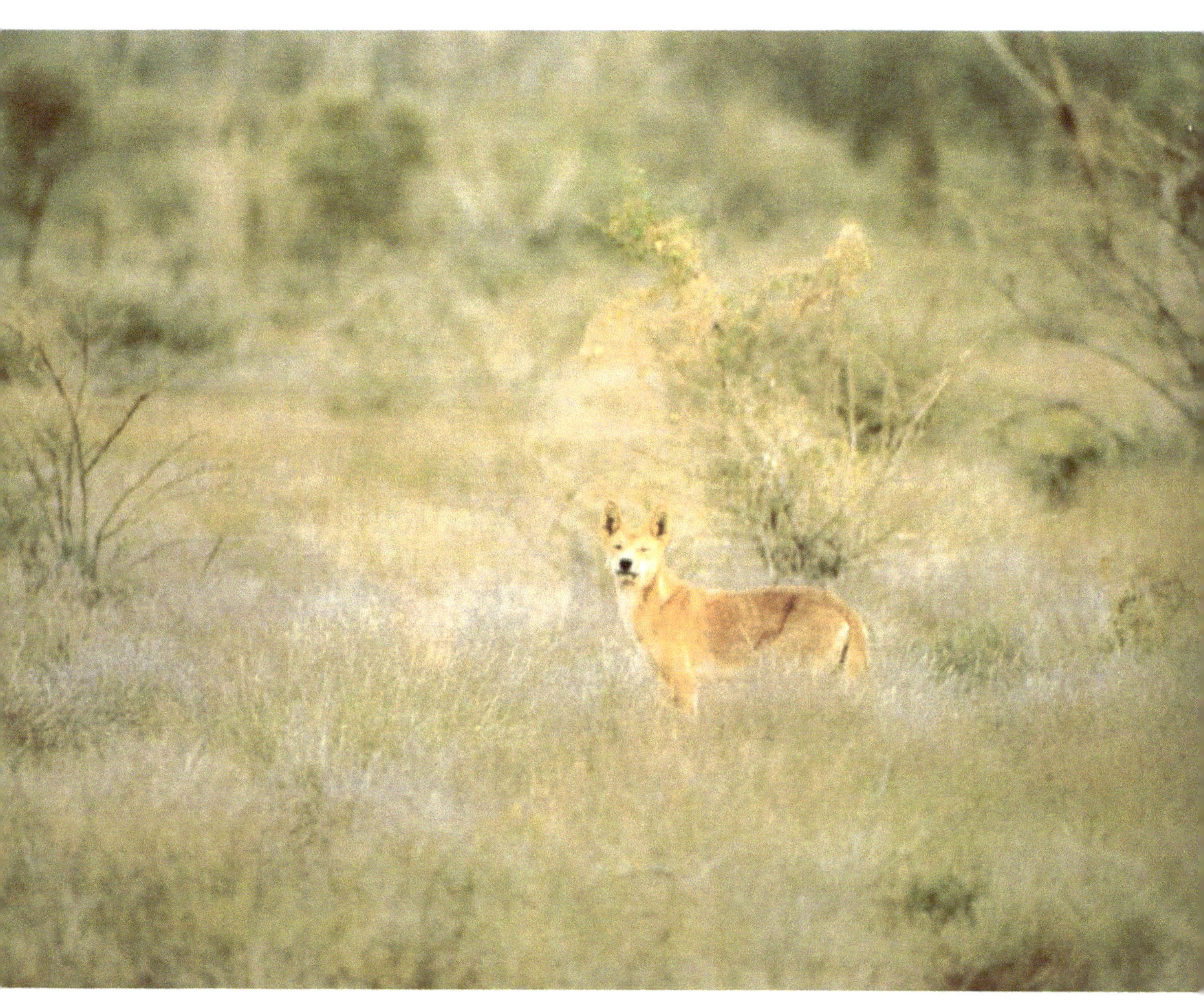

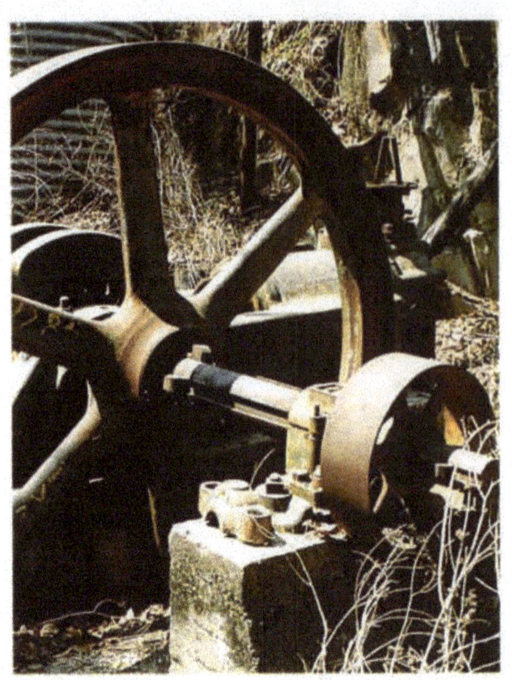

DALHOUSIE

While the sun sets
 over our shoulders,
the moon rises over the ruins
 of Dalhousie homestead.
Nearby are a few palm trees
 around the springs,
some rusted farm machinery
 and old fencing wire,
and many hectares of paddocks
 filled with nothing but gibbers.

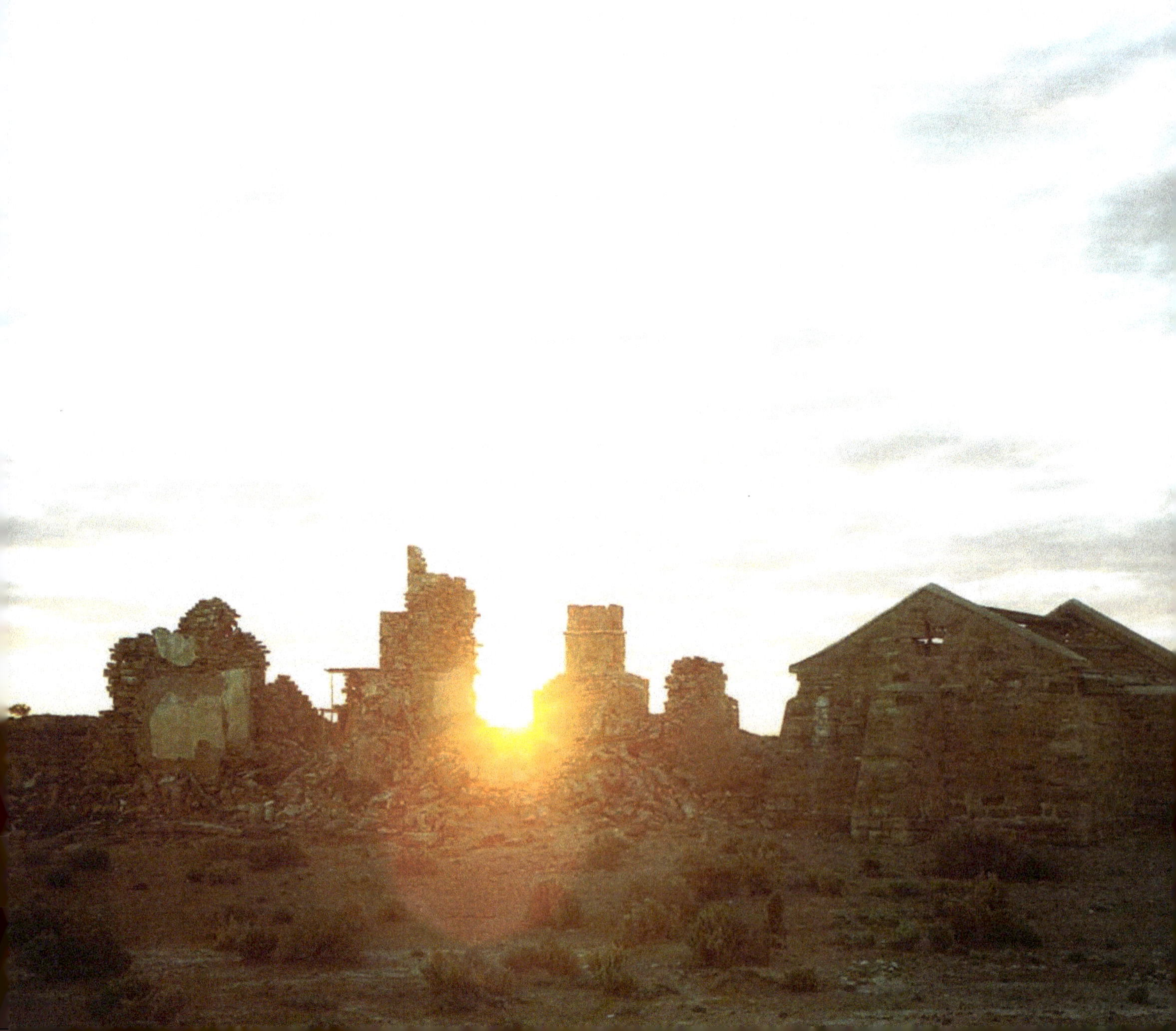

Once there had been topsoil here,
   and the trees, shrubs, and bush grass
   of the semi-desert country.
Birds sang here,
   and diverse tribes of marsupials
   went about their business.

Now only the ruins,
   the erosion, and the crops of stone —
grim witnesses to the desolation
   that follows human wilfulness,
   ignorance, or desperation.

Loving Creator, friend of the earth,
   how many millennia will it be
   before your patient renovation
   makes this place live again?

Loving Redeemer, friend of sinners,
   how long until we are converted
   from the wantonness of the arrogant
   to the stewardship of the meek?

PREWER

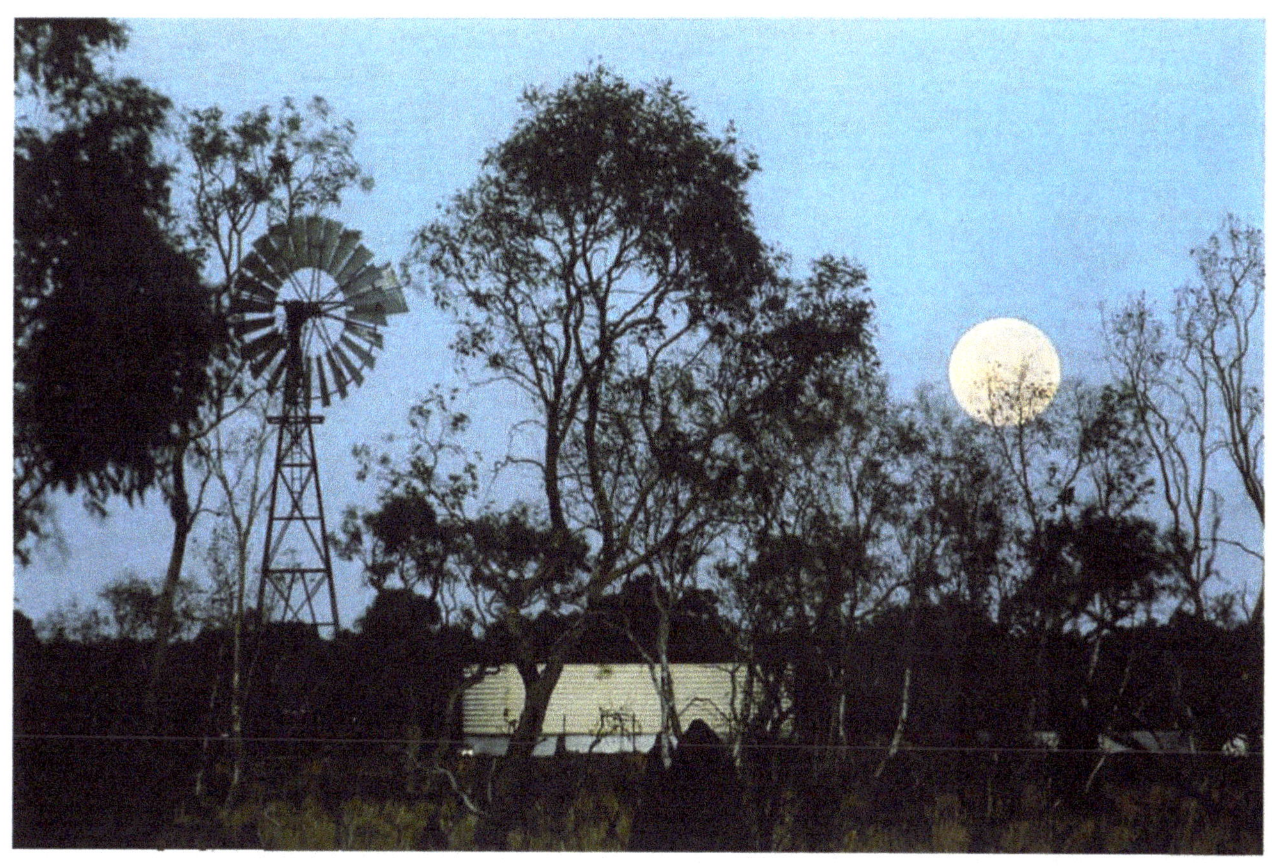

UPPER LEFT: *Rusted mining relics, Litchfield Park, NT*
LOWER LEFT: *Ruins, Oodnadatta Track, SA*
RIGHT: *Moonrise near Tennant Creek*

SOUVENIR

Choose a pebble
in this vast expanse of stones,
a single pretty one
that latches to your eye.

Take it home,
and when your journey's done,
let it bring to mind
this place it came from —
and something more.

Let it become
the little truth you grasp
of all that is good and true,
the single pebble
you made your own,
of an infinite stony plain.

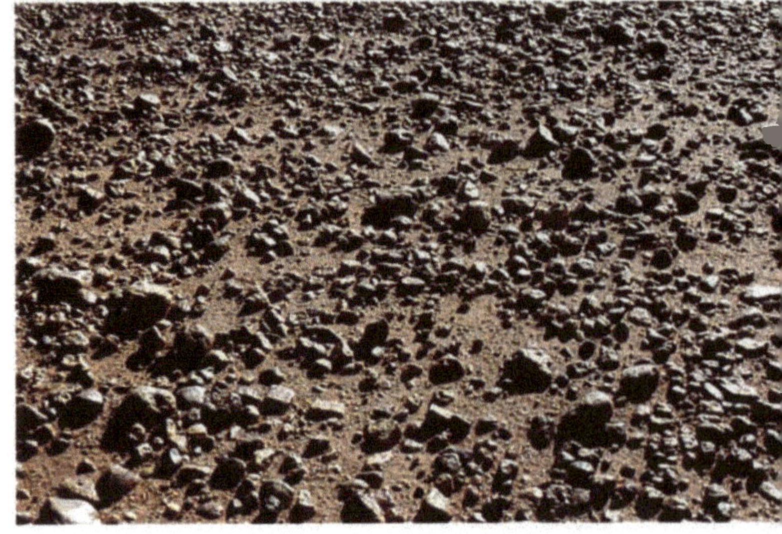

For it is good to understand
that the sum
of all your knowing
is that small stone.

PODLICH

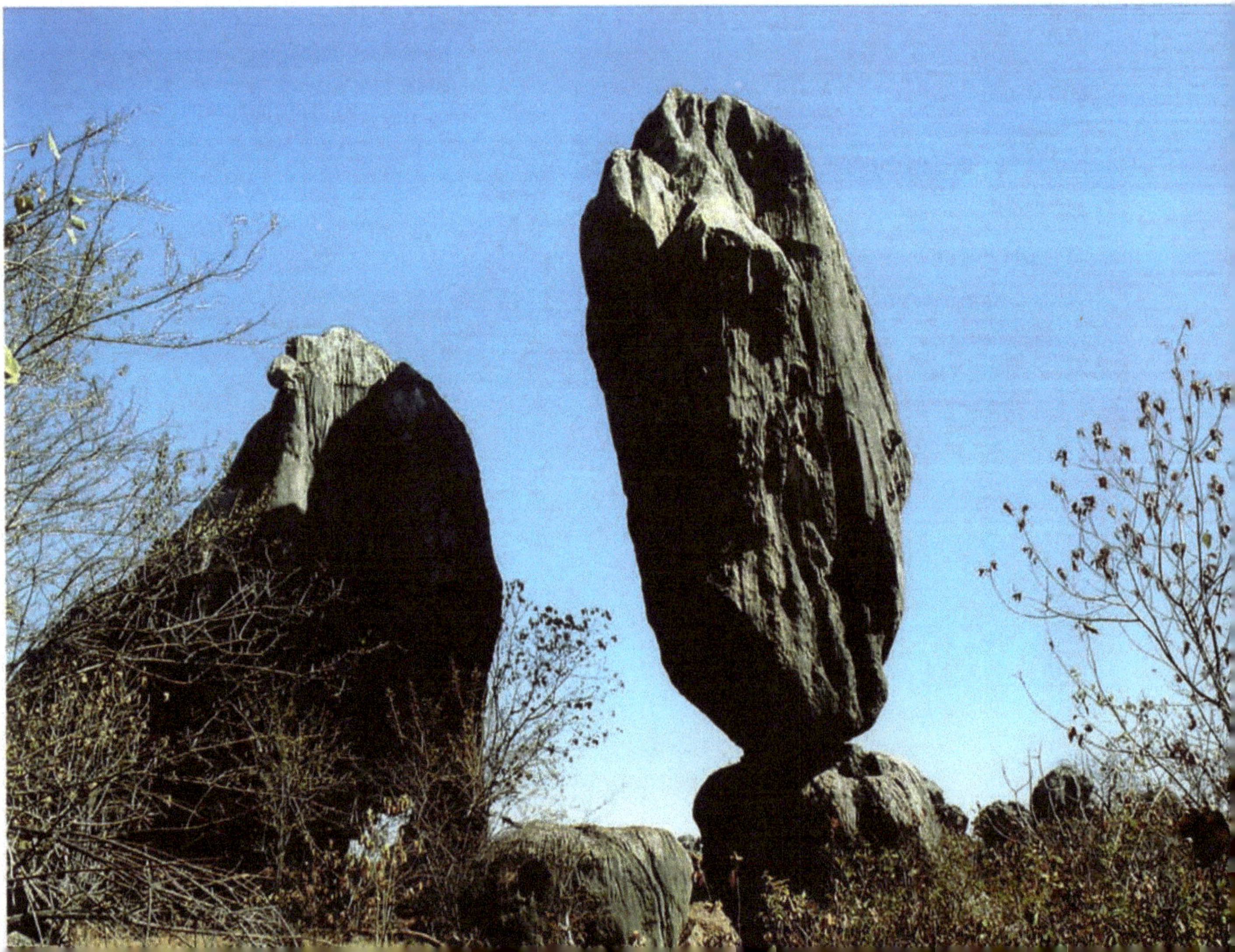

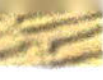

KALAYA PITI

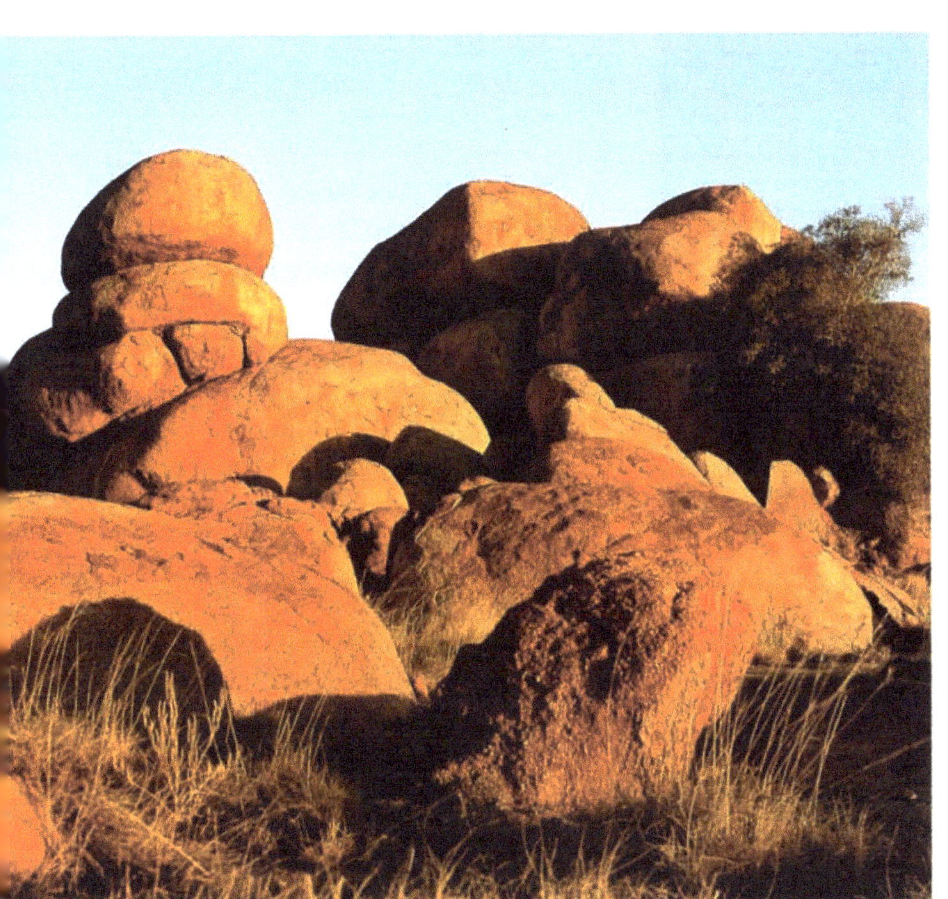

Blustery day of heat,
nothing moves on the plains
except some camels.

The great rocks of Kalaya Piti
seem to hold no promise,
dry as the desert and hotter.

But high up on one slope,
our breath jerking
with every step,

we find the place
where the old ones came
for the precious water.

Deep in a fissure
a cool dark cistern;
one must bend low to drink.

Strangely it reminds me
of Bethlehem's Church
of the Holy Nativity,

and the low door
through which one bends
to worship there.

PREWER

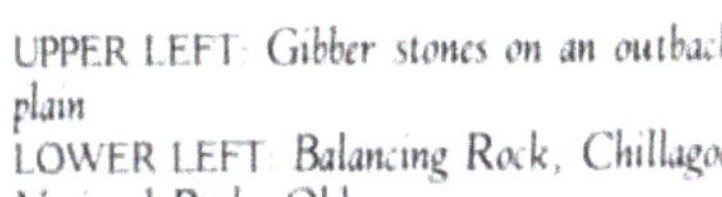

UPPER LEFT: *Gibber stones on an outback plain*
LOWER LEFT: *Balancing Rock, Chillagoe National Park, Qld*
RIGHT: *Devil's Marbles at sunset*

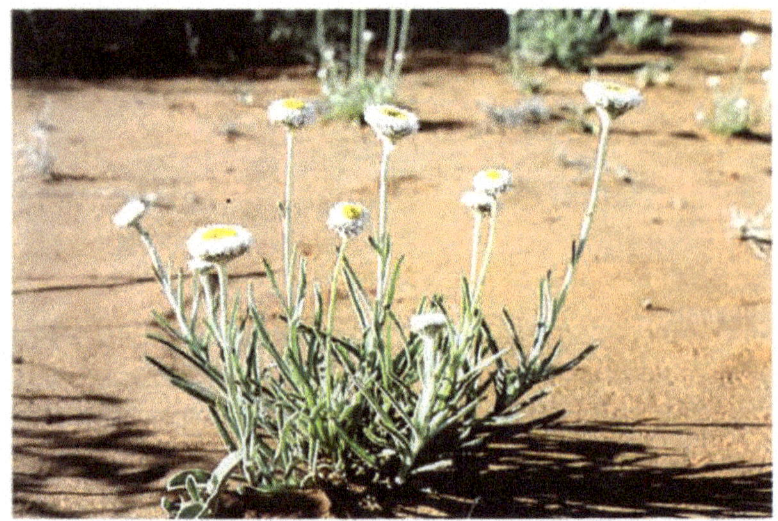

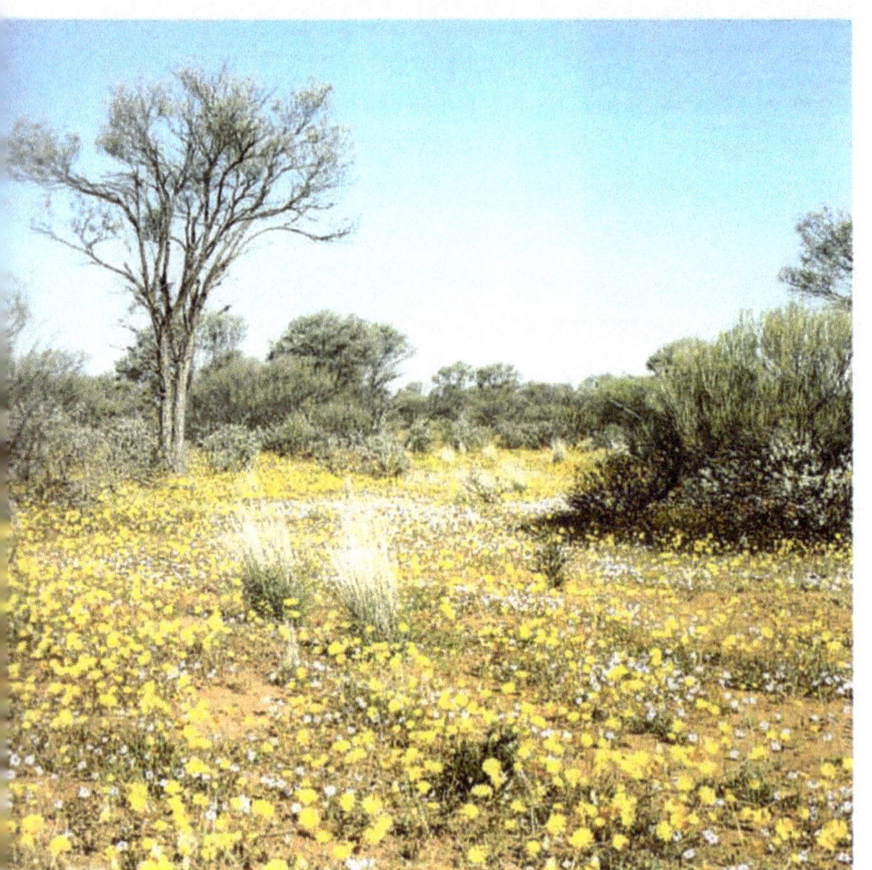

AFTER RAINS

Beautiful, ever beautiful
is the Creator-Spirit,
Friend of the good red earth!

Out from the red-spined ranges,
on the sweeping plains
after abundant rains,
one may know the beatitude
of wide desert fields,
blossoming as the rose.

A pageant of colours
which makes the poet's
'host of golden daffodils'
seem but a poor man's plot
compared with the raw immensity
of these prodigal gardens
of God.

Beautiful, ever beautiful
is the Creator-Spirit,
Friend of the good red earth!

PREWER

UPPER LEFT: *Poached egg daisies*
LOWER LEFT: *Spring wildflowers near Mount Magnet, WA*

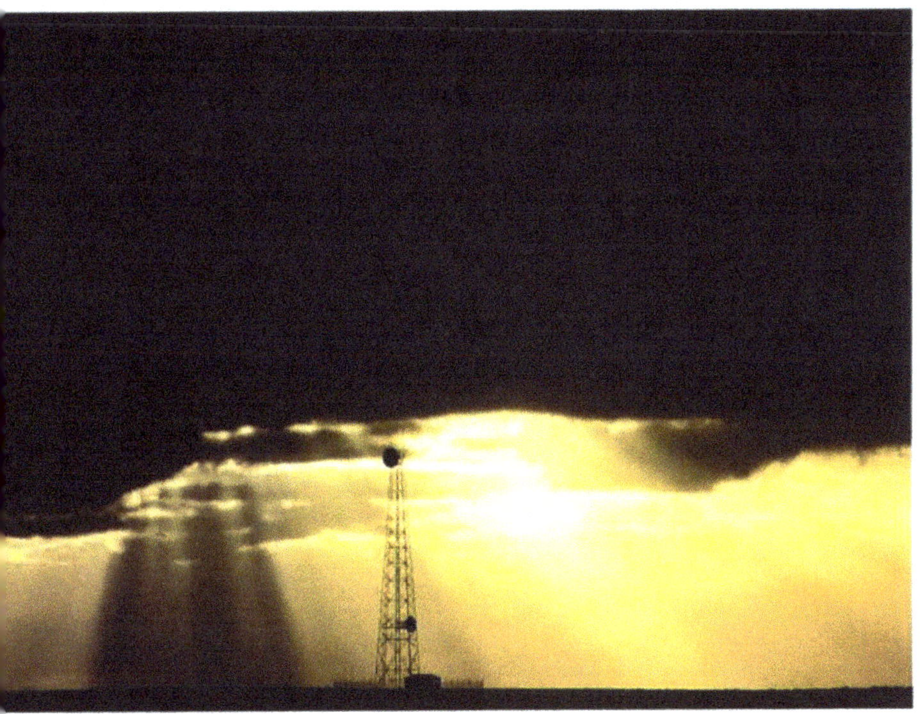

GREY DAYS

Even here in the centre
there are the grey days:
  clouds shroud the sun,
  dead mulga stand stark,
  grey falcons sit huddled,
  a mangy dingo pads by,
  and the gorges are colourless.

Have pity, Lord,
when we mirror such days:
  when feelings stay flat,
  the eye sees no grandeur,
  the heart misses the wonder,
  the spirit crawls low,
  and praise forsakes the lips.

Have pity, Lord,
  and kindle the light
  that comes only
  from within.

UPPER RIGHT: *Near Biloela, Qld*
LOWER RIGHT: *Repeater station, Stuart Highway*

PREWER

MIRAGE

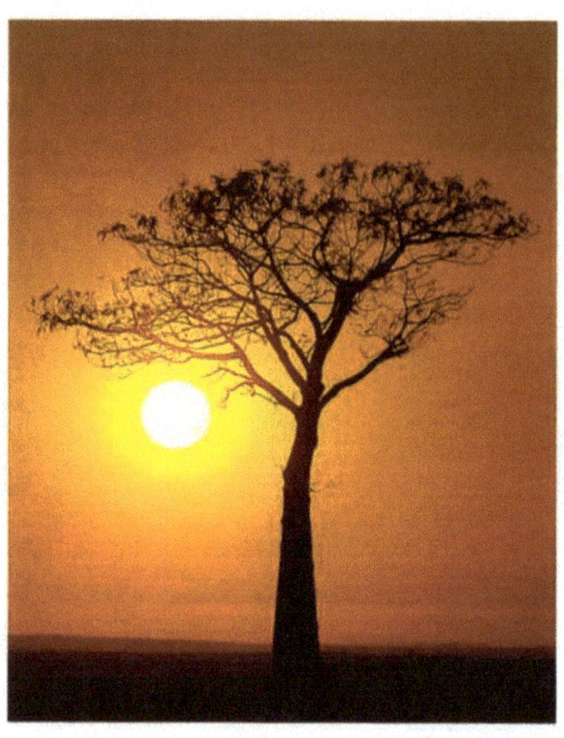

In the mirage
there's a single tree,
and on the tree,
a Man.

Our God is a mirage
without that Man,
'forever receding
as we forever advance', *
without the Man
on the tree
of the cross!

* *Words of Phillip Adams, 1991*

PODLICH

LEFT: *Boab tree at sunrise, east Kimberley, WA*
RIGHT: *Sunrise over riverine forest, Kakadu National Park, NT*
OVERLEAF: *Ayers Rock at sunrise, Uluru National Park, NT*

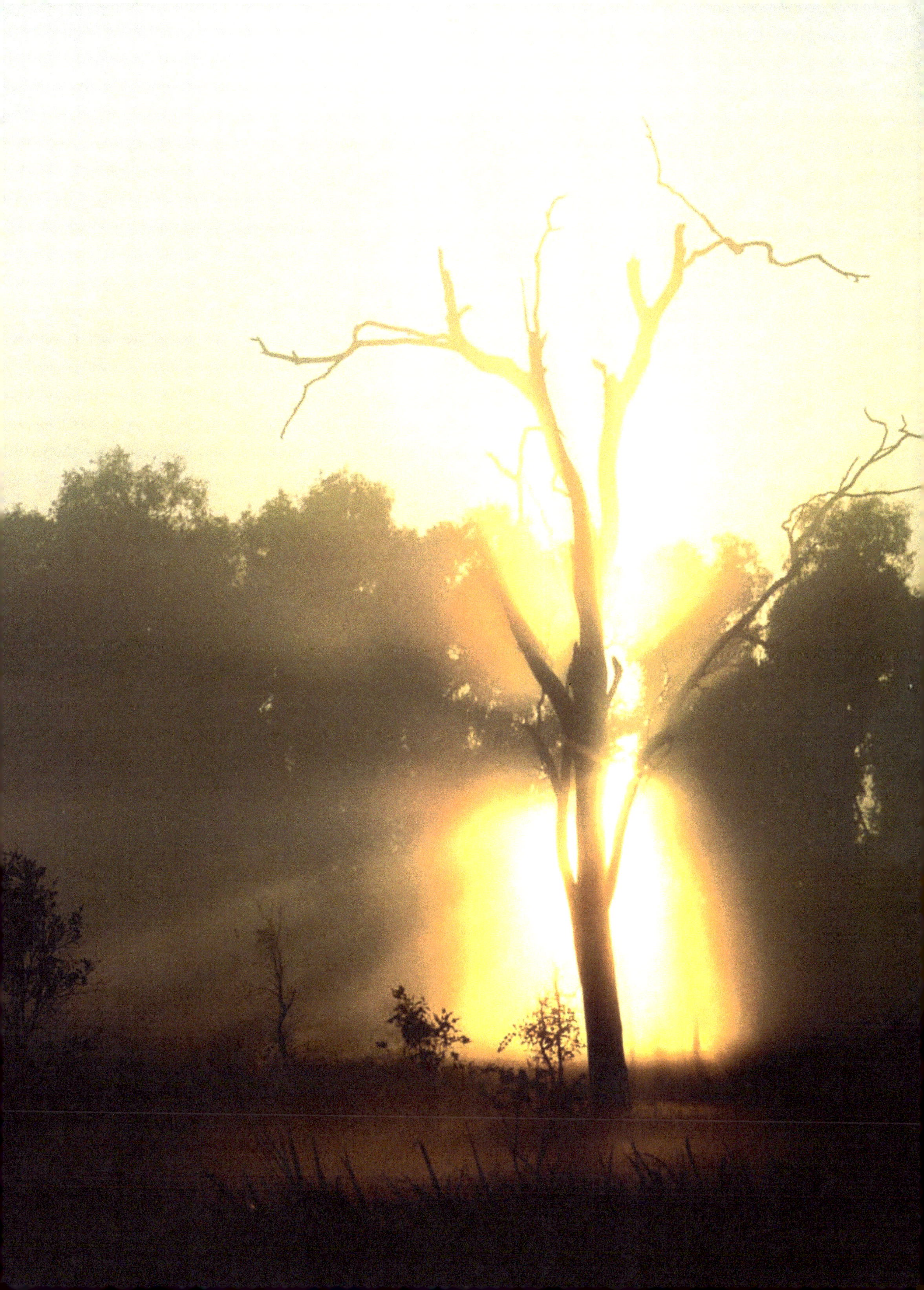

NOON AT KATATJUTA

From a distance,
   they looked mauve-mystic,
   ready for comfortable thoughts.
Now, among the Olgas at noon,
   the light is relentless,
   and will not adjust itself
   to the wants of city eyes.

Everything seems exposed;
   few shadows, no secrets,
   pretence seared away.
Reality, alarming reality;
   discomforting, painful even,
   yet somehow better, purer,
   than sentimental illusions.

God of God, light of light,
   we need you,
   yet we fear you;
Lord, I am not worthy
   that you should come to my house;
   but say the word,
   and I shall be healed.

PREWER

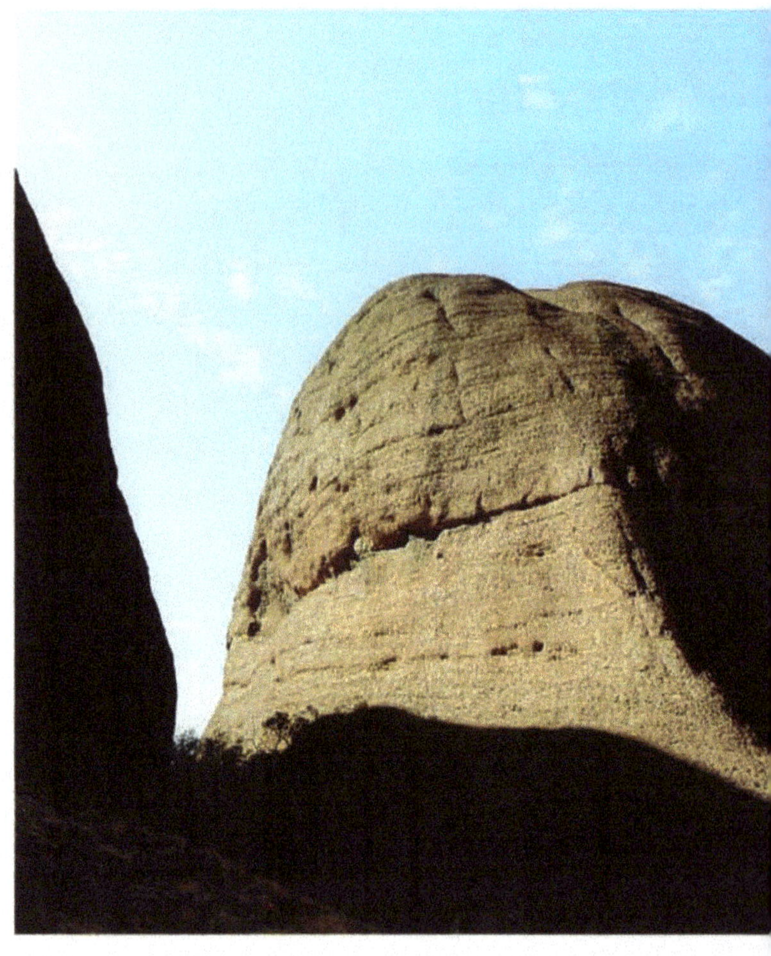

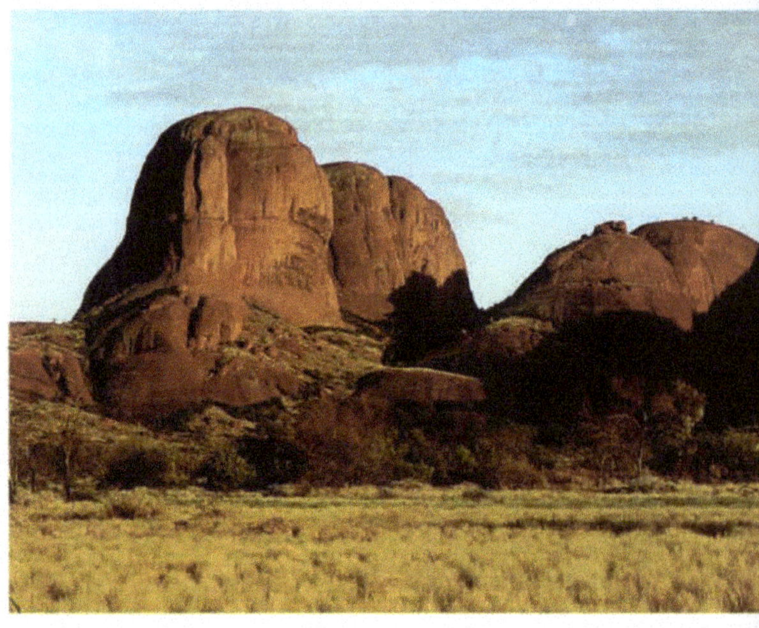

UPPER LEFT: Valley of the Winds, the Olgas, Uluru National Park, NT
LOWER LEFT: Dying Kangaroo Man, the Olgas
RIGHT: The Olgas at sunset

FOR THOSE WHO THIRST

Jesus, water of life,
when we are parched and desolate,
and all our hopes run dry,
teach us to draw close to you,
as the thirsty animals converge
at shrinking waterholes
when drought grips the land.

Blessed are those
whose thirst is so great
it can only be slaked
by eternal pools.

PODLICH

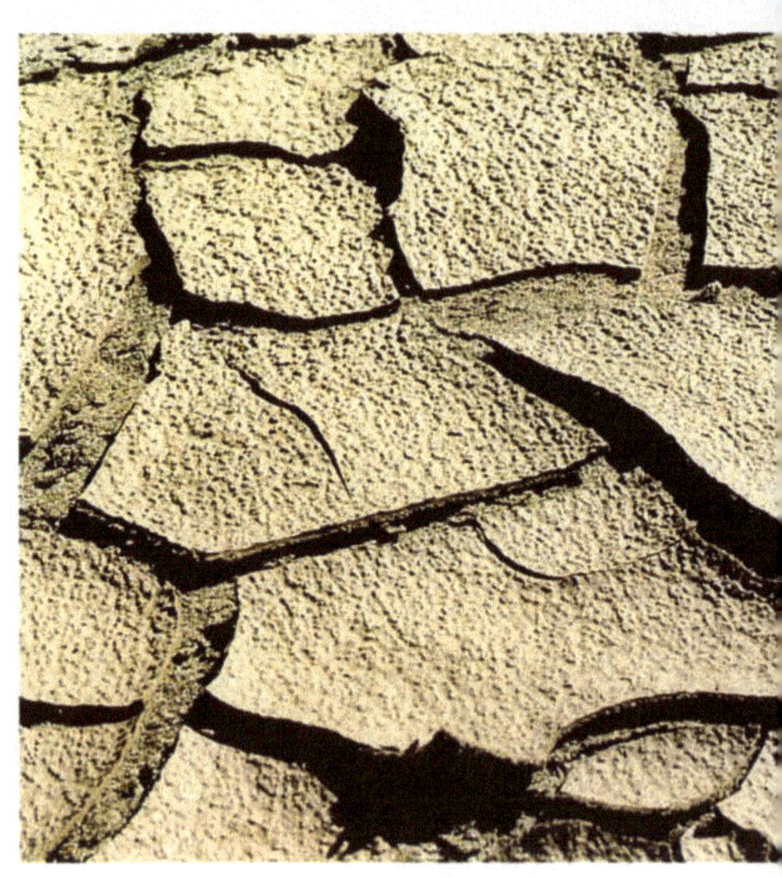

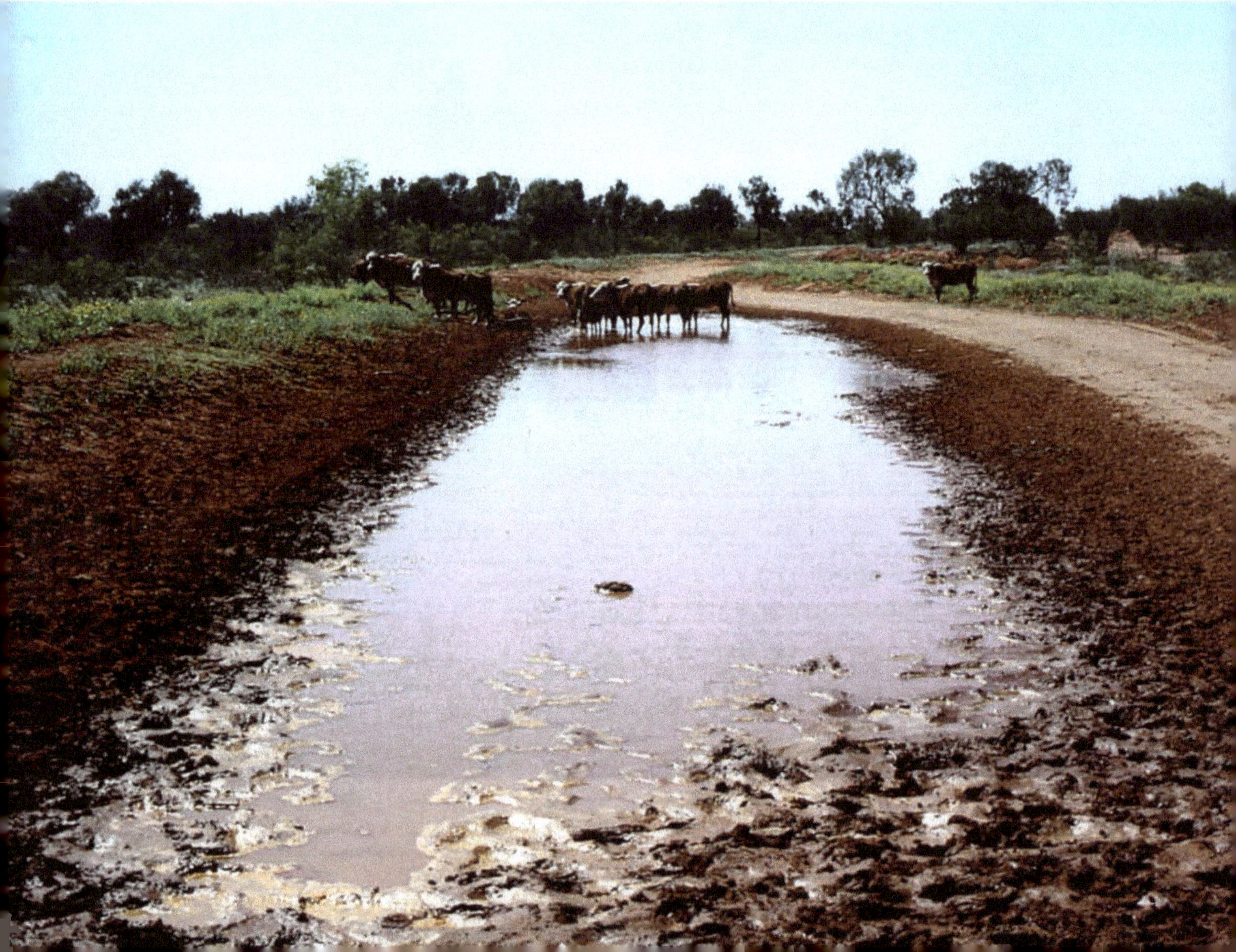

WILD ASSES

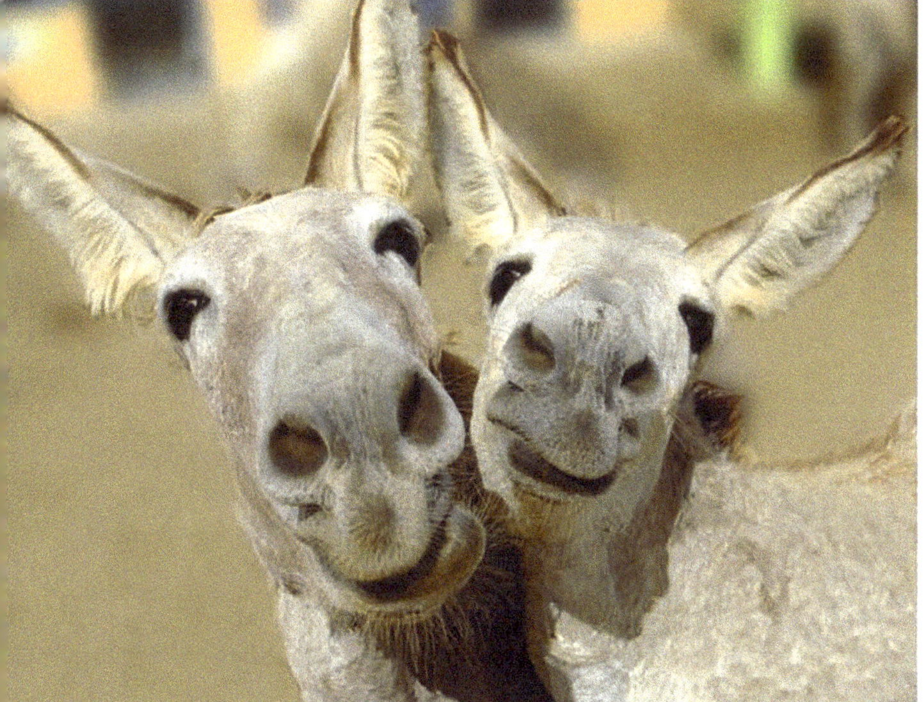

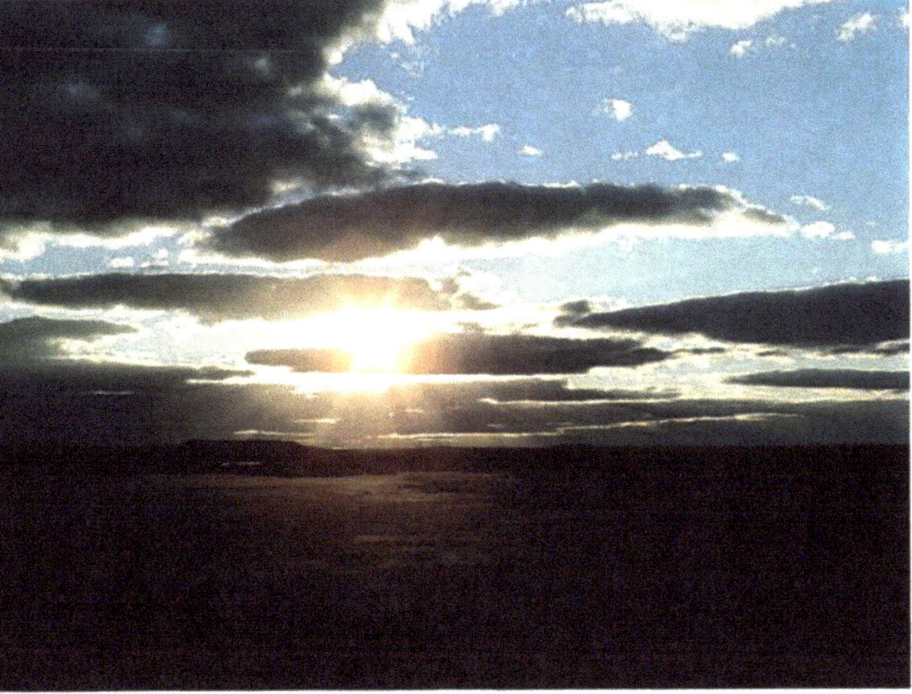

Somewhere south of Finke,
across the gibber country,
we travel under afternoon sun,
hoping this track leads
to the goal we seek.

No signposts.
But wild asses turn and watch us,
their comical heads steady,
seeming to contain
an ancient wisdom.

Another wisdom
gleaned in another land
in another time and story,
when stones were ready
to sing aloud their praises.

We make camp in a gully,
water scarce, and not sure
that this is the right track,
or that our goal is nearer
than when we started out.

Distant enthusiastic braying
of donkeys at dusk
is like sweet gospel,
telling us the springs we seek
are nearer than we feared.

Not fools, these creatures
that survive where we cannot;
they are to us
messengers of God
in a weary land.

PREWER

UPPER LEFT *Dried mud, outback SA*
LOWER LEFT *Cattle on outback road, near Maryvale, NT*
UPPER RIGHT *Donkey duo*, BIGSTOCK
LOWER RIGHT *Claypan, near Dalhousie, SA*

STURT'S DESERT PEA

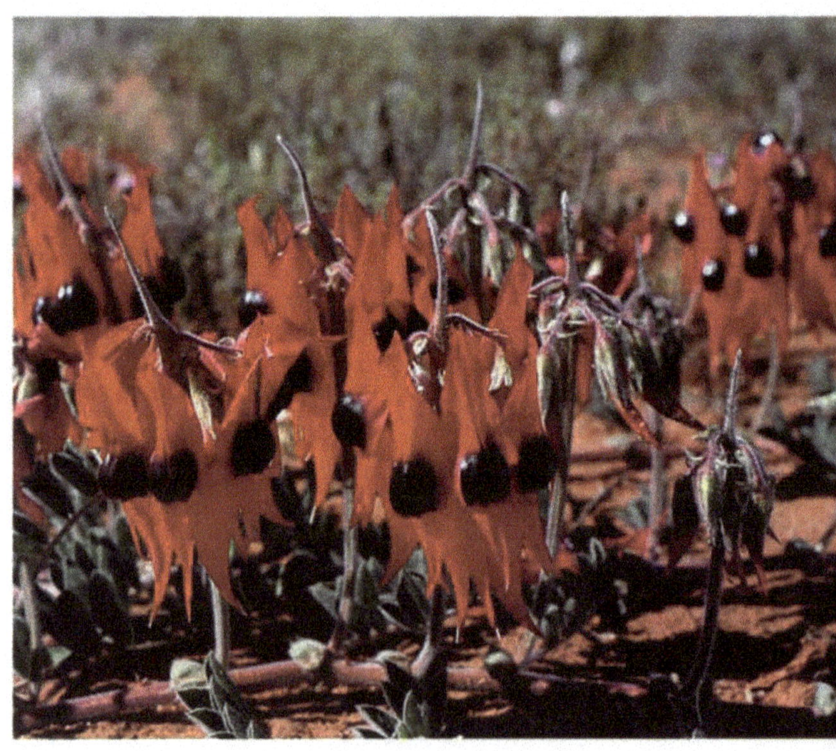

The land's allegories
  meet me everywhere
  and set me singing.
When I look intimately
  into the deep dark eyes
  of the blood-red desert pea,
I imagine I am seeing
  the love-deep eyes
  of my Lord.

PREWER

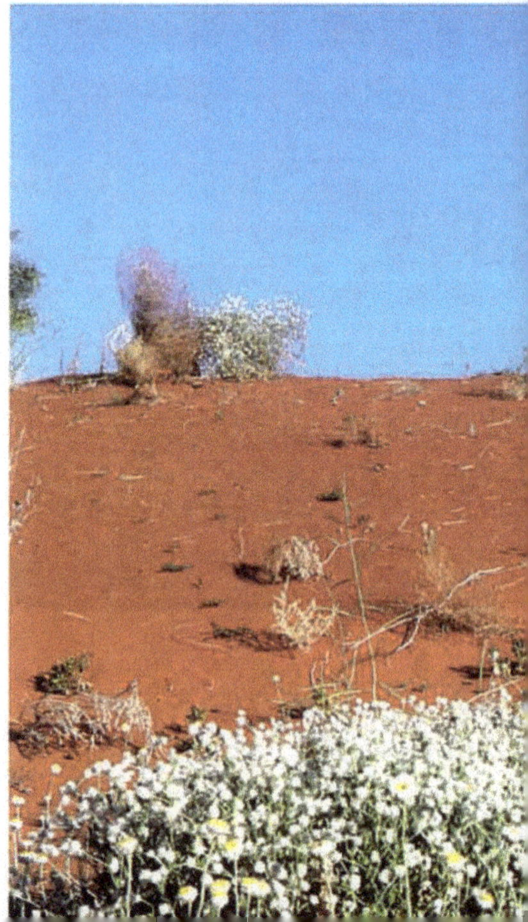

UPPER LEFT: *Sturt's desert peas*
UPPER RIGHT: *Daisy seed head*
CENTRE RIGHT: *Spring wildflowers, near Wubin, WA*
LOWER RIGHT: *Red sandhill country in spring, south of Alice Springs*

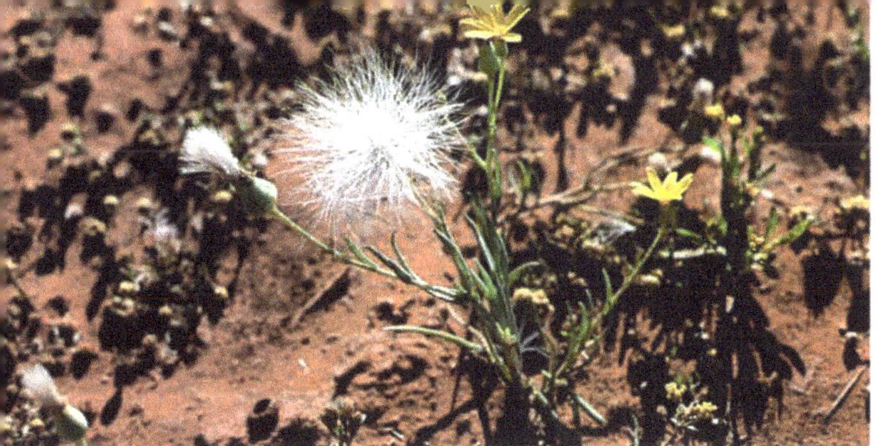

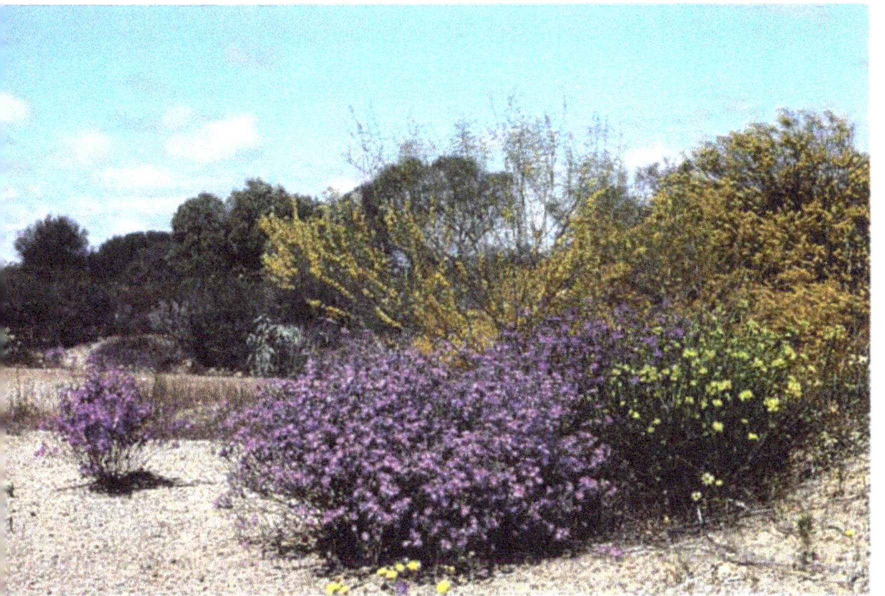

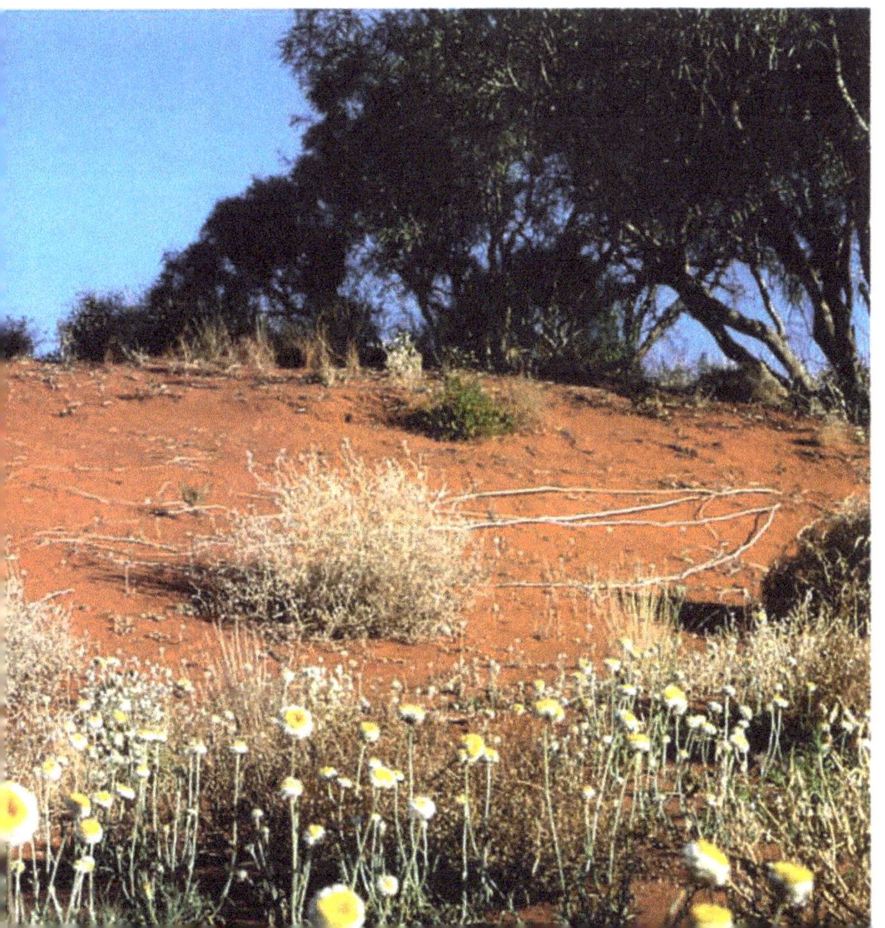

THE GENTLE SEEDS

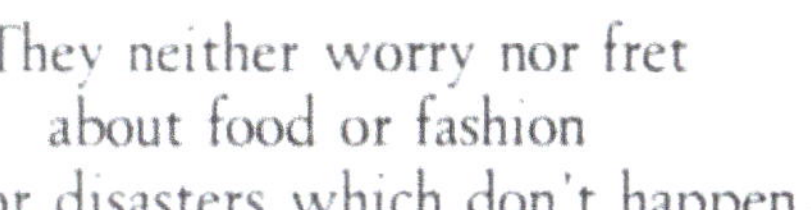

The seeds of the wilderness
beyond Ernabella
take no thought for tomorrow.

They neither worry nor fret
about food or fashion
or disasters which don't happen.

Seeds gently rest
in the warm womb of the land
and wait for the rains;

the rains that will come,
this year or next year,
or in twenty years' time.

Then they will awake,
dance up into life,
and clothe the inland with majesty.

All we who pass by
with cameras at the ready
may, if we wish, hear them speak:

'O you of little faith,
rest awhile with us and learn
how dearly loved you are'.

PREWER

STANDLEY CHASM

Soon the sun had moved
forty minutes beyond its zenith,
having briefly bathed the walls
with rich aboriginal red.

The midday hubbub is over,
the tourists up and gone,
the car park is empty,
the dust settled.

The gorge returns
to the serene solitude
it has known
from ancient days.

Some rock wallabies,
which have been in hiding,
hop out among the stones,
stretch and sun themselves.

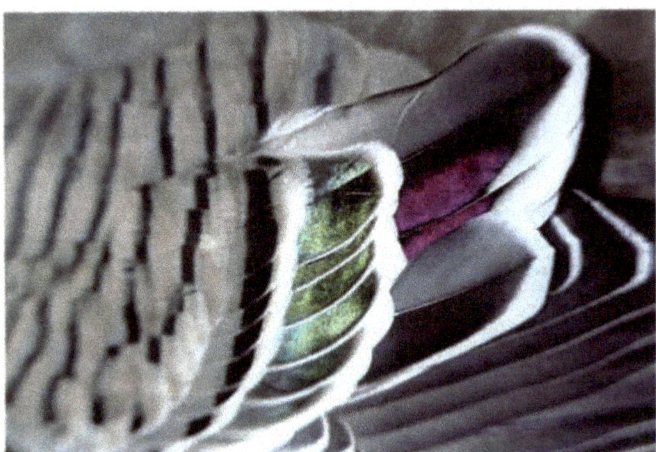

Little plumed pigeons,
colourful and energetic,
like kindy kids released,
run down to a pool to drink.

And you, Creator-Spirit,
having observed the noon rush
and smiled ruefully
at your human flock,

you watch these contented creatures
of the inland wilderness,
and you smile sabbatically
at their pleasure in simple gifts.

PREWER

LEFT: *Crested pigeon, wing detail* PODLICH
RIGHT: *Standley Chasm, MacDonnell Ranges, NT*

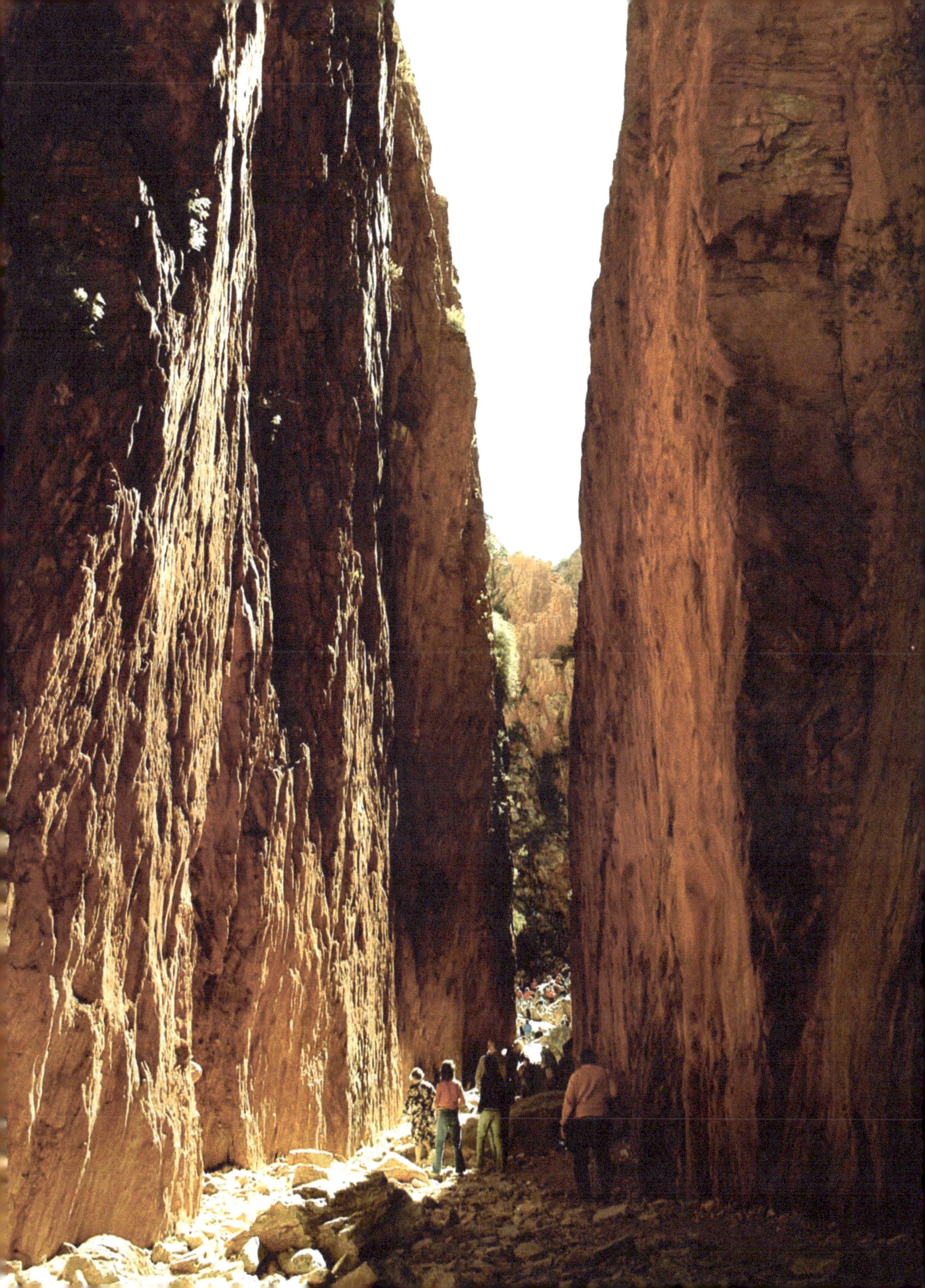

OUTBACK PEOPLE

At home in such harshness,
like saltbush and ghost gum,
you've put down your roots
and learnt to belong.

So you inspire us
to love as our home
the dry land around us,
and to reach deeper down,
keeping cool,
staying green.

PODLICH

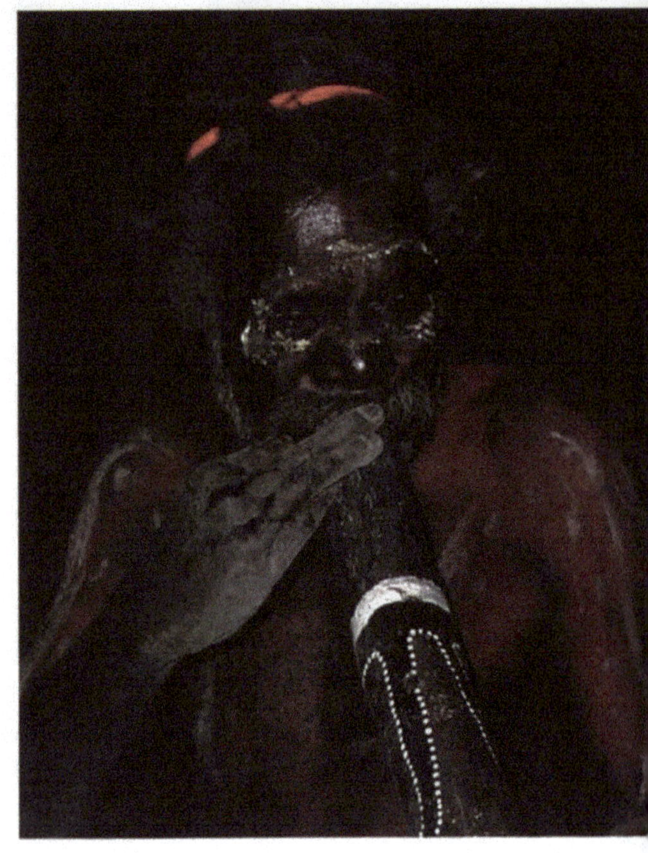

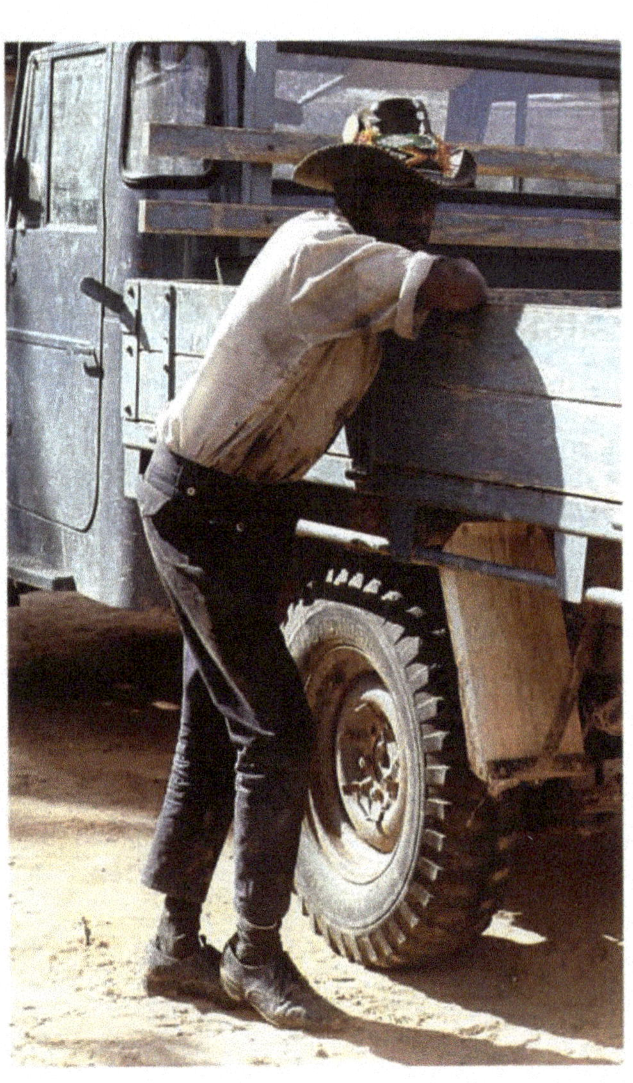

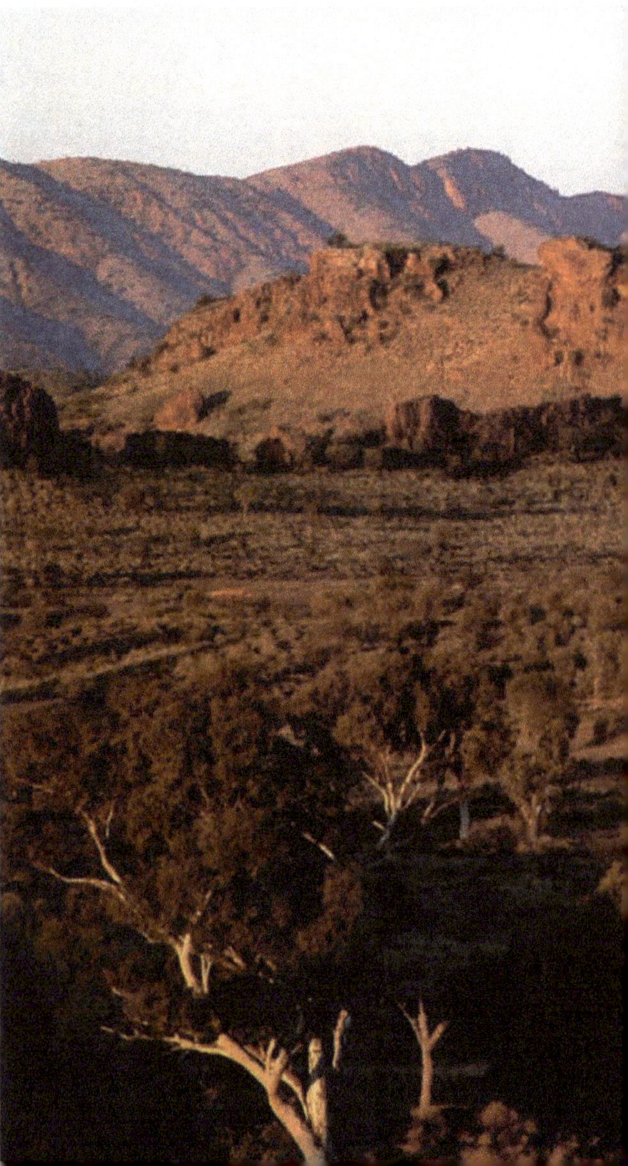

SWEET SANITY

Here,
where the red sand blows,
and distant mountains
elbow themselves up from the plain,
our being chairman of the board,
athlete of the year,
judge of the high court,
or much respected preacher
counts for nothing.

UPPER LEFT: *Aborigine playing a didgeridoo*
LOWER LEFT: *Aboriginal stockman, Birdsville Track, SA*
BELOW: *MacDonnell Ranges, NT*
OVERLEAF: *Reflections, Finke River at Glen Helen, NT*

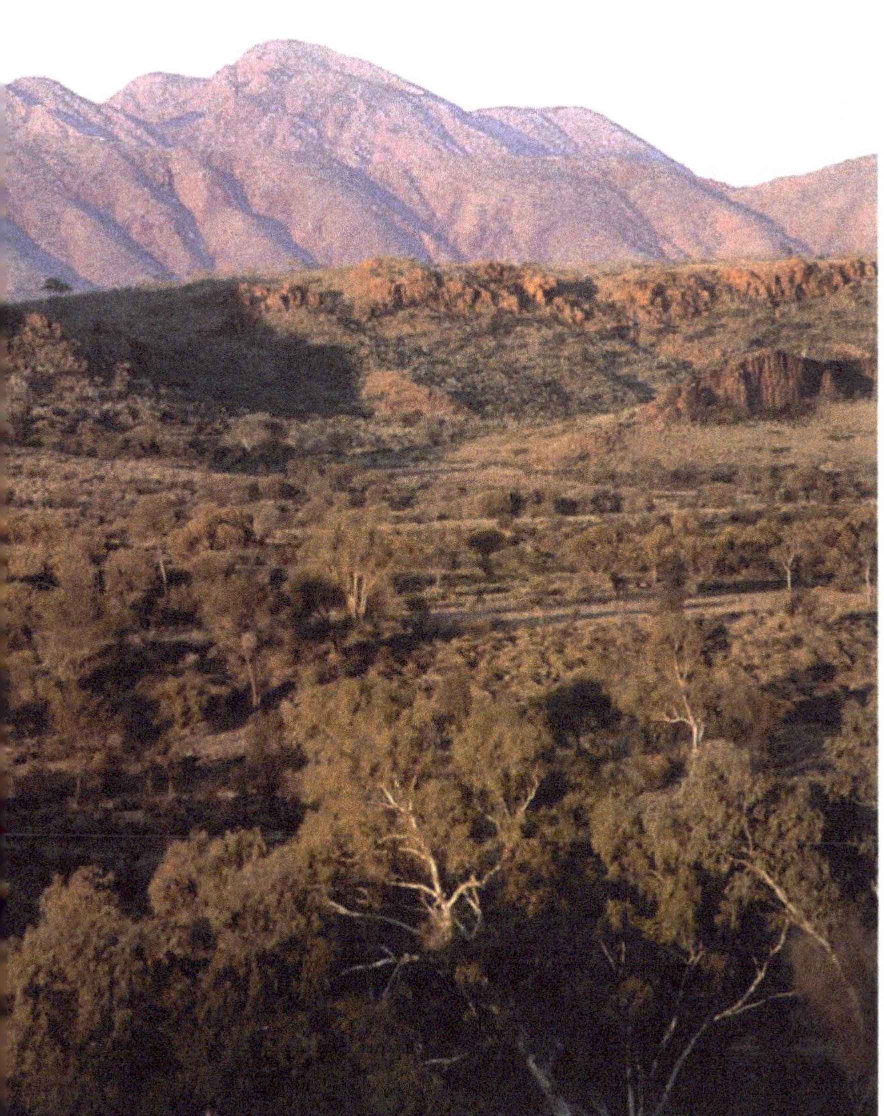

We
are the ignorant,
the outsiders
who cannot survive alone
for more than a couple of days,
or understand in a whole lifetime.

Here
the abrasive winds
blow away all pretensions,
and the dunes are ready
to quickly cover human bones.

We
are reduced to size,
and after the first shock,
the affront to our arrogance,
it becomes a healing thing.

Here
we have much to learn;
even the shy animals
can teach us lessons
that stand between life and death.

Here
things go on happening
as they always have, without us,
and in this sweet sanity
we find a new tranquillity.

Here
there is One who comes
from wilderness places, saying:
'Come unto me, all you
who labour and are heavy laden,
and I will give you rest'. *

* *Matthew 11.28*

PREWER

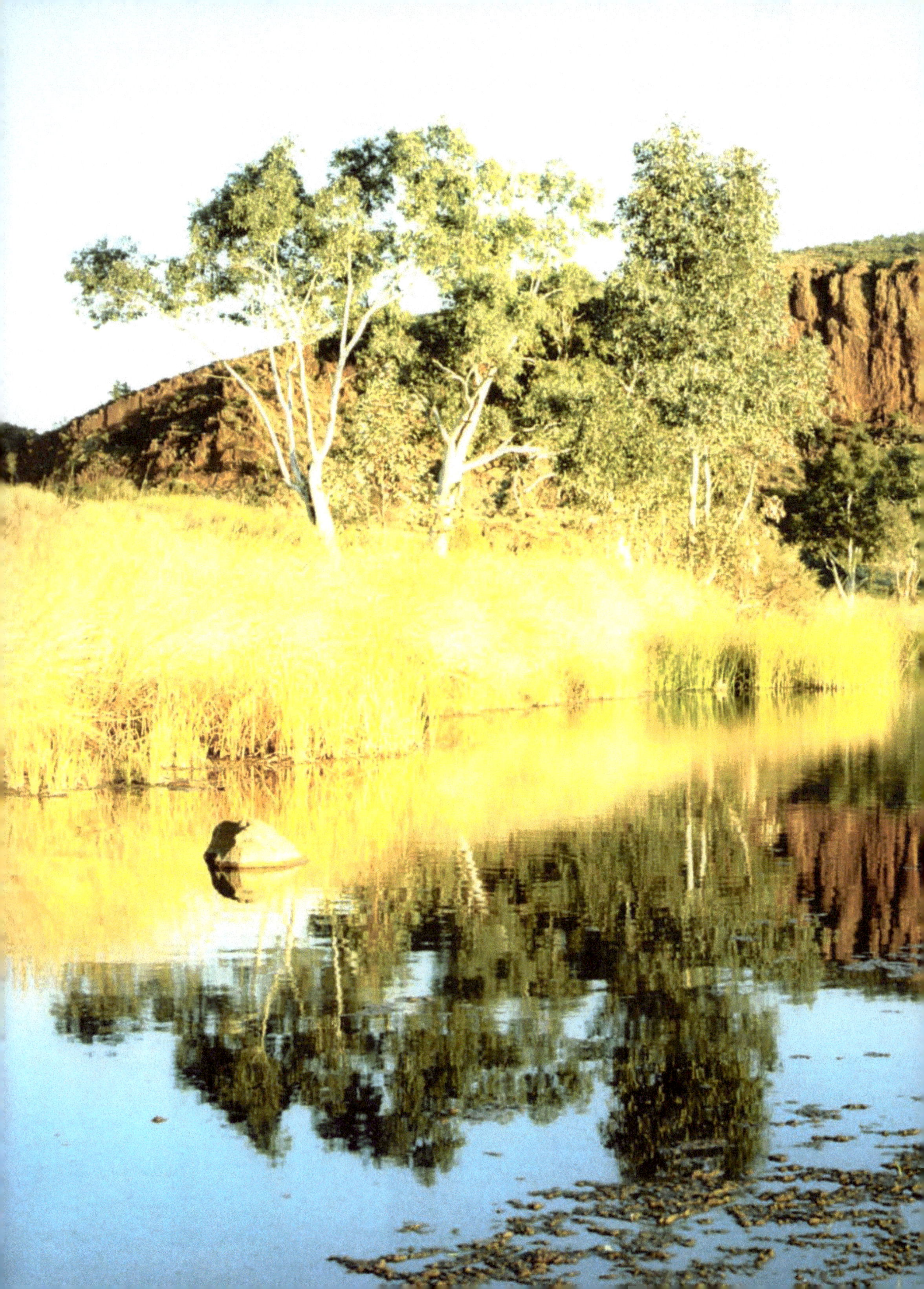

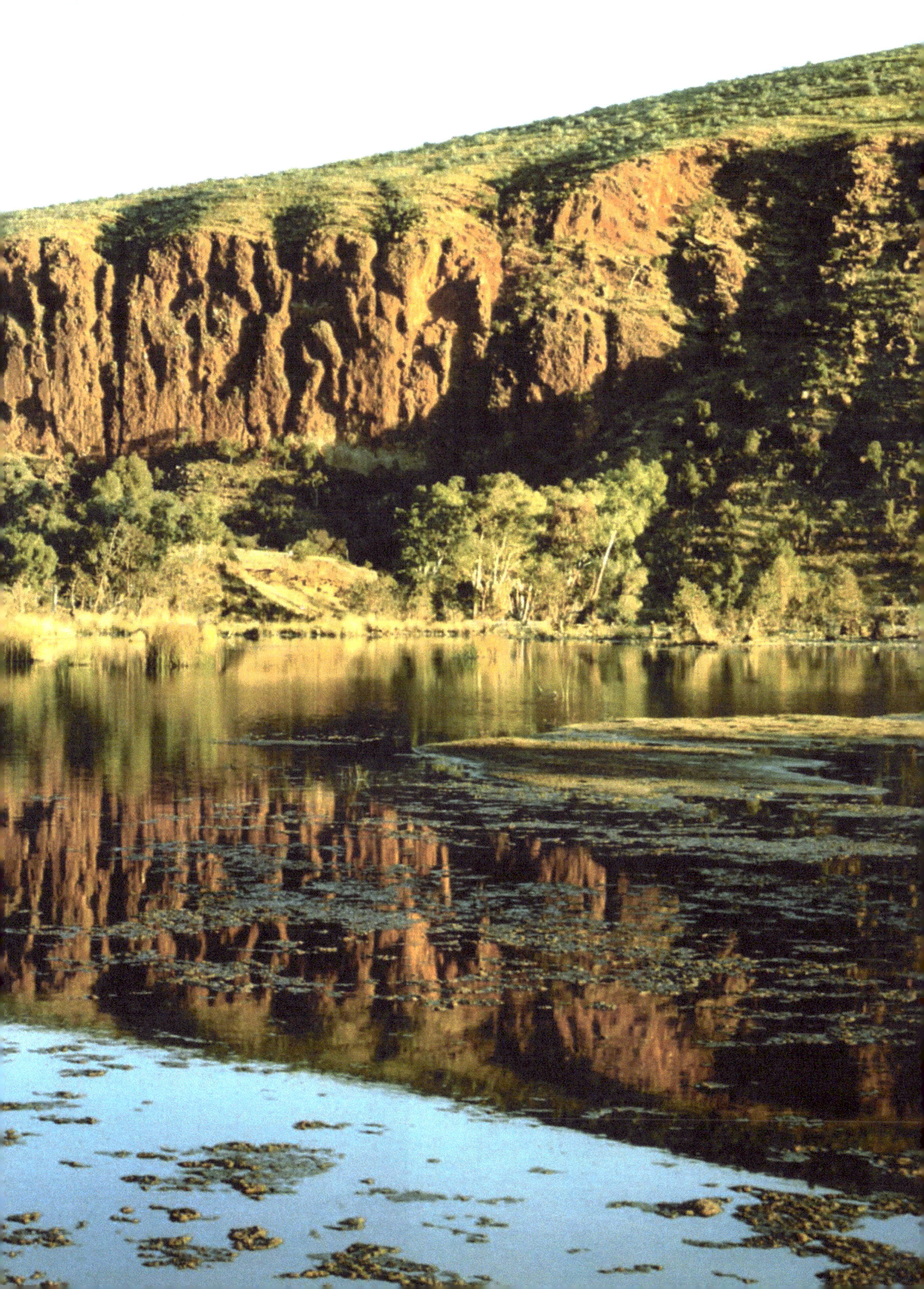

BAOBAB

'The creation waits in eager expectation.' *

Fat ladies, weary,
trudging on the plain;
fat ladies with petticoats
bulging with last year's rain,
and hair unkempt.

There's a distant roll of thunder,
and, etched against the flame,
they quicken to the wonder
of the fast-approaching storm.

And in the clouds they glimpse Him
who will claim them brides again,
these fat ladies, tight in skirts,
stepping lightly on the plain.

* *Romans* 8:19 NIV

PODLICH

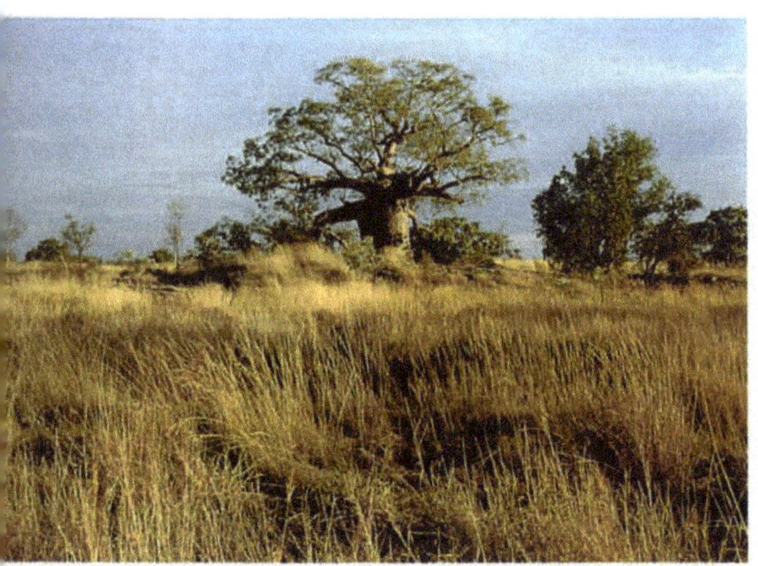

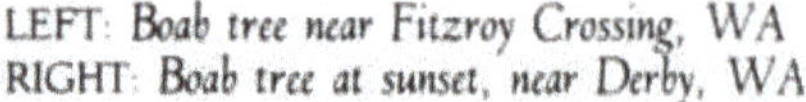

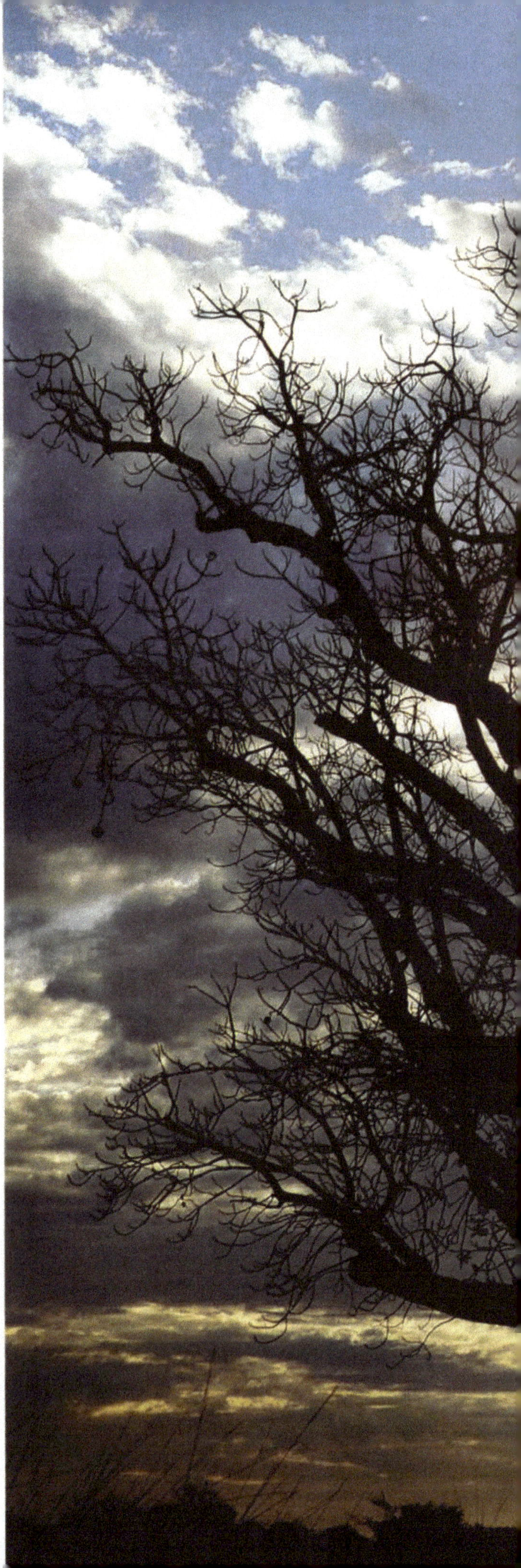

LEFT: *Boab tree near Fitzroy Crossing,* WA
RIGHT: *Boab tree at sunset, near Derby,* WA

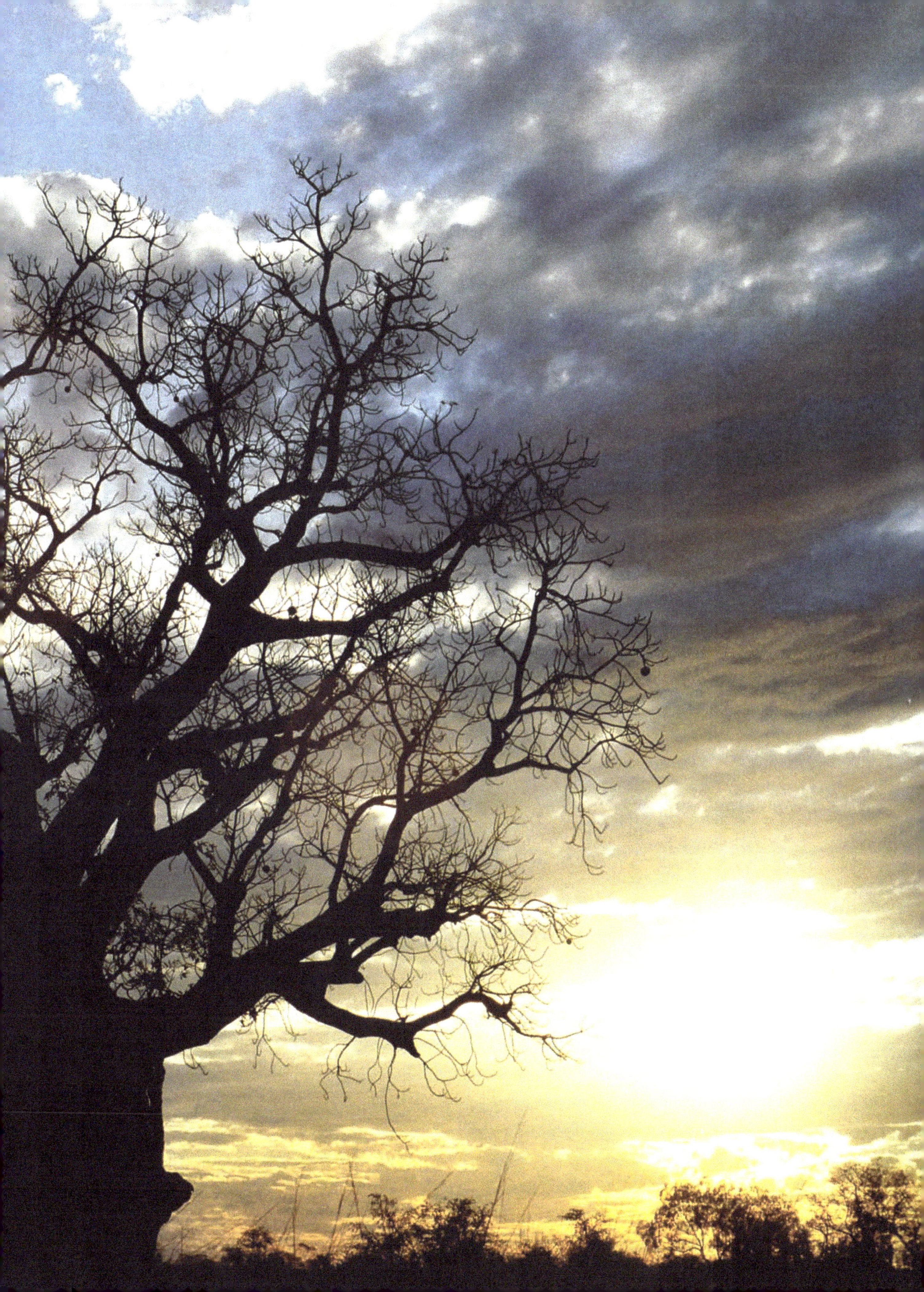

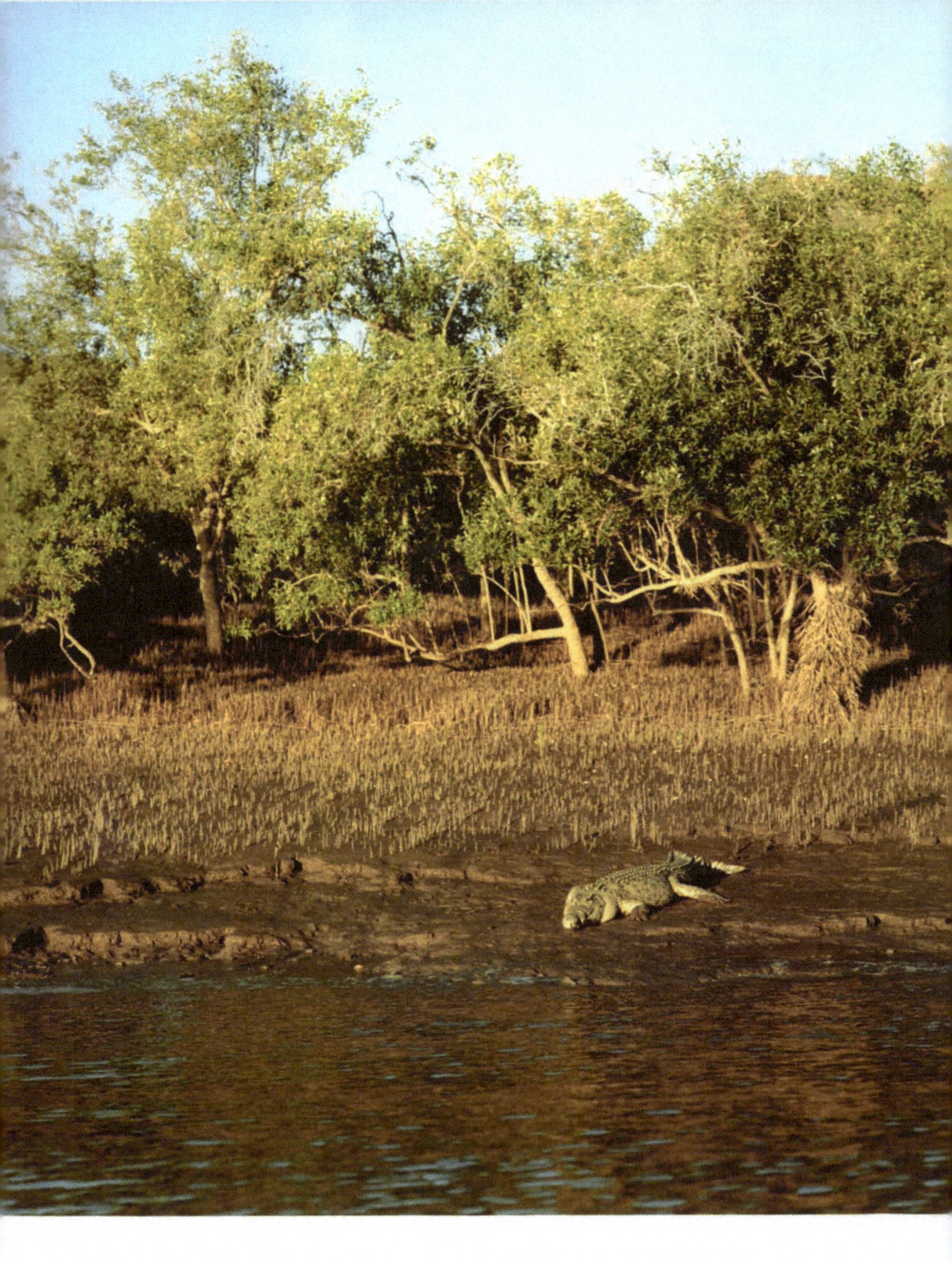

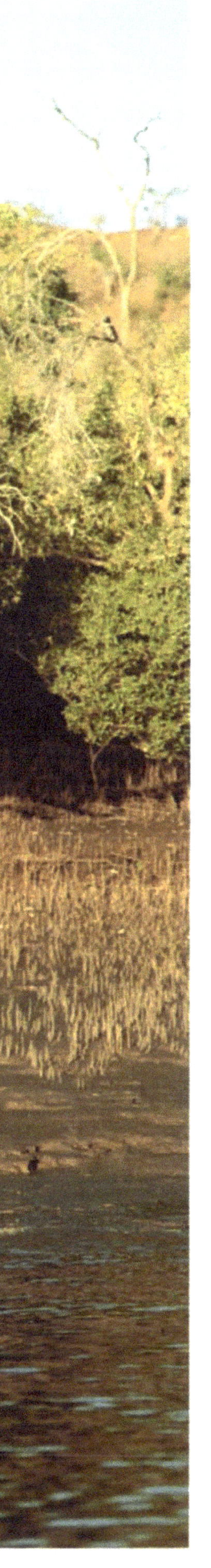

CROCODILE

What could be more tender
than these awful jaws,
jagged with terrible teeth,
gaping carefully,
gently conveying
its little ones
safely from nest to stream?

Who is more tender
than El Shaddai, almighty God,
bursting from such jaws as these
to carry me
to safety?

PODLICH

LEFT: *Saltwater crocodile, Wyndham, WA*
RIGHT: *Freshwater crocodile, Ord River, WA*

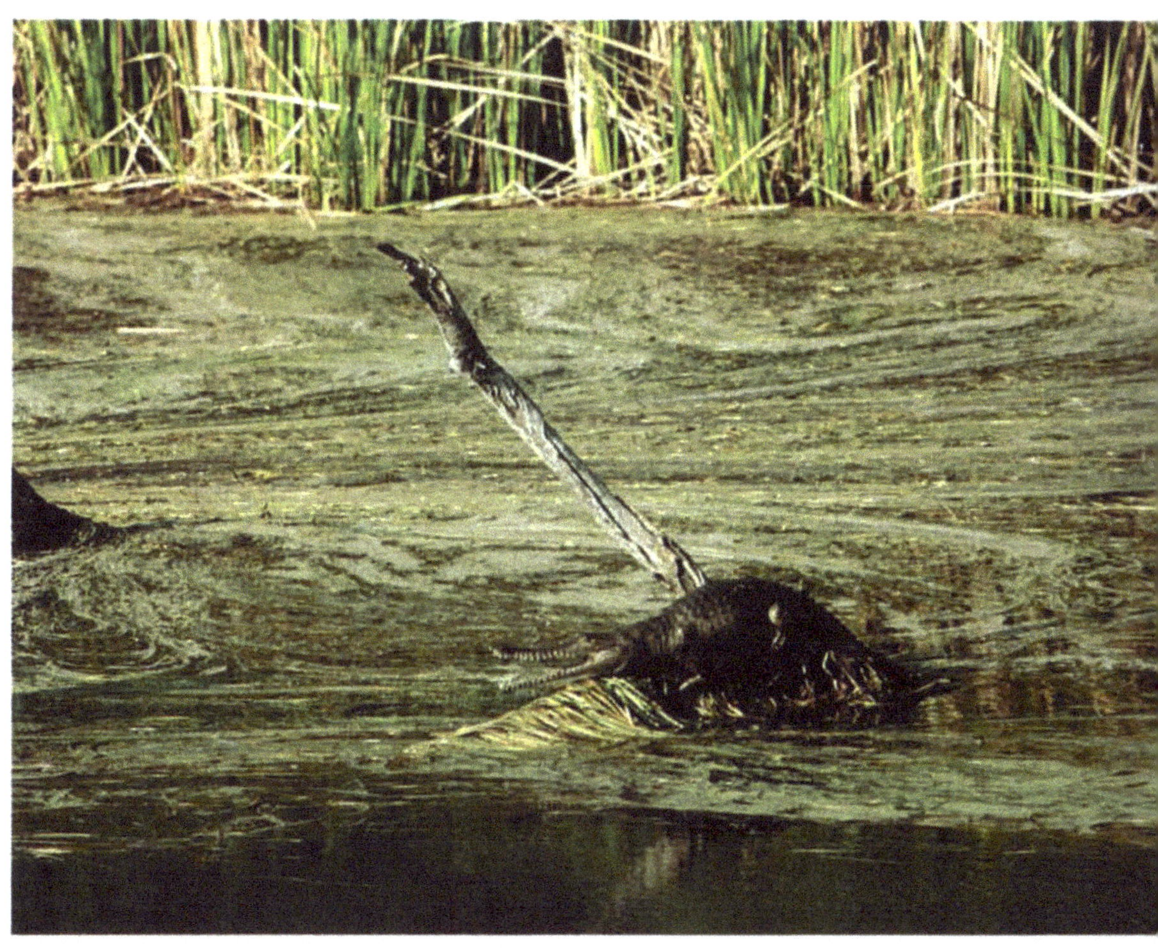

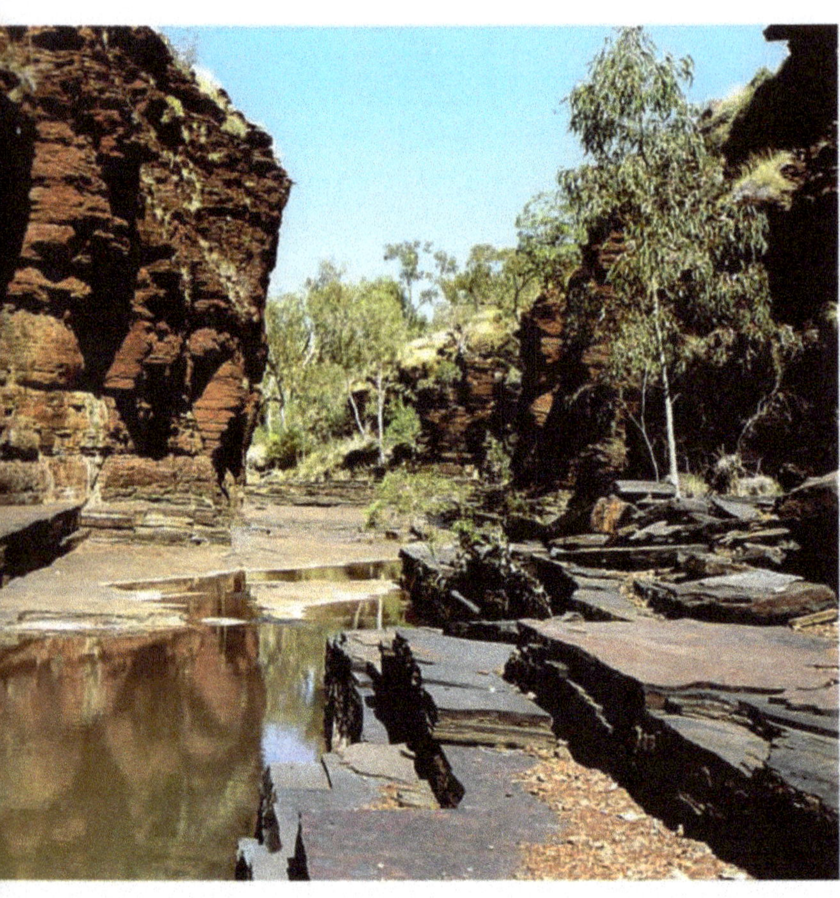

DESERT DWELLERS

Lord of the mystic inland,
  I only dare to visit
  the desert places of the spirit
  in the pleasant seasons:
when the rains have been
  and the red sand is carpeted
  with white and gold;
when one can find pleasant pools
  among the rocky places,
  where nymphs become dragonflies;
when the desert animals breed well
  and the dingoes, well fed and sleek,
  find the hunt an easy task;
in such seasons I go exploring
  and cope with minor difficulties,
  pretending I have embraced the truth.

But when the dry times come,
  and the desert shimmers like an oven;
when summer makes travel by day
  a distress and a danger;
when the red sand whirls
  on a fierce savage wind,
  and even shady places
  leave one weary and panting;
then, Lord, I shirk the pain,
  and stay far away in comfort.

Then I leave it to those bold souls
  who trust you in the desert places;
who know and read the summer landscape
  with a love which surpasses sentiment
  and willingly endures the pain.
These who choose to live here,
  not counting the cost,
  have a wisdom and peace
  which is your desert gift.
We, the comfort-holders,
  envy them and laud them,
  but wait for the pleasant seasons,
  and evade the harder learning.

PREWER

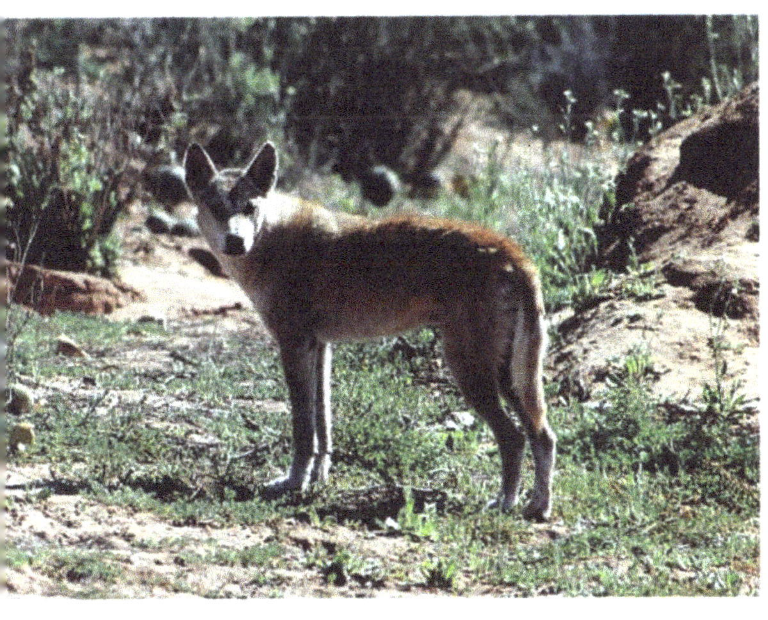

LEFT *Kalamina Gorge, Hamersley Range National Park, WA*
UPPER RIGHT *Dingo, Simpson Desert*
LOWER RIGHT *Hamersley Range, Pilbara, WA*
OVERLEAF *Windmill, NT*

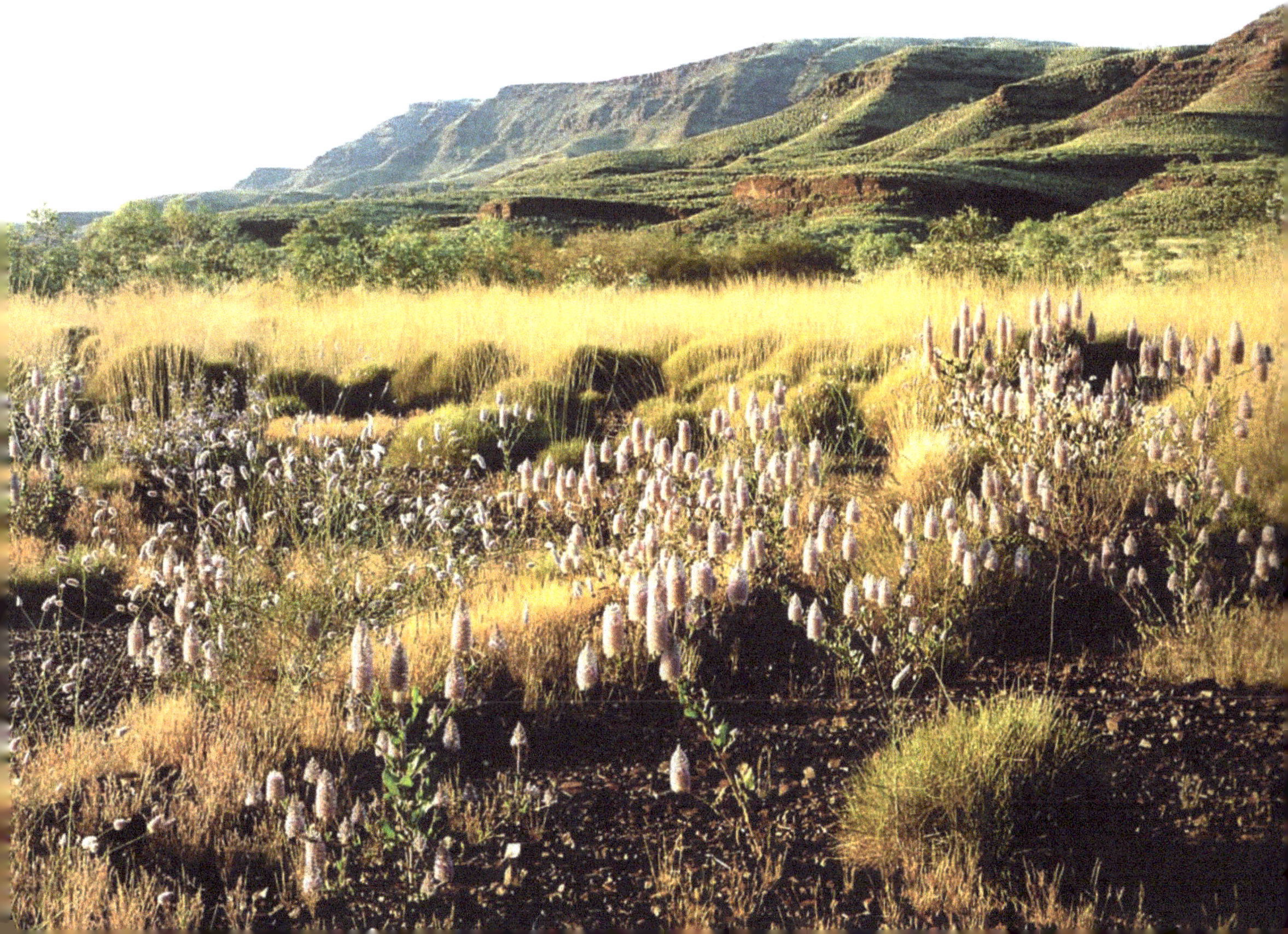

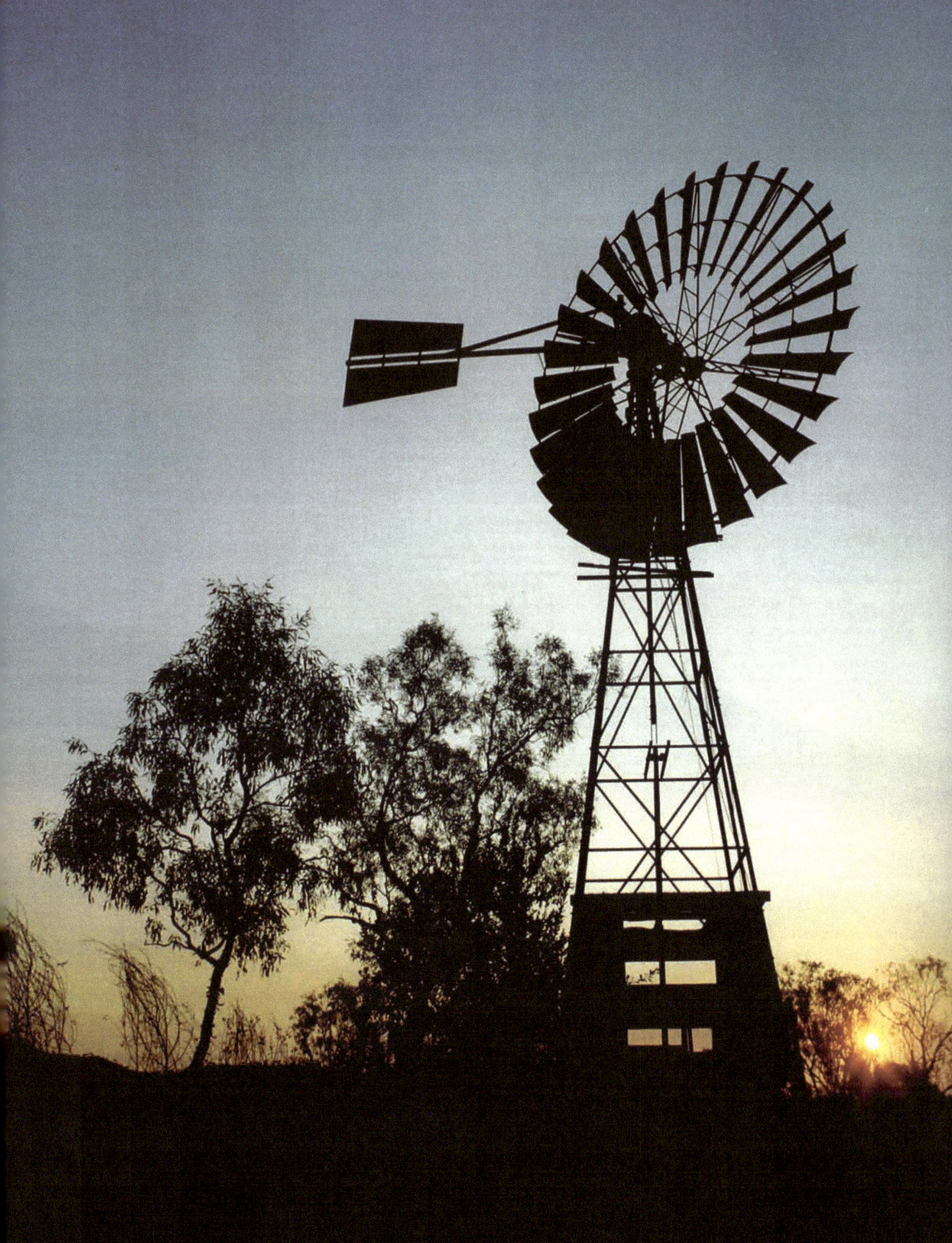

Although it has been inhabited by Aboriginal people for thousands of years, the Australian outback can be harsh and unforgiving to human beings. Yet for all that — perhaps partly because of it — the outback has a lure and fascination for Australians, and attracts the awe and admiration of people from overseas. The rich colours of the inland are beyond compare; and landforms and rock sculptures surprise and delight visitors. And over all the brooding and crumbling landscape hangs the impression of an ancient beauty sculpted and painted by time and hardship.

A closer look reveals a unique wildlife, from the kangaroos, wallaroos, plains turkeys, wedge-tailed eagles, and flocks of finches, galahs, and budgies, to the profusion of desert wildflowers after rain and the many gums, acacias, and casuarinas. Then there are the shy nocturnal creatures whose presence is indicated by a thousand footprints on the sand, and, deep underground, the ants and the frogs.

While for most people the outback is remote and exotic, there are others who have made it their home: the Aborigines, the white pioneers, the pastoralists, and the inhabitants of towns, mining camps, and missions.

Well-known authors Aub Podlich and Bruce Prewer here reflect some aspects of this remarkable land in inspiring poetry. With the spectacular full-colour photography of Jocelyn Burt and Chris Spiker, this book highlights the authors' deep love and respect for the Australian outback and its Creator.

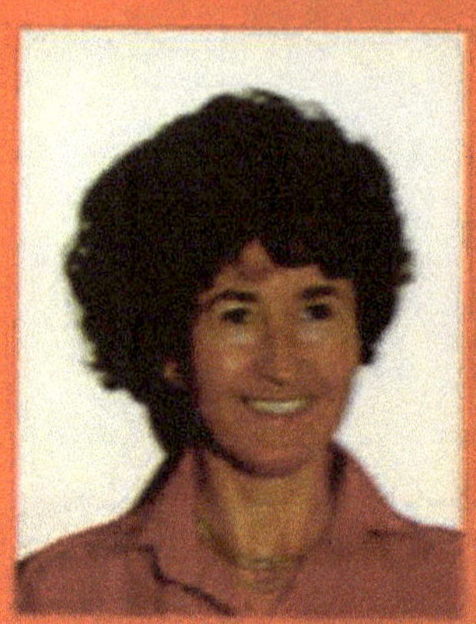

Jocelyn Burt, one of Australia's leading scenic photographers, has travelled extensively through Australia and New Zealand. She now works as a freelance photographer. Her work has been published widely and has won numerous awards. Jocelyn's many previous books on Australia include *The Earth Is the Lord's*.

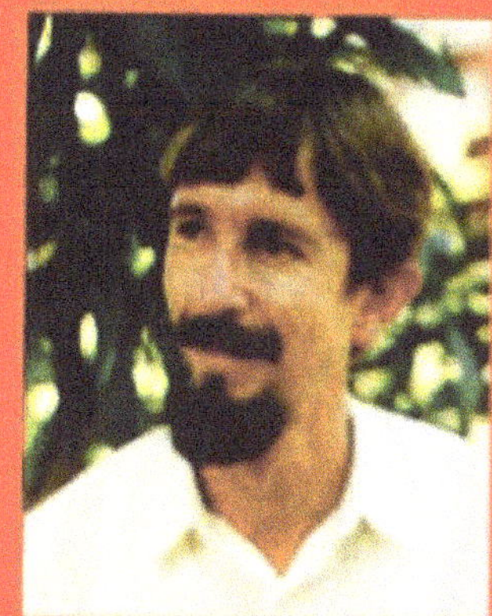

Aub Podlich's great love for nature and for the Creator shows in his writing, which reflects what he sees around him and the grace and power of God. His previous publications include *Barrier Reef Reflections*. Aub, who describes himself as a writer and dreamer and planter of trees, is married with four children, and presently is a pastor at Raceview, Queensland.

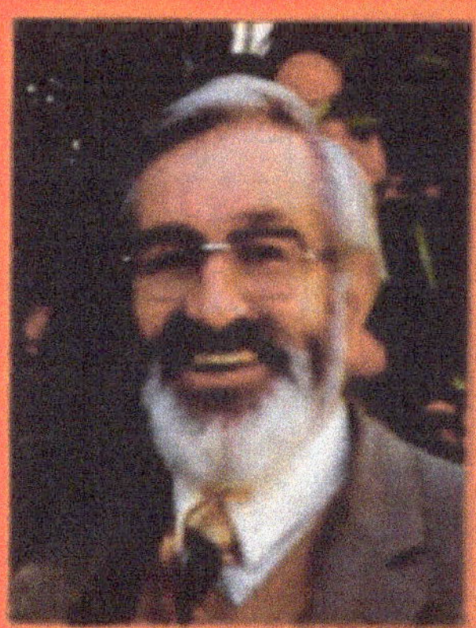

Bruce Prewer has become widely known through his popular Australian poetry and prayers, in which he shares his love for creation and for the gracious Creator-Redeemer. He wrote the text for *Kakadu Reflections*. A minister of the Uniting Church, Bruce has served parishes and the wider church in Tasmania, Victoria, and South Australia; he is now at Bendigo.

www.ingramcontent.com/pod-product-compliance
Lightning Source LLC
LaVergne TN
LVHW060638110826
845147LV00018B/1006

9781628801446